MRS COADE'S STONE

Other books by the Author

Decorative Wedgwood in Architecture and Furniture
Wedgwood Ware
Story of Wedgwood,
English Fireplaces

Contributor to
National Trust Studies 1980
Dictionary of English Furniture Makers (Furniture History Society)
Georgian Craftsmen (Geoffrey Beard)

and the forthcoming
Macmillan History of Art

MRS COADE'S STONE

ALISON KELLY

Published in 1990 by
The Self Publishing Association Ltd
18 High Street
Upton-upon-Severn, Worcs
A MEMBER OF

in conjunction with
The Georgian Group

British Library Cataloguing in Publication Data
Kelly, Alison 1913
   1. Buildings. Architectural features. Building materials.
Stone
   I. Title
   721.0441

ISBN 1 85421 055 6

Designed and Produced by The Self Publishing Association Ltd
Printed and Bound in Great Britain by The Eastern Press Ltd, Reading, Berks

Acknowledgements

Quotations from the Windsor Archives are by the gracious permission of Her Majesty the Queen.

Over the many years in which I have been working on Eleanor Coade I have been helped by so many people and organizations that it would not be possible to list them here. The notes and gazetteer will, I hope, indicate all of them. However, I am particularly indebted to a number of people whose names cannot be left out; and I take this opportunity of thanking Elizabeth Adams, Robert Breakell, Nancy Briggs, F.J. (Guy) Collins, J.F. Cordingley, J.A.K. Dean R.I.B.A., Clare Forman, John Fowles, Ian Freestone and Mavis Bimson, John Havill, Peter Hone, N.P. Neblett, Robert Oresko, Nancy Valpy and Jeffrey Williams. Mollie Adams has shown that Coade stone can be made today.

Photographic Acknowledgements

Archives Publiques du Canada
Ashdown House School, Sussex
James Austin, Cambridge
Borough of Brighton, Royal Pavilion and Art Gallery
Christies, London SW1
City of Nottingham, Museum of Costume and Textiles
Vera Collingwood, London W4
F.J. Collins, Fareham, Hants
Commissioners of Public Works of Ireland, Dublin
Country Life, London SE1
T. Crowther, London SW6
John Davis, London E9
P.J. Gates, London W1
Charles Gillespie, Madison WI, USA
Kenneth Gravett, New Malden, Surrey
G.L.C. Record Office, London E1
Guildhall Library, City of London
J.A. Havill, Exeter
Peter Hone, London W9
A.F. Kersting, London SW18
Library of Congress, Washington DC. USA
National Monuments Record, London W1
N.P. Neblett, Sterling VA. USA
St Peter's Hall, Oxford (photo Simon Nicholson)
Scottish National Monuments Record, Edinburgh
Sir John Soane's Museum, London WC2
Sotheby's, Billingshurst, Sussex
Studio Camm, Wilmslow, Cheshire
The Octagon, Washington DC. USA
A.J. Ventris, Brighton
Victoria and Albert Museum, London
Other photographs by the author.

Ham House, Surrey
River God, *1784 or later, by John Bacon R.A.*

CONTENTS

Sign for the Cocoa Tree, early 19th Century Chocolate House in the London area. Private Collection.

LIST OF ILLUSTRATIONS

Page No

FOREWORD

Much has been written of the impact of 'new technology' on the development of architecture through the centuries, whether it be that of concrete on Roman vaults, cast iron on the 19th century glasshouses of Paxton and others, or of yet more recherché materials on the so-called high-tech buildings of the late 20th century. The artificial stone patented by Mrs Eleanor Coade may not have revolutionised the architecture of the late Georgian period in any structural sense, but its aesthetic contribution was much more considerable than is generally realised; paradoxically, indeed, its popularity amongst architects and clients was in direct proportion to its subsequent anonymity, since its success in imitating the real thing was the reason both for its widespread use and for the fact that modern writers have tended to ignore its existence.

New materials and new techniques do not automatically produce aesthetic advances, as the widespread use of concrete in our own times has demonstrated; it depends to a large extent on the controlling sensibilities of architect and client. Coade stone made it possible for architects of the greatness of Soane and Wyatt to exploit, develop and deploy the infinite variety of the classical vocabulary of ornament in a way that reliance on natural stone would have rendered impractical. In this sense it was an invention which enormously enriched late Georgian architecture in England and further afield. Perhaps somewhere here there is a lesson for modern architects to learn. This book performs a great service in quantifying and illuminating Mrs Coade's achievement, and the Georgian Group warmly endorses its publication.

Roger White
Secretary
The Georgian Group
37 Spital Square
London E1 6DY

INTRODUCTION

Eleanor Coade was well-known and highly successful in her own time. She was employed by every eminent architect of her day, and her work can be found in all parts of the British Isles. It was exported to North and South America and the Caribbean, and to Poland and Russia. An article on it, "Ueber Herrn Coade's Lithodipira oder Kunst Backerstern [sic; should I think be Backerstein] Fabrik zu Lambeth in England", was published in the *Intelligenz-Blatt* magazine, Leipzig, for August 1788. Coade stone ornaments such well known architectural monuments as Buckingham Palace, the Royal Naval College (formerly Hospital) at Greenwich and St George's Chapel at Windsor, as well as many hundreds of other buildings, great and small. She made architectural ornaments of every kind, statues, fountains and other garden features, urns, commemorative and funerary monuments, chimneypieces, candelabra and other interior decorations, and heraldic achievements. Mainly she worked in a classical style, but she also had a large Gothic output, and made some Egyptian statues and architectural details. Once, for Twining's Tea Emporium, she designed two Chinese figures. Yet, of all this huge output, spanning, with the work of her successor William Croggon, a period of seventy years, only two or three pieces are well known – the lion on Westminster Bridge, the doorways in Bedford Square and the tomb of Captain Bligh.

It is not that her work has disappeared. Because her medium was remarkably resistant to the weather, most of her pieces are in as good condition now as when they were made, some over two hundred years ago. There are many hundreds of Coade pieces still to be seen, and it is surprising that they are not more often referred to in books on British architecture.

There are two reasons, I believe, for this neglect. One is that Mrs Coade's output was of architectural form achieved in a ceramic medium. Her work, to use the jargon of the day, was at an inter-disciplinary interface, and both architectural and ceramic historians feel that it is outside their field. Indeed, without some ceramic knowledge, her contribution to British architecture can hardly be understood. The second is that her work, in one respect, was too successful. She made a product which was intended to reproduce, in clay, a natural stone, and did so with such effect that natural stone is what people think they see. How many visitors to St George's Chapel, standing under the vaulting of the screen, know that they are looking at a roof of pottery? Mrs Coade's camouflage was perfect; and as one who designed camouflage for five years, I can salute her expertise.

In this book I hope to do something to remedy this neglect, and by showing the range and quality of her work to try to restore Mrs Coade to her rightful place among the bright stars of the Georgian decorative world.

A word must be said about the arrangement of this book, and the reasons for not making it the usual chronological survey. The Coade records emanating from the firm are patchy;

they are as follows:

1. The firm's catalogue of 1784, listing and numbering over 700 different designs. Copies are in the British Library (a) and the Royal Academy Library (b).

2. The handbook, dated 1799, of Coade's Gallery, the exhibition gallery opened in that year. Apart from many designs not listed in 1784, it contains a list, county by county and country by country, of the places where Mrs Coade had had commissions (not all of them, as she forgot some since discovered) for the thirty years from the foundation of the firm in 1769 until 1799. The only copy known to me is in the British Library.

3. The Nelson Pediment pamphlet issued to publicize the 40 ft. pediment sculpture at Greenwich Hospital in memory of Nelson. The only known copy, in the Scottish National Library, is undated, but the pencilled date of 1813 is likely to be correct, as the pediment was finished in 1812. It gives a short list of major works.

4. The work books of William Croggon, Mrs Coade's manager from the death of her partner John Sealy until her own death in 1821. Croggon was not made a partner, and when he was not left the business, he had to bring a case in Chancery over the sum to be paid for it. His order book, day book (accounts) and letter book came into the Public Record Office. The records for these eight years are complete for purchasers, prices and destinations. When Croggon had bought the firm he had to begin a new set of work books, and these, and all later records, are lost. If his son Thomas John retained them when he refounded the firm in 1835, they were lost in the blitz in the City in the last war.

Records of designs are:

5. The folio book of etchings in the British Library, bound in red morocco and stamped with the Royal Arms; it was George III's copy, which reached the library as part of George III's library, "given" to the British Museum by George IV. It is discussed in detail in the chapter on the Coade factory. It has two plates to a page.

6. The Guildhall Library book of etchings. This has one plate to a page.

7. Sir John Soane's Museum's book of etchings, marked proof copy and very defective, as many pages have been cut out, no doubt to send to Soane's clients. (He used Coade stone from the age of 27 until he was 75). This also has one plate to a page.

8. The Royal Academy book of etchings, which belonged to the architect John Yenn. It also has one plate to a page and is similar to the Guildhall book, with one plate extra. It is bound with No.1.(b).

9. A bill exists at Burton Constable for £3.7s.6d. for a book of drawings of artificial stone supplied by Eleanor Coade, probably in connection with the Coade work on the Orangery there in 1789, but the book itself has not yet come to light among 250,000 documents at the house.

No further assemblages of prints, nor catalogues, appear to have been issued. As late as the Regency, Croggon sometimes identified a design as "C. and S. plate . . ." though in fact all the known etchings were assembled before Sealy became a partner.

Except those in the British Library book, the designs have numbers, written in ink, corresponding to those in the catalogue, enabling comparable designs, such as the large number of similarly draped classical ladies, to be identified. The books have no title pages, but frontispieces taken from a design for the card of entry to the factory, drawn by John Bacon. These are undated.

Since this is the material available, providing a skeleton list of commissions from 1769 to 1799, a slight list of major works from 1799 to 1813, a complete and detailed list from 1813 to 1821, and nothing thereafter, it is clear that the normal chronological arrangement would not be possible. A very large number of commissions have been discovered from outside sources and the information of friends, but serendipity is not enough, and I am very conscious that much must have escaped the net.

In addition, the fact that many Coade designs were repeated over very long periods presents a further obstacle to chronological treatment. A Stourhead *Borghese Vase* of 1772 is exactly the same as a *Borghese Vase* at Coleorton Hall dated 1827, and no purpose would be served by describing them separately at the beginning and the end of the book. The *Vestal* appears to date from 1773, but was still in vigorous production in the Regency. While the plaques and swags of the Adam style went out of fashion by about 1800, and fountains were ordered in greater numbers as the more formal garden designs developed in the early nineteenth century, there was a continuous demand for figures based on classical originals, and for architectural features, such as capitals, throughout the firm's existence. The continuity was much more than the change.

It seems best, therefore, to describe first the biographical details of Mrs Coade and her family, then the precursors of the Coade firm, followed by information on the Coade factory. There follows the formula for Coade stone, as identified in the British Museum Research Laboratory by Dr Freestone and Miss Bimson. There is then a chapter on Coade's Gallery and its handbook, giving a general picture of production at the end of the 18th century.

There then comes the problem of dealing with the mass of Coade commissions, and, since a date scheme is ruled out, of dealing with more than 650 surviving commissions, as well as hundreds more of which there is documentation alone, and putting them into some kind of order.

It seems best to divide them into kinds; chapters will be found on garden features, external and internal decorative features, monuments and so on. There are also chapters on work for the Crown and Government, Gothic designs, and the major architects using Coade stone. (It is not generally realized that *all* the eminent Georgian architects, as well as a host of minor ones, were Coade patrons).

The later part of the book is arranged for reference, and consists of a list of all the architects using Coade stone, with what they used and where, and a Gazetteer of known pieces, both surviving and demolished, arranged, like Mrs Coade's own list, county by county and country by country.

A note on abbreviations

CG	The list of buildings mentioned by Mrs Coade in her exhibition handbook *Coade's Gallery*.
CD	Croggon's Day Book, for his accounts, now in the Public Records Office.
CO	Croggon's Order Book, filed with the above. C111/106
Letter Book	The book of copy-letters kept from 1813 to 1821. Filed with the above
Gunnis	*Dictionary of British Sculptors 1660-1851*, by Rupert Gunnis.
Pevsner	*The Buildings of England*, by Sir Nikolaus Pevsner et al.
Colvin	*A Biographical Dictionary of British Architects 1660-1840* by Howard Colvin

Plaque of the Oxford Canal Company, 1790s, originally on the Company's demolished premises, now transferred to the Master's House of St. Peter's College, Oxford, which was the Company's later headquarters. The shield bears the arms of the City and University, and St. Mary's Church and the Radcliffe Camera can be seen in the background.

CHAPTER 1

Eleanor Coade and the taste of her time

Women in business were few in Georgian times. Alice Hepplewhite produced her late husband's *The Cabinet Maker and Upholsterer's Guide,* on which his reputation rests; Hester Bateman belonged to a family of silversmiths, but had her own maker's mark; Anna Maria Garthwaite was an outstanding free-lance designer, for many years, of patterns for the Spitalfields silk weavers – the list could be extended but would not be very long. Eleanor Coade was an exception in that her firm flourished from 1769, with the Royal Appointment to both George III and George IV, until her death in 1821, and continued under her former manager William Croggon, for extensive work at Buckingham Palace and elsewhere, throughout the 1820s and into the 1830s. It is worth examining the history of her family for light on this remarkable achievement.

The Coad or Coade family originated in Cornwall,[1] where there is a village called Coad's Green; the telephone book shows that there are still Coads living there and elsewhere in the Duchy. However, one branch of the clan moved east in the 17th century, and established themselves in Lyme Regis, in Dorset near the Devonshire border, where they prospered.[2] On 31 May 1704, a George Coad (the final e came and went according to taste) married Elizabeth Fowler and had a large family. The eldest was called Robert Fowler after his maternal grandfather, and married Sarah Enchmarch of Tiverton, Devonshire. The second son, who is the most important to our study, was baptised George, after his father, in November 1706. After him came Margaret, who married Aaron Tozer and inherited Coade property when the Coade name had died out. Then followed more sons and daughters before the 14th and final child, Samuel, arrived in 1724. Another brother was Mayor of Lyme in 1780, and Robert Fowler Coade and his Sarah lived in some state in the Great House in Broad Street. They were wealthy enough to patronize the well-known painter Thomas Hudson and to dress in the way he would have thought suitable for his sitters;[3] Sarah is in satin and pearls, Robert in velvet with gold braid. In the summer, their house was let to Lord Camelford who owned land in Cornwall from which china clay and china stone were obtained – a possible link with later Coade ceramic activities.

George the younger married another Enchmarch sister, Eleanor, in 1732 and moved to Exeter about the same time. Because other Coades remained in the town, and Eleanor II had a house there later, almost every reference book concludes that George's family were in Lyme until they all moved to London. In fact, as John Fowles' and John Havill's researches show, George was in Exeter for nearly 30 years. His daughter Eleanor was born there on 24 June 1733 (as Elinor) and her sister Elizabeth in 1735. George was in the wool trade, very prosperous at that time, as a hot-presser (wool cloth finisher). He was joined by his brother Samuel, in the same trade as a fuller, and at one time they were in partnership.[4] Samuel, however, kept up his connections with Lyme Regis, only 30 miles away, and bought the house, then called Bunter's Castle and now Belmont, which he transferred to his niece Eleanor in 1784.

Southernhay, Exeter, Devonshire,
Coade Doorway as Bedford Square 1805-1825

George did well and bought 49 Magdalen Street, in what was then the commercial centre of Exeter, and several other houses and a warehouse nearby. In a letter[5] on crooked politics in Lyme in 1747 he boasted that he "would not scruple to lay out £500 out of my own pocket" to ensure a fair election. He enjoyed polemics, and wrote a practical and sensible "Letter to the Lords Commissioners of Trade and Plantations",[6] and a denunciation of Charles I[7] whose tragedy, in Coade's opinion, was wholly self-inflicted.

His wife Eleanor's sister, Mary Enchmarch, married James Sealy, whose son John eventually became Eleanor II's partner, and a fourth sister, Frances, married Walter Oke, who was connected with the Croggon family of Grampound, Cornwall which produced Eleanor II's manager and successor, William Croggon.[8]

There were so many Dissenters[9] in the South West that the Coades, and others of similar beliefs, led comfortable lives without being harassed for practising what Horace Walpole called "ugly Enthusiasm".[10]

When the meeting house needed rebuilding, George gave £55.5s.0d., Samuel Coade £40 and James Sealy £50 to the chapel which became known as George's Meeting.[11] Here the congregation wandered through several byways of non-conformism to end up as Unitarians.

By the end of the 1750s, the wool trade in Exeter was in decline and in 1759 George was declared bankrupt.[12] He left Exeter and next appears in London in 1762, when he became a Fellow – for one year only – of the Society for the Encouragement of Arts and Sciences[13] (now the Royal Society of Arts). He was then living in Charterhouse Square, but moved later to Charles Square, Hoxton on the north eastern outskirts of the City of London. His daughter Eleanor established herself as a linen-draper, and insured her stock for £200 in 1766.[14] In the next year, she was described as a merchant, and the value of her stock had risen to £750.[15] She moved to St Thomas Apostles, a street which became a short remnant after the building of Queen Victoria Street in the City. Her sister had lodgings in Eleanor's house, and insured her plate etc for £200.[16] I think it is possible that she kept her property with her sister so that their father could not lay hands on it. (Elizabeth had no part in the history of the Coade factory as she died aged 40).[17]

In 1769, two events occurred which are difficult to reconcile. George Coade went bankrupt again and all his Exeter property (which he must have regained after the previous bankruptcy) was sold.[18] He then died. In the same year, Eleanor Coade and her mother established themselves at what became the Coade factory at Lambeth.[19] Since any property owned by Mrs Coade, the widow, would have been controlled by her husband and lost in the bankruptcy, she personally can have contributed little. Samuel Coade remained wealthy, and in his will forgave Eleanor II's debts to him, so his money may have underpinned the project. Sarah, wealthy widow of Robert Fowler Coade, was described in her will as being of Lyme Regis and Lambeth, and may also have been involved.[20]

Since both mother and daughter had the same name, confusion has reigned over the contribution of each of them to the manufactory. The widow Eleanor was of course Mrs, and it has been assumed that any mention of Mrs Coade must refer to her. Rupert Gunnis,[21] for instance, believed that the widow ran the factory until her death, in her late eighties, in 1796. What is not generally realized is that women in business, in Georgian times, had the courtesy title of Mrs (like an Edwardian cook). So Mrs, in the Coade records, normally refers to *Miss* Coade. Bills were usually headed Eleanor Coade, but two, as early as 1771, for Hatfield Priory, Essex, and 1773, for work at Burton on Trent Town Hall,[22] are made out to *Miss* Coade, showing that from very early days she was in charge. The only references which specifically concern the mother are the first two entries for the factory in the Lambeth Poor Rate books, when the rate was paid by Widow Coade.[23] (After that there is a gap of two years in the records, and when they resume the rate is paid by Eleanor Coades [sic].) So George's widow had some contribution to make, though I believe only a small one. Charles Fowler,[24] an early 19th century architect who used Coade stone himself, referred to the Coade firm in a lecture on terra cotta and artificial stone to the Royal Institute of British Architects in June 1850, and specially mentioned that it was founded by Miss Coade. He was related to the Fowlers of Cullompton, the family of Miss Coade's grandfather, and could well have met his elderly relation as a young man. He commented on her scientific knowledge, not mentioned elsewhere.

So it is *Miss* Coade on whom we must concentrate. In accordance with Georgian practice, however she will hereafter be referred to as *Mrs* Coade. Fortunately, her will exists[25] and gives a striking picture of her character. She was deeply religious, and left many bequests to clergymen who were expected to distribute the money to their flocks. Though a Baptist,

23

she left legacies not only to the Baptist Minister in Lyme Regis, but in a pleasantly oecumenical way to the Independent Minister and the Church of England Vicar as well, so that the poor of Lyme of all denominations could get their fair share. She was a most careful planner – as well as an annuity, her maid was left all the bedroom furniture, the kitchen equipment, the silver spoons and the small tablecloths. The large tablecloths, with the silver coffee pot, went to a London friend.

Belmont, Lyme Regis, Dorset, Mrs Coade's house 1784, exterior Coade Ornament.

She never married, and clearly recognised the importance of her status as a free agent, a century before the Married Women's Property act gave a wife control of her own money. Most of her legatees were spinsters or widows, but three married women were mentioned, and the wording of their bequests is remarkable. Their husbands were not to touch their bequests, and though their husbands would normally have signed for them, they were to sign themselves for their legacies in front of the executors "notwithstanding their coverture". This odd phrase turns out to refer to their married status. A mare is covered by a stallion when she goes to stud, and the legal term, of the same derivation, has some interesting overtones relating to the Georgian idea of the position of women. It has

24

not been possible to find out if these bequests were granted, or if they were considered as void, being against public policy. But in making them Eleanor Coade joined pioneering people such as Mary Wollstonecraft in questioning traditional views on the status of women. Perhaps significantly, the Girls' Charity School at Walworth was left £100, but the Boy's school only half as much.

Some may have thought her a prig. The Town Clerk of Tiverton[26] remarked "I have many ... (word illegible) about the extent of the bounty of Miss C. She is too great a Saint to have many new Feelings for her poor Relations". But this was unfair, since she had heard of a small post with the East India Company at India House (she had had many commissions from the Company) and hoped to obtain it for an Enchmarch cousin, to whom she sent £10 for his travelling expenses. (She also left him £300 in her will, but he did not survive to get it; wealthy Samuel Coade only left him 19 guineas.)[27]

Family feelings may have been ruffled by relations who did not get as much as they hoped, but she begged those "who share less than others not to impute the difference to want of affection", but to the fact that the poor, and the spreading of the Gospel, made the primary claim on her estate.

This devout and independent minded woman had successfully run her own business for several years before she and her mother arrived at Narrow Wall, Lambeth.

Like her contemporary Josiah Wedgwood, Eleanor Coade set up in business at a moment peculiarly appropriate to their media. Robert Adam had returned from Italy in 1758, and his interpretation of neo-classical design during the subsequent decade had provided a perfect decorative style for a public overburdened by the formality of strict Palladian taste, and tired of the restlessness of rococo and chinoiserie. As the name neo-classical implies, it was based on the Roman certainties, but it was also new. As Sir John Soane said:[28]

> "To Mr. Adam's taste in the Ornaments of his Buildings and Furniture we stand indebted, in-as-much as Manufacturers felt, as it were, the electric power of this Revolution in Art. Our printed Linens and Paper Hangings exhibit such specimens of Decoration that the admirers of the Loggia of the Vatican could not see without their rendering due praise to them".

In the introduction to their book *The Works in Architecture of Robert and James Adam*[29] the brothers said that

> "We flatter ourselves that we have been able to seize, with some degree of success, the beautiful spirit of antiquity and transfuse it, with novelty and variety, through all our numerous works".

The spirit of antiquity they evoked was different from that of the classical buildings standing above ground, from which all traces of plaster and woodwork had been weathered away. This was the architecture of exteriors, and the corresponding Roman interior decoration was almost unknown. The excavations at Herculaneum (mainly from

25

1738-65)[30] demonstrated that it had a much lighter, almost "unclassical" atmosphere which Robert Adam fully understood. Soane perceptively refers to "admirers of the Loggia of the Vatican", and Adam also drew nourishment from Raphael's "grotesques" there.

The word grotesque has come down in the world; it was originally *grottesche* in Italian, meaning that it came from grottoes or caves. Nero's Golden House[31] in Rome had had (and still dimly has) similar decoration to Herculaneum and Pompeii. From the late 70s AD, the clearing of the site to build the Colosseum had resulted in huge quantities of soil being shovelled over the Golden House nearby, and burial was complete when Trajan built his Baths on top. The Palace was rediscovered at the end of the 15th century through workmen breaking through the roof into what they believed were caverns or grottoes. Its decorations proved an inspiration to Renaissance artists, and to Raphael in particular in his frescoes in the Loggie of the Vatican, painted between 1514 and 1516. Adam was therefore able to draw on Roman decorations as revealed at first hand in Herculaneum, and as reinterpreted by Raphael and others (drawing on similar classical material in Rome) in the Renaissance.

The motifs of Adam decoration have all been identified and carefully drawn by Marthe Blythe Gerson[32] in her "Glossary of Robert Adam's neo-Classical ornaments", and the comparison of her illustrations with the Coade etchings shows that most of them reappear there, including anthemion variations, acanthus scrolls, swags of husks, paterae, putti, guilloche, griffins, bucrania and so on. In addition, Eleanor Coade made copies and variations of his sometimes unorthodox capitals, and his plaques and medallions. Her individual commissions for Adam are referred to in other parts of this book and summarized in the section on individual artists.

His designs could be carried out in plaster indoors as easily as in Coade stone, and usually were. Where her medium came into its own was for exteriors, where it was wholly resistant to the weather. Adam's designs called for delicate and detailed bas-relief work typified by the South front of Kedleston. Here, beginning at the top, there are two oblong plaques with grotesque decoration and four figures in classical dress. Below is a continuous frieze of swags and paterae; below again, two round bas-reliefs of figures and finally two more statues in niches. At Kedleston, all this ornament, finished by 1765, is carved in stone, but all of it could have been carried out in the Coade factory if it had been founded in time. Adam brought back from Italy copies of the Medici and Borghese Vases, and Coade copies of these stand each side of the south entrance. They did not arrive at Kedleston until some years after he had finished work there, but he would have approved of them, and himself used Coade stone until a year or two before he died.

The same happy relations between Eleanor Coade and Adam continued with the Wyatts, James who used Coade stone more than any other architect, his brother Samuel and various subsidiary Wyatts including Sir Jeffrey Wyatville; Henry Holland; Humphry Repton; William Wilkins; John Nash and Sir John Soane. In carrying out work for all those eminent men, Eleanor Coade was at the centre of the neo-classical movement in this country, into the Regency and beyond.

Kedleston Hall by Robert Adam, 1760-70. All the motifs here carved in natural stone were later made in Coade stone. The Medici and Borghese Vases at the top of the steps are of Coade stone.

NOTES

1. See Boyd's Marriage Registers for Cornwall in the Society of Genealogists.

2. The genealogy of the Coade family has been researched by F. J. Collins, working with Ida Darlington, who first discovered the Enchmarch forbears of Eleanor Coade I, John Fowles who provided a genealogical table of the Coade family and John Havill who researched in detail the history of George Coade and his wife and daughter during their Exeter sojourn. His MS monograph has been deposited in the University of Exeter. I am most grateful to all of them for permission to publish their findings.

3. These portraits were shown to me in 1973 by Bertram Hume. He was descended from the Tozers. He has since died, and I do not know their present whereabouts.

4. John Havill has recently discovered the seals which were attached to lengths of wool cloth which have George's and Samuel's names together.

5. Lincolnshire Record Office, Fane 6/2/4, quoted by Havill op cit.

6. 1747. British Library 08218 b 14.

7. 1746. Published by J. Robinson, London. Three later editions.

8. Mr John Croggon, present day historian of the family, has traced a Walter Oke Croggon, but has not yet found the exact connection between him and William Croggon.

9. See Allan Brockett *Non-Conformity in Exeter 1650-1875* 1962.

10. Letter to John Chute, 15 October 1766.

11. Brockett, op cit p134.

12. Havill, op cit p12.

13. Royal Society of Arts' records of admission to the Fellowship. Information from Dr Allan, Librarian.

14. Sun Assurance Company – Guildhall MS 11936.
    Vol 169-233501 4/- Midsummer 1767 4/7
    Eleanor Coade in Charles Square. Linen Draper
    (Stock in the Brick Dwelling House of Robert Hollings, Labourer in Holywell Row Shireditch)

    | | 5 May 1766 | £200 |

    Information from Elizabeth Adams.

15. *Vol 176 – 246717 – 18/- – Midsummer 1768*
    Eleanor Coade at No 21 in Little St Thomas the Apostles Merchant.
    (Stock not hazardous in Brick Dwelling House)   £750
    (Printed books)   £50

(Wearing Apparel) £100

26 June 1767

See Ind. No 20 p195

Information from Elizabeth Adams

16. *Vol 176 – 248748 – 4/- – Midsummer 1768 4/3.*
Elizabeth Coade at No 21 Little St Thomas the Apostles Spinster
(Wearing Apparel and Plate in her Apartments in the Dwelling House of Eleanor Coade) £200

11 September 1767.

Information from Elizabeth Adams.

17. Bunhill Fields Burial Records. This was the Dissenters' Burial Ground. Elizabeth was buried with her parents, and Eleanor after specifying a burial in a "decent and frugal manner" later joined them. They are not buried in a Coade stone tomb, as Coade stone had not been put into production at the time of George's death.

18. Havill op cit. p. 16

19. Stated by Eleanor Coade in the *Coade Catalogue* of 1784 and *Coade's Gallery* of 1799.

20. Havill, op cit. Other financial assistance may have come from John Strange, otherwise unknown, who is listed as her partner in the first insurance policy so far found for the Coade factory.
Sun Assurance Company Guildhall MS 11936.

Vol 206 – 299458 – £5.5.0 – Midsummer 1772
Eleanor Code [sic] at Mr Demar's/Opposite the lying Inn [sic] Hospital in Bridge Row Lambeth and John Strange Esq.
Artificial Stone Makers.
On their Utensils and Stock in their Warehouse only situate on Narrow Wall Lambeth Timber not exceeding Fourteen Hundred Pound
N.B. Two kilns at the said Warehouse £1400

8 July 1771

Information from Elizabeth Adams.

21. *Dictionary of British Sculptors* 1953, Coade entry p106.

22. Hoare's Bank account, 25 September 1771 (ledger 84/101) for John Wright, of Hatfield Priory, Hatfield Peverel, Essex, made out to Miss Coade. Information Mrs Cowell.
Staffordshire Record Office, bill from Miss Coade, 30 April 1773 for two paterae, 190ft of "gulochi" (guilloche) and a panel with arms, supplied in 1771 and 1772 for Burton on Trent Town Hall, built 1771-2. The bill is addressed to Jos. Wyatt, brother of James Wyatt. If, as John Martin Robinson believes, the Town Hall was designed by James, this will have been the first encounter between him and Eleanor Coade.

23. Lambeth Poor Rate Books, Liberty of Marsh and Wall. There are no books prior to

1773. In 1773 "widow Coades" was assessed at £52, and paid £1.6s.0d. in rates. The next year she paid the same. There is then a gap in the records for two years, and thereafter the rates are paid by "Eleanor Coades" [sic]. Minet Library, Brixton.

24. He called her Miss Coode. This may be a printing error, but I think it possible that he spelt it as he pronounced it in a rounded, Devonshire way, unlike the modern pronunciation as Code. The gatepiers of her house, Belmont, Lyme Regis, had coots in low relief, and this is probably a rebus on the name. Her cousin John, the Mayor of Lyme, had "Arms – Argent, a chevron between three coots, all sable. Crest – a coot, sable." George Roberts *History of Lyme Regis and Charmouth*, 1834, p296. There were some armigerous Coades, but their crest was a chough – a Cornish bird; the Coades seem to have made their own illicit variation.

25. Deciphered and printed in full by John Havill, op cit.

26. Letter from Beavis Wood to Nathaniel Lord Harrowby, 19 December 1795, printed from the Harrowby MSS Trust by John Havill, op cit.

27. ibid.

28. *Sir John Soane Royal Academy Lectures on Architecture* edited by A. T. Bolton 1929, p180. Lecture XI, 16 March 1815.

29. Published in 1773.

30. *Herculaneum* by Amedeo Maiuri (translated by V. Priestley) 1959 p3-9.

31. Georgina Masson *The Companion Guide to Rome* 1967 p312-316.

32. Martha Blythe Gerson, "A Glossary of Robert Adam's Neo-classical Ornament", *Architectural History* 1981 p59-82.

CHAPTER 2

Precursors

Maps of London today show almost as much of Greater London south of the river as north of it; but in the 18th century the town was north of the Thames. South of it there were isolated villages and the built-up area of the Southwark Borough at the end of London Bridge, but the land nearest to the water was bleak and sodden. One of the "Liberties" into which the parish of Lambeth was divided had the name of "Marsh and Wall".[1] It was a "hope", the word used locally for an area of land reclaimed from the river, and its inland boundary was a small wriggling lane called Narrow Wall, on the line of a dyke which had kept the tides from spreading inland.

In the early 19th century, Narrow Wall was straightened and renamed Belvedere Road, a name it retains today. One end of it led to the eastern (Surrey) end of Westminster Bridge, newly opened in 1750; the other led towards the later 18th century Blackfriars Bridge. (The intervening Waterloo Bridge was not built until Victoria's reign).

This desolate area was sparsely populated, and the industries carried on there were those not acceptable elsewhere. Upstream, at Vauxhall,[2] the screech of grinding wheels on the plates made looking-glass manufacturers unacceptable in polite society; Lambeth air had been polluted by the smoke of pottery kilns since the 17th century. In one part of the parish, on a site bounded on one side by the river, on the other by Narrow Wall, was a piece of land given to Jesus College Oxford in the 1680s by Sir Leoline (Llewellyn) Jenkins,[3] and retained by the College until this century. The Royal Festival Hall, The Hayward Gallery, and the end of Waterloo Bridge are on the site today.

In the 18th century the Jesus property had an inn on the waterfront called the King's Arms, with the usual jetty, King's Arms' Stairs, projecting into the river, so that people could reach the area by water. By the waterside, in the early 18th century, was a pleasure garden belonging to a Mr Cuper,[4] conveniently near the inn, whence came the names of Cuper's Gardens and Cuper's Bridge, sometimes given as part of the Coade factory's address; later in the century a brewery was built on the site. A little lane, College Street, with small houses on one side of it, ran inland from the King's Arms to give access to Narrow Wall, and in the angle between the two lanes, and entered from Narrow Wall, was the Coade factory. Mrs Coade said that she opened her exhibition gallery in 1799 at the end of Westminster Bridge because visitors had had so much difficulty in finding the factory, and a glance at a Georgian map shows that she was not exaggerating.[5]

In the 1720s, Richard Holt came to the area and began to manufacture what he described as artificial stone. He took out two patents in 1722,[6] one describing a kind of liquid metal or stone, which seems likely to have been a form of ceramic material, which is written in such obfuscating language as to be incomprehensible today – no doubt to fool imitators –

and, in conjunction with Thomas Ripley, a formula for making china or porcelain without the use of clay, which appears to be nonsense. Holt wrote a pamphlet[7] about his artificial stone, asserting that a similar body had been used at Stonehenge and in many of the ancient cathedrals, and dedicated it to Lord Burlington, whom he described rather oddly as the nursing father of the arts. Holt also wrote a document (British Museum Add. MS. 11394) giving full details of his formula, and signed by friends who were sworn to secrecy about it. It is published in full in the *Transactions of the English Ceramic Circle* 1986, Vo.12 Part 3, plates 126-129, and need not be repeated here. Its importance in Coade studies lies in the fact that it contained lead ore, and so can be distinguished from the Coade body, which Mrs Coade therefore did *not* obtain from Holt.

Holt had premises near King's Arms' Stairs, and because the Coade factory was in the same area it has been assumed that both firms had the same site, Mrs Coade taking over from Holt. Holt, however, said in his pamphlet that visitors coming at high or half tide could land directly at his factory, indicating that he had a river wall with steps. Visitors at low tide had of course to use the jetty belonging to the inn. Holt also mentioned that he put vases and other pieces along his water-front, so that his premises could be easily identified by those coming across the Thames. From the plans in possession of Jesus College it is clear that the Coade factory never had a river frontage, but was a couple of hundred yards inland. The name of King's Arms' Stairs was sometimes used in the Coade address, since most visitors came by boat and had to use the inn's jetty. The College did not grant leases to individual small leaseholders, and there are no records of Holt's name among the papers of the College's Jenkins estate. (Mrs Coade's and William Croggon's names appear on the plans and elsewhere, but as sub-tenants). Holt may indeed not have been on Jesus land at all, if he was upstream, instead of downstream of King's Arms' Stairs.

Holt mentioned being harassed by someone who said that he "knowd how to elude and set aside any patent whatsoever" and was going to use Holt's formula. This was Batty Langley, well known for a large number of architectural books and a certain amount of actual architecture. He established himself in neighbouring Southwark at the Hercules Head,[8] near the Faulcon Stairs on the Bankside and from there engaged in advertisement and counter-advertisment with Holt in the pages of the *Daily Advertiser* for some months, Langley on 25th May, 24th June and 12th July; Holt on 28th and 29th May, 1st and 24th June and 1st July 1730. The argument died down after a time, and there is as yet no information as to when either of them gave up. (The London directories only cover the Cities of London and Westminster until the 1770s.) Langley died in 1751, and the date of Holt's death is not known. Daniel Pincot, in 1770,[9] said that the Holt business flourished for a time, but "the proprietor dying, the affair died also". He added sharply that this was only to be expected, as Holt's pieces were neither well designed nor well finished. I have found no evidence for the story, given in *Concrete*,[10] that Holt convalesced after an illness at Lyme Regis, and sold his business to the Coades.

Though no Langley or Holt pieces have been identified, it is interesting that both offered the same types of architectural feature – capitals, friezes, chimneypieces, etc as well as vases and figures – that were later made by Mrs Coade.

Interest in artifical stone seems to have developed again in the 1760s. In January 1767, Daniel Pincot (spelt Pincat in the catalogues of the Society of Artists' exhibitions, but correctly spelt in his advertisements and pamphlet) advertised that he had set up a manufacture of artificial stone in Goulston Square, Whitechapel, offering the same things which Langley and Holt had made, but asserting that they were "executed in a Manner far exceeding any thing of the like Kind that has hitherto been offered to the Publick". By July 11 he had opened a warehouse in Long Acre. However, by October,[12] George Davy had begun to put advertisements in the *Daily Advertiser* saying that *he* was making artificial stone at Goulston Square, and Pincot had moved across the river to Narrow Wall, to the address which later became the Coade factory, where he also made artificial stone. Here he made a copy of the Borghese Vase which the committee of the Free Society of Artists would not allow in their exhibition, because it was not an original design, but which they put in the lobby at the entrance to the exhibition room "on account of its being a very fine performance".

Both were making the same kind of thing. Pincot offered "all sorts of rich carved Ornaments used in Buildings, viz. Tablets, Frizes, Medallions, Ionic and Corinthian Capitals, Statues, Bustos, Vases etc".[13] Davy said he sold "near 100 different Subjects, such as Figures, Busts, Tablets, Friezes, Medalions, Vases, Capitals of the different Orders of various Sizes".[14] Moreover, though they were of artifical stone, he offered them "at the same Prices as the same Things are sold in the Plaister Shops" and cheaper, he pointed out, than in wood.

In December 1767, the year's production from Goulston Square (presumably this meant Pincot's as well as Davy's) was sold at Christie's. The catalogue has survived in Christie's archives and the prices were very poor, being in most cases half, or less than half, what Mrs Coade later charged.

After that, Davy changed to another auctioneer, John Moreing,[15] whose records have been lost. He went on advertising in 1768 and 1770, changing to yet another auctioneer, Mr Blyth.[16] By April 1771,[17] a desperate note sounds in Davy's advertisements – the goods were to be sold without reserve. He advertised that his pieces were the Product of the Original ARTIFICIAL STONE MANUFACTORY, and pointed out that they had stood "Seven Years Trial" when he had only been in business for four. His last entry in the *Daily Advertiser* was on April 27th 1771. Among the Northumberland Archives at Alnwick is a frantic letter from him to the Duke, dated October 5th 1773,[18] asking for payment for "4 pieces of Cornis . . . 4 Pattras [paterae] with Lyons heads . . . 2 Medallions of Your Graces Head" costing in all 14.8s.0d. "for I must Actually go to Prison in a City Action if I can't raise fifteen Pounds by the 15th or 16th of this Month".

The existence of this letter suggests that it may have been Davy who made the artificial stone decorations on Robert Adam's Brentford Gateway at Syon House, home of the Duke of Northumberland. These decorations crumbled at the first frost, and Eleanor Coade, in her catalogue,[19] complained that they had injured her reputation, since people thought they had been made by her. The Coade firm had to replace most of this decoration later.

Croome Court, Worcestershire, Druid 1795

Another candidate for the Syon decorations might be a Mr Bridges. On May 26 1755 [sic; it was in fact 1775] Christies sold "the remaining stock in trade of artificial stone at the manufactory in Knightsbridge belonging to Mr Bridges, quitting that business, consisting of figures, Pedestals, Bustos, Vases, Tablets, a remarkably fine figure of a Druid . . . etc".[20] The Syon Screen is dated 1773; if the decorations failed in the winter of 1773 or 1774, this would provide a reason for Mr Bridges to go out of business in 1775. At the sale, Mrs Coade bought the Druid and various other pieces, and it appears she bought the factory as well, since in December 1778[21] she sold all the equipment of "Mrs COADE's Manufactory at Knightsbridge . . . The Whole to be sold extremely cheap, on Account of clearing the Premises, the Business being carried on only at King's Arms' Stairs Lambeth". The equipment then sold will be referred to later.

Yet another artificial stone factory was opened in February 1780 at No.1 Upper James Street., Golden Square by Arnold and Co. as their *Daily Advertiser* entry states. By 12/14 April, however the partners John Lynch, Samuel Arnold and Thomas Sharpe had split up leaving only Lynch and Sharpe in charge. They said that "all favours received will be gratefully acknowledged", but whether they got any is not now known. They did not advertise again.

On June 20th 1780,[22] there was a sale on the premises in Princes's St. Lambeth of the Artificial Stone Manufactory of William Brooks, deceased. His interesting stock, including "Aphers and Pudlocks . . . Hatters and Malsters chaffering Slap Jacks" seems to have been for the manufacture of builders' fireclay objects rather than decorative pieces. He was presumably succeeded by Joseph Chandler, of Prince's Street, Lambeth, artificial firestone manufacturer, who can be found in *Bailey's Directory* of 1784.

All these manufacturers had one thing in common – failure. Most of their names were unknown until Mrs Nancy Valpy undertook her researches in the *Daily Advertiser* of which the only complete run is in the Library of Congress in Washington. How was it that Coade factory, making the same kind of thing, survived?

Keystone, early 19th century, 57 South Lambeth Road

NOTES

1. St Mary Lambeth Poor Rate Books, Minet Library, Brixton

2. Geoffrey Wills, *English Looking Glasses,* p.61.

3. Documents (uncatalogued) of the Jenkins Bequest, Jesus College Library, Oxford. I am most grateful to the College librarian for allowing me to examine them.

4. Survey of London vol XXIII p.25.

5. *Coade's Gallery* handbook of Coade and Sealy's exhibition rooms, 1799.

6. Patents no 447, dated 31st May 1722 and 448 dated 13th June 1722.

7. *A short Treatise of Artificial Stone as t'is now made* . . . 1730.

8. Information from Mrs Nancy Valpy who discovered the advertisments of the early artificial stone makers in the *Daily Advertiser.* The full text of all these *Daily Advertiser* advertisements is printed in *English Ceramic Circle Transactions 1986.*

9. *An Essay on the Origin, Nature, Uses and Properties of Artificial Stone* . . . Daniel Pincot 1770.

10. Jenny Cupial "The Coades and their Stone" *Concrete* October-November 1980 pp. 18-22, 27-29.

11. *Daily Advertiser* 31st January 5, 11, 13, 20, 24, 27, February.

12. *Daily Advertiser* 23, 30 October 1767.

13. *Daily Advertiser* 31 January. February 11, 13, 20, 27.

14. *Daily Advertiser* 23, 30 October.

15. *Daily Advertiser* 23, 24, March 1768, 27 May 1768, 4, 15, June, 12 December 1768.

16. *Daily Advertiser* 5, 8, February 1770.

17. *Daily Advertiser* 17, 18, 19, 27 April.

18. Syn V I 28 – Information from Dr Colin Shrimpton, Archivist to the Duke of Northumberland.

19. *A Descriptive Catalogue of Coade's Artificial Stone Manufactory,* 1784.

20. Archives Messrs. Christies's.

21. *Daily Advertiser* 24 December 1778.

22. *Daily Advertiser* 20 June 1780.

CHAPTER 3

The Coade Factory

Mrs Coade, in the handbook of her exhibition rooms, *Coade's Gallery*, specified the date of the foundation of her factory as being 1769, yet as we have seen Daniel Pincot had been in the same place, making the same product, for the previous two years. It is time to put together the scraps of information we have about her first manager.

It is not known how Pincot and Mrs Coade got in touch with each other. As both were Dissenters, they may have met through their chapel or dissenting friends. Hoxton, where George Coade was in 1767,[1] is not very far from Whitechapel where Pincot began production at Goulston Square; and, particularly when they were not as welcome as they were in the easy-going south-west, Dissenters congregated together.

Like Holt, Pincot wrote a pamphlet on artificial stone, which was published in 1770.[2] It is an engaging mixture of sense and nonsense. Houses in London, he thought, were "stuck about with carvings in a most execrable taste", but judicious people would not be satisfied with "a dull Apollo, a limping Diana, a knock-kneed Hercules or an impotent Mars". Not only was the standard of carving poor, but the resistance of natural stone to the weather was unsatisfactory, and people needed some new material. Yet when he showed some samples about three years before, (no doubt at the Free Society of Artists' exhibition), "the only encouragers were persons who had some understanding of these burnt bodies".

Like Holt, he believed that our ancient cathedrals were built in part of artificial stone, but he went further in flights of fancy. "Stones of baked earth", he thought "were discovered almost directly after the Flood . . . or more probably long before the Deluge". The Great Wall of China was of artificial stone, since the "Chinese are most probably the offspring of Abraham and his concubines, which I could prove, were it worth the pains". In spite, however, of the advantages of design, cheapness and ease of manufacture, the building trade rejected it, as it ran counter to accepted practice.

> "The masons are decrying the material and deterring modellers from working in the manufactory; telling them they will be despised by the whole trade as forwarding a work which it is in their interest to suppress . . . Again, when their employers signify an inclination to use this material, they immediately cry out "Oh, Sir! Why will you have artificial stone? Nature must be better than art; it is but an imitation, a meer makeshift. Is it not more to your credit to have real stone than to stick up earthenware?"

Pincot made the point that glass in windows must be a makeshift, since horn was natural, but clearly felt frustrated by the opposition he and others were encountering, and his pamphlet ends on a rather dejected note. This must have been reinforced by the results of a sale at Christies in 1771[3] of artificial stone. Again, there is no indication of the seller, who could have been Davy, Bridges or even Coade and Pincot, but whoever it was, the results were abysmal. Eighty-nine lots, some of them consisting of several pieces, went for a total of £34.9s.6d.

Nowhere in Pincot's little book is there any mention of Mrs Coade's name, nor is she mentioned when in 1771 he obtained a subscription for a copy of the *Borghese Vase* from Henry Hoare of Stourhead.[4] (It survives in the Temple of Flora there). In 1771 also he wrote on his own authority to Matthew Boulton, telling him that the *Borghese Vase* was ready for Mr Wyatt, and that the *Medici Vase* would be modelled soon. Sir Nicholas Goodison, who found the letter, kindly pointed out to me that this Wyatt was Samuel, then Clerk of the works at Kedleston, for which Matthew Boulton was doing work at the time. It is therefore satisfactory that the very fine pair of *Borghese* and *Medici Vases* has survived on the steps of the south front of Kedleston. In relation to the history of the Coade firm it is interesting that the *Borghese Vase* is not marked, but the *Medici* is marked Coade. Possibly because in the pamphlet and in these two orders Pincot had given no hint that anyone else was concerned with the factory, Eleanor Coade went into action. In the *Daily Advertiser*[5] of September 11th 1771 (and also in the *Gazetteer* and *New Daily Advertiser*) she stated that:

> "WHEREAS Mr Daniel Pincot has been represented as a Partner in the Manufactory which has been conducted by him; Eleanor Coade, the real Proprietor, finds it proper to inform the Publick that the said Mr Pincot has no Proprietry in this Affair; and that no Contracts or Agreements, Purchases or Receipts, will be allowed by her unless signed or assented to by herself."

Customers were to apply to her at Mr Demar's, Bridge Head, Lambeth. Three days later,[6] she inserted an announcement that:

> "Eleanor Coade gives notice that Mr Daniel Pincot having now no further Employ at her Manufactory at King's Arms Stairs, Narrow Wall, Lambeth; all Orders relative to the Manufactory are desired to be sent to Eleanor Coade at Mr Demar's, Bridge Head, Lambeth."

That was the end of Pincot's connexion with the Coade firm. Nothing further has been found about him, except for the fact that he died in 1792 and was buried, like other Dissenters, in Bunhill Fields Cemetery. It seems that she may have taken over, from him, designs which he had already produced, since in her September 11th announcement she said that:[7]

> "Whereas her present intention is the making such Things only as are bespoke, those Goods which were at first produced as Specimens to the Publick, such as Bustos, Figures and Various Ornaments, Chimney-Pieces,

Frizes etc. shall now be allowed at a Price sufficiently low to encourage any Gentlemen or Builder who chuses to treat about them."

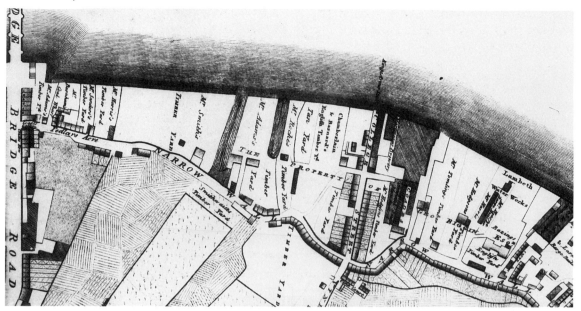

Richard Horwood's plan of London 1799, showing the sites of the factory and of Coade Gallery, at the end of Westminster Bridge.

View of the Coade factory in the 1790s. Note the workman leaning on a font like that at Debden.

Bedford Square, London, Doorway c.1775.   *Coade etching of a doorway of Bedford Square type 1775*

Pincot may have been unwise, indeed not very truthful, in leaving Mrs Coade's name out of his correspondence, but the break between them may have been precipitated by the fact that she had found a much more promising collaborator. On September 23rd and 25th she announced in the *Daily Advertiser*[8] that:

> "Her Manufactory at King's Arms Stairs, Narrow Wall, Lambeth, lately conducted by Mr Daniel Pincot, is now under the Superintendance of Mr JOHN BACON, Sculptor, whose Merit as an Artist being too well known to need any Encomiums, she promises herself the Continuence of that Encouragement she has hitherto received from the Publick . . ."

Bacon was extremely astute choice. He began life in humble circumstances, and it need hardly be said that he was a Dissenter.[9] He was apprenticed to Nicholas Crisp,[10] who had a shop opposite St Mary le Bow Church and a kiln in Lambeth, to model little porcelain figures, and was said to have been so impressed by the large terracotta busts being fired in the kiln that he formed a resolution to do something of the kind himself. (If he had seen the busts of Roubiliac they would have been worth emulating). Crisp was a founder Fellow of the Society for the Encouragement of Arts and Manufactures, and an important figure in its proceedings until he was involved in a financial scandal; and it is possible that he drew the Society's attention to his able apprentice.[11]Bacon at any rate won a number of the premiums given by the Society to encourage youthful talent.

The foundation of the Royal Academy in 1768 came at an important time for Bacon. He was one of the first students at its art school, and became an Associate of the Royal Academy as soon as it was possible to do so in 1770. At this early date, the Associateship did not have the prestige it later acquired, but it was an indication of the eminence later to be achieved by Bacon as one of the foremost neo-classical sculptors of the later 18th century.

Mr Timothy Clifford discovered, in the British Museum Print Room, an early trade card of John Bacon, giving his address as "at Mr Pincot's, Spitalfields".[12] So it may have been Pincot who brought Eleanor Coade and his supplanter together. Bacon's religious feelings must have struck a responsive chord in Eleanor Coade's heart.

Bacon wrote an epitaph for himself:

> "What I was as an artist was of some importance to me while I lived: what I really was as a believer in Jesus Christ is the only thing of importance to me now"[13]

Such sentiments at the end of his life were only the culmination of a belief in divine preservation following a childhood accident, and would have been a recommendation to Eleanor Coade, even if he had not been a man of outstanding talent.

The book of Coade etchings in the British Library has a title page hand-written in indian ink on which somebody, at some time, has written in faint pencil "Published only for private circulation in the years 1777, 1778 and 1779, no doubt under the superintendance of John Bacon, the sculptor who was for many years the real proprietor of this Artificial Manufacture". As I will show later, the book must have been put together after 1784, and I believe that the statement that Bacon was the proprietor must be equally an error. Certainly in the early years, the position was one of Eleanor Coade as the employer and Bacon as the employee. "Miss Eleanor Coade, sculptor, S. of A." [Society of Artists] as the catalogue described her, exhibited annually at the Society of Artists' exhibitions from 1773 to 1778 and again in 1780.[14] In all, she exhibited figures of *Urania*, a *Vestal*, two *Sybils* [sic], two *Floras* and two *Pomonas*, *Minerva*, a *Charity Group*, *Hymen* and *Psyche*, two *Lions*, two *Bas-reliefs*, a *Naiad*, two *Tripods*, a *Medici Vase*, another*Vase*, several *Pedestals for Candelabra*, a *Chimneypiece* from a design of Mr Johnson's, a *Pedestal* intended for a Sundial by James Paine Esq. and a *Group of Figures* for the Marine Society (another Charity group). Apart from mentioning the two architects Johnson and Paine, she gave no suggestion that any other designers were responsible for her exhibits. Yet when we turn to the handbook of *Coade's Gallery*, published in 1799 after Bacon was dead, we find Mrs Coade attributing to Bacon a number of works which she had exhibited as her own twenty years before – *Urania*, a *Vestal*, a *Flora* (I cannot identify which) a *Naiad*, *Hymen* and *Psyche* (small sized figures for Mr Locke) *Minerva* and the *Group* for the Marine Society. Collation of the list of her Society of Artists' exhibits with her statement of 1799 shows that each year from 1773 to 1778 she showed as her own at least one, and in 1777 three, compositions which she later allowed to be by Bacon. This hardly suggest that in the 1770s Bacon was the proprietor and Eleanor Coade the employee – rather the reverse. The same relationship can be seen in a commission for Sir John Griffin Griffin, at Audley End, of 1773.[15] Sir John paid Mrs Coade 15 guineas for the figure of a *Vestal*, and in addition gave Bacon £12.15s.0d as a present, thus suggesting to me that it was a new design completed to Sir John's particular satisfaction. If Bacon had been the proprietor, the whole cost would have gone to him. But he receipted it "Bacon for Coade", and she exhibited it as her own at the Society of Artists' exhibition the next year.

Etching of the Charity Group for the Marine Society by John Bacon RA, and a Minerva.

In 1799 she also attributed to Bacon a set of the *Seasons, Contemplation, a Tyger* and its *Companion* and the huge 9 foot *River God*. It seems therefore that Bacon's original postion was subordinate, but with his rising reputation she was happy to stress his association with the firm. In Ducarel's *History of Lambeth* (1784) there is a print of the *River God*, and the writer says of the factory:

> "Here are many statues which are allowed by the best judges to be master-pieces of art, from the models of that celebrated artist John Bacon Esq., a specimen of which Mrs Coade has given us liberty to present to our readers".

The work shown, the *River God* – was the most expensive item, at 100 guineas, in the Coade catalogue of 1784.

Bacon had been intelligent, as well as lucky, in attracting the interest of the King. In the early 1770s,[16] a bust of George III was commissioned for Christ Church, Oxford, and the King gave sittings. It was customary for clay modellers to take a mouthful of water and spit on the clay as they worked.[17] Bacon thought it would be unseemly to do this in the royal presence, and had a little silver filter made for the purpose. This elegant behaviour pleased the King, whose influence later secured many commissions for the sculptor.

In 1771 Mrs Coade had referred in her advertisement to the "Superintendance of Mr Bacon". On May 8th 1772 she advertised[18] that the firm was "under the Inspection of Mr Bacon, of Wardour Street, Soho", and I think that this must imply that Bacon was not at Lambeth every day, though important pieces would receive his consideration. However, his influence went far beyond the particular designs attributed to him. One statue could easily be altered into another by changing the poses of arms and heads, and giving them various emblems. Only two sets of plaques are specifically associated with Bacon's name, for Chelmsford in 1789[19] and a repeat set, almost duplicates, made after his death for Lewes; but dozens of related plaques, all with reclining girls, are strongly Baconian. *Agriculture* (or Ceres), with corn could easily be turned into *Hibernia*, with harp, *Hope*, with anchor, *Architecture*, with set-square and so on. His influence therefore extended far beyond the particular designs attributed to him, and permeated the whole of the figure work of the firm. His graceful, gentle neo-classical style was exactly appropriate to the architecture of Adam and the Wyatts.

Mrs Coade, too, designed in a Baconian style. Though she purloined some of Bacon's work to show at the Society of Artists' exhibitions, at least half the pieces she exhibited appear to have been her own, and of a sufficiently high standard to be shown in a professional artists' exhibition. Most of them were based on engravings or plaster casts of classical pieces, and the guide lines were there, but none the less much skill had to be employed to render them in three dimensions on the scale required. When she showed her version of the *Medici Vase* there was no nonsense about its being exhibited in the lobby; it was in the main exhibition.[20] It will be remembered that she lodged, in 1771, with Mr Demar, who can be identified as John Emmanuel Diemar who lived "opposite the Lying-in Hospital, Westminster Bridge". He was a modeller in wax and was one of the directors of the Society of Artists, where Eleanor exhibited. He seems likely to have been her tutor.

Bacon's Coade connexions continued for most of his life. Mrs. Valpy found an advertisement in the Daily Advertiser as late as June 14th 1776 showing the factory was still under Bacon's superintendance. The Chelmsford plaques and the enchanting *Charity*[21] figure surviving in the Fishmonger's Hall were made in the decade before his death. His association with the firm was important in giving it a quality of design and a cachet which none of the other manufacturers could approach. By March 1773,[22] Mrs Coade could advertise that:

> "The Proprietor of this Manufactory, instead of enlarging on its Merits, in the usual Stile of Advertisements, begs leave to mention the single fact of her being employed by many of the Nobility and first Architects of the Kingdom, apprehending that to be a more powerful Argument in its favour."

If this was a slight exaggeration in 1773, it very shortly became a plain statement of fact. At the most recent count, more than 140 architects and builders were on the list of Coade stone users, including all the best known; no list has been made of Mrs Coade's titled customers, but, from George III downwards, it must have included a handsome fraction of Debrett.

Early on, when Pincot was about to be sacked,[23] she announced that "her present Intention is the making of such Things only as are bespoke". Subscription lists were also kept for some designs: on May 8th 1772[24] she advertised that she had on show "the superb and elegant *Borghese Vase*. The number of Subscribers being compleat, those Orders will be immediately attended to".

I have already referred, in connexion with Mr Bridges of Knightsbridge, to the fact that Mrs Coade bought his premises and appears to have run them for three years. Her announcment of Christmas Eve 1778[25] gives the details of her closing down sale addressed:

> "To Builders and Others. Artificial stone now selling by Hand at Knightsbridge, constisting of various Ornaments, a great Number of Ballusters, Blocks for Cornices, Rustics for Frontispieces, Facia, and Coping at 10d per Foot run, a Pair of Piers erected in the Yard, Egyptian Sphynxes and other odd Things; likewise a Horse-Mill, with a cogged Wheel of 16 Feet Diameter, a Bed-Stone and two Runners, with an apparatus for a Beating Mill, some Moulds, a very large Quantity imperfect, to be sold as waste Plaister, which not having been injured by Oil is preferable to what is generally to be met with. The Whole to be sold extremely cheap, on Account of clearing the Premises, the Business being carried on only at King's Arms Stairs, Lambeth, where a Variety

of elegant Designs are to be seen. Attendance at Knightsbridge from Ten to Four".

The Horse-Mill was for grinding the materials used for Coade stone or other ceramic bodies. When the Lambeth Coade site was excavated in 1949-50 in connection with the clearing of the area for the Festival of Britain, a horse-mill was found by Mr F.J. Collins, then of the LCC Historic Buildings Department, together with some wasters (pieces distorted in the kiln) and a quantity of plaster moulds, or pieces of them. The plaster and Coade stone relics are now in the Museum of London, and the bed of the horse-mill has been incorporated on the paving in front of the Royal Festival Hall. Unfortunately as there is no information on an adjacent plaque; few realize what this circular motif can be.

Plaster moulds were oiled inside to facilitate the removal of *plaster* casts from them. Ceramic bodies such as Coade stone would not require a mould to be oiled, since the body would shrink as it dried, and so would easily drop out of the mould. We must assume that Mr Bridges was making some kind of a ceramic body related to Mrs Coade's, and so he too would have used un-oiled moulds. Broken moulds sold by the large group of plaster-cast manufactures, on the other hand, would have included many oily fragments.

We must assume that the bespoke orders came in in large numbers, since in 1784 Mrs Coade issued a catalogue, containing 778 items, including *figures, busts, paterae, capitals* and all kinds of other architectural pieces, *vases, urns, chimneypieces* etc. It is worth pointing out here that as moulds were expensive, and would not have been made unnecessarily, each piece in the catalogue must have been made in Coade clay at least once. While a large number have been traced, there remain many more of which the catalogue is at present the only evidence, and which eventually may come to light.

An engraver was available, and plates were made, so that prints could be sent out in answer to customers' enquiries. These were outline illustrations, and not particularly good; a Coade figure usually looks better than its printed representation. An exception was the *River God*, a fine etching with the figure fully modelled. There is a tradition that this plate was made by William Blake, and while I have not yet found any documentary evidence, apart from the graffito on the British Library etchings, it seems a reasonable suggestion, since he is known to have done commercial illustations for Josiah Wedgwood,[26] and probably for others. We have already investigated the business relationship between Eleanor Coade and John Bacon. The statement about the dates is equally suspect. Far from all being dated 1777-1779, fifty-eight of the plates (there are two whole-plate etchings) have no dates at all. Of the remaining twelve, four are dated 1777, eight are dated 1778. None is dated 1779.

The British Library copy of the etchings does not have numbers for the designs, and so it is not possible, without referring to the numbered designs in the other books, to disentangle *Urania* from *Clio* or a *Vestal* from a *Sibyl*. By collating the numbers of the designs on the plates with those in the catalogue, it can be seen that several have numbers higher than any in the catalogue, while some have no numbers at all - merely the size and price written in. Such designs must have been made after the issue of the catalogue. The presence of such plates in *all* the books indicates that the plates were assembled into books after 1784. If I am right in assuming that one of the monument designs (unnumbered, and with only the size and price - 30 guineas - written in) is related to Repton's Babworth monument[27] (demolished), this print may be late as 1790.

Coade factory yard, 1790s showing the River God like that at Ham House and other pieces.

George III's interest in Coade stone may date from the end of the 1780s, when Henry Emlyn was reconstructing the Screen in St George's Chapel (see chapter on Commissions for the Crown.) I have found no later etchings in book form; if there were other, later prints, they must have been kept as loose sheets in the factory, and been lost.

Bacon died in 1799. By this time old Mrs Coade, the widow, had been dead for three years.[28] John Sealy, Mrs Coade's cousin, son of Mary Sealy, old Mrs Coade's sister, had been working in the factory for some years (he was there in 1792) and by 1799 he was made a partner. From being COADE, or in the 1780s COADE'S LITHODIPYRA, (the meaning of this made-up word will be discussed in the chapter on the manufacture of Coade stone) the firm's stamp became COADE & SEALY. Sealy must have been a capable modeller, since in

The Picture of London, Richard Phillips in 1804 (p.263) reports that "Mr Sealy has lately finished a colossal statue of his Majesty to be placed . . . at Weymouth" where it still is.

In 1798, a row of houses was built and named Coade's Row at the eastern (Surrey) end of Westminster Bridge and Coade's exhibition gallery was opened there and is described in Chapter 5 Coade's Gallery.

A nephew of John Sealy was also employed at the factory, since *The Times* of January 11th 1804 records that he struck himself against a post in the dark at Pedlar's Acre and was so badly injured that he died. John Sealy's son, another John, was a sculptor, but I have not yet found any evidence that he designed for the firm; in any case he died only four years after his father.

In the Coade Gallery handbook, the new designer for the firm now that Bacon was dead is given as John Devaere,[29] and his design for the Pelican Insurance Company's overdoor group was used as the frontispiece. This is not up to Bacon's standards, with a Pelican Insurance representative, in the guise of a Roman Centurion, calming some distraught ladies who are presumably widows being told that their claims would be met by the Company. (It has survived, and is in the garden at the back of the Horniman Museum in South London).

Horniman Museum Garden, S.E. London, Pelican Insurance Company Group by Devaere, pre 1799.

Apart from a candelabrum, I do not know of any other designs which can be specifically attributed to Devaere, but towards the end of the 18th century, the Coade firm had been able to call on John Charles Felix Rossi, a more robust sculptor. He modelled the *figure* of Coke on a column at Stoke Poges[30] and the *bust* of Warren Hastings at Melchett Park,[31] among other pieces for the firm, and he was said according to its text to have modelled the huge group of *Acis* and *Galatea* at Coade's Gallery. (In the early 19th century he set up on his own, the artificial stone caryatids on New St Pancras Church being his).

Coade and Sealy were at the height of their success at the beginning of the 19th century, and in 1810 obtained the commission for the huge memorial, 40 feet long, to Nelson at the Royal Naval College at Greenwich. The pamphlet[32] written to describe this "epic poem in stone", mentions a number of the firm's commissions between 1799 and 1813. At Greenwich another modeller was employed, Joseph Panzetta, who worked on the designs of Benjamin West. Panzetta,[33] in 1830, said that he had worked for the Coade firm for 26 years, which would suggest that he first worked at the factory in 1804, and his name can frequently be found in the firm's records from 1813 to 1821.

Exterior of the Coade factory in the early 19th century.

In October 1813,[34] John Sealy died, aged 64. Since he was younger than she was, the elderly Mrs Coade might have expected him to survive her, and his death must have been a blow. Too old to go back to managing the firm by herself, she took on William Croggon,[35] a man from Grampound, Cornwall, who was in some way related to her aunt Frances Enchmarch, who had married Walker Oke. A Walter Oke Croggon appears in the Croggon family tree, but the present-day historian of the family, Mr John Croggon, tells me that he had not been able to work out the exact relationship between Walter Oke Croggon and the William Croggon who managed the Lambeth factory. There seems to have been a remote cousinship between him and Mrs Coade, however, and such relationships counted for a good deal in the Georgian period.

William Croggon was 45 years younger than Mrs Coade,[36] and was not made a partner. The firm reverted to being Coade. He managed the factory for the eight years from Sealy's death to her own in 1821 when she rated an obituary notice in the *Gentleman's Magazine*, 1821 vol 2 page 572:

> "November 18th at Camberwell in her 89th year, Mrs Eleanor Coade, sole inventor and proprietor of an art which deserves considerable notice. In 1769 a burnt artificial stone manufactory was erected by Mrs Coade at King's Arms Stairs, Narrow Wall, Lambeth. This manufactory has been carried on from that time to the present on a very extensive scale, being calculated to answer every purpose of stone carving, having a property peculiar to itself of resisting the frost and consequently of retaining that sharpness in which it excels every kind of stone sculpture and even equals marble itself".

On her death Croggon found that he had not been left the business. He seems to have engaged in some litigation in Chancery with the executors and in consequence his Order Book and the Work Book in which he recorded accounts as they were sent out, and the Letter Book which had been begun by Sealy at the beginning of 1813 and continued by Croggon, all remained in Crown custody, and are now in the Public Record Office.[37]

They were discovered by John E. Ruch, who made an extensive study of them, "Regency Coade, a study of the Coade record books 1813-1821" *Architectural History* 1968 p.34-56. Coade students are much indebted to Mr Ruch for this discovery.

While the earlier history of the firm is only sparsely documented, these Croggon papers shed a flood of light on the work at Lambeth. We know what was made, for whom and what it cost. At the end of his Work Book Croggon jotted down how much he had paid to various workmen, so that the names of Coffee, Griffith, Ilam, (or Ham) Murray, Wilcoxon, Morgan, Cooke, Pyke, Harrison, Hill, Wilson, Watkins, Thomas, Young, Henesey, Calleghan, Barnett, Dunn, Wheeler, Durand and Kelly come out of the shadows. Jones and Robinson had charge of the horse and cart. It is not clear if they were all there all the time, but Panzetta (called Panzetti by Croggon) and another designer called Thomas Dubbin seem to have been in continuous employment. Dubbin, usually referred to as Mr

Dubbin, seems to have been sent out to interview clients and to do drawings on the spot.[38] When scagliola manufacture was begun he seems to have been responsible for the capitals and bases of columns. On Mrs Coade's death he and Croggon attested the will, and while Croggon called himself Artificial stone manufacturer, Dubbin, surprisingly, described himself as Gentleman. (PCC 651 Mansfield).

Wages, when recorded, seem to have ranged from 4s.6d to 9s.0d per day. Senior modellers had 12s.0d. Packing cases, to stand up to the rigours of Georgian travel, had to be strongly constructed and were quite an expensive item. There seems to have been no allowance for "Returned Empties", and customers often had to pay £5 or £6 for them.[39] The pieces were usually taken to an inn which served as the depôt for travel by regular carter – East Anglian orders waited at the Blue Boar in Whitechapel. Some pieces went by Pickfords;[40] this firm, now renowned for removals by road, had at that time recently begun a service of "Flying Boats" which travelled along the developing canal system.

When he had bought the firm, Croggon, of necessity, had to begin a new set of work books, and these have been lost, so that for the last period of the firm's history there are no internal records at all. Fortunately, Croggon's most important work after 1821 was for Buckingham Palace, and full records of this are in the documents of the King's Works. Things would have continued successfully, it would seem, if Croggon had not become involved in work for the Duke of York, as detailed in the chapter on Scagliola. He went bankrupt in 1833 and died in 1835. His younger son Thomas John refounded the firm, which – as Croggon (1835) and Co – survived until at least 1977, making wire netting, but has now disappeared from the industrial lists, possibly through takeover. Though Thomas John retained the factory, and the moulds and some remaining pieces were not sold until 1843,[41] little more Coade stone seems to have been made, though there are pieces dated as late as 1840.

A *History of Lambeth* – no date and no author (Minet Library 12/64) probably circa 1821 – states that "This extensive concern has recently been purchased by Messrs. Croggan [sic] and Co. who are removing it to the New Road leading from Somers Town to Paddington". This has been repeated, by Mrs Esdaile[42] and others, and taken to mean that the whole concern was moved to Marylebone Road – Euston Road, to be in a good position to attract customers in the newly developing Regent's Park area. The *factory* remained where it always had been, and both addresses are recorded for Croggon in the Trade Directories up to the 1830s.[43] The Pedlar's Acre showrooms were given up, they were now too far from the fashionable areas to be of much use. The great composition over the entrance to the original showrooms was however removed to the new site, as the *Builder* (August 22nd 1891 p.140-141) states that "on the front of Messrs. Smart and Co's fringe and upholstery workshops within 110 yards of the end of Hampstead Road, may be found the original bas-relief, a mythological composition (or replica of it) that distinguished the factory at Lambeth. That bas-relief is now partly hidden from view by two shops, nos. 268 and 279 Euston Road, which have been built in the forecourt".

This writer is not correct in saying, as did Mrs Esdaile, that the business passed to

Austin and Seeley, of the New Road. Felix Austin was indeed in the New Road, from 1830,[44] but his premises were in a different part of the street and he described himself in the directories as an architect, statuary mason and sculptor as well as artificial stone manufacturer. As he also advertised himself as *Roman* stone maker, his medium was not a ceramic but something like the reconstructed stones of today, which harden by chemical action. His advertisement (*Concrete* 1980, November, p.13) reproduces Austin & Seeley's designs, made "in their own peculiar Composition, without either the use of Roman Cement or the application of Heat". He was not joined by Seeley until 1843, some time after the Coade works had ceased production.

Thomas John Croggon seems to have diversified in several ways[45] being an agent for scotch whiskey, anchor chains and other ventures before settling down as one of the pioneers of bituminous felt, and by the 1840s he was in business in the City. If any records of the Coade phase of his family business were kept by him and passed down, they were all blown up in the last war.

J. M. Blashfield was said by Gunnis[46] to have bought the Coade moulds and to have manufactured artificial stone. He did indeed make artificial stone of good quality but of a yellower colour than Coade stone, as can be seen in the fine gates at Castle Ashby. As the Coade moulds etc. were sold in 1843, and Blashfield did not begin artificial stone manufacture until after 1851, he cannot have bought them, and indeed the designs shown in his catalogue in the Victoria and Albert Museum library are quite different.

Blashfield remarked in his essay on terracotta[47] that he had been inspired to make something of the kind by seeing the pieces for which Mark Blanchard had been awarded prizes at the Great Exhibition of 1851, and it seems to have been Blanchard who for a time carried on the manufacture of something in the nature of Coade stone. Though he changed over later to the strongly coloured terracotta preferred by the Victorians, and his name can be read on the decorations in the courtyard of the Victoria and Albert Museum, Mark Blanchard made some pieces which, apart from his stamp, are indistinguishable in medium and design from Coade pieces. His advertisement in the *Builder*, as late as December 29th 1855, will serve to conclude this chapter.

He was, he said:

> "late of Coade's original works, and successor to them in the manufacture of this invaluable material that has been so successfully adopted for nearly a century in this country by our eminent architects and others, and in the adornment of our noblest buildings and is the only tried material that is capable to stand the ravages of time unimpaired".

NOTES

1. At Charles St Hoxton, George Coade executed a deed as surviving trustee for an Exeter Charity, appointing Samuel Coade and others as trustees in his stead. It was witnessed by Eleanor Coade Junior. Information from J.A. Havill.

2. *An Essay on the Origin, Nature and Uses and Properties of Artificial Stone 1770.*

3. Catalogue in Messrs. Christie Manson Wood's archives.

4. Information from Kenneth Woodbridge.

5. Information from Nancy Valpy.

6. Information from Nancy Valpy.

7. Information from Nancy Valpy.

8. Information from Nancy Valpy.

9. 1. *John Bacon* RA by Ann Cox-Johnson.
   2. *Dictionary of British Sculptors*, Rupert Gunnis, article on John Bacon RA.

10. "Nicholas Crisp founding member of the Society of Arts" John Mallet, *Journal of the Royal Society of Arts*, December 1972, January, February, May 1973.

11. Ibid.

12. Mr Mallet records Crisp being a member of a dissenting meeting in Bury Street, and a Methodist, but also a member of the Vestry of St. Mary le Bow, the Church of England church opposite his premises.

13. Ann Cox-Johnson op.cit. p.43.

14. *The Society of Artists of Great Britain, the Free Society of Artists*, Complete Dictionary, A. Graves, 1907. Coade entries.

15. Essex Record Office. Audley End Archive D/DBy A 30/2.

16. There seems a difference of opinion over its date. Gunnis gives 1770. Ann Cox-Johnson (p.11) implies that it was after 1771.

17. Cox-Johnson ibid p.11.

18. *The Daily Advertiser.*

19. See section on plaques, chapter on External Architectural Details.

20. Unlike Pincot's Borghese Vase, which was not allowed into the main exhibition room as it was a copy.

21. 1791. Fishmongers' Company's records.

22. *Daily Advertiser* 26 March 1773.

23. *Daily Advertiser* 11 September 1771.

24. *Daily Advertiser.* The vase had been modelled by Pincot.

25. *Daily Advertiser.*

26. He illustrated Wedgwood's 1817 Queen's ware catalogue. *Dictionary of Wedgwood* Robin Reilly and George Savage p.49.

27. See chapter on Funerary Monuments.

28. Gunnis op.cit.

29. Or de Vaere.

30. See chapter on Commemorative Monuments.

31. See chapter on Commemorative Monuments.

32. *Description of the Grand Model of Neptune giving up the Body of Nelson with the Dominion of the Sea into the Arms of Britannia, executed from a Design by Benjamin West Esq. for Greenwich Hospital at Coade and Sealy's Ornamental Stone Manufactory, Lambeth.* Undated but probably 1813. Scottish National Library Acc 5111 box 12.

33. Gunnis op.cit. Panzetta entry.

34. Monument in St Mary Lambeth churchyard.

35. Many writers, including Gunnis, incorrectly spelt the name Croggan.

36. Information from Mr John Croggon.

37. All filed together as C 111/106.

38. He was sent for instance to do drawings at Deane Church near Basingstoke. See chapter on The Gothic Style.

39. Lord Rosebery had to pay something approaching £1000 for packing his Coade stone for Dalmeny House, Lothian Region, Scotland.

40. See chapter on The Gothic Style. i.e. CD May 1814. "Earl of Plymouth sent by Pickford's barge from Paddington to Hewel [Hewell] Grange near Bromsgrove, to be left at Tardebag [Tardebigge] wharf
    1 Medicean   )
) vases with pedestals £105".
    1 Borghesian)

41. Sale by Rushworth, Jarvis, Savile Row, on the Coade premises, July 21st 1843 and the three days following. Card of admission to view in Minet Library Brixton. (12/64).

42. *Architect and Building News*, K.A. Esdaile, January 19th-26th 1940, pp 94-96 and 112-114.

43. Until 1822 the trade directories (Robson's and the P.O. Directory) list E. Coade Narrow Wall. In 1823 the name changed to Croggon and Co (Kent's Directory). There are no directories for 1824. In 1825 Croggon and Co Narrow Wall (Kent's Directory). Between 1826 and 1835, Croggon, William and Co are at Narrow Wall Lambeth and New Road St Pancras in Kent's and Pigot's Directories, the latter address sometimes being expanded to 6 Palace Row, New Road and once as "next to the Duke of Grafton". In 1835 the New Road address disappears and the firm is listed

only as at Belvedere Road (which Narrow Wall had become). In 1836 the firm becomes Croggon T.J. and Co. and in 1837-1839 Croggon Thomas John, son of the late William Croggon, at Belvedere Road. In 1840 both T.J. Croggon and Routledge Greenwood and Keene are listed at the same address in Belvedere Road (Robson's Directory), but in 1841 Routledge Thomas and Co. were in sole possession there and Thomas John Croggon had gone to 17 Fenchurch St. (P.O. Directory).

44. At 1-3 Keppel Row, New Road, Fitzroy Square (Robson's Directory). He remained there until 1843 when he was joined by Seeley. They later opened premises at 24 Church St. Rotherhithe.

45. 1843 Post Office Directory.

46. Gunnis op.cit. Blashfield entry.

47. *An Account of the History and Manufacture of Ancient and Modern Terracotta and its use in Architecture as a durable and elegant Material for Decoration* 1855. In the Victoria and Albert library.

CHAPTER 4

The Making of Coade Stone

As the illustrations show, the standard of design of the Coade firm was high, and the range wide; but unless there had been a satisfactory medium in which to carry out these designs, little would remain for us to study. The results are for us to see, and we must try to investigate how they were achieved.

The story that the formula for Coade stone has been lost has been repeated so often that it is now generally believed. It has been asserted that the secret died with Mrs Coade herself, without taking into consideration the fact that thousands of pounds worth of Coade stone decorations were used in the building of Buckingham Palace and elsewhere in the decade after her death. There is even a charming story that the secret formula was stolen from a locked drawer in her desk. This is romantic, but untrue. As we have seen, a number of people were making what they referred to as artificial stone before Mrs Coade came on the scene, with what appear to be unsatisfactory results. No pieces made by the manufacturers mentioned in Chapter 2 have so far been identified, and though some may come to light through the discovery of bills etc., I think it more probable that most will have crumbled away. (There are in fact occasional records of faulty firing of Coade pieces, necessitating replacements, and the Coade stone Sealy family tomb at St Mary Lambeth is in a poor state).

From Holt's patent it is clear that he was making a form of *ceramic* body; so was Mrs Coade, and we must now try to identify what it was and how it differed from what is offered as artificial stone today.

Most modern artificial stone is a type of concrete. The materials used harden by chemical action, without the addition of heat. The Romans knew how to make it; and for the last century vast quantities of concrete have been made for structural use. Very large sizes can be made without great difficulty – the walls of the 2nd century Pantheon in Rome are twenty feet thick – and therefore large pieces of artificial stone are not likely to arouse great interest.

The principles used in making a *ceramic* artificial stone are quite different because the raw materials are not converted into the final product until they have been subjected to considerable heat, for a considerable time, in a kiln. The conversion of clay into ceramic bodies has of course been known from antiquity, and anyone who has stood astonished in front of the life-size Etruscan Sposi in the Villa Giulia in Rome, or has seen the six-foot pottery warriors which have recently come to light in China, will know that civilizations with primitive equipment have been able to produce breath-taking results.

But if the raw materials and technique may be simple, such results are produced by a highly sensitive balance between the clay and the fire. Mrs Coade's contemporary, Josiah

Wedgwood, the cleverest ceramic chemist of his day, made hundreds of experiments before succeeding in perfecting his jasper ware, and thousands of his experimental pieces in general have survived to show how patiently he built up his chemical knowledge in relation to the firing temperatures possible in his time.[1]

Without modern chemical analysis, without accurate methods of measuring the temperature in the kiln, with primitive means of achieving and controlling that temperature, so that a change of wind might act as a bellows and ruin a kiln-load of pieces by over-firing, the achievements of someone like Wedgwood or Mrs Coade are remarkable; and apt, even today, to be underestimated. As Pincot remarked in his pamphlet, the only encouragement he received was from those with some understanding of baked earths, and this statement is true at the present time. Take an average architectural historian to see the nine-foot reclining figure of the *River God* at Ham House, tell him it is a form of pottery, and he will express polite interest. Show the figure to an average ceramic historian, and he will have difficulty in believing his eyes. His previous experience will have suggested to him that such a thing is not possible.

There are three kinds of ceramic body – earthenware, which is porous, and has only a small part of the clay vitrified (melted to a glassy consistency) in the kiln; stoneware, which is non-porous, and in which a larger proportion of the clay has vitrified; and porcelain, which is the most highly vitrified, is virtually translucent, and is extremely difficult to make into large-scale objects as the clay almost liquifies in the kiln. The strongest of the three bodies is porcelain, but the difficulty of making it would rule it out for statues, capitals and so on. For practical architectural purposes, stoneware is the toughest available ceramic body, and this is what Coade stone is.

Stoneware is made in large quantities by craft potters, and most households contain at least one factory-made piece of stoneware in the form of a casserole, but Coade stone is no ordinary form of stoneware. A striking feature of the Coade stone body was its extraordinary small rate of shrinkage. Clay vessels are expected to shrink from 10%, and in some cases up to 20%, in drying and firing. Yet the Coade body shrank only half an inch per foot in drying, and a further half inch in firing, or just over 8%. To achieve this remarkable result, a large part of the materials used must have been unshrinkable. Since clay once fired will not shrink again when put back into the kiln, the Coade formula must have included clay which was already fired, and so *pre-shrunk*.

Such a body is not unusual. Pre-fired clay, ground to powder and called "grog" is often used in the stoneware body of the "kiln furniture", used to support and hold wares in firing, which is still to be found in potteries today. We can be certain grog was included, even without laboratory tests, since Mrs Coade told her customers so – those who knew Greek – in the name she used for her product for about ten or fifteen years before 1800. She called it *Lithodipyra*, a word put together from three Greek words meaning *stone, twice* and *fire*. The *di* (twice) element in the word refers to the grog part of the formula and also to the crushed glass which was included, both of which were of course fired twice – once to produce them, and a second time when kneaded into fresh clay to form the Coade body.

Confirmation of this can be found in what I believe to be the most accurate contemporary description of the making of this material. In his sumptuous book on his Custom House[2] David Laing said it was:

> "a material which, although composed of various ingredients, may be described as a species of terracotta. It combines in one mass pipe-clay, flint, sand, glass and stoneware, that has already passed the furnace. These are ground to a very fine powder, and are mixed in the proper proportions, and the whole is well kneaded together by means of the addition of water. In this state it forms a kind of paste which has the ductility of the clay usually employed in modelling; it is now wrought into the form desired . . . and when finished it is left to dry gradually. When thoroughly dessicated, the performance is placed in a kiln, where it undergoes an intense white heat; and being allowed to cool it is now complete".

"Stoneware that has already passed the furnace . . . ground to a very fine powder" is a precise description of grog, as we have just seen.

Albury Park, Surrey. Capital by Sir John Soane 1800-1802, back of a capital, showing construction.

When the Coade factory site was excavated c.1949-1950, some of the materials thought to have been used for making Coade stone were found with the relics already described. They included calcined flints and a clayey compound which was taken to be Coade stone before firing. The Building Research Station of the then Department of Scientific and Industrial Research was given samples of this clay, and S.B. Hamilton, in the *Architectural Review* of November 1953 (pp.295-301) reported on their findings. At that time, it was concluded that the clay was kaolin (china clay) and not ball clay. The other ingredients were finely-ground flint, quartz and glass. The Building Research Station fired its sample and noted that something like Coade stone could be produced at temperatures of 1100°-1150°C. which would be a heat comparable to the white heat mentioned by Laing.

Since the 1950s, techniques of chemical analysis have progressed. In the 1970s, I was given a fragment of one of the gate-pier tops of Belmont, Lyme Regis by its present owner. This house was taken over by Mrs Coade from her uncle Samuel in 1784, and owned by her until her death. It was built by a Mr Bunter – hence its early name of Bunter's Castle – but it is reasonable to suppose that the Coade decoration with which its façade is covered was put there by Mrs Coade soon after she took over, as a kind of three-dimensional catalogue. So this piece of Coade stone is satisfactorily attributable to the Coade factory and the mid 1780s.

I gave some of it to Miss Bimson of the British Museum Research Laboratory, and she made an analysis of it at the time, and has recently carried out, with Dr Ian Freestone and M. S. Tite, a further investigation of the body using the most advanced techniques.[3] The stone has been analysed by optical microscopy, x-ray diffraction (XRD), a Cambridge S600 scanning electron microscope (SEM), atomic absorbtion spectrometry (AAS) and a Cambridge Instruments Geoscan microprobe fitted with a Link Systems energy dispersive spectrometer. Samples were refired at temperatures from 1100°-1200° C. in a Pt-wound furnace and examined by the SEM. I am grateful to these researchers for permission to summarize their findings.

They conclude that Coade stone was manufactured from a ball clay (not, as earlier thought, a china clay). Coming from Dorset and Devon, the main sources of ball clay, the Coade family would have been in touch with suppliers among friends and relations.

"10% or more of grog, possibly crushed stoneware, 5-10% of flint and 5-10% of fine sand were added to reduce shrinkage. About 10% crushed soda-lime-silica glass was added as a vitrifying agent. While the body is not as vitrified as porcelain or china materials, it is comparable with some stonewares, and was fired at temperatures of 1100°-1150° C, well in excess of those of earthenwares and many earlier terracottas. Salt glazed stonewares of this period were fired at these temperatures or higher. Thus the available kiln technology was sufficient to achieve the required temperatures. The skill and expertise involved in the firing of Coade stone was that which enabled maintenance and control of such temperatures for up to four days in kilns of a size sufficient to accommodate the larger pieces of sculpture. The ability to produce ceramic sculptures that could be fired at such temperatures depended on careful selection and mixing of raw materials and careful preparation. It is the highly vitrified nature which is responsible for the hardness of Coade stone and this in turn is responsible for its resistence to weathering.

There is no evidence for the deliberate addition of marl, felspar or titanium dioxide, which have previously been suggested as fluxing agents."

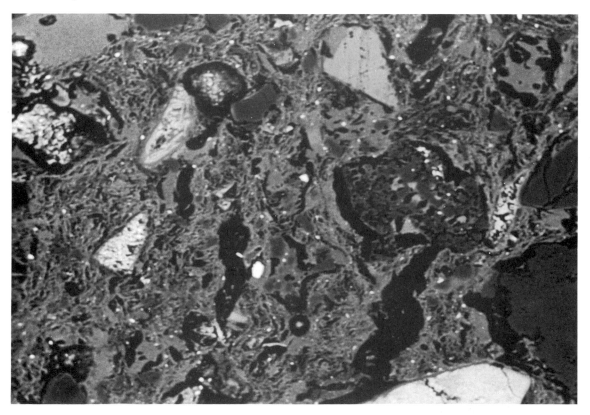

Belmont Lyme Regis 1784. Microscopic section of Coade stone. British Museum Research Laboratory.

Dr Freestone, Miss Bimson and Mr Tite point out that the Coade formula corresponds very well on most points with a formula quoted by Charles Fowler in his paper on terracotta, of 1850, which I have already mentioned. He gave a formula which he had obtained from the great building firm of Thomas Cubitt, and which they said was in general use for builders' ornaments:

"white potters' clay forming about one half; pulverised stone ware from one-third to one-fifth; ditto glass, from one-fourth to one-ninth; and some add, for finer purposes, a small portion of white Reigate sand and powdered flint, about one-tenth part of each".

As the decorative details on houses of the Regency period and on into the 1850s are invariably painted in with the plasterwork, I believe that this continuance of a similar formula to Coade's has not been previously noticed. If it came out reddish in colour, this did not matter as the paint concealed it; Bubb's decorations in Regent's Park and Rossi's caryatids at Montpellier Walk, Cheltenham are noticeably red under their cream paint.

The elements of the Coade body were therefore far from a secret in the mid-nineteenth century, and probably were known to the capable ceramists of the late Georgian period, from whom it was difficult to hide anything. It was the meticulous preparation of the raw materials combined with the high temperature of a long (and expensive) firing, which distinguished the Coade product from those of competitors, and provided for its remarkable resistence to weathering.

As Miss Bimson pointed out to me, a body of this kind, with not much more than half of it clay, would not be very plastic. (In view of the modern use of the word, I must point out that I use it in the potter's sense of being capable of being shaped with the fingers). It would not have been possible to model direct into the clay as a craft potter or sculptor would do. Moulds would have to be made, and the Coade clay would have to be rolled out in a "bat" like pastry and pushed into them. Mr F.J. Collins has pointed out to me that he has seen very small fingerprints inside some Coade pieces, and thinks that perhaps children may have been employed for this fidgety job.

For a new design, someone like Rossi or Panzetta would have made a model in modelling clay. This would be at a scale of 13 inches to the foot, to allow for shrinkage to the correct size in the kiln. Then a plaster mould would have been made from it; and finally the Coade clay would have been pushed into the mould and later fired. This meant that even "one off" designs required moulds, even though it would have been more convenient if it had been possible to work direct in the Coade clay.

Two *pedestals* for Royal Lodge, Windsor,[4] for instance, cost more than £53 each for modelling in clay and making moulds, and only £42 for producing in Coade stone.

Good moulds were therefore of the greatest importance. They were expensive and had to be carefully kept. When the Festival of Britain site was excavated and the factory site found, Mr F. J. Collins discovered a mould with "Altar Pelian Office" written on it in pencil. It belonged to the classical altar on the *Pelican Office's over-door composition*, and the detail moulded from it can clearly be seen today. Devaere modelled this design before 1799, so the mould must have been carefully kept for something like forty years.

The use of moulds also had the advantage that a successful design could be repeated at will. The first *Borghese Vase* was modelled in 1771; the last I know of is stamped 1827. Nor did the fact that moulds were used mean a standardized, mass-produced job. All kinds of variations were possible, using supplementary moulds. A garden vase, for instance, could be plain, or with lion-head handles, or it could have swags of drapery or the family coat of arms. If it was needed for the top of a funerary monument, its normal finial would be replaced by flames signifying resurrection.[5] The various details would be moulded separately and stuck on, using slip (liquified clay) as an adhesive. The firing fused the ornaments permanently on the background. The little white bas-relief figures on Wedgwood jasper ware are stuck on in exactly the same way today.

Complicated pieces would be made up from a number of moulds. The various parts, when sufficiently dry, would be assembled together by someone similar to the "repairer" who put the arms, legs and bodies together of the little china figures made at Chelsea or Bow. The joins of the moulds usually leave seam-marks, and further hand work would have been needed "fettling and towing" to remove them, since they are very rarely to be seen. Probably women were employed in this work – Mrs Coade remembered two women "at my manufactory" in her will. Further work with modelling tools would be needed for sharpening up detail, undercutting and incising lines and inscriptions before firing. (The head of the *River God* at Ham has received a great deal of handwork in deepening his eye sockets, detailing his hair and the shells tangled in it and defining his eyebrows).

If the grog and other ingredients meant a loss of plasticity, and hence the reliance on moulds, it had compensating advantages. There was greater than normal stability in firing, so that thin slabs of very large size could be fired without distortion and to precise measurements. The sizes of small items in the Coade catalogue were specified down to $^{1}/_{8}$ inch. This dimensional control meant that friezes and other pieces could be made to fit successfully into masonry work, as precisely as if they had been carved in stone.

The grog, I believe, also gave Coade stone its characteristic texture. The broken surface of a piece of Coade stone is indistinguishable from a piece of natural stone. The moulded surface is smoother, varying from something like slate,[6] to something like emery paper,[7] but never approaching the high polish of Victorian terracotta. Coade stone harbours lichens exactly like natural stone,[8] and this is probably the reason why so few garden ornaments made at Lambeth are recognised for what they are. In general, it is very difficult to distinguish between Coade stone and natural stone apart from the sharpness of detail.

When Coade stone had been taken from its mould, neatened and dried, it was ready for the kiln. Mrs Esdaile[9] quotes a letter of 1790 from John Lygo, the Derby factory's London representative, who tried to get the man in charge of the kilns to give him the secret of the Coade process. This man told him that there were three kilns, all, considering what came out of them, of remarkably small size. The largest was 9 feet in diameter, he said, though I cannot think this was right. An interior view of the kiln, published in the *European Magazine*,[10] shows the *River God* and the *Four Seasons* figures, as well as other pieces all inside it. There were two smaller kilns. There were only three fire holes (the places where the fires were stoked) in each. Saggars, the stoneware boxes used to keep the ceramic pieces from the flames, were not used, and the great size of most Coade pieces would have precluded their use, even if the kilns had not been muffled to prevent too much heat reaching the pieces. This is a very early date for a muffle kiln. The muffle wall can clearly be seen in the *European Magazine* illustration. The fireman told Lygo that muffling, as well as all the other work connected with firing, was his responsibility.

Engraving of the interior of the Coade kiln. The River God and Statues of the Seasons being fired together, 1784.

Firing went on for four days and nights continuously, and the fireman relied on his own judgement to get the temperature right. Sometimes this failed him, and exhibited as a curiosity in Coade's Gallery was a figure so over-fired that the whole of the surface was vitrified.[11] Wedgwood had invented a pyrometer for checking kiln temperatures as early as 1783, and among the Wedgwood archives is a note of one being sent to John Bacon. Beside it is the letter G which is thought to mean gift or gratis.[12] Either Bacon kept it to himself, or the fireman was not prepared to use it. Hartley coals were used for firing and the fireman got an extra allowance for firing nights, apart from his guinea a week. Lygo called him a "drunken bad chap", but lured him to Derby all the same. Mrs Coade had some cold words to say in her will about drunken workmen, and her views may have been coloured by his behaviour.

The Coade factory appears in a number of prints and drawings.[13] At first, it appears to have been simply a converted house, with a porte cochère allowing the carts to get into the yard at the back. In later years, the porte cochère was improved, and had an elaborate composition of the Royal Arms over it. A 1798 print showing this version of the premises in the GLC collection has caused confusion, as someone has written, under the print, "Pedlar's Acre". The Pedlar's Acre site, Coade's Gallery, had not yet been built at the time the print was made, and, as we shall discover in the chapter on it, looked quite different.

With the generally held view that the formula is lost, it is often said that Coade stone could not be made today, but this, again, is untrue. The formula is known, and the probable firing time can be postulated. Mollie Adams consulted the British Museum team and used their formula to model the figure illustrated here in 1987. It was fired by Diogenes Farri of East Sydney Technical College N.S.W. Its colour and surface conform to Coade examples. With the resources of the pottery trade today, there is no reason why Coade stone should not once more be made commercially.

Seated figure by Mollie Adams, Coade stone 1987

NOTES

1. They are in the Wedgwood Museum, Barlaston, Staffordshire.

2. David Laing, *Plans etc of Buildings Public and Private executed in various parts of England*, 1818. In spite of the title, almost the whole book was concerned with the Custom House, the construction of which, as it turned out, was a disaster. All the Coade stone disappeared in the rebuilding.

3. I.C. Freestone, M. Bimson and M.S. Tite. "The Constitution of Coade Stone," *Ancient Technology to Modern Science* ed. W.D. Kingery, The American Ceramic Society Inc. Columbus, Ohio. 1985.

4. Bill for pedestals. Windsor Archives 16736.

5. I.e. Bligh tomb.

6. I.e. the capitals in the library at Ickworth.

7. I.e. the urns at Mottisfont Abbey.

8. The quantity of gold-coloured lichen on the vases in the garden at Killerton led early viewers to think they were looking at traces of gilding, with the consequent belief that the vases must once have been indoors.

9. Op.cit. Lygo's letter was owned and printed, in his *The Ceramic Art of Great Britain from Prehistoric Times Down to the Present Day* (1878) p.141, by Llewellynn Jewitt. He also owned and printed a letter from Eleanor Coade to William Coffee dated 1792. Among the many unaccountable mistakes made by Jewitt in his description of the Coade firm, he confused the unnamed fireman referred to in Lygo's letter with the Coffee mentioned in the letter from Mrs Coade, even though this is dated two years later. Coffee eventually went to Derby as a modeller, where Lygo was dissatisfied with his work: "The figure no.359 is very vulgar about the bosom, for sure never such bubbys were seen and so much exposed. The design is pretty enough". (*Old Derby Porcelain and its Artist Workmen* by Frank Hurlbutt, p.44. No date but from appearance c.1910.)

10. European Magazine 1786.

11. No.55 Triton fountain. "The effects of inattention to the kiln fires at the time this statue was burnt, is worthy of observation, its surface being almost vitrified, the preservation of any part of the remaining contents of the kiln, depended on the hasty extinguishment of the fires".

12. Information from Gaye Blake Roberts, Curator, Wedgwood Museum, Barlaston.

13. The Guildhall Library print collection has a number, several of which are reproduced here.

CHAPTER 5

Coade's Gallery, 1799

Towards the end of the 18th century, the Coade firm must have been at the height of its success, and it is fortunate that a document has survived which gives us a vivid picture of its production at that time.[1] John Sealy was now a partner, and I think it may have been he who had the idea of setting out an impressive showroom where visitors could see the whole range of Coade pieces. Instead of merely labelling and pricing the items, he and Mrs Coade issued a booklet which took the visitor on a conducted tour of the premises, embellishing each description with quotations from the best authors, classical and modern. For instance, the particulars of a *bust* of the *Duke of Clarence*, (who was in the Navy) included a line from Virgil and its translation "He has the command and governance of the sea"; while a *fountain nymph* prompted a passage on Sabrina, the spirit of the Severn, from Milton's *Comus*. The booklet makes lively and enjoyable reading, and it is fortunate that a copy of it has survived in the British Library. (T.16(7))

The Gallery was a few hundred yards upstream, of the factory, at the Surrey end of Westminster Bridge and approximately where County Hall now stands. The site was a piece of land known as Pedlar's Acre. The Records of the Commissioners of Westminster Bridge (PRO Works 6/37) show that Mrs Coade asked for permission to build new premises near the Surrey abutment of Westminster Bridge "where she proposes, to erect a Building with an elegant Front much to the Ornament of the place". On 16th May 1798 she was granted a 31 year lease at 15 guineas "only requiring that a substantial Brick Building be erected with a handsome outward appearance". Building went on in 1798 but the Lambeth Rate books[2] show that the Gallery was not then occupied, as no rates were paid until 1799. The great Coade *lion*, made in 1837, has now been placed near the site. The gallery itself had disappeared by William IV's reign, but the terrace that housed it, Coade's Row, survived into this century.[3]

The Westminster Toll House and the Ordnance Tavern nearby were decorated with Coade stone, but the great set piece was at the entrance to the Gallery. John Bacon had designed a "card of direction to the Manufactory" which appears as the frontispiece of the Guildhall and Soane Museum books of engravings. At Westminster Bridge it was enlarged to a bas-relief symbolizing "the Attempts of Time to destroy Sculpture and Architecture, defeated by the vitrifying Aid of Fire." Fire, with flowing hair and a torch in her right hand, took a flying leap at Father Time, gripping his arm so that he dropped his sickle, his attitude being, as Mrs Coade said, "finely emblematical of dismay and confusion." In the background, a kiln was visible, open so that a triple-figure candelabrum could be seen inside. Keen-eyed visitors could read a quotation from Ovid round the top of the kiln. This great panel was supported by four male terms on pedestals eleven feet high;

Mrs Coade remarked that "the anatomical parts of these statues are worthy of observation", and those who wish to observe them today can see a set supporting the porch at Schomberg House,[4] Pall Mall, and the surviving, but battered, chimneypiece in the hall at Seaton Delaval.

Frontispiece to the books of Coade etchings, taken from John Bacon's Card of Entry to the Gallery, and enlarged as a bas-relief, over the entrance to Coade's Gallery.

Over the side door was another large panel, listing all the types of Coade stone, warning against unsatisfactory substitues, and reminding the public that the firm had been honoured by commissions from the King, the Prince of Wales and the Duke of York.

Schomberg House, Pall Mall, London. Porch 1791

Schomberg House, Pall Mall. Term Figure 1791

Schomberg House, Pall Mall. Plaque symbolizing painting 1791.

A selection of the items will give the flavour of Coade and Sealy's display and show how their designs were attuned to the architectural tastes of the times. "Athenian" Stuart's renowned book the *Antiquities of Athens*[5] is the source not only of versions of the *Erechtheion caryatids*, already used by Soane at the Bank of England and Pall Mall, but also of a figure of *Decelia*. "This Athenian statue is seated with great dignity, girt with a lion's skin, and in her hands is the tripod won by Thrasyllus – *Stuart's Athens*. 6ft. high", said Mrs Coade. It is possible to identify the figure from Plate 6, vol. II of Stuart's book. I have not seen an exact version of this figure, but believe that she lost her lion's skin, received a shield, and arrived on top of the dome of Liverpool Town Hall as *Britannia* in James Wyatt's reconstruction.

Nearby in the Gallery were *Flora* and *Ceres*[6] "from the Farnese Collection" (a pair is to be seen at Heveningham Hall) and a chimneypiece with pilasters ornamented with "profile figures modelled from designs found in the ruins of Herculaneum" (as at Capesthorne, Cheshire)[7]. There was "an antique *Sybil*[8] [sic] from the Barberini collection (as at Burghley House) and the favourite *Medici* and *Borghese Vases*[9].

After these discreetly classical pieces, the visitor came upon a *coup de théâtre*:

Engraving of the entrance to Coade's Gallery, 1799, at the end of Westminster Bridge

"This stupendous design is conceived at the moment when Polyphemus discovers, from the summit of the rock, the nymph *Galatea* with his rival *Acis,* upon whom, in his fury, he hurls a fragment of stone, and kills him. This work occupies a space of 20 feet in height and 12 in width, the Polyphemus is a statue of 10 ft. 6 ins., a cave is formed in the rock, at the entrance of it lays [sic] the *Acis* and *Galatea*, much larger than life".

It is a great pity that though this astonishing composition survived until at least 1824, when L., a writer in the *Somerset House Gazette*, saw it,[10] there appears to be no illustration of it. For the frontispiece of their handbook Coade and Sealy chose the much more insipid *Pelican Insurance Office Group*, an engraving we could manage without as the actual group survives at Forest Hill.[11]

In a suitably melancholy setting inside the cave were shown a group of tombs which survive in a number of places, and which are described in the chapter on Funerary Monuments.

There were also two angels, one with a trumpet and the other with a sword "in the character of *Admonition and Reproof*" for which Mrs Coade (or John Sealy) found suitable quotations from *Paradise Lost*.

Mrs Coade seems to have been allowed to model from "*an antique sarcophagus*" at Stowe. It was originally in the dining-room there, and is described in the 1797 handbook to the house by J. Seeley (no relation). On the top, in Mrs Coade's words there was "a naked figure laying [sic] on a serpent" and an inscription saying that it was made in the time of Trajan. Mrs Coade was clearly delighted with it, saying that "it is impossible to give an adequate description of the exquisite workmanship of this piece of ancient sculpture", and to prove her words, the Coade sarcophagus was rediscovered in spring 1989 by Mr Peter Hone. It is very small – only 2 ft. 3ins long – but admirably worked. The figure which lay on top, surrounded by a snake, is now missing and was presumably moulded and fired separately. The original is still lost.

In the Gallery was a copy of the Gothic *font* made for St George's chapel.[12] Mrs Coade was naturally pleased with this Royal commission, and devoted pages to a description of the figures on it, which were taken from Sir Joshua Reynolds' window at New College Oxford. Other Royal connexions were emphasized by *busts* of the King and the Duke of Clarence, and a *medallion* of the Prince of Wales. (None of these is now known). There was also "an elegant tripod for three lights . . . modelled for the Queen's Lodge at Frogmore", and a copy of a *plaque* erected by Lord Howard de Walden at Audley End, to celebrate the King's return to sanity in 1787. (It still survives there, see Chapter on Commemorative Monuments.) Coade's Gallery contained two Venus statues, the designs for which must have come from a book with an Italian text, since they are described as "131 The *Venus Callipygis* uscita dal bagno – Nell palazzo Ffarnese" and "132 A Statue of Venus in atto d'andare al Bagno". The first can easily be identified, and is now in the Museo Nazionale at Naples. She is illustrated and described in Francis Haskell and Nicholas Penny *Taste and the Antique*, p.316-318. In John Evelyn's accurate but inelegant description, she is "that so renouned piece of a Venus pulling up her smock and looking backwards on her buttocks". A Coade example of this piece has not yet come to light, but recently a Venus figure of exceptionally small size – less than three feet – appeared at an antique dealer's and is now in a private collection. The figure, which is delicately modelled, is nude except for a length of drapery held in her hands, and could well be described as "in atto d'andare al Bagno". If the two Venuses are meant to be a pair, the Venus Callipygis may also have been of this previously unknown small size. A clothed version appeared at Sotheby's Billinghurst sale on June 1st 1988, lot 770 (unprovenanced, stamped 1804).

Coade and Sealy, it appears, sold plaster casts as a sideline, but without enthusiasm. They remarked upon plaster's fragility, and "though casts may appear to be a saving of expense at first, yet it frequently happens, either through the carelessness of servants, accidents by carriage, or likewise, they have been rendered unfit for their situation, and Coade stone pieces had to replace them". A few pieces, however, were on show in plaster, for which orders were taken, and when a sufficient number had been received – ten, thirty or fifty –

Coade examples were to be modelled. John Wesley's bust was one of these, and clearly sufficient commissions from Dissenting friends must have come in for Coade examples to be made.[15] Another plaster bust was of Mrs Siddons as *Ophelia*; so many busts of her by Flaxman, Mrs Damer, John Hickey, Charles Rossi and even herself were available that there may not have been enough orders to Coade and Sealy to warrant manufacture.

Small Venus, possibly "Venus in atto d'andare al Bagno" of Coade's Gallery 1799

The Coade Gallery handbook includes a list of hundreds of places for which Coade stone had been supplied. This is not a complete list of commissions for the 1769-99 period since I have found dated pieces which Mrs Coade had forgotten, but in general it gives a good picture of the firm's activity. It is also extremely useful to the researcher of today in suggesting where to look. To take one county, Essex, as an example, Coade stone was supplied for "Chelmsford, Woodford, Wanstead church, Audley End, Debden Hall and church, Saffron Walden, Copped Hall, Dunmow church, Hill Hall etc." Debden Hall has been demolished, and I have not tracked down any Coade stone that was (or possibly still is) at Copped Hall; but at all the other places it survives, and at Chelmsford and Audley End survives in abundance. The Coade Gallery handbook is not only, therefore, an entertaining and enlightening period piece; it is an essential compass to point the Coade enthusiast in the right direction.

Coades Manufactory, Narrow Wall

NOTES

1. COADE'S GALLERY or EXHIBITION of ARTIFICIAL STONE, WESTMINSTER BRIDGE ROAD of STATUES, VASES, BUSTOS, PEDESTALS, and STOVES Medallions and Pannels in Bas-Relief, MODELS from the ANTIQUE, CHIMNEYPIECES, MONUMENTS, FONTS, COATS OF ARMS, ETC Specimens from the Manufactory AT KINGS ARMS STAIRS, NARROW WALL, LAMBETH, PRINTED BY S. TIBSON, NO.7 BRIDGE ROAD, NEAR ASTLEY'S AMPITHEATRE 1799.

2. Minet Library, Brixton.

3. *Survey of London*, vol. XXIII p.69. A house with a tablet inscribed "Coade's Row 1798" survived until 1908.

4. *Survey of London*, vol.XXIX p. 375-6. The Polygraphic Society, makers of very poor copies of pictures, put up the porch c. 1791. One of the figures is dated 1791; the date of the installation of the chimneypiece at Seaton Delaval, with duplicate figures of those at Schomberg House, is not known.

5. James Stuart and Nicholas Revett, *The Antiquities of Athens*, vol.1 1762, vol.2 dated 1787, published 1789.

6. See chapter on Statues.

7. See chapter on Interior Decoration.

8. See chapter on Statues.

9. See chapter Mrs Coade's classicism.

10. *The Somerset House Gazette*, 1824 page 381.

11. The composition is in the garden behind the Horniman Museum, Forest Hill, London S.E., and is attached to the back wall of the Museum, which does not own it.

12. See chapter on Commissions for the Crown.

13. See chapter on Statues.

CHAPTER 6

Georgian Architects and Coade Stone

Josiah Wedgwood complained to his partner Bentley, when he put his chimneypiece plaques on the market, that "we could not prevail upon the architects to be godfathers to our child".[1] The exact opposite could be said of Eleanor Coade. Over 140 architects and builders who used her work will be found listed at the end of this book, and it is only the more important, or more prolific, who will find a place in this chapter.

Robert Adam

20 Portman Square, London, by Robert Adam 1773-6, Plaques, Paterae, String Courses.

As suggested in the first chapter, the influence of Robert Adam was crucial in the development of the Coade style. Adam's well-known interest in Liardet's Cement had, I believe, diverted attention from his very considerable use of Coade stone. One of the earliest commisssions is Home House, 20 Portman Square. In her book *Home House* (1969) Margaret Whinney is, as far as I know, the only writer to identify Adam's use of Coade stone anywhere. At Home House there are oblong *plaques* with swags and paterae on the front of No.20 and also on the matching frontage of No.21. There are *string courses* of a guilloche pattern, and some round *paterae*, now overshadowed by a later balcony. On the back are round *medallions* of girls riding on mythical creatures, and on the back portico an *Ionic Order* which Margaret Whinney has identified as being from *Della Magnificenza ed Architettura de' Romani*, plate XX, by Adam's friend Piranesi.[2] Mrs Coade very rarely specified what was at the sites for which she had had commissions in her 1799 list, but for this house, probably recognising its importance, she said she had orders for "Pannels of oak [the plaques on the front] Capitals, Medallions, Ballusters etc."

73

The house has had an extra storey added, and it is not known if the balusters are now the original ones from the lower cornice. Nor is it known, since they are painted, if the bucrania on the porch are Coade stone or not.

Alnwick Castle and Luton Hoo are on the 1799 list. Anything that was at Luton Hoo has been lost in later reconstructions, but at Adam's Hulne Priory and Brislee Tower, Alnwick, Mr J.H. Cordingley has found bas-relief plaques of the Duke and Duchess of Northumberland in Coade stone. A few spare plaques kept at the Castle and shown to Mr Cordingley have the Coade stamp on the *edges* of the pieces, so that when inset in the masonry, the mark would be hidden. This is an important discovery, since there may well be many other built-in pieces invisibly marked in this way.

Caenwood (Kenwood) is also on the 1799 list. The fiasco of the medium used for the decoration of the south front is well known; but can it be that there is some Coade stone on the north portico? The large medallion in the pediment is in very high relief and perfect condition. As it is painted it is unlikely to be natural stone, and if it is plaster it is remarkably well preserved. Can it, and the capitals of the columns which follow a Coade pattern fairly closely, be of Coade stone?

At Croome Court, Worcestershire, Adam used Coade stone at the Island Temple. It is shown among the drawings in Sir John Soane's Museum[3] and is described as "Design for a building to be placed between the woods at Croome". Clearly to be seen are two circular bas-reliefs of the *Phrygian Shepherd and Shepherdess*, a long plaque of the *Aldobrandini Marriage* (the Grecian Wedding) and two panels of *Griffins and Ornament.* All survive in it today, and interestingly the bill was paid through Capability Brown. The bill was modest, the Grecian Wedding costing 8 guineas, the two griffin panels 10 guineas, and the whole thing, including "cases and cartage to ye inn" £26.13s.0d.[4]

Other orders for the Coade firm include Bury St. Edmunds Town Hall, (natural stone on the ground floor, Coade panels above), Newby Hall (*plaques* as Home House on the Adam extensions) Wedderburn (*heraldry*) and Dunbar Castle, later Castle Park Barracks, with the Lauderdale winged *sphinx* on its cornice. At Glasserton, Wigtownshire (now Dumfries and Galloway Region) the 1799 list mentions a "Statue for lights". At Culzean,[5] the Cat Gates are not surmounted by domestic cats but by *Egyptian Lionesses* copied from those on the Campidoglio in Rome. Also recently observed at Culzean are armorial *plaques* surmounting the archways leading into the formal garden on the landward side of the castle. At Stowe,[6] more *lions* were ordered for the North Portico, the £40 bill for them being receipted in February 1778. At Cullen House,[7] Banffshire, there is a gateway with *heraldic animals* for which there is a drawing by Adam (vol. 36, 68-70) in Sir John Soane's Museum, though it does not seem to have been carried out until 1816. At Castle Upton,[8] Co. Antrim, Ireland, there is a mausoleum by Adam in which Coade stone was used, including two *medallions* of mourners, *vases* and an *urn*, dated 1789.

The Brentford Screen at Syon was first decorated by someone unknown and had to be restored by the Coade firm in the early 19th century (see Chapter 2). Long after Adam's death, this design was re-used for the gateway of the zoo in Rio de Janeiro,[9] with its Coade

Stone decorations, (chapter on Coade Stone Abroad). Another copy of an original Adam work is the floor of the Ante-Room at Syon,[10] in scagliola

One of Adam's last commissions, at Gosford, near Edinburgh, dates from 1790, and combines the whole range of Coade designs which he had used elsewhere. This house has a stable block attributed to Adam, c.1790,[11] and decorated with a number of *plaques* and *roundels*. Several of the designs, such as the *Judgment of Paris*, have not been traced elsewhere, and were presumably special orders, but the *roundels*, here, with large heads, are catalogue items.

Gosford House, Scotland. Plaques on the stables, Robert Adam c.1790

The main house had a chequered career; it originally had two pavilions connected by wings to the central block, but only about a decade after completion, the wings and pavilions were pulled down, to be replaced at the end of the 19th century by Adamesque new structures by William Young. About ten years ago, Miss Catherine Cruft, of the Scottish National Monuments Record, found a large number of Coade *plaques* and *roundels* lying in the long grass in an uncultivated part of the Gosford estate. If the plaques came from the pavilions, they must have been there for something like a hundred and sixty years. There is unfortunately no record of how they were used, as no drawings of Gosford appear to be in the collection at Sir John Soane's Museum. They consist of oblong *plaques* of standard designs, and a dozen *roundels*, all showing over life-size heads, a few of which can be found among the etchings, but the majority being clearly designed specially. They include a girl in a helmet inscribed 'SCOTIA', a man in a turban, a man wearing an elephant-head helmet and a Red Indian. These last four suggest to me that there was a scheme symbolizing the Four Continents, with Scotia representing Europe.

A drawing of sphinxes wearing necklaces was discovered a few years ago at the house.[12] It came from the Adam office and was addressed to John Sealy, no doubt one of many drawings for the special items at Gosford. The *sphinxes* survive, and with the heraldic *swans* and *lions*, as well as the *plaques* and *medallions*, (1799 list – "Arms and supporters, Pannels, Medallions etc. at the Earl of Wemyss") make the Gosford collection unique, and a fitting conclusion to a collaboration between Eleanor Coade and Robert Adam which had lasted for most of her firm's existence.

Sir William Chambers

Sir William Chambers gave a very just report on Mrs Coade's disagreement with Horace Walpole; he went on to use Coade stone himself at his major work, Somerset House,[13] where twenty-nine *vases* along the parapet are of a particularly portly shape, with a spiral gadrooned top, which may reasonably be called the Chambers pattern. He also used Coade stone at his own house, Whitton Place, and at Stanmore House. Both are on the 1799 list, but as both have been demolished, it is not known what features he incorporated. At Rathfarnham Castle, Co. Wicklow, however, Mrs Coade's 1799 list give us more details; "Pannels of the Sciences, Patteras etc." were used there. The *panels* would probably have been the usual reclining ladies with scientific instruments. He also used Mrs Coade's work in a doorway in the base of the portico at Manresa House, Roehampton.[14]

Sir Robert Taylor

Sir Robert Taylor was another towering figure among the older architects. His splendid portico at Gorhambury[15] owes its Corinthian *capitals* to Mrs Coade. In recent years, the house has been refaced in Portland stone, which matches the Coade stone exactly. It would not have been possible to attribute the capitals to her if the bills for them had not survived in the Hertfordshire Record Office, where we read in the acount book of the 3rd Viscount Grimston that he paid "to Mrs Coade in part of her bill for capitals at the new house £250." (April 9th 1782). He paid the remaining £92. in March of the next year. Another Taylor site is Heveningham Hall, Suffolk,[16] where a line of *medallions* of the design known as *Griffins and Ornament* runs above the first-floor windows, and there is an elaborate composition of *figures*, *vases*, bas-relief *plaques*, and a *frieze* of swags above the centre of the front. Later work at Heveningham was by James Wyatt.

James Wyatt

James Wyatt made his name with the Pantheon, in Oxford Street, London, of 1770-72, and in Mrs Coade's 1799 list she mentioned *capitals*, *paterae* and *arms* for it, but the connection between Wyatt and Eleanor Coade may go back even earlier. The Town Hall at Burton-on-Trent was built by Benjamin Wyatt, the father of James in 1770-2, and it is now assumed that the design was a very early work of James. In 1771 and 1772, *Miss* Coade supplied "4 ornamental Patteras, 190 feet of Gulochi [guilloche string-course] and a coat of arms."[17] With his huge practice, he continued to use Coade stone throughout his working life, in about twenty-nine commissions. I have only found two occasions on which he used Coade Gothic motifs, at Sheffield Park[18] and Milton Abbey, where the now missing Gothic *font* may be attributed to him; the rest of the Coade-Wyatt collaboration is classical.

Heaton Hall,[19] Greater Manchester, is the first of a series of houses by both James and his elder brother Samuel where a bow-fronted two-storeyed façade has *plaques, medallions* or *paterae* between the storeys. The attached columns at Heaton have beautifully detailed *capitals,* and since they were made in 1772, only three years after the Coade firm's foundation, it is possible that the design may have been made specially for him. Mr James Lomax drew my attention to the fact that while *capitals, string course* and *paterae* are of Coade stone, the plaques on the garden side are of natural stone, and not very well carved. Since the Wyatt brothers used Coade plaques by the dozen later, it is possible either that Wyatt suggested to Eleanor Coade that she should make something of the kind herself, or that she saw the opportunity.

The Radcliffe Observatory[20] is a case in point. The back has three long bas-relief panels modelled by J.C.F. Rossi symbolizing *Morning, Noon* and *Night,* and in addition there are *plaques* of the *Signs of the Zodiac.*

At Liverpool Town Hall,[21] remodelled by Wyatt, the dome is crowned with a statue of Britannia by Rossi, again now gilded. More *figures* commissioned by Wyatt can be seen in a room at Bowden Park, Wiltshire, of 1796.[22] Being for indoor use, they could be "bronzed". Gunnis[23] mentions two figures at Hothfield Place, now demolished, and statues of *Flora* and *Pomona* are on the Orangery at Heveningham Hall,[24] surmounted by bas-reliefs of the Borghese Dancers.

Heveningham Hall, Suffolk, Orangery by James Wyatt 1780s, with Coade decoration.

In Coade's Gallery, Mrs Coade exhibited a *tripod* consisting of three figures with a circular abacus on their heads, which, she said, was designed by Wyatt for the Queen's Lodge at Frogmore. It is now untraced there, but what I believe to be the same design appears at West Wycombe Park,[25] where there are four *torchères* consisting of three girls linked by garlands. It also appears among the Coade etchings, and a similar design, with the girls' arms raised to support the abacus, was sold at Godmersham Park, Kent on June 6-9 1983.[26] A late commission for *figures* was at Purley Park, Reading in 1813,[27] again with bronzed, lamp-holding girls. Other Coade work must also have been supplied for the house, since it is on the 1799 list. Wyatt may also have been responsible for the *Druid*, now decapitated, at Erddig when he was working there, since another *Druid* at Croome Court, dated 1795, together with the Coade rusticated *"Dry Arch Bridge"* of 1796 and a gateway of 1794 surmounted by Coade *vases* all appear to belong to the period when Wyatt was designing garden features there.

Lord Portsmouth's Gateway in the 1799 list must be the entrance to Hurstbourne Priors. The house has been demolished, and the *mermaids* on top of the gatepiers there have now been transferred to gatepiers at Farleigh Wallop. Another gateway is at Blagdon,[28] Northumberland. Confusingly called the Kale Cross, it was made as a gift to the city of Newcastle by the Ridley family, and later given back to them; *lions* and *vases* are on its top. The Holgate monument[29] at Brocklesby, Lincolnshire, is attributed to Wyatt. It is a slim tapering structure surmounted by an *urn* and supported on three *tortoises*. The same design appears at Mount Edgcombe, Plymouth, and Stanmer Park, Brighton, all being of Coade stone. A puzzle is the fourth of this group at Lucan House, Co. Kildare, Republic of Ireland. There is decoration on a *bridge* and *plaques* on the gate-piers in Coade stone, but the monument has been discovered recently by Dr David Griffin to be of Portland stone.

Wyatt used Coade decoration on his own house, 1 Foley Place,[30] St Marylebone. The 1799 list, noting another important customer, specifies "Capitals, Pannels, Consoles, Trusses, Balusters etc. at the house of Mr James Wyatt". Three *plaques* of reclining ladies and four oval *paterae*, together with *Corinthian capitals,* may be seen on an ancient photograph of the front. Further *plaques* of these reclining ladies can be seen on the lodges of Ottershaw Park, Surrey, where at present they shock the viewer, as the owners have painted them in natural colours, with pink putti.

Antony Dale refers to Coade *plaques* at Charlton Park, Wiltshire,[31] and at Wilton House,[32] where he noted classical bas-reliefs in the Wyatt Cloister, now sadly removed.[33] He also refers to a Coade *chimneypiece* at Pishiobury Park, Herfordshire, as being by Wyatt, a rare example of a Coade *chimneypiece* being attributable to a particular architect.[34] For Stoke Park,[35] Stoke Poges, Wyatt designed the memorial column, with a statue of Sir Edward Coke in Coade stone, again by Rossi. Apart from these traced Coade examples, a number of James Wyatt buildings appear on the 1799 list, without it being possible to trace what was used; they include Henham Hall, Suffolk; Sunning Hill Park, Berskhire; Copped Hall, Essex; Bryanston, Dorset.

Samuel Wyatt

Samuel Wyatt was almost as devoted a user of Coade stone as his brother, employing it in much the same way. Doddington Hall[36] in Cheshire has *panels* and *medallions* between the storeys, and Neale's Second Series *View of Seats* (1829) shows Hooton Hall, also in Cheshire, to be almost a duplicate of Doddington. Only its lodges, with Coade *plaques*, survive. At Holkham,[37] the Vinery and East Lodge both have Coade decoration; the Vinery of 1780 has *paterae* and a strip of guilloche *string-course*, and the East Lodge (1799) has a specially designed round *medallion* with an ostrich crest and a wreath of oakleaves said to have been modelled by Bernasconi.

Herstmonceux Place[38] is another example of the Wyatt, two-storeyed house with *plaques* between the ground and first floors, but the *plaques* here are unusual and not in the catalogue, having larger and bolder motifs than normal. In this they are nearest to the *plaques* at Woodhall Park, Hertfordshire, by Leverton. It is a pity that the Herstmonceaux *plaques* have been painted white. Probably the most appealing of this group, by either brother, is Belmont,[39] near Faversham in Kent (1792). Here the basic design of Herstmonceux has been refined by Samuel, and includes a full range of Coade details, oblong *plaques* with leaf swags as at Portman Square, other oblong *plaques* with festoons of flowers which I have not seen anywhere else, a pair of bell *kraters* with human-head handles, only one of which survives, guilloche *string* courses, and round *medallions* of putti representing the *Seasons*. In the middle of the South front a standard Coade *reclining lady* lolls in front of Belmont house itself.

Belmont, Faversham, Kent, 1792 by Samuel Wyatt

At Shugborough,[40] Samuel Wyatt added a portico with Ionic Coade stone capitals. He may also have added the Coade Druid (now in the ruins). Also possibly at Wyatt's order, a Coade *plaque* of *griffins and ornaments* has been added to the memorial to Admiral Anson's cat.

In London, Samuel Wyatt was responsible for the *Arms* of the elder Brethren of Trinity House,[41] City of London, and in Birmingham he designed the exterior of the Theatre Royal,[42] for which he ordered medallions of *Shakespeare* and *Garrick*. In addition, a number of other houses by Samuel Wyatt appear on the 1799 list, including Temple House, Hurley, Berkshire; Penrhyn Castle near Bangor, Gwynedd; and Kinmel Park, Clwyd, which has been rebuilt but still retains its *Egyptian Lionesses* on the gate piers.[43]

Shugborugh, Staffordshire, Colonnade, 1790-98, Samuel Wyatt

The next generation of Wyatts - Lewis, Benjamin Dean, Philip and Sir Jeffry Wyatville used small amounts of Coade stone and scagliola, and their contributions can be found in the architects' list and the gazetteer.

Henry Holland

Henry Holland worked frequently with his father-in-law Capability Brown, and the Orangery at Broadlands, Hants,[44] with its spare Coade decoration of a triple-swag *plaque* surmounted by an *urn*, is likely to be his. A *Borghese Vase* in the garden could have been placed there by either of them. Berrington Hall, Herefordshire, is unquestionably Holland's, and has small details of Coade stone inside the portico. Here, the Coade cream colour, which I believe could have been modified, seems unhappy against the rich brown-pink of the sandstone used for the house; the effect must have been better at Carlton House,[45] where the Portland stone would have harmonized with the *trophies of arms* supplied from Lambeth in 1795. Holland also used Coade stone *figures* at the first Royal Pavilion at Brighton. In *Coade's Gallery*, Mrs Coade mentioned the *statue* of Fortitude as being a duplicate of one of six "supplied in 1788 for his Royal Higness's Pavilion in Brighthemlstone". A similar subject appeared on Nash's Buckingham Palace,[46] as one of a set round the dome on the garden side. Henry Holland's Debden Hall, Essex, is on Mrs Coade's 1899 list. It has been demolished and illustrations do not indicate what the Coade work was.

Henry Holland was responsible for the development of Hans Town in Chelsea. Most has been rebuilt, but at the time of writing there are still five houses, 188-193 Sloane Street, which may have been designed by him, and which have Coade stone doorway decorations.

Lancelot "Capability" Brown

Capability Brown was also a user of Coade stone. Apart from his collaboration with Adam at Croome Court, Worcestershire, he also used the Lambeth product at Burghley[47], where Coade *lions,* now lost, were supplied; at Tixall[48], Staffordshire, where some more Coade *lions* were used on a screen wall; and at Redgrave Hall[49] Orangery, where Coade *Seasons* were appropriate with some *paterae.*

John Johnson

John Johnson was not a particularly renowned architect, but since he used a great deal of Coade stone he should be mentioned here. He was County Surveyor for Essex, and built Chelmsford Shire Hall,[50] a serene building decorated with three specially designed *plaques* by John Bacon the Elder. Johnson was proud of the Shire Hall, and in 1808 published a fine volume of plates of it,[51] in which he said that "all the ornamental parts of the front including Plate XIV [detail of the Bacon plaques] are all finely executed in artificial stone by the late eminent artist J. Bacon R.A." Apart from the plaques, the Coade work consists of *capitals* of two sizes of a particular Ionic design.

Chelmsford Shire Hall, Essex, by John Johnson, Plaques, 1790-92 designed by John Bacon RA.

Not far from the Hall, Johnson designed a *Naiad Conduit*,[52] of 1793. Also in the town centre is Moulsham Bridge,[53] a delightful high-arched structure, with rotund Coade *balusters* and oval *plaques* of River Gods' heads.

In 1800 there was further work for the County Surveyor, as Chelmsford parish church,[54] now the Cathedral, collapsed and Johnson re-built the *south arcade*, the *ceiling* and *angel figures* between the clerestory windows (see chapter on Gothic Coade).

The remainder of Johnson's Coade commissions were in a neo-classical style, the church work having been a necessary excursion into Gothic. Woolverstone Hall[55] (in Suffolk near the Essex border) has a full range of Coade details – *vases, consoles*, a large circular *medallion* of *Diana the Huntress*, and the same *capitals* as at Chelsmford Shire Hall. Of the three *urns* on the pediment one, ingeniously, is a chimney pot. Lewes County Hall[56] repeats the *plaques* by Bacon from Chelmsford, as well as forty *balusters*, sixteen *imposts*, ten female head *blocks* (squeezed into the top corners of the first-floor windows) sixty *medillions* and a *coat of arms*.

Johnson had family connections with Leicester, and there built the County Rooms,[57] in

Hotel St. and originally a hotel, with the front expressing the assembly rooms inside. At first floor level, three great tripartite windows within blind arches reach up into what would normally be the second floor. Two plaques of the *Borghese Dancers* diversify the large area of plain stonework. Between the windows, which have small Coade Ionic *capitals*, are niches with statues which, for once, are in natural stone. As at Lewes, *balusters* are used at the windows, and again as at Lewes, the little oblong *blocks* with their squeezed faces are used, here in aedicules which surround the niches; very small *paterae* run in line along their friezes. Also at Leicester was St Mary's School, with two *Charity Children*,[58] which have now been moved to the modern St John's Primary School.

In her exhibition gallery, Mrs Coade exhibited a chimneypiece "from a design of Mr Johnson's", but I have been unable to identify it among the Coade etchings. Yet further Johnson work can be seen in London in New Cavendish St., St Marylebone.[59] Opposite the end of Mansfield St. and forming an arresting eye-catcher, three of the Bedford Square doorways are set side by side, two of them being entrances and the middle one a window. Johnson used the same doorway again for Hothfield Place, Hatfield Peveril.[60]

John Nash

Both Nash and Soane are thought of as early nineteenth century architects, but both were born in the 1750s and both were using Coade stone in the 1790s. Nash used Coade stone when he had to retire to Wales after his early bankruptcy. Ffynone, Hafod and Llysnewydd (spelt Llesnewydd) are on Mrs Coade's 1799 list. At Ffynone, Gunnis[61] says that two Corinthian *capitals* were supplied in 1796 at a cost of 16 guineas, which meant that they were not very large. Hafod was destroyed by fire thirteen years after Nash worked there, so it is not now possible to find out what was used at the house, though Sir John Summerson kindly showed me a pre-war photograph of a *gateway* in the Garden of Adam and Eve, which appeared to be a standard Bedford Square design. For Llysnewydd, there is no further information about the Coade work.

Back in London, Nash continued his Coade connections. Grovelands at Southgate, the Casina at Dulwich, Sundridge Park at Bromley and Worcester Park in Surrey are all on the 1799 list. Grovelands (Southgate Grove) is shown in Richardson's *New Vitruvius Britannicus* as having a *sphinx* on the cornice, a pair of *urns* of the Somerset House variety, and Ionic *capitals*. The sphinx and vases have gone, but the *capitals* remain. Worcester Park has gone and I have found no illustrations of it, and the Casina at Dulwich has also disappeared. Sundridge Park at Bromley survives, but it was also worked on by Humphry Repton and Samuel Wyatt, and all of them used Coade stone. The exterior of the house is now painted, and identifying what is attributable to which architect will require an extensive search.

With later Nash orders, we come to the period covered by the Coade records in the Public Record Office. In the Coade letter book beginning in January 1813, there is a letter (p.6) reminding Lord Foley that a bill for £86.14s.0d had been sent to him on 11

September 1811 and requesting payment. Summerson[62] dates Nash's reconstruction of Witley Court c.1810, which would fit in well with the Coade bill, but unfortunately the letter does not specify the work. The house was Victorianised and is now a ruin, so that identification of the Coade work is unlikely. Chichester Market House, by Nash, has the *arms* of the town in Coade stone, and in view of his taste for this material, there is no reason to suppose that the order came from anyone but himself.

Nash's long residence in the Isle of Wight brought some commissions. East Cowes Castle, his own house, is mentioned in the 1799 list, not long after he bought the site. A venture in a Gothic style was a Marine Villa for Sir John Hippisley Cox at West Cowes, for which "5 octangular *pinnacles* at 16 guineas each" was supplied early in 1814.[63] Nash's friend George Ward ordered from Nash a curious dual-purpose structure – a tower for West Cowes church[64] which contains a memorial chapel for the Ward family on the ground floor. The entry in Croggon's order book for November 1816 is addressed to John Nash Esq. for George Ward Esq. and specifies "4 serpents on an outside ground 4 ft. diam. within 12 gns., 1 shield of arms and crest, 18 gns. one pannel . . . with Doves in Glory and one round pannel with inscription encircled by serpents 6 ft. diam. 25 gns". Serpents swallowing their tails were symbols of eternity; on the West Cowes tower they surround clocks, one on each face. The *Doves in Glory* (the Paraclete), the coat of arms and the panel with inscription are not now visible in photographs, and may be inside the mausoleum.

Langham House[65] was built by Nash opposite his All Souls Langham Place (which has Coade stone *capitals*) as part of the Regents Park-Regent Street developments. In 1817, Sir John Langham, Bart. ordered four *figures* to hold lights on *pedestals* with his coat of arms on the front. A *Pomona and Flora* were also ordered at the same time and all were to have the fashionable bronze finish. While Nash's name is not specifically mentioned in this order, the figures would have been part of the interior fittings of the house, no doubt the hall, and probably ordered at his request. The Nash connection seems the more certain because he had ordered similar figures for his own house in Dover St. Croggon's Day Book for April 1814 specifies "2 figures of sculpture and architecture, 4 do. geometry, music, painting and poetry for 150 guineas". The four *figures* which were intended as a set can be seen in illustrations of the house,[66] standing between the three horizontal oval windows of the attic story. The other two may have made themselves useful indoors, like those at Langham House. Doubtless because of the orders received from Nash, only a nominal 12s.0d. was charged for delivery from Lambeth; less favoured customers usually had to pay several pounds.

Two of Nash's castle residences, Ravensworth Castle[67] at Gateshead and Lough Cutra Castle[68] in Co. Galway, had *chimneypieces* from the Coade factory. Luscombe Castle in Devonshire, another Gothic job, is ornamented with the family *arms* in Coade stone.

Mrs Coade's death in 1821 meant that Croggon had to begin a new set of work books, which are lost, so that Nash's later commissions for the Coade firm have to be identified from other sources. As Nash used Coade stone so often before, it is likely that there remain commissions from him which have not yet been found, possibly for some of the Regent's

Park developments. Fortunately his most important work at Buckingham Palace is fully documented; (see chapter on Commissions for the Crown)[69].

Nash also worked at Royal Lodge, Windsor,[70] and in 1825 ordered a pair of *Borghese* and *Medici Vases.*

Buckingham Palace, London, John Nash 1826-9, Consoles Frieze, etc.

Sir John Soane

Sir John Soane also used Coade stone a great deal, though the rate of survival of his works is less than Nash's, particularly in London. He started using Coade stone at the age of 27, at Adam's Place, Southwark,[71] where Professor de la Ruffinière du Prey identified an elaborate Coade *frieze,* and continued to use it at several Norfolk houses – Earsham, with a Coade *plaque* in the pediment of the Music Room (1784), Shotesham Park, with Ionic pilaster *capitals,* (1785-8), Langley Park, (1791) with ornament on the lodges. Another Norfolk house, Taverham is not, as the others are, on the 1799 list, but may be the site referred to as Norwich, which is nearby. Soane also provided a *porch* for Wood Eaton

Manor, Oxfordshire,[72] where unexpectedly the *shafts* as well as the *capitals* were of Coade stone, and *capitals* for a reconstruction at Albury Park,[73] Surrey (1800-2), which was again reconstructed by Pugin, who naturally threw Soane's work out.

Pitzhanger Manor, Ealing, Middlesex, 1802
Sir John Soanne, showing Caryatids

A Wyatt type of house was Cuffnells in Hampshire,[74] with plaques between the storeys. At Tyringham,[75] Bucks. Soane used Coade stone, but the bills in the Soane Museum do not make it clear what, and the house was much altered at the beginning of this century. A fine *Father Time*, for a sundial, may have been ordered by him. Soane's two house 13 Lincoln's Inn Fields[76] and Pitzhanger Manor,[77] Ealing, incorporate Coade stone, and show his use of a favourite motif, the *caryatids* from the Erechtheion. There are two in Lincoln's Inn Fields and four at Pitzhanger, where he also decorated the front parlour with four *figures* designed originally, as the Coade etchings show, for the sides of chimneypieces, and the main eating room with two lamp-holding *figures*. The *caryatid* theme appeared again at Buckingham House, Pall Mall, where, with *capitals* on their heads, they supported a drum with a dome. The house has disappeared but what I believe to be six of the figures are now at Anglesey Abbey, Cambridgeshire.[78] They are stamped with the same date as Buckingham House, 1793.

The main commission of Sir John Soane, lasting for a great part of his working life from 1788-1833, was the Bank of England,[79] and here the *caryatids* appear again. The Rotunda and the Transfer Office had twelve each, arranged round a drum as at Buckingham House. All these were in place by 1799. In the new century Soane began the Lothbury Court, where he used Coade stone *vases* over a Corinthian colonnade, and four large Coade *statues* of the Continents, each side of an archway. Sir Herbert Baker swept all this away, though the Continents landed up on the roof and the caryatids were all reassembled in one hall, with artificial lighting.

Soane did less Gothic work than many of his contemporaries, and the only commission I have discovered was for a Perpendicular window in a chapel at Bramley Church, Hants,[80] for a Mrs Brocas who was already a customer, presumably for classical work. It is in a hard and bony Gothic, which the Coade firm carried out for 100 guineas in 1802. It is not surprising that it was replaced in a natural stone, more correctly, later in the century.

Scagliola became an important part of the firm's production in the Regency period and also after William Croggon had taken over, and Soane found it useful, particularly for public buildings. He used it for the Royal Entrance of the House of Lords, and at the Board of Trade, and finally, in 1828, for the Freemasons' Hall.[81] He had begun to use work from Lambeth in 1780 and the last example I have traced is of 1828 – a long collaboration.

William Wilkins

William Wilkins, Junior, was another user of Coade scagliola, in the Hall of Downing College Cambridge,[82] where it forms the pilasters. He also used it at Dunmore Castle, Falkirk in 1820,[83] this time for columns as well as pilasters – the house has been demolished. His most important commission for the Coade firm was Dalmeny House,[84] a remarkable Gothic design based on East Barsham Manor, Norfolk, for which *panels, battlements,* Tudor *chimneys,* a *coat of arms, pinnacles* etc. were provided.

Among the many commissions for statues on pillars which came the Coade firm's way, William Wilkins, a Norfolk man, had his opportunity for the Nelson Column at Great Yarmouth, Norfolk.[85] Instead of a statue of Nelson, the monument is crowned by a huge statue of Brittania, supported by a ring of smaller figures symbolizing Victory. (see chapter Commemorative Monuments).

Very many other architects and builders used Coade stone, and only the most important are listed here. The work of the rest may be traced by following the works listed in the Architects section.

The Paragon, Blackheath, S. London, by Michael Searles c.1793, Colonnade.
Mrs Coade had property in the Paragon

The Paragon, Blackheath, S. London, Michael Searles c.1793. Rusticated Quoins, as at Belmont, Lyme Regis

NOTES

1. Alison Kelly *Decorative Wedgwood in Architecture and Furniture* (1965) p.76.
2. Margaret Whinney, *Home House* (1969) p.26.
3. Vol.44 104-6.
4. Bill paid 12 July 1779, photocopy supplied by Mr John Hardy.
5. Information, David Learmont, Scottish National Trust.
6. Michael McCarthy, 'The Rebuilding of Stowe House 1770-1777' *The Huntington Library Quarterly*, May 1973.
7. CO May, June 1816
8. *Country Life* 13 July 1978, p.2126, figure 2.
9. Alison Kelly 'An Expensive Present', *Burlington Magazine* September 1984.
10. Syon MS U III. Information Dr Colin Shrimpton. William Croggon supplied the scagliola floor complete in January 1832 for £900.
11. Photographs in the Scottish National Monuments Record.
12. Information Miss Catherine Cruft.
13. 1799 list.
14. 1799 list
15. Hertfordshire Record Office, Grimston MSS account book XI 17.
16. 1799 list.
17. Staffordshire Record Office D/603/F/3/13/14.
18. Pinnacles, a few Gothic flowers, a rather flat coat of arms and a much more vigorous coat of arms dated 1809.
19. 1799 list.
20. 1799 list.
21. Monthly Magazine 1799, p.904.
22. 1799 list.
23. Rupert Gunnis *Dictionary of British Sculptors 1660-1851* p.105.
24. I assume they are still there, but no contact with the owner of Heveningham is at present possible.
25. Alison Kelly 'Coade stone at National Trust Houses' *National Trust Studies 1980* p.110.
26. Christies.
27. Coade Letter Book, September 1813, p.7.
28. 1799 list and additional information from Lady Ridley.
29. John Harris and N. Pevsner, *Buildings of England, Lincolnshire* p.200.
30. Reginald Turnor *James Wyatt* 1950, plate on p.74.
31. Antony Dale *James Wyatt* 1956 p.33.

32.   ibid. p.164.

33.   Information from the Earl of Pembroke.

34.   Dale op.cit. p.52.

35.   N. Pevsner *Buckinghamshire* p.246.

36.   Christopher Hussey *Mid Georgian* 1963 plates 322, 323.

37.   J.M. Robinson 'Holkham' *Country Life* 21 November 1974.

38.   1799 list.

39.   1799 list.

40.   1799 list and N. Pevsner *Staffordshire* 1974 p.237.

41.   The 1799 list mentions Arms, Statues etc. at the Trinity Houses at Water Lane, Tower Street and Tower Hill.

42.   1799 list.

43.   Discovered in 1989 by Peter Hone.

44.   G. Jackson Stops in an article on Broadlands, *Country Life* 18 December 1980 attributes the extension of the Orangery to Holland. Dorothy Stroud *Capability Brown* 1975 attributes it to Brown.

45.   The Survey of London volume XX, 1940, Chapter 8 Trafalgar Square.

46   History of the King's Works vol. VI see below.

47.   Dorothy Stroud *Capability Brown* 1975 p.78.

48.   ibid. p.154.

49.   ibid. plate 22b.

50.   Essex Record Office Q/S Bb 348/1.

51.   John Johnson *Plans, Sections and Perspective Elevations of the Essex County Hall at Chelmsford* 1808.

52.   Information from Miss Nancy Briggs.

53.   Essex Record Office Q Fabb 66 East Packet 52/1 no.25 EP 1787.

54.   A full description of the rebuilding, with the relevant correspondence is in *Essex Review* XC, July 1931 p.100ff by the Rev. J.F. Williams.

55.   1799 list.

56.   R.F. Dell *Sussex Archaelogical Collections* Vol C p.9 ff gives details the commission. Information from Dr Brian Austen.

57.   1799 list.

58.   N. Pevsner *Leicestershire* (2nd edition) 1984

59.   Dorothy Stroud *Institute of Psychoanalysis Report 1953* attributes these houses to Johnson, 1778.

60.   Information from Nancy Briggs.

61.   Gunnis op.cit. p.108.

62   Sir John Summerson *The Life and Work of John Nash, Architect* 1980 p.49, 50.

63.   CO June 1814.

64.   CO November 1816.

65.   CO January 1815.

66. Terence Davis *John Nash, the Prince Regent's Architect* 1966, plate 38.
67. CD August 1815.
68. CD December 1818.
69. H. Colvin, J. Mordaunt Crook and M.H. Port *History of the King's Works* vol. VI 1973 pp. 270-301.
70. Windsor Archives 26736.
71. Pierre de la Ruffinière du Prey *Soane the Making of an Architect* 1977 p.225 fig.117.
72. Alison Kelly 'Sir John Soane and Mrs Eleanor Coade', *Apollo* April 1989 p.249
73. ibid. and plate 4.
74. ibid. p.249.
75. ibid. p.249
76. ibid. p.251.
77. ibid. p.251, plates 8, 9.
78. ibid. plate 5.
79. ibid. p.250, 251, plates 8, 9.
80. ibid. p.252-3, plate 10.
81. ibid. p.253.
82. CO July 1819.
83. CD February 1821.
84. CD October 1815 to August 1816.
85. CD June 1818 to September 1819.

CHAPTER 7

Mrs Coade's Classicism

The Coade factory was founded when the rococo taste had almost finished its course, and the neo-classical taste of Adam was in the ascendant. She wasted no time with Hogarth's "line of beauty"; C-scrolls and serpentine trails were not for her. From the beginning she copied the well-known festoons of husks, the oval paterae, the plaques with classical figures in low relief, which were the hallmarks of the Adam style.[1] These motifs were also being copied by plasterers, carvers, metal founders, textile designers, cabinet makers and upholsters. A whole section of the 1784 catalogue lists such details, to be stuck on furniture, chimneypieces, pedestals and so on, in a wide range of sizes.

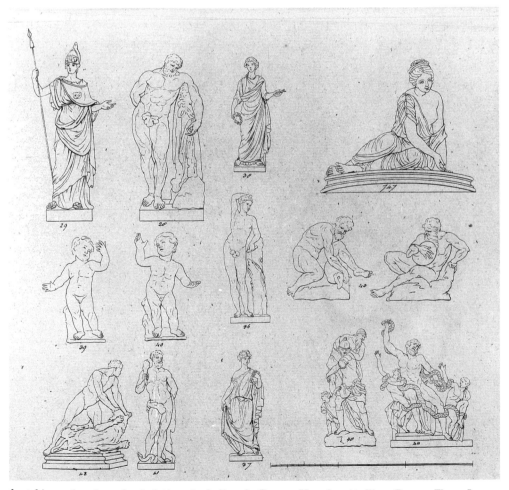

Coade etchings of various classical pieces including the Farnese Hercules, Apollino, Farnese Flora, Laocoon, etc.

91

In this, her designs show that she was like the rest of the up-to-date craftsmen, but she also had available to her a wider opportunity to satisfy customers who had a real knowledge of classical sculpture, and who wanted an Apollino, a plaque of the Borghese dancing girls or a Farnese Flora. To many people these would be merely attractive figures, but to those who were informed about antique art, the allusions and history which these pieces carried with them gave an extra patina to their purchases. We are apt, today, to forget how deeply people of education were steeped in the classics. Dr Johnson said that "Latin is like lace. A man should have as much of it as he can", and at public school or university the history men studied was by Livy rather than by Clarendon. Gibbon's *Decline and Fall of the Roman Empire* was a masterly exposition of well-known facts. In English literature, the latinized construction of Milton's verse was particularly admired; *Coade's Gallery* includes quotations from Milton, as well as numerous Latin quotations, thoughtfully translated.

Rome was the central point of the Grand Tour, and a classical fragment the essential souvenir. Statues were immediately recognised from engravings, and their attributes understood. *Taste and the Antique* by Francis Haskell and Nicholas Penny has admirably explored this field in general, but in this chapter I shall concentrate on the way in which Mrs Coade in particular responded to this stimulus with models taken directly from classical sources. Without visiting Italy, information could be obtained from the plaster-cast men who could offer a range of favourite pieces. At least four firms in London could earn their living from selling classical copies, including the sculptor John Flaxman's father, who since he had the same name as his son, and sometimes receipted bills for him, has caused confusion in Flaxman studies. Books of engravings were available, though often expensive ("Count Caylus will *cost us money*" complained Josiah Wedgwood to his partner),[2] but provided excellent illustrations from which to work.

The Coade firm either owned, or had access to, the four great volumes on the Capitoline Museums at the Campidoglio in Rome.[3] *The Piping Boy* is illustrated among the Coade etchings, and though I have not yet traced an example, there was one in a Sussex antique shop in the early 1970s, its present whereabouts being unknown. Another piece from the Museum Capitolinum was a large "Pannel Diana and Endymion", which Mrs Coade credited to Rossi, but which is based on a bas-relief there which was also copied by Josiah Wedgwood. A huge keystone in the Museo dei Conservatori known either as "A Weeping Province" or "Weeping Dacia" has a seated mourning woman with a trophy or arms beside her. The Coade version substituted a classical lamp, and in this less warlike form it became suitable for a funerary tablet. It can be seen on the monument to Edward Wortley Montagu in the cloisters of Westminster Abbey, and the Green monument in Bramber church, Sussex. From Pevsner's description in his Warwickshire volume, I believe that it also appears in St John the Baptist, Lea Marston.

Another borrowing from the Capitoline Museum was *"Pietas Militaris, or the Death of Pallas"*, shown in Coade's Gallery and specified as being "from the Museum Capitolinum, vol IV plate 39". This has not yet come to light. A quotation from the Aeneid was added to its description.

Coade etching of a chimneypiece ornament, Roundel of "Weeping Dacia", etc. 1770-1780s

At the bottom of the Scalinata leading down from the Campiloglio there are two Egyptian lionesses imported to Rome in Imperial times.[4] They are in the catalogue and shown in the etchings (see chapter on Fauna).

The Vatican collection provided several interesting Coade designs. C.H. Tatham's book *Etchings of Ancient Ornamental Architecture drawn from the Originals in Rome and other Parts of Italy during the years 1794, 1795 and 1797*, was certainly available at the manufactory, as Croggon sent a bill for £38.2s.0d., in June 1818[5] to "Rhodes architect's office, Woods and Forests, Whitehall" for "4 vases with birds per Tatham's book". However, the most interesting pieces which were copied from his Vatican etchings were the pair of *seats* now at Parham House, Sussex, based on classical thrones. Tatham's drawing shows lotus flowers as the finials, which are not now on the Parham pieces; however, small holes at the top of the backs show where finials, separately made, could have been dropped in. These pieces came from a dealer, and are unprovenanced, but Hope's illustration of his picture gallery in *Household Furniture* (1807) shows an identical pair of pieces.[6] In the text they are described as being of stone, but there is at present no means of knowing if the Parham pieces belonged to Hope or are merely duplicates.

Parham House, Sussex, Throne copied from a classical example in the Vatican by C.H. Tatham c.1800

Tatham seems to have been a personal friend of Croggon or Mrs Coade, since he was given a pair of *pineapples* for the gate of his house in Lisson Grove,[7] and also a bust of Wesley, which suggests that like others of the Coade circle he was a Dissenter.

Further Vatican copies are the pair of Egyptian *figures* dated 1800 and now at Buscot Park, Oxfordshire (formerly Berkshire). Though they have the characteristic Egyptian stance with one foot forward and the hands clenched at the sides, the modelling is softened and humanized, and though this might have been thought to have been done in the Georgian period, the figures turn out to be exact copies of a statue of Antinous made for the Emperor Hadrian and found at his Villa.[8] His favourite Antinous drowned in the Nile, and among many portraits of him as an ordinary Roman youth, the Emperor had this statue made of him as a Pharaoh. Again, there is no known provenance for the Coade figures, but Hope's Egyptian room at Duchess Street contained a similar figure.[9] Many pieces from the Deepdene (Hope's country house) found their way in the 1930s to Buscot Park, and these statues might possibly have been among them.

Buscot Park, formerly Berkshire now Oxfordshire, Egyptian Figure from the original in the Vatican from Hadrian's Villa, 1800.

There is a whole gallery devoted to candelabra in the Vatican, and one of these, of the 2nd century AD, was copied by the Coade firm. It has a triangular base with sphinxes at the corners (hence the reference to it as a tripod at Tatton Park) surmounted by a baluster with delicate low relief decoration, and a gadrooned bowl-shaped section on top. The example in a private collection is left in its natural cream colour, but the other, at Tatton Park, Cheshire, has been bronzed.[10] This is dated 1815; the other is of 1816. The original was illustrated in Eileen Harris's book on the *Furniture of Robert Adam*, plate 77; though she does not appear to link it with any actual Adam piece, the design is very much in the Adam spirit.

Yet another Vatican piece was a heavily draped statue of a woman who went by several names, Pudicitia and Livia among them.[11] A *Livia* was made, for Chicksands Priory, Bedfordshire in 1816 for Sir George Osborne at a cost of 40 guineas, so the figure was either unusually large or was a special order.[12] Unfortunately, all that remains is a section about a foot high of her feet and a portion of her drapery.

Probably one of the most famous groups in antiquity was the Vatican group of the Laocoon, in which a man and his two sons struggle with a huge serpent. The original is about eight feet high, but the Coade version[13] is reduced to a size to stand on a chimneypiece, its base 14 inches by 8 inches. William Dennison, father of Lady Conyngham the mistress of George IV, was offered a "Laocoon, repaired and bronzed" (no doubt to conceal any damage), and paid 10 guineas for it in July 1816.[14] It has not been traced.

Another Roman collection containing admired pieces was that of the Farnese family. A delightful figure, which went from the Villa Farnesina to Naples in Mrs Coade's lifetime, was the Venus Callipygis,[15] a girl holding up her draperies and looking back over her shoulder.

Drastically reduced was the *Farnese Bull*,[16] a turbulent composition in which five people and a dog try to restrain the rearing animal. The base for the Coade piece is catalogued as only 16 inches square. Haskell and Penny record, however, that a small bronze version about 18 inches high was in the Borghese collection, and it may have been this which was copied. No example has come to light. The Farnese *Flora*,[17] however, was not so drastically reduced, and is a life-sized figure. Examples are at Tehidy Park, Cornwall and St John's College, Oxford.

The Villa Borghese provided one certain Coade design and possibly another. the Borghese Dancers,[18] a group of five girls linking hands, was popular in England, and copies were at Moor Park, Badminton and Rokeby, besides innumerable versions by Josiah Wedgwood with the addition of seven extra girls by Flaxman. The Coade etching only shows four figures, possibly because the model was made in a special size for James Wyatt for the Orangery at Heveningham, Suffolk, where it survives. *The Borghese Gladiator*,[19] is a figure which lunges forward in a diagonal pose which would have been very difficult to support in the kiln. In a letter to the Earl of Jersey, of Middleton Park, Oxfordshire, Sealy wrote, on May 25 1813, that another *statue of Gladiator* was in hand, and he hoped for better luck with it. Clearly wishing to be allowed to drop a difficult commission, he asked if a majestic statue of Hospitality, with cornucopia, might not be better. A large figure with a cornucopia, of a design not previously known, was sold by Christies in 1989, and could be this statue.

The most succesful design from the Borghese collection was the *Borghese Vase,* made from the firm's earliest years up to the later 1820s. It was one of the most admired pieces of classical art in the 18th century, featuring in Panini's painting in which the most important antique works were assembled in an imaginary gallery.[20] The best known Borghese Vase was the example made for George IV at Royal Lodge, Windsor, to the order of John Nash in 1825. (It is now at Wrest Park, Bedfordshire.)

The Barberini collection provided the Coade manufactory with another best seller: "the Antique Sybil [sic] in the Barberini Collection, bronzed" was the description of the figure in Coade's Gallery. Ten *sibyls* (called the Wise Virgins because they hold lamps) can be seen in the chapel at Burghley House, Northants,[21] and many more were made, usually with Vestals to accompany them, in the Regency period, when they were particularly useful as lamp-holders on stairways or in halls.

A curiously titled group shown in Coade's Gallery is called *Salmacis* and *Hermaphroditus.* The name comes from a passage in Ovid's Metamorphoses IV, given to a group in the Fede collection in the Palazzo Fiorenza in the 18th century, for what seem mistaken reasons. A near duplicate is in the Capitoline Museum and shows a boy and a draped figure, presumably a girl, embracing each other, and has always been known as Cupid and Psyche.[22] The Fede piece, now lost, apparently had one of the heads turned away which gave rise to the conception that this figure was a hermaphrodite trying to escape from the embrace of Salmacis.[23] Why Coade and Sealy chose this version of the group in place of the Capitoline one, and what Mrs Coade, with her Baptist upbringing, thought of the subject, cannot now be discovered.

The Florentine collections of the Medici were almost as well-known as those in Rome, and the *Medici Vase*[24] was copied as frequently by the Coade manufactory as the *Borghese Vase,* to which it made an admirable pair. A *Medici Vase* (now in Kew Gardens) was made to match the *Borghese Vase* at Royal Lodge Windsor. Both vases were in the 18th century thought to be the work of Phidias and admired accordingly.

The *Apollini*[25] [sic; it should have been Apollino] was another Medici piece copied at Lambeth. It is a rather flaccid figure, with one hand raised to its head. The Coade version, shown in the etchings and in the catalogue, was another of the small sized figures, less than two feet high. None has been traced. The *Florentine* or *Medici Lions* stand with one paw on a ball. One of them is antique,[26] and its pair is a Renaissance copy.[27] They were useful for entrance gateways, and Preston Hall, Lothian Region, has a fine pair from Lambeth.

The problem of translation from the Italian arose again when a copy of the Medici Dancing Faun was modelled. In Coade's Gallery it is described as "The Bachanal, or, Faun – CO CIMBALI NELLE MANI",[28] and the figure does have cymbals in his hands and a form of bellows, for making a squeak, under one foot. This was a favourite piece and many plaster and marble copies exist in this country, but I have not yet found a Coade one.

Coade's Gallery contained a "Roman Procession to the Capitol from the Villa de Medicis now at Florence". This was a piece designed to be used as the "tablet" in the middle of the frieze of a chimneypiece, and showed about a dozen figures in togas similar to those, of a larger scale, on the Ara Pacis Augustae now (though not in Mrs Coade's time) to be seen in Rome. An example in a chimneypiece can be seen at Seaton Delaval, and another, presumably from some demolished chimneypiece, is built into a passage wall at Chicksands Priory.

Coade etchings of the Borghese and Medici Vases.

One of the very rare painted panels to survive from antiquity was known as the Aldobrandini Marriage. It showed three groups of people so casually linked that Josiah Wedgwood FRS could make the design into three separate medallions. Mrs Coade kept them all together, and an example can be seen in Island Temple at Croome Court, Worcestershire.[29] Another example can be seen in the back parlour of Sir John Soane's Pitzhanger Manor at Ealing. It is now painted, but considering the amount of Coade ornament at the house, I think it reasonable to assume that the plaque came from Lambeth.

Coade etching of Medallions of girls and animals, and Plaque of the Aldobrandini Marriage 1770s-1780s

Herculaneum, as it was uncovered, provided new insights into Roman interior decoration, and Mrs Coade kept abreast of the discoveries. A stool supported by three monopodia (lions' legs surmounted by lions' faces) from the House of the Cervi was supplied to Sir John Griffin Griffin at Audley End as early as 1783.[30] It stands rather incongrously on top of a pedestal used elsewhere as a sundial; both were intended together from the first, since they are charged as one. The same design appears over twenty years later in an illustration of the Picture Gallery in Thomas Hope's Duchess Street,[31] though the medium used for it is not specified, and it is not possible to be certain that it is a Coade piece.

Audley End, Essex, copy of Tripod from Herculaneum 1783

A *chimneypiece* shown in Coade's Gallery had profile relief figures on its pilasters "modelled from designs found in the ruins of Herculaneum", and the Coade etching shows that they were two of the dancing girls modelled from murals discovered there, and used frequently by Mrs Coade's contemporaries; Josiah Wedgwood used them for a number of jasper plaques. Several examples of these chimneypieces survive, including specimens at Washington DC, Capesthorne, Cheshire and Wollaton Hall, Nottinghamshire.

A number of Coade pieces were copied from sculptures in British collections. A favourite design, copied also in glass-paste, Wedgwood jasper and various semi-previous stones, was the Marlborough Gem of the Marriage of Cupid and Psyche.[32] The original is small, but the Duke of Marlborough had had it enlarged and used as the "tablet" of a marble chimneypiece at Blenheim, and thus set a fashion. The Coade etchings and the catalogue give several chimneypiece designs including this piece.

The Townley collection of marbles was justly famous, and the Townley Vase, with figures similar to those on the Borghese Vase but arranged on an amphora, was copied by the Coade firm. A very late example, dated 1840, was sold at auction in May 1988.[33] Also from this collection came the bust of Isis Aphroditis, which was exhibited in Coade's Gallery, but which has not been identified. In Coade's Gallery also was a figure described as "a Statue of Brito Martis found in the Verospi Villa at Rome, a setting figure from Mr. Townley's collection."[34] The engraving of it, however, shows that it was the Nymph with a Shell, in the Borghese Collection in Mrs Coade's time. Though it had various other names, Brito Martis does not seem to be among them, and seems borrowed from Spenser. Townley seems to have had a duplicate figure, which is now in the British Museum. The Sarcophagus from a classical piece at Stowe is described in chapter 7.

Taplow Court, Buckingham, George III 1804, based on a statue of Hadrian.

For his Jubilee in 1809,[35] and also in 1804[36] for a reason as yet unidentified, George III was modelled as the Emperor Hadrian, from a statue in the British Museum. (The piece is now in the Orangery at Hampton Court, where it accompanies Mantegna's Triumph of Caesar.) The King appears in Roman armour, and only his shield with the Royal Arms indicates that this is not a classical piece. Another model from the same source was "an eagle from one at the British Museum" ordered by Sir George Osborne of Chicksands Priory, Bedfordshire.[37] A number of fine Coade *eagles* exist, but I have not been able to establish if they are from the Museum original (see chapter on Fauna).

The Warwick Vase arrived in England not long after the Coade factory began,[38] bought for the Earl of Warwick by Sir William Hamilton, but permission to copy it was not given for some time. A mould was however made for it by 1818, since in Croggon's December stock-taking in that year it was listed as "Warwick Vase and foot and an ornamental pedestal for do 110 guineas". I have not traced a customer for it, and the only example I know is of 1840, in a private collection.

The Elgin Marbles had not yet arrived in England at the time when Soane introduced the Erechtheion caryatids into his work at the Bank and elsewhere, and Mrs Coade had to copy the design from an engraving. In Coade's Gallery she showed "A statue for holding a light – modelled from STUART's Athens, introduced as Cariatides . . . by Mr. SOANE the Architect". The figures were not exactly copied from Stuart, however, as the Coade girls have arms, and are in fact similar to the statues which surround the oblong pool at Hadrian's Villa. (The only exact copy of the Erechtheion figure in the British Museum was not made until the Hon Frederick North, later Lord Guildford, ordered in October 1816 "in six months a statue abt. seven feet copy of Caryatis [sic] from one of the Elgin Marbles in the British Museum at 50 guineas to be copied as it now appears." (See chapter 9)

A further borrowing from Stuart, shown in Coade's Gallery, was as I have suggested, the Decelia/Britannia at Liverpool Town Hall.[39]

Marble or bronze busts to stand on the tops of bookcases were essential features of the well furnished Georgian library, and the Coade firm could supply a number of designs, though far fewer than Josiah Wedgwood could do in his black basalt ceramic formula; his 1779 catalogue lists eighty-seven. The Wedgwood models all came from the plaster cast sellers,[40] John Flaxman Senior, John Cheere of Hyde Park Corner, Richard Parker "opposite the new church in the Strand" (St Mary le Strand), Hoskins and Oliver, later Hoskins and Grant, and Mrs Landré. It seems probable that the Coade models also came from the same sources.

The Coade classical designs so far identified are *Antoninus Pius*, which was bought by Lord Rockingham of Wentworth Woodhouse, at the 1767 Pincot sale at Christies and continued in the Coade catalogue; the *Isis Aphroditis* from the Townley collection, a *Venus* and *Caracalla* in the sale of an "Eminent publisher retiring from Business" at Christies on February 24 1809,[41] and also in the catalogue, the Venus being described as Grecian; a *Homer*; a *Marcus Aurelius*; a *"Vestinia"* (should be Faustina); a *Horace*; a *Cicero*; and a *Commodus*. Extant copies of these have not been traced, but since they were probably "bronzed" in a close imitation of an actual bronze, and of a similar weight, it is likely that some may stand unrecognised on undisturbed cornices.

Mrs Coade made a variety of classical *capitals*, but it is not easy to correlate the orders for them with the descriptions in the catalogue (see chapter 9) The sources of some, however, can be identified. The sixth century BC temple, miscalled the Basilica, at Paestum, supplied the *capitals* at Hammerwood Park, Sussex, designed by Benjamin Latrobe; an illustration from Thomas Major's book on Paestum supplied the details.[42] Latrobe also used a Greek model in the *capitals* at Ashdown House, also in Sussex. The capitals from the North Porch of the Erechtheion are used here. Stuart's *Athens* (volume 2) again provided the design.

Greek Ionic *capitals* were supplied for Arthur Browne of Cambridge, but cannot be identified more precisely than "6 ionic capitals, ancient Grecian order" sent by the Cambridge waggon from Bishopsgate in April 1814.[43] The building, Grove House, Trumpington Street, has fortunately survived.

A special order for classical *capitals* is also recorded in an order from Sir John Soane for Wood Eaton Manor, Oxfordshire.[44] Here the design specified was "Ionic capitals . . . from the Temple of Apollo at Miletus", and these had to be modelled to the scale required at a cost of 3 guineas. The porch for which they were made is very small, and conveys little of the majesty of the huge Miletus capitals; Mr Weyland, for whom they were made, might have saved his money by having a standard design. Grecian Ionic *capitals* were also supplied to Thomas Hope at the Deepdene, Surrey in August 1815.[45] Since there is little over a fortnight between the order and its execution, it seems probable that this was a design in stock. The Deepdene was demolished in the 1960s.

Wood Eaton Manor, Oxfordshire, 1793 by Sir John Soane, Capitals from the Temple of Apollo, Miletus.

These examples will show that, whenever her customers required it, Mrs Coade and her later manager William Croggon could produce the desired classical copies. Sometimes the sources used were the splendid books of engravings which by the end of the 18th century depicted the main classical sites or collections. Sometimes the models seem likely to have come from the plaster cast sellers. On a few occasions the firm may have been lent a sculpture to work on, either an original or a copy. We know, for instance, that Robert Adam brought back copies of the Medici and Borghese Vases, and it is possible that he may have allowed Mrs Coade to examine his Medici Vase for her own version, since she worked for him from the earliest years of her firm. From whatever source they come, the Coade pieces reflect that reverence for the classical past which inspired the neo-classical movement.

Small sized figures, mainly for interior decoration

Mention has already been made of the nude figure, probably a *Venus*, which might have been copied from an Italian book of engravings. This was the only known statue of this size until its variant, wearing drapery, appeared at Sotheby's sale on June 1st 1988. However, the Coade etchings include a page of very small figures, none of which has yet come to light. They could have been bronzed, as were many of the small pieces intended for use in saloons or dining rooms.

These include a *Farnese Hercules* 2ft 6ins high. The original is enormous, being over 10ft high,[48] and had, of course, to be viewed from below. The head and shoulders therefore lean forward. Another smaller *Hercules* 1ft 9ins high, stands upright with his club on his shoulder. Yet a third *Hercules*, in a robust pose, is fighting the Nemean Lion, kneeling on its side and wrenching its jaws open; it also is 1ft 9ins high.

There is a very small *Farnese Flora*, only 1ft 8ins tall, and a *Ceres* of the same size which could make a pair to it. Two more pairs are portly *putti* 1ft 6ins high, and *River Gods* reclining in left and right versions at 2ft.

A *Minerva*, 2ft 6ins high, presents a puzzle. In pose she closely resembles the Pallas of Velletri, but as this figure was not discovered until 1797,[47] and the *Minerva* was in the Coade catalogue of 1784, there must have been another similar classical figure to use as a model.

A very small and very complicated group is *Aeneas* and *Anchises*, with Aeneas carrying his father, and his small child holding the edge of Aeneas's garment as they all escape from Troy.

NOTES

1. Martha Blythe Gerson "A glossary of Robert Adams Neo Classical Ornament" *Architectural History* 1981 p.59-82.

2. *Recueil d'Antiquités*, from 1752-1767, Alison Kelly, *Decorative Wedgwood in Architecture and Furniture* p.17.

3. G. G. Bottari (vols 1-3) and P.F. Foggini (vol 4) *Musei Capitolini*.

4. Piranesi *Vedute di Roma*, Piazza del Campidoglio S. Maria in Aracoeli.

5. CD.

6. David Watkin *Thomas Hope and the Neo-Classical Idea*, figure 8.

7. CD June 1819 "C.H. Tatham for 4 pineapples agreed to be a present". 35 Alpha Road, Lisson Grove.

8. James Stephens Curl *The Egyptian Revival*, plate 5.

9. Watkin op.cit. figure 14.

10. Alison Kelly "Coade Stone at National Trust Houses" *National Trust Studies* 1980, plate 18.

11. Francis Haskell and Nicholas Penny *Taste and the Antique* plate 157.

12. CO March 1816. The remains are stamped Livia Coade Lambeth.

13. Coade catalogue no.44.

14. CD October 1816. It was sent to Pall Mall.

15. Haskell and Penny, plate 168.

16. Op.cit, plate 85.

17. Op.cit. plate 19.

18. Op.cit. plate 101.

19. Op.cit. plate 115.

20. Op.cit. plate 45. The painting is now at the Staatsgalerie, Stuttgart.

21. They are in Mrs Coade's 1799 list and are thought to have been bought c.1790.

22. Haskell and Penny, plate 98.

23. Op.cit. plate 52, drawing by Pompeo Batoni.

24. Op.cit. plate 167.

25. Op.cit. plate 26.

26. Op.cit. plate 127.

27. Op.cit. plate 128.

28. Op.cit. plate 106.

29. Sir John Soane's Museum, Adam drawings vol 44, nos.105-106.

30. Essex Record Office A1/5 1783.

31. Watkin op.cit. figure 8.

32. Haskell and Penny op.cit. plate 27.

33. Sotheby's Billingshurst, Sussex.

34. Haskell and Penny op.cit, plate 148.

35. In a niche on the Bargate, Southampton.

36. At Taplow Court, Buckinghamshire.

37. CO May 1817.

38. Haskell and Penny op.cit. p.67. The vase was discovered in 1771.

39. The statue of Britannia was modelled by Rossi, and was put up as part of James Wyatt's reconstruction. *Monthly Magazine* 1799, p.904.

40. Alison Kelly *Decorative Wedgwood in Architecture and Furniture* pp.47-50.

41. Rupert Gunnis *Dictionary of British Sculptors 1660-1851*, Coade entry, p.106.

42. Thomas Major *The Ruins of Paestum* 1768. Nikolaus Pevsner *Studies in Art, Architecture and Design*, volume I, p. 201 (no 14) reproduces Major's detail.

43. CD.

44. Sir John Soane's Museum, Soane Bill book 4, 1793.

45. CO August 12 1815. CD August 30 1815.

46. Haskell and Penny op.cit. plate 118.

47. Op.cit. plate 150.

CHAPTER 8

The Gothic Style

"Ruder than Gothic" said Millamant of a gentleman who came into her presence in his boots,[1] and probably the majority of Georgian people would have agreed with her usage, and considered anything Gothic to be automatically uncivilized. If they had been customers of Mrs Coade they would have bought classical ornaments for their houses. But gradually, towards the end of the 18th century more and more architectural enthusiasts began to take an interest in the Gothic past, and the word itself in time lost its barbaric associations, became a neutral architectural term, and even developed romantic overtones. There were enough of such people to provide Mrs Coade and William Croggon with a steady supply of orders, fewer than the classical commissions, but in some cases, as St George 's chapel and Dalmeny House, both significant and lucrative.

In 1772 Horace Walpole[2], the original popularier of the Gothic Style, who had been embellishing his house Strawberry Hill, Twickenham, for more than twenty years, decided to add a new *Gateway.* It had, of course, to be Gothic, and Mrs Coade, who had only been in business three years, was called on to make it. Acrimony ensued. Mrs Coade charged £150, and Walpole thought this far too much and went to arbitration about it. He appointed Sir William Chambers, a towering architectural figure, Comptroller of the Works and friend of the King and the Dowager Princess of Wales, to act for him; Mrs Coade employed a Mr Kemble Watley, a Lambeth neighbour. (His name is in the Lambeth parish poor rate books.)[3] Chambers took a great deal of trouble, talking to the workmen employed, inspecting the books and so on; and in the end Chambers and Watley issued a joint statement that, in their view, the commission had cost Mrs Coade £151.15s.10d. exclusive of profit.[4] Horace Walpole is unlikely to have ordered anything else from Mrs Coade. There is a Coade stone *plaque,* probably of Thomas Gray, on the outside of Strawberry HIll, but Walpole could have bought it earlier. However, the controversy must have been very helpful to Mrs Coade. Very early in her career she had been commended as a scrupulously honest trader by the most influential member of the architectural establishment, and Chambers later commissioned pieces from her. What might have been a disaster turned out greatly to her advantage.

The *Gateway,* which has now disappeared, was designed by James Essex, based on the tomb of Bishop de Luda at Ely, and can be seen in illustrations of Strawberry Hill.[5] Since moulds had had to be made, and would have been available for other orders, it is worth examining the Coade etchings to see if there is anything which might seem like Walpole's commission. I believe it is the pair of *Gate-piers,* no.503. These are 13ft 6ins high and extremely slim – only 2ft square. They have pinnacles at the top, each surrounded by four needles. Gothic tracery covers every available surface, and all the pinnacle edges are decorated with dozens of minute crockets. A modified version was used for the gate piers of Charleville, Co Offaly, Ireland, a house designed by Francis Johnston, in 1813 (Letter Book 12.8.1813, p14).

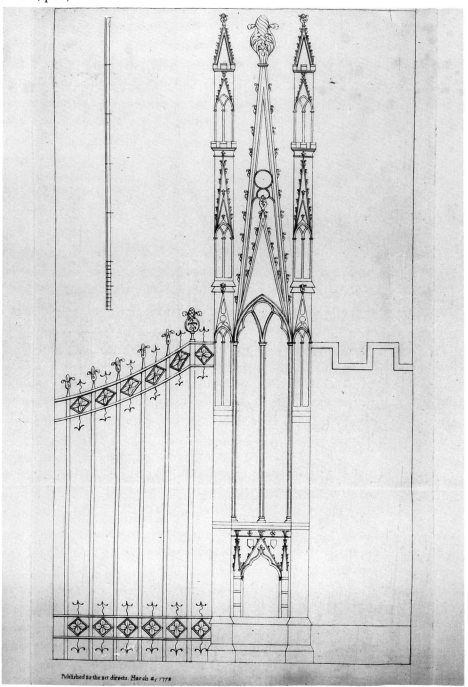

Etching of Horace Walpole's Gate-pier, designed 1772 by James Essex from the tomb of Bishop de Luda.

Churches with extensive Coade work: Chelmsford, Debden and Deane

In 1800, the Coade firm was presented with a great opportunity when Chelmsford Church, now the Cathedral, largely fell down. Both arcades collapsed, one completely, leaving only the stumps of the piers standing. John Johnson, was called in to rebuild. Correspondence in connexion with it has fortunately survived in the Cathedral archives, and was summarized by the Rev J.F. Williams.[6] John Sealy, not long elevated to be Mrs Coade's partner wrote to Johnson in 1801, saying that:

> "I have not the least shadow of doubt that they (the piers) will stand for ever. A core of some sort, of course, is carried through them, either rough pieces of stone or brickwork, and that grouted in properly, and there is not the least danger of their bearing any weight."

The Phoenix Fire Office had a Coade *Phoenix*[8] on top of its elegant classical temple to house the fire-engine, and it seems that Coade work was supplied for the engine-house as well, for Sealy added, in a rather lordly way,

> "My Mason is now at Chelmsford, fixing the Works for the Phoenix Engine House etc. If your people want any Advice or Assistance, he can give it to them."

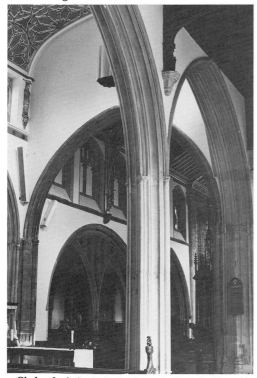

Chelmsford Cathedral (formerly Parish Church), Essex, Arcade rebuilt by John Johnson 1800

Johnson reconstructed the south arcade *Piers*, following the design of the remains, in Coade stone, where they bear out Sealy's confident prediction. Few visitors to the Cathedral know that these clustered columns are anything other than a hard-surfaced natural stone. The clerestory had to be reconstructed as well, and this has Gothic windows with simple tracery, divided by draped *Figures* standing on winged cherubs' heads. These are now gilt, so the underlying material is hidden and could not be claimed as Coade stone without the bills.[9] As well as the *figures*, decoration was provided for the roof. A bill of November 1801 refers to the "Gothic tracery ceiling with the figures between the upper windows and the cherub corbills that support them, per agreement, £262.10s.0d.," which, considering the amount of work involved, was cheap. Window tracery was also supplied, since in June 1803 Sealy had to apologise because a waggoner had refused to collect a case containing a *Window*, from the Blue Boar, Whitechapel.

Another waggoner lost the top of the Font.

The *Font* caused difficulties in other ways. The Rebuilding Committee wanted it for £25 (the list price being £30) on the grounds that they had only wanted to spend £6 or £7.[10] It has been removed from the Cathedral, and is now in Chelmsford Museum, Oaklands Park; it has Tudor roses repeated round its octagonal bowl and a fairly plain pillar, without figures. If the "top" that was lost was in fact a font-cover, it still has not got one.

Debden Church, Essex,
Font designed by Richard Holland 1786

A *Font,* designed by Richard Holland which does retain its cover is at Debden Church near Saffron Walden, Essex. This is on the same lines as that at Chelmsford, but more elaborate. Alternating with the roses round the bowl is the heraldry of Mr R.M.T. Chiswell, who commissioned it; and there is an inscription round the rim recording his gift of it to the church. Below the bowl are niches with very small figures of the Virtues, taken, Mrs Coade tells us,[11] from Sir Joshua Reynolds' window at New College Oxford. the cover, trumpet-shaped, is also elaboratley decorated, with small quatrefoils round its edge. The *Font,* and Debden House[12] nearby, which has now been demolished, were designed by Richard Holland, a cousin of the better-known Henry, and there was Coade work there too, of some kind, as the house, as well as the church, is on Mrs Coade's 1799 list.

The *Font* was in place by 1786, and in 1791 Mr Chiswell decided on further additions to his church; this time the architect was John Carter, then well known for his knowledge of mediaeval architecture. He designed an octagonal brick extension, with Chiswell arms on small *Shields* at the corners, and quatrefoil *Plaques* with his initials. The detail of these architectural ornaments, after nearly 200 years outdoors, is as sharp as that of the *font* inside.

Debden Church, Essex, Font designed by Richard Holland 1786 - detail.

Towards the end of the Regency Mr Wither Bramston, of Oakley Hall near Basingstoke, Hampshire, decided to build a church at Deane, nearby. Almost all the decorative work for the church was supplied from Lambeth, and as the date is within the period of Croggon's work books, we have all the details. The original order,[13] given early in 1819, lists six *Gothic Windows*, four large *Pinnacles*, four *Finnials* [sic] a *Cross* for the porch and a *Skreen* [sic] 20ft wide, with the *Royal Arms* on top. Apart from the *Royal Arms*, removed at some date unknown, and the *Cross*, which disappeared between my visits in 1971 and 1973, everything is still there, and the church is a delightfully unspoilt example of early 19th century design.

No architect is known for the church, and I think that there may not have been one and that Bramston and Croggon managed it between them. Thomas Dubbin, whom Croggon employed to visit customers and take orders, was sent down to Oakley Hall in January 1819[14] to draw designs for the *Screen* for approval on the spot, and this seems to have been done before Croggon got a firm order. In June and July,[15] as they became ready, *Windows* (£48 each) and *Pinnacles* at 12 and 15 guineas, went to Deane, and finally the *Screen* was finished in December (£312.19s.4d.) It is a charming piece; as early as 1819 strict historical accuracy was not to be expected, and the dog-tooth round the arches does not belong to the period of the Perpendicular brattishing along its top, but the scale of the decoration is right for the screen, and the proportions of the three arches are harmonious. The window tracery is simple but agreeable, and the pinnacles are enthusiastically crocketed. *The Royal Arms* presumably stood on the middle of the screen, as at Lydiard Tregoze; fortunately its removal did no damage to the decoration.

Deane Church, Hampshire, Tower and Window 1818

In January 1820, Dubbin was again at Oakley Hall, "drawing for Plaisterers", and presumably designing the delicate Gothic tracery on the East wall. From February, Lambeth workmen went down for eight weeks to put the *Screen* up. Finally, in March, a *Cross* for the porch and a larger one for the chancel were sent to Deane, and the Coade work was finished. It had cost £823.10.4. Outside, the colour of the Coade stone blends with the cement rendering of the building, and inside all is painted white, so without the Croggon work books it would not have been possible to identify this beguiling example of Coade craftsmanship. The incumbent of Deane church was Jane Austen's brother, but she died before the work was carried out.

Deane Church, Hampshire, Screen 1818

Pinnacles

The Coade etchings illustrate a number of Gothic *Pinnacles* which could be bought as catalogue numbers, costing 2½ to 4 guineas. As they were made hollow with a hole at the top into which a finial could be dropped, it was easy to make a fatter model, leave off the finial, and use it as a chimney. I have not yet identified one of these, but ordinary Coade *Pinnacles* survive on the gothic Mausoleum at Duff House, Banffshire. The house was on Mrs Coade's 1799 list. For the 1800-1813 period, I have not found any, but there are one or two orders in Croggon's work books. In 1821 the Committee for rebuilding Harwich Church, Essex[16], ordered sixteen matching *Pinnacles* for the body of their church, and another six of assorted sizes and shapes, including two with "five cants", which probably fitted on to the polygonal chancel. The church, designed by M. G. Thompson survives, and is in the fishbone-thin Gothic of the 1820s. Mr Thompson, possibly the same man, ordered two octagonal *Pinnacles* in the same year for a place which Croggon called "Lendon, Colchester". There is no such place in that area, but a Lexden church on the outskirts of Colchester was rebuilt in 1820-1, in a similar style to Harwich, and is still there.[17]

Windows

Richard Elsam and Thomas Chawner enlarged Chertsey Church, Surrey, in 1806-8, by adding new aisles to the mediaeval nave. The aisle windows have *Label-stops* stamped Coade and Sealy, and the window tracery is Coade as well.[18] The *Label-stops* are an amusing collection, including a death's head in a crown, winged cherubs' heads (as at Chelmsford) and, when invention ran out, what appears to be a bit of the Laocoon, which the firm made, in a very small size. This appears to be the only Coade work in the church.

Chertsey Church, Surrey, Gothic Window detail 1806 R. Elsam or T. Chawner

Not long before, Mrs Coade received a commission which must have given her great satisfaction. Passing her childhood in the shadow of Exeter Cathedral, a few hundred yards from her home, she must have been familiar with the cream-coloured intricacies of its West Front, and would have been pleased to know that Coade stone was to be used to repair it. We have already met John Carter at Debden Church. He was not strictly qualified as an architect; his chief interest was in recording mediaeval antiquities and buldings, and in writing articles for the *Gentleman's Magazine* condemning the demolition or uninformed restoration of old buildings. He was called in at Exeter, since we read in his obituary notice that:

114

> "The Great West Window of Exeter Cathedral, by Coade, about eight or nine years ago, under Mr. Soane, was from the designs of Mr. Carter."[19]

This gives a date of 1808 or 1809 for the restoration, but this turns out not to be right. The Assistant Librarian of Exeter Cathedral Library, University of Exeter, has kindly told me that there is a record of repairs to the lower part of the mullions of the West Window, in Coade stone, in 1802-3, under the supervision of "Mr. Carter, the architect". I am told that none of the Coade stone survives. The Mr Soane referred to cannot, I think, be the eminent architect who by then would not have worked to anyone else's designs. Possibly the name is as inaccurate as the date. H. M. Colvin, (*Dictionary of British Architects*), however believes that Sir John Soane is the man.

Evidence on the windows at Tetbury Church is circumstantial but, I believe, convincing. Francis Hiorne was called in, as architect and mason, to rebuild the church in the 1770s, and the huge windows, with their filigree tracery, immediately strike one as Coade stone, by their precision and unaltered cream colour. Various drafts in the Gloucester Record Office[20] specify Tetbury stone for the building and "the same" stone for the windows, columns etc. In the final draft "proper and suitable stone" replaces "the same stone" and this is followed in the final agreement allowing Hiorne to use what medium he wanted. Since Coade stone is cheaper than natural, Hiorne would have done well.

Tetbury Church, Gloucestershire,
Gothic window 1781 by Francis Hiorne

Screens

As well as the Screen at Deane and the St George's chapel examples (see chapter on Commissions for the Crown), another fine example is found at Langley Marish, outside Slough, Buckinghamshire, where the Kederminster family added a chapel to the parish church. In the 18th Century, the chapel passed to the Harveys. David Harvey was commemorated in 1788 by one of the standard catalogue *Monuments* of a *Vestal* embracing an urn, and in 1792 the family, probably being pleased with it, decided on a special order from Lambeth. To separate the chapel from the rest of the church, there is now a *Screen* of verandah type (like St George's Chapel) with three arches, very slender quatrefoil piers, and a vaulted roof. It is as elegant in Gothic terms as the Vestal is in classical. H. M. Colvin believes the design was by Henry Emlyn.

Fonts

Apart from the *fonts* at St George's Chapel, Debden and Chelmsford Church, there was a further copy on show in Coade's Gallery in 1799, and yet another at Milton Abbey in Dorset.[21] What happened to the Coade's Gallery one I have no idea, and the Milton Abbey example is also missing. The dismembered pieces of a font at Plush, not far off, and thought by the Royal Commission on Historical Monuments (Dorset) possibly to be from Milton Abbey, seem to me not to be Coade stone. However, a late example of the design, of 1838, survives at Chignal St James, a few miles from Chelmsford, and in a water-colour of the outside of the Coade factory (undated) one of these *Fonts* stands in the road awaiting collection, with a workman leaning gracefully upon it. (See Chapter 3 on Coade Factory.)

Other *Fonts* of various designs appear in Croggon's Order Book. In 1817,[22] the East India Company had a *Font* "highly wrought, with cherubs" (the mould for the cherubs, as we know, being already made) and the Churchwarden of Welwyn Church, Hertfordshire, had a 12 guinea *Font* in 1818.[23] "A Rich Gothic Font" was ordered by David Laing in 1820 when he reconstructed St Dunstan's in the East,[24] in the City of London, and possibly it is the design which has been mentioned so often. The church was bombed in the war. All those *Fonts* are missing, but an interesting little portable *Font*[25] belonged to the Foundling Hospital and is now in the Court Room of the Coram Foundation, 40 Brunswick Square, Bloomsbury. It is based on a tripod classical altar, which seems strange for a Christian rite. Its three supporters are monopodia in the usual way, but instead of having lions' or rams' heads, the heads are those of lambs, Christian symbolism having broken in.

Gothic Monuments

Rahere, the founder of the church and hospital of St Bartholomew on the edge of the City of London, was so venerated that, centuries later, the 15th century monks of St Bartholomew the Great made him a new tomb, with an effigy, monks reading holy texts, and a delicate canopy over his head. This decayed, like the church, and in 1815[26] the churchwardens commissioned Croggon to repair it. Croggon made a charge of 50 guineas for "men's time and materials in cleaning and restoring a rich Gothic monument, including sundry new pinnacles, corbels etc." It took them three months. The tomb is partly painted, and partly natural stone colour; I believe that the coloured parts are the original, and the unpainted parts the Coade work.

A fine Gothic *Tomb* survives in Stanton Harcourt Church, in Oxfordshire, in memory of the 2nd Earl Harcourt. It was made in 1813,[27] and stands in a Perpendicular chapel which already contained two fine 15th century tomb chests with recumbent figures. It was decided to represent Lord Harcourt on a similar gothic tomb chest, with appropriate heraldry; and the problem of his Georgian clothes was ingeniously evaded by showing him in Peer's robes. Gothic tracery decorates the tomb chest and a long panel on the wall, his feet rest on a peacock, and his arms and supporters are behind his head. The tomb was expensive; Croggon sent a bill to the Countess Dowager of £262.10s.0d for "a Rich Gothic tomb with figure of the late Lord Harcourt, arms, crest, Gothic panels etc." Extras were the "Gothic pannels at the foot for full arms and supporters, inscriptions highly wrought with trellis work pinnacles, 80 guineas", and in addition Lady Harcourt had to pay more than £9 for the long inscription, and the wages of a Lambeth workman for more than three weeks to put it up (9s. 0d a day and his keep).

Stanton Harcourt Church, Oxfordshire, Tomb of Lord Harcourt 1814

A curious commission can be found in Croggon's Order Book for 1820:[28] "Mrs. Smyth, Ballinatre, Athlone, Ireland . . . a statue 6ft 2ins high, per drawing, St. Molanfide 50 guineas." This Celtic saint is very obscure, and it has required some research to find out who he was; the Coade firm however took the order in their stride. After all, Coades and Croggons had been married or buried for generations under the protection of such dim Cornish saints as St Blazey, St Endellion and St Veep. St Mola, or St Mola n' Faidh, was a 6th century Irish Bishop, who founded Mola Abbey, the ruins of which still stood in the grounds of Ballinatray House. This was owned by Mr Gryce Smyth; and when he died, his

117

widow had the romantic notion of erecting a statue to him robed as St Mola, and standing in the ruins of his Abbey. As we read of it, the world of *Nightmare Abbey*,[29] ruins shaggy with creeper, moonlight and ghostly monastic figures, rises before our eyes. Mrs Smyth would have had the owls and ivy on the estate, but she ordered half a ton of cement to be sent with the figure on board the Susannah, to be sure that it was solidly erected. This it was, since Mr John Ruch records that it is still in situ.

A minor Gothic monument is at All Saints, Coleshill, Oxfordshire (formerly Berkshire), to Mark Stuart Pleydell, 1802. This has a frame of Gothic ornament round a large plaque, and is a curious elephant grey colour, suggesting that it has been painted or stained at some time. It is marked COADE & SEELEY, an error which suggests to me that the letters of the names were impressed separately, in this case by a semi-literate workman.

Domestic Gothic

Chimneypieces

An early *Gothic Chimneypiece* can be seen in Stapleford Church, Leicestershire, installed when the church was rebuilt in 1783.[30] The Squire's pew is a West Gallery, giving a fine dress-circle view of the preacher and congregation, and furnished with a set of good mahogany dining chairs. The *Chimneypiece* is of ordinary 18th century shape, made as Gothic as necessary by overall Perpendicular tracery. The *Tablet*, instead of showing *Cupid and Psyche,* or something similar, has the story of *Abraham and Isaac* in low relief. A Gothic Coade *chimneypiece,* of similar size without a tablet, came to light in a private collection in 1989.

I know of no other Gothic chimneypieces of the 18th century, but several can be found in Croggon's work books of the Regency. Since this was long after the time of the catalogue, with its numbered designs, none of which were Gothic, Croggon identified each order by saying its was "As Mr. So and So", and it has required some patience to disentangle them. I think the following is an accurate summary of what was produced between 1813 and 1821.

In 1814, Sir H. A. Liddell, of Ravensworth Castle, Co. Durham[31] had a *Gothic Chimneypiece* costing 140 guineas for the house which had just been designed for him in a romantic Gothic style by John Nash. This price would have bought an elaborate specimen. In 1820[32] Mr Edward Harman had "a Gothic chimneypcs [sic] similar to Sir. H.A. Liddell" for Clay Hall, Enfield, Middx. No doubt because the moulds were available, it only cost him £109. Both houses have been pulled down; according to Pevsner's *Co Durham,* the demolition of Ravensworth Castle in 1953 was a great architectural loss.

In 1815, Sir Godfrey Webster[33] had what I assume to be a fairly plain *Gothic Chimneypiece,* since it only cost him 40 guineas, for Battle Abbey (see below). In 1816 Mr Edward Harman of Clay Hall[34] had what could have been something similar, since it was originally invoiced at the same price. By delivery time, in 1817, it had gone up to 50 guineas, possibly through a change of design. He did not like it where he first put it, and had to pay a further two guineas for "Wilson's attendance 3 days taking down and refixing in another room a Gothic Chimneypiece".

In 1817[35] a bill was sent to Mr Evelyn Shirley, of Ettington Park, Warwickshire for "expenses at Windsor, Dubbin taking drawing and dims. of chimneypiece £4.10s.0d." Fortunately, though the house was largely redone later in the 19th century, the Regency library survived, and the Coade stone chimneypiece with it.[36] It has a Tudor arch for the fire opening, pinnacles at the ends, and a frieze with late Perpendicular motifs – portcullises etc. In style it is not unlike the fireplace in the Abbot's Lodging at Muchelney Abbey. It is now painted a dark colour, probably the "bronzing" which was often the finish for Coade stone used indoors, and cost him £69.16s.0d. Next year Croggon took an order from "Lord Gorst 9 Cadogan Place" for a "chimneypiece as Shirley's".[37] He was Lord Gort, who had commissioned John Nash to build him a Gothic Castle on the shore of Lough Cutra, Galway, Ireland. Like Ettington Park, it was regothicised later, but the *Chimneypiece* survives.

The last variety of *Chimneypiece* in Croggon's books was what was described as "a rich gothic chimneypiece with a centre", costing 180 guineas, for Richard Watt Walker of Mitchell Grove, Sussex.[38] The order was in November 1816, and one of Croggon's work notes in the back of his order book shows that the centre, whatever it could have been, was made in the same month. The whole construction, however, was not ready until a year later. Neale's *Views of Seats* 1818-29, shows a castellated house; it was built c.1536. It was demolished, and so we have no means of finding out what Mr Walker's elaborate piece looked like.

Three houses: Battle Abbey, Dalmeny House and Arundel Castle

Battle Abbey, Sussex was, of course, a mediaeval foundation of which considerable remains survive now. There was more in the early 19th century. In the autumn of 1814, Croggon gave estimates to Mr Godfrey Webster for Mr Vidler (probably the builder) for an "archway 40-60 guineas, Arms, 30 guineas, pedestal for lion, 20 guineas, chimneypieces from 40 guineas, window labels 8s.0d. per foot, corbels 30s.0d. to 60s.0d. window . . . (illegible) at 5s.0d. per foot, and window heads 10s.0d. to 13s.0.d" A month later Croggon recorded an order from Sir Godfrey Webster[39] (the name had been corrected, or he had been knighted interim) for "22 Gothic corbels (label stops) for supporting window weatherings". Four each of different designs were unspecified, but a later order was for "6 corbelles, 2 Men carrying Stone, 2 miser and Thief, 2 Friar and Beggar". These sound more suitable subjects for a mediaeval setting than the scratch collection put together for Chertsey Church.

In September 1815, Sir Godfrey got his *Large Gothic Archway* for £147,[40] and by November the *Gothic Chimneypiece* was finished for 40 guineas, and next month "Arms, crest on circular tablet 30 guineas" was sent "per waggon for White Hart" (The Battle Inn.) Mr Henry Clutton swept away much earlier building in 1857, and may have included Coade work. The chimneypiece was lost in a fire in 1931. The *Archway* has fortunately survived on the outside of the house and the dripstones with their decorations seem all to be in position. The *coat of arms* is broken but remains in the garden. More label stops were seen in the garden in the 1950s but have now disappeared.[41] They may have come from 1857 demolitions.

Battle Abbey, Sussex, Gothic Detail 1815

Battle Abbey, Sussex, Gothic Head label-stop 1815

A more rewarding building to study, since not only did it have much more Coade decoration, but all of it is complete today, is Dalmeny House near Edinburgh. William Wilkins Junior is probably better known for such classical buildings as the National Gallery, London, but he also designed in a Tudor Gothic style, and in 1814-18 he was busy with two very similar houses, Tregothnan in Cornwall and Dalmeny House, both based on the genuinely early Tudor East Barsham Manor. I can find no orders for Coade stone at Tregothnan, and must assume that all its decoration is carved natural stone, but at Dalmeny House all the ornament is Coade.

120

Apart from the Buckingham Palace orders, it represents the most lucrative domestic order of which records survive. Over a period of nearly three years,[42] more than £3,800 worth of Coade stone was shipped to Leith in more than 300 cases. The individual items were quite cheap, battlements 3-3½ guineas, embrasures only a guinea or 25s.0d.; the sheer quantity of Coade stone was therefore enormous. Croggon made a summary in 1818 of "sundry work supplied". It included:

> "171 plain chimney stones, 756 figured ditto, 74 small panels with crests or letters, 59 small embrasures, 30 large ditto, 103 Gothic heads and spouts, 21 panels with crockets, 79 double battlements, 31 single ditto, 29 caps and tops for chimneys, 20 ditto for offices, 2 large rich turrets for fleur-de-lys cornices, etc., 4 less rich ditto, 28ft 7ins rich fleur-de-lys frieze, (supplied in two sections) 6 long Gothic panels, 5 square panels with shield of arms, one ditto with full arms and supporters, 4 caps and tops for turrets, and a shaft, cap and base for an octagonal chimney."

All this blends so well with the masonry work that, except in one area, it is hard to detect. The exception is on the North side, where a fire blackened the stone early this century.[43] The Coade stone was blackened too, of course; but since it is impervious, the rain has washed it back to its original colour, and it stands out starkly.

Dalmeny House near Edinburgh by William Wilkins Jnr. Gothic Detail 1815-16

Dalmeny House near Edinburgh Gothic
Detail by William Wilkins 1815-16

The house is battlemented all round. *The Merlons* (battlements to Croggon) mostly have two traceried panels, though some for corners have only one (single battlements). The *Embrasures* in between the merlons are decorated with a quatrefoil flower. *Panels* with shields of arms, the central one with supporters, can be seen on the porch, and *Blocks* with the letters P and R, for the family names of Primrose and Rosebery, appear on the entrance front. The *Fleur-de-lys Ornament* which crowns the screen at Deane appears on top of the porch (finished off by two Coade *Pinnacles*) and runs round a bay to its left. The *Large Rich Turrets* are near the centre of the entrance front. Probably the most effective ornaments of the house are the *Chimneys,* which, as at Hampton Court, are made a great feature. Each has a star top, which Croggon calls a crown. In the service part of the house, the shafts are plain, but show *Chimneys* have shafts with decoration in relief. Each shaft consisted of twenty-eight quadrant shaped stones, with Tudor roses, fleur-de-lys and heraldic animals; and every chimney stack is made up of three or six *Chimneys*, exhibiting all the patterns. The effect is splendidly rich. It is a pity that, as far as I have been able to find out, the Coade firm had no other comparable opportunity of showing off what variety and interest could be provided from easily made and comparatively inexpensive units.

Arundel Castle, a mediaeval foundation, is, as it stands today, mostly a Victorian Gothic creation; the work then undertaken, however, obliterated an earlier, Georgian Gothicization, since the Castle was almost entirely rebuilt in the later 18th century by the 11th Duke of Norfolk. J. M. Robinson in *Country Life* – Magna Carta and Pretty Ladies' Maids - [44] said that the East wing was dominated by a Coade stone relief panel modelled by J. C. F. Rossi which showed King Alfred instituting Trial by Jury on Salisbury Plain.

Mr Robinson dates this wing 1801. However, the Castle is on Mrs Coade's 1799 list, and in a letter of 19 July 1983 Mr Robinson informed me that the relief was dated 1797. It was 20 feet wide and about 10 feet high. It survived into the age of photography, but the image is so faint that a better representation is in a little handbook to the house dated 1851, plate opposite page 88. It would have been impossible to have made such a large panel in one piece, and the design, with the twelve jurymen standing at the back ready for duty, is ingeniously planned to be broken into sections. There was also a great *coat of arms*; and two giant *statues* of 9ft high of *Liberty* and *Hospitality*, and dated 1798, were in niches flanking the front door. Open Gothic cartwheel *decoration* in the balustrades by the door was also of Coade stone. All these Georgian items were sold by the local auctioneers in April 1891, and the *Builder* of August 22nd 1891 (p.140-1) recorded that "two terracotta figures 10ft high formerly at Arundel Castle have been presented by Mr. Edgley to Lambeth Vestry and, we understand, will be placed upon the Albert Embankment. They were burned at Coade's artificial stone factory in 1798, and if, as is said to be the case, they were modelled by Bacon the elder, sculptor, must be among his last works, for he died the following year". The writer in the *Builder* was no doubt right in attributing the figures to John Bacon RA, since he kept up his connexions with the Coade firm untl the last years of his life. Apart from this reference to the presentation of the figures to Lambeth Vestry, there appears to be no trace of them.

Battlements and Gothic decoration, Dalmeny House, Scotland 1815-16. William Wilkins Jnr.

NOTES

1. *The Way of the World*, William Congreve.
2. Horace Walpole bought his house in 1747 and began to Gothicise it at once. (Letters to Horace Mann June 1747 etc.)
3. Minet Library Brixton.
4. B.M. Add MS 41133. Gunnis op.cit. Coade entry, gives the story.
5. I.e. a print reproduced in "James Essex" by Donald R. Stuart, *Architectural Review* November 1950 plate 15.
6. "The rebuilding of Chelmsford Church" by Rev J.F. Williams, *Essex Review* vol XL July 1931 pp.100-166.
7. Williams ibid.
8. The Phoenix survives in a garden at Gray's Brewery, Chelmsford.
9. Williams op.cit.
10. Williams op.cit.
11. A duplicate was at St George's Chapel Windsor and Mrs Coade exhibited a 3rd copy in Coade's Gallery. In the handbook of the Gallery, she took up several pages in describing the figures in detail.
12. Colvin. op.cit.
13. CO February 1819.
14. CD January 1819 "Dubbin's attendance drawing design of screen."
15. CD July 1819, September 1819, December 1819, January 1820, February 1820, March 1820.
16. CD August 1821 "To the Committee for rebuilding Harwich Church 6 Gothic pinnacles at 6gns." Packing etc. brought the bill to £43.19s.0d. In September 10 more were ordered, and also in the same month 2 of five cants at 8gns each. In October four more of a larger octagonal size (16 gns) completed the order.
17. Colvin attributes Lexden Church to Thompson.
18. Pevsner (*Buildings of England, Surrey*) mentions the label stops but does not mention the tracery. Each of the eight windows has two different designs of label stop.
19. Gentleman's Magazine, Part II, October 1817 p.365.
20. All the papers on the rebuilding are filed together as D 566 R2/5. The first document is called The Particulars. In the draft of the Articles of Agreement "the same stone" is crossed out and "proper and suitable" written in. In the final, sealed, Articles of Agreement this amendment has been incorporated in the text. Hiorne's fee remained the same – £3484 for the whole job. Since Hiorne was his own master mason, bills from subcontracting craftsmen would have gone to him and not to the Rebuilding Committee.

21. Mentioned in Coade's Gallery handbook.

22. CD November 1817. It cost £36.15s.0d. The cherubs would be the winged cherub heads as used at Chelmsford etc.

23. CO July 1819 "James Walker, Churchwarden, Brickmaker, Welwyn Herts a font for church 12 guineas". No further details.

24. CO July 1820 "St Dunstan's Church East ordered by Mr. Lang a font abt. 25gns, a Royal Arms 20 gns".

25. Information from F.J. Collins.

26. CD "Churchwardens of St. Bartholomew the Great, August, September, October to Men's time and materials in cleaning and restoring a rich Gothic monument including sundry new pinacles corbels etc . . . 50 guineas".

27. CD May 1814. Both the Coade tomb and the 15th century tombs are painted in natural colours. The Coade tomb is stamped Coade & Sealy, probably one of Sealy's last works.

28. CD July 1821 "Mrs Smythe Ballinatre Athlone Statue of St. Molanfide £42.0s.0d." John Ruch "Coade Stone in Ireland", *Irish Georgian Society*, 1970, p.8.

29. Thomas Love Peacock.

30. It is attributed to George Richardson, who began his career as a draughtsman for Robert Adam and might well have known of Mrs Coade through her Adam connexions.

31. CO July 1814.

32. CD June 1821 "Harman Clay Hall Enfield a rich Gothic chimney piece with pinnacles".

33. CD November 1815.

34. CD July 1817, August 1817. Harman therefore had two Coade Gothic chimneypieces, one plainer and one more elaborate.

35. CD October 1817.

36. CD "Evelyn I. Shirley Esq. A rich gothic chimneypiece copied from one at Windsor Castle 60 guineas."

37. CD December 1818 "Lord Corst a rich Gothic chimneypiece from one at Windsor Castle 50 guineas". (The modelling costs had been absorbed in Shirley's bill, so Gort's was cheaper.)

38. CO November 1816. He also had, in the same vein "2 candelabra as Prince Regent – (CO March 1816). See chapter on Commissions for the Crown.

39. CO October 1814.

40. CD September, November, December 1815. 38 label stops (corbels to Croggon) were supplied between December 1814 and September 1815. The coat of arms remained in the hall over the fireplace (the Coade one?) until a fire in 1931. The mysterious spare label stops were photographed by F.J. Collins in 1950s and were still there as late as 1970 when L.J. Harper sent a photograph of them to the letter page of *Country Life* 9.7.1970.

41. I am grateful to Miss Mumford then of Battle Abbey School for showing these features to me.

42. The first orders are in COB October 1815. In August 1818 Croggon sent a detailed account of the whole. The bill included three guineas to the College of Heralds for drawing the Arms and over £50 for "men's time packing putting into lighter, shipping, Leith Vessels and expenses, 343 packages at 3s.0d. each".

43. Information, the late Dowager Countess of Rosebery.

44. "Magna Carta and Pretty Ladies' Maids", J.M. Robinson, *Country Life,* July 7 1983.

CHAPTER 9

Statues, Busts and Portrait Medallions

Statues, preferably from a classical source, were popular decorations in Mrs Coade's period. Poised on an exterior pediment (Buckingham Palace),[1] forming a focal point in a garden (Ham House),[2] standing indoors holding lights (Burghley House),[3] or enriching the design of a staircase (Preston Hall)[4] statues could play an essential part in a Georgian decorative scheme. Robert Adam, at Syon House, had demonstrated that not merely one or two, but a whole series of statues could be incorporated into the design of a room (six in the dining room and no less than a dozen in the anteroom) and this lavishness had set a pattern.

While plaster casts were often used indoors, Coade figures had the advantage of being much more robust, as well as more finely detailed; and of course outdoors they had the outstanding advantage of being more resistent to the weather than all but a very few particularly hard stones. Mainly, Mrs Coade's figures were for domestic decoration, but emblematical figures were also often needed, *Justice*[5] (Beverley Sessions House), *Britannia* (Liverpool Town Hall),[6] *Minerva* (Huntingdon Literary Institute),[7] and so on. Most of the figures are Roman classical, but Mrs Coade also made a long series from the Erechtheion caryatids. A pair of Egyptian figures is known, and there are even a couple of Chinamen for Twining's tea emporium[8] and an Indian god at Sezincote.[9]

A few portrait figures were made, and there were also the busts necessary for a gentleman's library or hall. A few medallions with portrait heads, on the lines of Renaissance bas-reliefs, have also come to light, and there are more listed in the Coade catalogue. We can therefore see what a good market lay open for Mrs Coade to exploit, and this chapter will give some indication, I hope, of the way in which she and her successors grasped this opportunity.

Statues

The Coade catalogue begins with a *River God* at 100 guineas. This was not too high a price for what was a remarkable feat of potting. The nine-foot *figure*, fired in one piece, reclines on a block of Coade rockwork. At Ham House, Petersham, where an example survives in fine condition, the figure and the Coade stone rock are placed on a base of natural stone which, as far as 90% of visitors are concerned, appears to be exactly the same substance as the figure.

Reclining River Gods were a cliché of classical sculpture, and several survive in Rome today; John Bacon's design, however, seems to be his own without a specific Roman model. He was fond of it, and repeated it in bronze on the base of the statue of George III at Somerset House. The King does not appear to have objected to something which was already in the Coade catalogue being reused with his portrait statue. Another Coade *River God* was at Llewenny Hall, Denbighshire[10] (now Clwyd), but has now disappeared, and a third, in the Terrace Gardens in Richmond,[11] has been badly damaged.

Thought of as a companion to the *River God*, and used with him at Llewenny, was a Naiad who has also disappeared. Both decorated in a surprisingly grandiose way the Bleach Works at Llewenny designed by Paul Sandby.[12] Another *Naiad*[13] at Croome Court in Worcestershire only survives in a very poor state – a pity since she is charmingly placed, and originally water fell from her amphora into two shells and then into a lake, while behind her is what is described as a grotto but is in fact a low wall of rocks. Again the design is by Bacon, and relates to a classical figure usually called Cleopatra[14] in the Vatican which at one time was arranged as a fountain. Reclining girls were one of the trademarks of the Coade factory, being used in the round for funerary monuments and in bas-reliefs for any number of different plaques. The *Naiad* however seems to be the only one intended for a fountain and so it is unfortunate that only part of her remains; the Coade etching shows what she should be. Both the Llewenny and the Croome Court *Naiads* were in place by 1789, so that the *Naiad* shown in Coade's Gallery in 1799 must be a third copy.[15] The Croome Court *Naiad* was not far from the Severn, and either Mrs Coade or John Sealy showed some literary knowledge by referring to the figure, in their handbook, as Sabrina, the nymph of the Severn in Milton's *Comus*. Possibly this *Naiad* was the one which Mr F.J. Collins told me was in Gunnersbury Park until after the war. (Now missing).

Croome Court, Worcestershire, Naiad by John Bacon, 1770s, damaged.

Coade etching of a reclining Water-nymph by John Bacon RA. 1770s

The *Four Seasons* were standing figures of natural size, 5 feet 9 inches. In the usual Coade manner, three of them were swathed in elaborate draperies, but the fourth, *Autumn*,[17] wears merely a square of drapery leaving her leg and shoulders bare.

The more usual size for a Coade girl, however, was 4 feet 6 inches, and there were a number of these. Probably the most successful, spanning the whole history of the firm, were the *Vestal* and the *Sibyl* (or, to adopt Mrs Coade's spelling, *Sybil*). I have not had the opportunity of examining the back of a *Sybil*, but the back drapery of the *Vestal* is particularly elegant, so that the figure can be placed in a focal position where she looks well from all sides. Both figures were versatile, and could be adapted to hold candlebranches or lamps, and in this form can be found frequently among the Coade orders of the Regency period. An early pair, bronzed, is in the chimneypiece at Audley

End,[18] and indeed the earliest *Vestal* is the one at that house already referred to in Chapter 3. More *Vestals* and *Sybils* went to the Assembly Rooms in Edinburgh New Town, where they survive in store.[19] A *Vestal*, turned into *Faith* by the addition of a chalice, used instead of the normal cross, has recently been acquired by the Metropolitan Museum, New York. Its provenance is unknown before 1964 in New York.[20] Four more, holding lights and on scagliola bases, were at Langham House, Portland Place,[21] London, and yet another pair, accompanied by an *Ancient Briton* and a *Norman*[22] (what could these have looked like?) went to Malvern Hall, Solihull. It would be tedious to enumerate all the orders for these figures which have come to light, but they will be found in the Gazetteer. It is only necessary here to say that the earliest was made in the 1770s and the latest for which records are available are at the beginning of George IV's reign. The Coade figures were admired abroad, since a *Clio* and a *Urania* (dressed as Flora, with a sheaf of flowers and more flowers in her hair) have recently come to light at the Essex Institute at Salem, Mass. They are recorded as being there from at least 1820, as garden ornaments.

Coade etchings of a Vestal, a Sybil (sic), Urania and Clio 1770s-80s.

130

The *Vestal* could also droop her head and put her arm round an urn to become a funerary monument.[23] *The Sybil* (who can be seen from the engravings to be merely a scaled down version of *Winter*) could be given a lamp to hold in both hands, and then became a *Wise Virgin*[25] in the chapel at Burghley House, Northamptonshire. With her head raised a little more, and one hand held up to command silence, she was *Contemplation*,[26] a variation which Mrs Coade tells us in the *Coade's Gallery handbook* was first made for the celebrated Dr Lettsom, who had many figures and plaques at his house in Camberwell, and an extraordinary medallion for the Medical Society of London.

As will be seen from the Coade etchings, all the Coade girls were very much alike, and without the design numbers written in, as they are in the Guildhall, Royal Academy and Soane Museum books, it would be almost impossible to collate them with the Coade catalogue. Figures similar in style, which could be used with the *Vestal* and *Sybil* to make up a set, were Urania and Clio. The four were used, and survive, in the magnificent hall at Downton Castle.[27] A similar set, modified to hold amphorae on their heads, is at Bowden Park, Wiltshire.[28] Earl Fitzwilliam, had a set of *Seasons*, and ordered a further set in June 1814[29] for his estate, Wentworth Woodhouse in Yorkshire. They were to be 4 feet 6 inches high, and as we have seen, the Seasons were much taller, so what in fact he got were a *Vestal*, a *Sybil*, *Urania* and *Clio*. They are now in a private collection.

Many of these figures are derivatives from classical originals, familiar to connoisseurs both from plaster casts and from the books of engravings published in several counties. Mrs Coade made a copy of the *Flora* in the Farnese collection, as well as another of her own (or Bacon's) design. One survives in Oxford,[30] and another, together with a *Pomona*[31] is at Heveningham Hall. Two sizes of *Pomona* were to be had, while no less than four *Floras* from 5 feet down to 1 foot 8 inches reflect a demand for this popular garden subject. In 1789, *Flora*, *Pomona* and *Ceres* arrived on top of an Orangery[32] at Burton Constable, Yorkshire (together with medallions of the *Seasons*, *putti* and a *pineapple* or two) and remain intact.

A *Venus*, presumably rising from the sea since dolphins played about her feet, was not so lucky; she was in the car park of a public house in Hampstead[33] and was complete until the 1950s. Requests to the brewery company either to sell her or put her in a safer place were ignored, and as was inevitable she was smashed a few years ago. Another victim was a *Diana as Huntress*, (as far as I know a unique design and perhaps relating to the large medallion of the same subject at Woolverstone Park, Suffolk) which was in the courtyard of Heslington Hall, York, until it became part of York University, but has since been vandalised. (Information from the Hall).

Justice was ordered for several Court Houses, at Beverley,[34] Waterford,[35] Canterbury,[36] Tower Hamlets[37] and Thetford,[38] and for Hothfield Place, Kent;[39] I believe that only the Beverley and Thetford examples survive.

Minerva was used for a fire insurance office at Charing Cross,[40] and on the cornice of Huntingdon Literary Institute; this figure survives and has recently been restored.

Heveningham Hall, Suffolk, Statue of Flora and Pomona, Orangery by James Wyatt 1780s

Hampstead, London, "Old Bull and Bush", Venus rising from the Sea 1803

Britannia[41] was ordered for Liverpool Town Hall and for the Custom House in London, and "an old figure of Britannia" was frugally ordered by a Dulwich customer.[42] The lamentable story of the Custom House (which also had a statue of *Neptune*), will be found in the chapter on Commissions for the Crown.

From all these rather repetitive ladies, it is a relief to turn to special orders. A large and expensive standing *Naiad*[43] was designed as a conduit by John Johnson to complement his Shire Hall, Chelmsford, nearby. Being an impediment to traffic it was dismembered many years ago, but is now happily reassembled inside the Shire Hall.

A *Charity*[44] group (quite different from the Marine Society's group) is at Greenwich Hospital, with a seated girl and three small children, and it was repeated in a niche on Nuckel's Almshouses at St Peter in Thanet.[45] A standing *Charity*[46] also with three children, was designed by Bacon for Fishmongers' Hall, and all these appealing groups survive.

Governors of Orphanages had been in the habit of indicating their charitable status by putting figures of their children on the exteriors. Usually they were of wood, painted and made to order; but Mrs Coade could offer them ready made. They are engaging little figures about the size of a child of eight or so, and the costume shown in the engraving could be modified to suit the uniform of the institution. That worn by the pair on the Fanmakers' Guild building, formerly a school, behind St Botolph's Bishopsgate,[47] differs slightly from the Coade etching, and the *Charity Boy* on Vintners' Hall[48] (who lost his *Girl* in the war) has been dressed in the fashion of his date – 1840 – by giving him a pair of long trousers instead of breeches.

Fanmaker's Hall, City of London, Charity Boy and Girl 1821, originally on an orphanage.

Vintners' Hall, City of London, Charity Boy, 1840. Note his Victorian trousers instead of breeches.

Male Coade figures are far outnumbered by the Coade regiment of women, but there are a few designs. As we have seen, Mrs Coade bought a *Druid*[49] when Mr Bridges gave up, and it was probably this model which she repeated a number of times. It is a seated figure with enveloping robes and hood, and a staff in one hand. Complete, it can be found in Priory Park Chichester[50], and at Croome Court,[51] Worcestershire. *Druids* in various stages of decay are at Erddig,[52] Clwyd; the Vyne, Hampshire;[53] and Shugborough,[54] Staffordshire. This last, placed in the pre-existing mock ruins by the river, probably by Samuel Wyatt, has lost his middle, possibly by a fall of rock, and only the head and legs remain. A fine *Druid*, complete except for his staff, from a Sussex house, was recently in the hands of a London dealer.

On the same page of the Coade engravings is *Father Time*. This is one of the finest Coade pieces and was used on the Henniker monument at Rochester Cathedral. *The Gentleman's Magazine*[55] attributed it to Thomas Banks, and it appears to be the only Banks design so far found among products of the Coade factory. Another *Father Time*[56] is at Tyringham, Buckinghamshire, appropriately used as a sundial. Yet another, probably of the same design, was sold to a customer at Turnham Green.[57]

An *Apollo* Belvedere went to the Earl of Buchan, and *Apollos*[58] were sold to Sir Charles Cockerell at Sezincote, at the same time as his Indian sculptures there. They are not now in his house, and at least one was for the East India Company's headquarters, where Sir Charles was an important figure, and for which other Coade pieces were bought.

Special commissions for the Regent of Portugal, then in exile in Rio de Janeiro, were *St George* (with shield) and *St John* (with eagle) for the Royal Palace.[59] They were part of a series of orders which included *Truth, Justice,* the *Arms* of Portugal, statues of *Flora* and *Pomona* and elaborate bases for them, with dolphins, and a copy of the Syon gateway by Adam. The *Gateway*[60] survives at the entrance to Rio Zoo, but I have been unable to find any information about the fate of the other pieces.

Mrs Coade and her partner Sealy were influenced, like others interested in design, by Egyptian art. The figures on the Egyptian House, Penzance, are still in situ and are of Coade stone.[61] Two remarkable Egyptian figures,[62] dated 1800 and wearing Pharonoic headdresses, are in the garden of Buscot Park, Oxfordshire. They are discussed in the chapter on Mrs Coade's Classicism since the originals were made for the Emperor Hadrian.

Another exotic, of a different kind, made by the Coade firm, was a statue of *Suraya*,[63] an Indian God, made for Sezincote, Gloucestershire, and this is discussed at greater length in the chapter on Garden Ornaments.

Greek art and architecture had a profound influence on the connoisseurs of the later Georgian period. Sir John Soane was a good customer for *Caryatids* based on those of the Erechtheion, of which he ordered more than three dozen. They appear at the Bank of England[64] (placed in a new position by Baker in the 1930s) and at Soane's own houses in Lincoln's Inn Fields[65] and Pitzhanger Manor, Ealing.[66] He also used them at Buckingham House, Pall Mall;[67] All Soane's *Caryatids* have been provided with arms, and are in fact like those made for Hadrian at his Villa. The model was designed for Soane at the Bank before Lord Elgin had brought the *Caryatid* back from Greece, and so must have been modelled from the *Antiquities of Athens* or a similar book. The Earl of Plymouth was another customer for *Caryatids* for Hewell Grange,[68] Worcestershire, but the house has been demolished.

Mrs Coade refers in *Coade's Gallery* to *caryatids* being supplied for the Picture Gallery, Pall Mall, by which she could have meant Dalton's house, where the Royal Academy held its exhibitions until 1779, or Christie's premises, used by the Free Society of Artists; both buildings have been demolished.

The Hon. Frederick North ordered half a dozen of the usual Coade *girls* for his house in St. James's,[69] but in October 1816[70] gave the Coade firm a very different commission, for them to make "six months time a statue abt. 7ft. copy of caryatis [sic] from one of the Elgin Marbles British Museum at 50 guineas to be copied as it now appears". In other words, it was not to be a free version from Stuart's engraving, but an exact copy of the Erechtheion statue Lord Elgin had brought from the Acropolis, with all the damage time and its journey inflicted on it.

Lord Guildford, as he became, was a passionate Philhellene, who founded a University on Corfu of which the academic dress was ancient Greek, and is said to have worn this in London. His exact copy was sent to Athens,[71] and I can only suppose it was intended to replace the pile of stones which supported the Erechtheion entablature in place of the missing figure. However, I fear that his plan to mitigate the damage caused by Lord Elgin seems not to have been successful. The pile of stones remained until Victorian times, when it was replaced by a terracotta copy (itself since replaced by marble). Coade stone can be described as a terracotta, but it seems unlikely that the Coade figure lay about unused in Athens or the Piraeus for about thirty years. I think it must have been lost in the turmoil of the Greek War of Independence, and, like Lord Byron, to have been its victim.

Portrait Statues

The Coade firm made a number of portrait statues for commemorations, including several *George IIIs*, some *Nelsons* and *Lord Hill*, and these are dealt with in the chapter on commemorative monuments. We are concerned here only with that small group of figures which are portraits without being public memorials.

Shakespeare was made for the Opera House, Haymarket, and is now in front of the Public Library, Romford Road, Newham, its route there being unknown.[72] This is the usual 18th century version of the dramatist, with his stiff Jacobean clothes softened into something more acceptable to Georgian taste. Another *Shakespeare* was on the pediment of the theatre in Edinburgh, accompanied by the *Comic* and *Tragic Muses*.[73] The *Muses* disappeared on the demolition of the theatre, but *Shakespeare* was taken to Bonaly, on the outskirts of the city, where it survives in the garden.

Panel, Griffins and Ornament, Gosford House Stables, 1790. Scottish National Monuments Record.

CHAPTER 10

External Architectural Details

The Coade firm made such a variety of architectural ornaments that it is essential to discuss each type of detail separately. This means that some buildings, such as Woolverstone Hall or 20 Portman Square, each of which is decorated with several different architectural ornaments, will appear in three or four places in this chapter, and also elsewhere in this book. It is hoped that the Gazetteer section at the end of the book, with its summaries of the Coade work at each site, will give the reader a complete picture of such houses.

The Classical Orders

Everyone with pretensions to architectural taste knew the characteristics of the Doric, Ionic and Corinthian Orders and wished to use them. Great houses were built with porticos of giant columns; if these could not be afforded pilasters took their place. Smaller houses might have porches supported by columns perhaps eight or ten feet high, which would suggest the correct Roman allusions. Inside the house, columns and pilasters appeared in the more formal rooms; and when Croggon embarked on scagliola work he was able to supply not only the capitals (which the factory had been making since the 1770s) but the columns as well. Very small columns often appeared as the supports for a chimneypiece. So it is not surprising that the early water-colour of the factory yard should show a huge Corinthian capital awaiting despatch, while forty or more years later L., a writer in the *Somerset House Gazette* of 1824, p.381, describing his visit to the factory and the making of Coade stone and scagliola, should have remarked upon the stacks of capitals, one on top of another, which reminded him of the flower-pots in a market garden. Clearly, from its beginning until near its end, the classical Orders supported the Coade factory.

Mrs Coade listed the types of capital, in the 1784 catalogue, in what we should now consider a back-to-front manner, beginning with the Corinthian, and going on to the Ionic and "Composed". (There were no Doric capitals in the catalogue or the etchings.) Since every architectural book, however, puts them in the opposite order, I shall do the same.

Doric Capitals

There are *Doric Capitals* at the Paragon, Blackheath, and Mrs Coade made them, but they are a Roman variation on the Doric theme, with an egg and dart decoration on the echinus. Mrs Coade had property in the Paragon, mentioned in her will, and may have touch of Poussin in a Wordsworthian landscape, built by John Plaw in 1774, and I believed its Ionic capitals were Coade stone. Recent investigation has however, shown that these capitals are of wood. The reference must therefore be to some piece, or pieces, now missing.

Banbury is on Mrs Coade's 1779 list, and Mr Nicholas Cooper has found evidence pointing to the fact that the *Ionic Capitals* in the church there, a sophisticated design by S.P. Cockerell of 1792, are of Coade Stone.[4] (They are now brightly coloured.)

A late church commission came from John Nash, since the *Ionic Capitals* of All Souls, Langham Place were designed for him by Croggon in 1822. The *capitals* have the odd detail of a tiny cherub's head, with wings, between the volutes. At Watermen's Hall, City of London, little dolphins standing on their heads between the volutes of the Ionic capitals emphasize the watery connexions of the Guild's members.

More correct were orders for other customers. Thomas Hope ordered a pair of *Grecian Ionic Capitals* for his house Deepdene in 1815,[5] an unnamed customer in Exeter ordered capitals "from the Temple of Ilyssus" in 1819, and six "*Ionic Capitals, Ancient Grecian Order*" went to Trumpington St., Cambridge in 1814. It seems that only the Cambridge examples survive.

What I believe to be a unique Coade Ionic Order is at Hill Hall, Essex. Its Elizabethan courtyard had capitals of an order illustrated by Hans Blum in his book *de qvinqve colvmnarvm*, Zurich 1550. Restoration by Humphry Repton involved replacing the upper Ionic capitals in Coade stone to Blum's design. Paul Drury, the archaeologist in charge of the restoration after a fire, also pointed out to me that the giant columns on the east and south fronts have bases marked COADE LAMBETH 1791, but apparently their original shafts and capitals.

Hill Hall, Essex, C.1815.
Capital copied from Hans Blum "de qvinqve colvmnarvm" 1550, Zurich.

There are too many examples of Coade *Ionic Capitals* to be listed here, but a word may be said on Mrs Coade's method of charging for them. They were paid for by the number of faces required. A free standing capital needed four faces, a capital on an engaged column needed three, and a pilaster (I suppose) one. Small sized capitals for porches etc. might be 12s.0d. to 14s.0d. per face, while a large complicated design like that at Heaton Hall could be as much as 4 guineas per face.

Corinthian Capitals

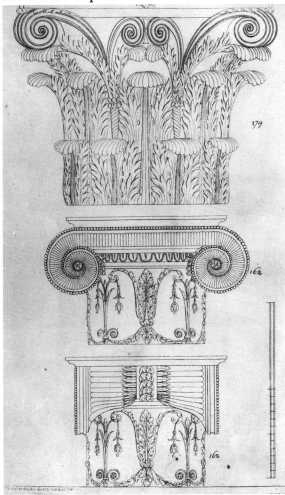

Corinthian Capitals were listed in several sizes in the catalogue, but in only one etching. It is a particularly elaborate design; the edges of the acanthus leaves are very finely serrated, and small spiral ornaments appear between the leaves of the upper row. The method of moulding these pieces in Coade stone made such complication easy; each leaf could be modelled separately and stuck on to a tub-shaped core of clay. At Audley End I was shown a capital which had lost a leaf or two and showed the technique clearly.

The largest sized *Corinthian capital* in the catalogue was priced at £3.10s.0d. per face, or £14 per capital, but this is smaller than the *Corinthian Capitals* made for Gorhambury, Hertfordshire, in 1782. The house was designed by Sir Robert Taylor in 1777, and has an unusual arrangement of the columns, with three grouped together at each end of the portico. The capitals for these, with those also for pilasters and engaged columns on the other side of the house, cost Lord Grimston £342.[6]

Coade etchings of a Corinthian and an Ionic Capital 1770s-80s

Handsome *Corinthian Capitals* were bought by Lord Howard de Walden, formerly Sir John Griffin Griffin, for his Temple of Concord at Audley End, built to celebrate the return to sanity of George III in 1787. This building is dealt with at greater length in the chapter on Commemorative Monuments, but the capitals should be mentioned here. There were twenty of them, of large size. Their cost is not known; the bill has been lost, though curiously the Essex Record Office has the bill for sending them by waggon to Essex – £6. 10s.9d.[7]

Gorhambury House, Herts, by Sir Robert Taylor, Corinthian Capitals 1782

At about the same time, the architect Thomas Hardwick built the handsome classical church St Mary at Wanstead, with a five bay arcade supported by Corthian columns. It is fortunate that the buildings accounts survive in the Essex Records Office,[8] since the Coade *Corinthian Capitals* have been painted, and so could not be recognised without documentation. The pale green and white colour scheme enhances Hardwick's airy, harmonious interior.

Another 18th century order for *Corinthian Capitals* is unfortunately not traceable. In 1799 Mrs Coade mentioned that some had been sent to Boston, Mass., but as she mentioned neither the purchaser nor the building, they have not been found with certainty.

Orders for *Corinthian Capitals* were still coming in during the Regency and can be found in Croggon's Order Book, but I have not been able to trace any in surviving buildings. Pilaster capitals were bought for St John's Lodge,[9] Regent's Park, at the same time as a pair of Flaxman *Lions,* but they were removed in Barry's reconstruction.

Leeds Court House 1811-13 by Thomas Taylor, Coade Capitals and Plaques.

Composed Capitals

The Coade catalogue lists two capitals which Mrs Coade descibed as *Composed* (nos 165, 166) and one which she called *Fancy* (no. 181). All three are illustated among the Coade etchings, and seem to be variations on the design of the capitals on the porticos of the Tower of the Winds in Athens. Since these were illustrated in the first volume of the *Antiquities of Athens,* good clear engravings of them had been available since 1762. Mrs

Coade's *Fancy Capital* is the nearest to the original. Such capitals survive in the oval hall of Latrobe's Ashdown House.

Robert Adam evolved a number of Composed *capitals* of his own, one of them being on the Brentford Screen at Syon House, Isleworth. Mrs Coade's "Composed Capital no. 166" resembles this. On the back of 20 Portman Square are other composed capitals, the design being taken by Adam from his friend Piranesi's *Della Magnificenza ed Architettura de Romani.*[10]

Beaumont Lodge, Old Windsor, Berkshire, c.1792 by Henry Emlyn, Coade Capitals and Figures.

Probably the most bizarre commission for capitals to be carried out for the Coade firm was that for Beaumont Lodge, Old Windsor c. 1790. Henry Emlyn, whose Gothic work at Windsor is described in the chapter on Commissions for the Crown, conceived the idea of a new Order of Architecture, which he called the British. In an article on it in the *Gentleman's Magazine* (Feb. 1782)[11] he explained that the idea came to him from a tree at Windsor, the trunk of which split in two. Interesting dendrology does not make good architecture, but a Mr Griffiths allowed him to put his idea into practice, and Mrs Coade was called upon to make the capitals and other decorations. At the base, Emlyn's columns are oval in section, and about a quarter of the way up, split into two round columns, tapering in the normal way. At this point there are large medallions of Coade stone based, Emlyn said, on the shield of the Knights of the Garter.

The conjoined capitals come from the plumes in the Knights' hats, but also include "a lion's snout rising out of a rose". This fortunately stillborn Order can be seen as pilasters on the garden side and columns on the front. Mrs Coade praised in great detail Emlyn's Gothic work at St George's Chapel in her handbook, but suppressed any mention of his British Order, merely mentioning the name of the house. She also made figures for niches on the garden façade; Emlyn's invention had given out here, and he was satisfied with *Vestals*, instead of asking for Boadicea or King Arthur.

Rusticated Blocks

The London 1774 Building Act provided great opportunities for the Coade firm. The Act reduced exterior woodwork to the absolute minimum in an attempt to make the house as nearly incombustible as possible. Wooden porches and other decorations were banned, and window frames were set behind the embrasure, with very narrow glazing bars. As Sir John Summerson pointed out, in *Georgian London* (p.108-110), some form of fireproof decoration was needed, if house fronts were not to become intolerably boring and repetitious, and this is exactly what the Lambeth factory was able to supply in great variety.

Coade etchings of Keystones 1770s

With Coade units the doorway could be built into an imposing feature. A door could be set within an arch formed of rusticated *Blocks* and *Voussoirs* of Coade stone. As front doors were more or less standard sizes, the sets of blocks could be made in large numbers and were very cheap. One of the *Voussoirs* to go round an arch was only 6s.6d.[12] The usual way of using them was alternately with brickwork, so that the lighter-coloured stone made striped accents round the arch. The springing of the arch was marked by an *Impost Block* (see below) and the apex was emphasized by a *Keystone* (see below). The surface of the *Blocks* and *Voussours* was usually vermiculated, a rough texture resembling worm-casts; but at Belmont, Lyme Regis and at the Paragon, Blackheath the blocks have a different, more rocky surface which I have not seen elsewhere.

Bedford Square, Bloomsbury shows this decoration to the best advantage, since the complete square, of uniform houses, has happily survived. The square of c.1775 is usually attributed to Thomas Leverton, but recent research shows that he worked on the scheme at a fairly late date. Research by Mr Frank Kelsall, of English Heritage, indicates that the designs for the houses, by someone unnamed, were deposited in the Bedford Estate Office and have now disappeared. William Scott, brickmaker, and Robert Grews, carpenter, agreed in 1776 to carry out these designs, and Mr Kelsall believes that they were fully capable of producing the designs themselves under the superintendance of Robert Palmer, the Estate steward. Leverton said in 1797 that he "had had a principal concern in the finishing of

Bedford Square, and built among other houses that of the Lord Chancellor, beside several on my own account".

The effect is of great dignity, though the original cost was very small. A set of *Blocks* and *Voussoirs* could be bought for less than £3, while a suitably-sized *Keystone* cost 2 guineas, so that a handsome doorway could be had for £5. Variations of the Bedford Square design can be seen all over the area between the British Museum and Edgware Road, and between Marylebone Road and Oxford Street. Much has gone in recent years, but a good deal still remains. The north end of Harley Street, and to a lesser extent Wimpole Street, shows the pleasing variety to be had from quite a small number of different *Voussoirs*, *Keystones* and *Impost Blocks* combined in different ways. Of the forty houses with Coade decoration remaining in Harley Street at the time of writing, there are no less than sixteen models of front door. A walk in the surrounding streets will disclose other examples. Baker Street was rich in these doorcases, and in the 1945 edition of *Georgian London*, Sir John Summerson noted 27 examples. Now there are only four (one a reconstruction).

Keystone 1791, originally in London, Author's collection.

As mentioned in Chapter 6, an effective piece of Coade rusticated decoration can be seen in New Cavendish Street, W.1. Nos. 61 and 63 are on the axis of Mansfield Street; and to close the vista, the two front doors, and a window between them, have been combined into a triple arcade of Coade rusticated *Blocks* and *Keystones* with classical heads. A related design is shown among the Coade engravings, and is described in the catalogue as no.476 "An Arch to the left-hand entrance to Stratford Place, 5 guineas". The picture shows three arches, for a doorway and two windows, all linked with rusticated blocks; presumably the 5 guineas covered one arch only. The left-hand entrance to Stratford Place, off Oxford Street, was demolished in the 1930s for a shop, but fortunately a house, No 16, with this decoration still survives on the west side, further down this cul-de-sac.

61-63 New Cavendish Street, London, 1778 John Johnson Linked Doorways.

Outside London, the Bedford Square type of doorway can be seen at Southernhay West in Exeter,[13] a town where Eleanor Coade spent her childhood and where she still probably retained many friends. They also appear at the Terrace and the Mount at Torquay – by then old-fashioned, as the houses date from 1831. Mostly such doorways were for town houses, but Miss Nancy Briggs found a country house with one, Langford Grove, Essex, the architect being John Johnson again. Another was used as a gateway at Hafod.[14]

Eleanor Coade's own house at Lyme Regis, originally called Bunter's Castle and now Belmont, is a showcase of almost every type of Coade decoration, (see below under

Keystones, Fascia and *Friezes* and *Impost Blocks*) and has rusticated *Blocks* and *Voussoirs* round the doorway and blind arches round the windows. She took over the house from her uncle in 1784, and the decoration must date from then.

A fine, and probably unique, piece of Coade rustication is at Croome Court, Worcestershire. An estate road is carried over another at right-angles to form what is known as the Dry Arch Bridge.[15] On the lower level, the viewer is in a cutting, facing a mass of rusticated Coade stone with an arch in the middle. All the *Voussoirs* and *Blocks* were modelled specially to fit the space. The *Keystone* is a large one, no.439, of the *River God*, which cost 5 guineas in 1784. The design is repeated on the other side of the bridge.

Keystones

Even if a householder could not afford a whole Coade doorway, a *Keystone* would be likely to be within his reach. He could buy a small *Minerva* for 12 shillings, or a modest little *Lion*, 6 inches high, for two. A whole page among the Coade engravings shows the *River God*, as at Croome Court, a *Jupiter*, a bearded head less dishevelled than the River God (much used in Harley Street), a *Pan* and a *Satyr* (the latter to be seen in Charterhouse Square) a *Wood Nymph* with her hair done in a particularly Coadeish way, the front locks tied in a bow under her chin, *Minerva* in a feathered helmet, a *Female Head* with drapery round her face, (particularly popular) two *Lions* (one can be seen in Gloucester Place, W1) a *Goat* and a *Bucranium* (oxskull).

All of these face straight ahead; but an attractive group, added I think later, have the heads three-quarter face. These are a *Girl* (to be seen at Torquay) *a Baby* (probably the design known to Pincot as *Young Hercules*, since Hercules was said to have strangled a serpent in his cradle; this also can be seen at Torquay) and a man wearing the floppy turban Georgian gentlemen put on when they took off their wigs. He has a Hogarthian leer, and I think is the design to be found in Croggon's Order Book as the *Laughing Philosopher*. Two of these can be seen at the entrance to Bedford Square from Bayley Street.[16] The rest of the Bedford Square keystones are mostly *Jupiters* and *Female Heads*.

The northern part of Manchester Street, W.1. retains a very good selection of Coade keystones. This was built as a quite modest residential area and the *Keystones* are fairly small, costing 12s.0d. to £1. at most. They include *Minerva*, a *Faun*, a small *Jupiter*, small *Female Head* and the girl looking sideways.

South of the Thames, a large number of new streets were being laid out in Mrs. Coade's lifetime, in the development planned by George Dance. Coade *Keystones*[17] of the Manchester Street size can be seen in South Lambeth Road, Kennington Road, Wandsworth Road and smaller streets in this area. (See Gazetteer.)

At Belmont, Mrs. Coade had a specially designed *Keystone* for her front door, showing the *River God* wearing a crown. Over the windows, however, she made do with the draped *Female Head*, which was reproduced in large numbers.

160

Impost Blocks

These were decorative blocks, less deep than the rusticated blocks, which were set at the springing of an arch. The Coade catalogue listed four patterns. *Waterleaf with projecting mouldings, Guilloche with rich Flowers,* and *Honeysuckle in Flutes* in two sizes, none of which is illustrated in the Coade etchings. There are therefore difficulties in identifying them. The latter two appear quite often in Harley Street, where there can also be seen *Impost Blocks* with oval paterae and with vermiculated rustication.[18]

At Belmont, Mrs Coade had a delightful design, with a relief of a dolphin. Like the front door keystone, it seems likely to have been made specially for her; I have never seen either elsewhere.

Friezes, Fascia and String-courses

Mrs Coade did not include in the catalogue anything by the name of a string-course. However, what we should call string-courses appear in Coade stone on a number of buildings (from her *Fascia* range) and she herself was not very clear on what was the distinction between *Friezes* and *Fascias* (strictly, wider and narrower bands of a classical entablature) so it seems best not to divide them into separate categories, but to treat them all together.

Under what she spelt *Frizes*, Mrs Coade could offer: *Flute and Patera; Oxhead with Festoons of Fruit; Vase and Festoons of Husks; a Reversed Festoon of Husks, Scrolls and Honeysuckle; Foliage and Honeysuckle; Griffin and Ornaments; Foliage; Festoon of Laurel.* All these designs, of course, are arrangements of the motifs which appear many hundreds of times in the work of the Adam brothers or the Wyatt family, as part of the alphabet of the neo-classical style. Honeysuckle, here, is the Greek honeysuckle or anthemion ornament, and scrolls are the spidery coils and trails which Robert Adam borrowed from later Roman decoration. Husks, by themselves, are treated in greater detail in the chapter on Interior Decoration.

Flute and patera frieze can be seen at Belmont, Lyme Regis. It is each side of the front door, and then goes inside and follows the dado up the staircase. Mrs Coade (see below, Paterae) was fond of putting an animal's or a human face in the middle of her paterae, (circular or oval medallions with a design radiating from the centre) and at Belmont she used lions' faces. As the frieze is quite narrow the faces are hardly bigger than a penny, but quite distinct. The same design, appears at the Paragon, Blackheath.

Oxheads (bucrania) with swags can be seen on the Rotunda Hospital in Dublin, originally designed by James Gandon for an Opera House. The design does not exactly correspond to the Coade etching, but in any case this would have been a special order, as the sections of frieze would have had to be made on the appropriate curve. The frieze is continuous round the top of the building, with vases and oblong panels of swags lower down. *Oxheads with festoons of fruit* is a design used by Sir John Soane in his earliest house, 1780-2 at Adams Place, Southwark.[19] Another variation, on a smaller scale, was used by him at the Manor

House, Wood Eaton, Oxon. for a porch inspired by the Temple of Miletus in 1791.

Coade etchings of Friezes including a Bull's Head design used by Soane at Adam's Place, Southwark. 1780-82

Griffins and Ornament, with the griffins facing each other and a vase or other details between, was frequently made. The original design also comes from the Temple of Apollo at Miletus. A small section of it could be a plaque, to be seen on the watchman's box at Stratford Place, London W.1. and on the pedestal of the Cat Monument (in honour of Admiral Anson's cat which circumnavigated the globe with him) at Shugborough, Staffordshire, the cat itself being carved in stone. Long panels of it, with three repeats, and of particularly fine quality, can be seen in the Island Temple at Croome Court, Worcestershire.

Repeating Festoons can be seen as a *frieze* at Heveningham Hall by Sir Robert Taylor, and, in another variation, at Belmont, Lyme Regis; while the *frieze* of swags on the Skinners' Company's Hall, in the City of London (by Jupp), is made up of skins, not material, to symbolize the Company's occupation. A very charming *frieze*, not among the etchings, is on one of the lodges at Heveningham Hall (by James Wyatt) which has swags of drapery, and girls' faces; it is probably of the early 1780s. It has recently been stolen.

Fascia, in Mrs. Coade's catalogue entries, represented something usually narrower and simpler than the "Friezes". There were several variants of *Guilloche* (she spelt it guiloche), one pretty example having alternate bunches of grapes and vine leaves framed in the intertwined curves. The most usual pattern, however, has a little quatrefoil flower within each guilloche, and was described in the catalogue, rather inadequately, as *Guiloche with Bands*, and cost 2s.4d per foot. At the factory, however, it must have been made not by the foot but by the furlong.

Coade's insi
the etching
intended to
the size of b
identified in
them, rescu
they were in
Museum of

Heveningham Hall, Suffolk
Frieze on Lodge
by James Wyatt, 1780

Heveningham Hall, Suffolk
Console on Lodge
by James Wyatt, 1780

The little fa
times amon
with a bear
John Johns
Johnson ha
Balusters at
remarkably
this decorat

There are
designs can
George Byf

Iver Lodge, Bangors Road South,
Iver, Buckinghamshire.
String Course and Plaques, 1792

It see:
later,
house
and i
runni:
list).
Bang(
reveal
LAMF
  A d
and I
in th
Vitru:
Strou
Comr
stone
  Wit
gener
charr
unad
doorv
belies
Coad

Pater

As p1
from
their
desig
comr
Ther
  Th
Pater
grou
the s
its o1
deter
else,
  Pa
2½ g

must come from him, though the firm's chief modeller would not need his assistance to turn such a figure into *Astronomy* (with telescope), *Architecture* (with set-square), *Industry* (with spinning-wheel) or whatever else might be required. The usual size of these *Panels* was two feet by four, and so they could be combined with the *Festoon Panel* (with or without patera). This arrangement was at Cuffnells and survives at Belmont, Kent.

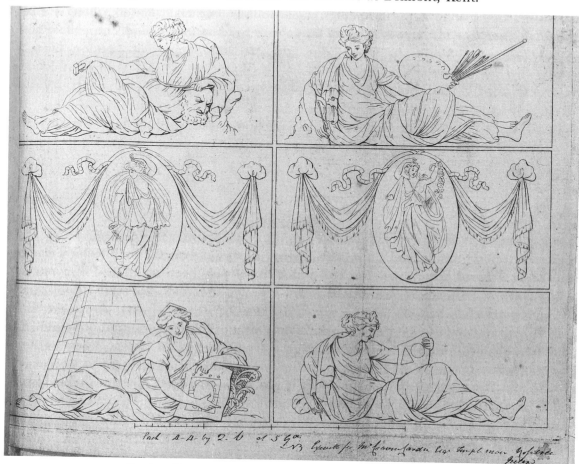

Coade etchings of Plaques of Reclining Figures by John Bacon RA.

The figures could be made to look in different directions, and were sometimes provided with an attendant putto. *Hibernia* (from Cuffnells) has a ship, and a map of Ireland. To make her into *America*, at Whiteford, near Callington, in Cornwall, on a decayed garden-house, the ship remains, but the map has been suppressed and her name written in.[33] At Schomberg House, Pall Mall, the reclining girl, with palette and paint-brushes, is Painting.

Architecture was on James Wyatt's house in Marylebone (demolished) and on a house in Blackfriars Road,[34] also demolished, though Mr F. J. Collins tells me that the *plaque*, and a Coade *vase*, are on the wall of a garage nearby. Another *Architecture* survives at Sledmere,

Yorkshire. Sir Christopher Sykes greatly enlarged this house in 1781-8, probably designing it himself, and on the first floor each of the triple windows, set in a blind arch, has a Coade plaque in the tympanum. On the south-west and north-east sides they represent *Architecture, Agriculture* and others whose symbolism I could not identify. On the south east side there are specially made plaques with swags and a motif from Sir Christopher's heraldry.

At Belmont, Kent, there is an amusing variation of *Architecture*. In low relief behind the reclining girl is the house itself (with plaques and medallions clearly visible). It is not meant to be in Kent, however, as a palm tree leans over the lady, and more grow beside the house. Lord Harris, who built Belmont, was the conqueror of Tippoo Sahib, and must have wanted some reminder of his Indian glory.

Belmont, Faversham, Kent, Samuel Wyatt 1792, Plaque showing the house itself.

All the houses so far discussed belong to the 18th century. It is an interesting reflection on the longevity of some Coade designs that the Bank of Canada, in Montreal, ordered a set of the reclining girl *plaques* as late as 1819.

A large number of *plaques* were made for Gosford, Lothian Region. Most of them, including a number found with the *medallions* in the grounds, were of standard designs, but several, built into the stable block, must have been special orders and include a fine *Judgement of Paris*.

All the plaques so far discussed are in normal low relief, and were quite inexpensive; but there is a further series precisely attributable to John Bacon which display the same themes in a different way. John Johnson's Shire Hall in Chelmsford was also decorated

171

NOTES

1. Thomas Major. *The Ruins of Paestum* 1768.
2. Ashdown House, probably 1794.
3. Dated 1787, but published 1789.
4. The contract for the masons *excluded* the carving of the capitals. The Trustees being short of money offered bonds at 5% instead of payment. Two of £25 each were taken up by Mrs Eleanor Coade of Lambeth. Information from Nicholas Cooper from documents in the Bodleian Library Oxford.
5. CD August 1815 "2 Grecian Ionic capital, £16.16s.0d. 4 pateras 18 ins diam. £8.8s.0d." for the Deepdene. Customer unnamed in Exeter, CO "4 Ionic caps. . . from Temple of Ilyssus at Athens". These were ordered in July and sent off "per Russett's wagon" in November 1819, at a cost of 12 guineas each. Four more, cheaper at 8 guineas each, were sent in January 1820. Presumably the customer was so well known to Croggen that there was no need to put his name in the résumé of the accounts, the name of the town being sufficient. They have not been traced. CO April 1814, 6 Ionic capitals, ancient Grecian order for Christopher Pemberton, ordered by Arthur Browne.
6. Hertfordshire Record Office. Account book of the 3rd Viscount Grimston XI 71. April 19th 1782 "To Mrs Coade in part of her bill for capitals for new House, £250". March 26th 1783 " To Mrs Coade the remainder of her bill in full £92".
7. Essex Record Office, D/DBy A 48/11 1790.
8. Essex Record D/P 292/28/5.
9. CDB July 1818 "C.A. Tulk Esq. Marylebone Park, 2 Corinthian pilaster capitals 16 guineas".
10. *Home House* 1969 by Margaret Whinney p. 26.
11. And in his book *A Proposition for a new Order of Architecture with Rules for several Parts 1781.* It went into 3 editions.
12. *Coade Catologue* 1784
13. John Havill has also discovered a pair in Fore St Heavitree, Exeter, and a number of houses with keystones only; see Gazetteer.
14. Information from Sir John Summerson.
15. It is marked 1797.
16. A variation, with curly hair, dated 1791, is in the author's possession.
17. I.e. 57 and 274 South Lambeth Road, 350, 352, 362-366 Kennington Road Montford Place, Kennington Road.
18. More are in Bedford Square.
19. *Soane, the Making of an Architect,* Pierre de la Ruffinière du Prey, 1977 p. 225,

fig.11.7.

20. *George Dance*, Dorothy Stroud 1971 p.136.
21. The whole doorway is numbered 470. "Flute and wheatears" is no. 224, "Flute and cable, plain "is no. 220, the impost block "Guiloche with rich flowers"is no. 434.
22. Q Fab 6 East 52/1 Packet 25.
23. Colvin II states that the centre was altered or rebuilt by Sir Robert Rich c1789 and the paterae etc. must date from then.
24. CDB September 1815 "Thomas Hope Esq. 4 pateras 18 inches diam. 8 guineas". An order for 2 Grecian Ionic capitals at 8 gns. each and 2 antics (?) to ditto 4gns. and the paterae, had only been given on August 12th, so that the items must have been in stock.
25. By Robert Mylne 1800-1.
26. "Coade's Artificial Stoneware", Henry Clay, *Connoisseur* October 1928 shows photographs. pp. 79-87.
27. Information from John Mallet.
28. In a list sent to Lord Rockingham.
29. A. Graves op. cit.
30. Information from the Secretary of the Society.
31. All these houses are on the 1799 list.
32. Information from Anthony Grant.
33. Information from Cyril Staal.
34. *Georgian London*, Sir John Summerson, 1945 edition, plate XXV.
35. Essex Record Office Q/s/Bb 348/1.
36. R.F. Dell, *Sussex Archaeological Collections* vol c. p. 9.
37. An old photograph is in Millicent Rose, *The East End of London* 1951 plate X.
38. Informatiom from the late Edward Joy, then Curator at Ickworth.
39. Information from the late Bertram Hume.
40. CD "Earl of Buchan, Apollo Belvedere, a circular pedestal with the 9 Muses modelled in the die, enriched with laurel leaves, £119.4s.0d." It went to Dryburgh Abbey.
41. Information from Sir John Summerson.
42. See note 23.
43. Gunnis, op. cit.
44. CD December 1819 "Earl Brownlow, Mr Jeffry Wyatt architect, 170 ballusters, small bottoms, £90.14s.0d." He had not yet changed his name to Wyatville.
45. Company's records.

Caryatid figures, male (then called Persians) or female. The jambs supported a frieze and cornice, the cornice projecting far enough to make what we should call the mantelshelf, and they called the mantle. (The word mantelpiece, to denote the whole surround of the chimney opening, had not yet come into use.) To add interest to the frieze, there was often an oval or oblong plaque called the Tablet in the middle. The section each side of the Tablet retained the name of Frieze, while ornaments at the top of the Jaumbs, at the outer corners of the chimneypiece, were called Blocks. The moulding round the fire opening was called the Architrave.

Several plaques with small-scale decoration were particularly suitable for the Tablets. The most used was probably *The Marriage of Cupid and Psyche*, a design based on an antique gem belonging to the Duke of Marlborough which had been carved on a chimneypiece at Blenheim. From there it became popular in all media, and I have seen it in marble, wood and Wedgwood jasper as well as in Coade stone.

Coade etching of a Chimneypiece design with figures on the Jambs used separately by Sir John Soane at Pitzhanger Manor. The Tablet is the Marriage of Cupid and Psyche.

Other suitable designs were the *Phrygian Shepherd* (adapted from the round design seen at Croome Court) a *Bacchanalian Procession* and a *Roman Procession*[13] (more sedate than the

188

Bacchanalian one) and the *Aldobrandini Marriage* (also at Croome Court). This last design had been available at Lambeth for a long time; it appears on one of Pincot's lists, described in his rather incompetent spelling as the *Grecian Wedden*.

Many of the narrower *Friezes* already described could be used in chimneypieces, while for the *Blocks* there were several wreaths, little vases, paterae, etc. which could ring the changes. There is also a *Medusa* who has been given by the engraver an expression of acute apprehension, as if she were at the receiving, rather than the emitting end of her own death-rays. I have not seen an example. In all, the catalogue listed 139 suitable items. All these motifs could be bought separately by the customer or his builder, to attach to custom-made wooden chimneypieces; but if the buyer did not want to go to the trouble of evolving his own design, Mrs Coade could sell him a complete wood chimneypiece with its Coade decorations already on it. No less than thirty different designs (or rather combinations of a limited number of units) are listed in the catalogue ranging in price from 14 guineas for an average-sized one, down to 25s. 0d. for a tiny one, plain except for the frieze, and suitable for a small room for an unimportant member of the household. I believe that the remaining late 18th century chimneypiece at Mrs. Coade's house, Belmont, which is now painted, may well belong to this group.

The catalogue listed eleven *Chimneypieces* made entirely of Coade stone, and the etchings show up to sixteen. (Four large scale illustratons are in the Guildhall book, and another dozen little pictures in the British Library copy). The grandest of the illustrations leans heavily on Robert Adam (at Mellerstain) and has a fully modelled *Faun* and a *Bacchante* standing in front of the *jambs*. The figures are 4ft 6ins high (a standard Coade size) and raise their hands to support a festoon of grapes which trails along the frieze. This *Chimneypiece* could have a richly-detailed or a plain cornice, and cost 40 or 35 guineas (nos. 514 and 515). An example has recently come to light. It came from Bretton Hall, in Yorkshire, and was sold in 1946 but did not reappear until 1985, and was sold at Christie's in 1986. In place of the tablet shown in the Coade engravings was the crest of the Beaumont Wentworth family.

No. 514 reappears at Caledon, Co. Tyrone, Northern Ireland, in the former front hall designed by Thomas Cooley from 1779. In place of the heraldry at Bretton Hall, it has a plaque of "Griffins and Ornament".[14]

The next design (no.516) has smaller caryatid figures, standing on pedestals. The frieze is *Griffins* and *Ornament* (not as large as that at Croome Court) and the *Tablet* is the *Marriage of Cupid*. The third design (no. 517) in the Guildhall book of engravings has yet smaller figures on the *jambs,* taken from the mural of dancing girls at Herculaneum, and these can be seen on one of the Capesthorne, Cheshire chimneypieces.[15] The fourth design (no.518) looks as if it had been designed for a naval man, with an anchor, cables and seaweed on the jambs, Ionic capitals composed of curled-up dolphins, and festoons of fishing net in the frieze. It cost 16 guineas. A chimneypiece similar to this was sent to Washington.

Chimneypiece formerly at Bretton Hall, Yorkshire c.1790.

Coade etching of a Chimneypiece as at Bretton Hall 1790s.

190

When we turn from the lavish collection in the catalogue and etchings, records and surviving examples are scarce. The Fishmongers' Company had four Coade *chimneypieces* at a cost of £205 in 1790 but they had a short life.[16] The Company's Hall was rebuilt in 1831, and by then such designs were out of date, and they disappeared. Gunnis refers to two Coade *Chimneypieces* made for Boreham House, Essex, for which he found records among the Hoare's Bank archives, but I have not been able to trace either the chimneypieces or the records. Also not traced are the specimens which Mrs. Coade said she had sent to Amsterdam and "Zarsko Zelo" – Tsarskoe Selo, Catherine the Great's palace near St. Petersburg. (Now called Pushkin.)

However, it is possible to refer to some extant Coade pieces. Antony Dale[17] found in the Recreation room of Pishiobury Park, Herts., a house where James Wyatt made alterations, a chimneypiece of artificial stone which he identified as Coade, which has a frieze of cornucopiae, scrolls and sphinxes. It dates from 1782. A fine specimen survives in North London, with a Vitruvian scroll *Frieze*, a *Tablet* of figures and a *Vase* which I have not seen elsewhere, and *Jambs* with Ionic pilasters.[18]

A very fine pair of Coade Chimneypieces is at Capesthorne in Cheshire c. 1790. After a fire and rebuilding, they were taken there in the 1860s, having previously been in the family's house in Belgrave Square, London.[19]

Capesthorne, Cheshire, Chimneypiece 1789

Wollaton Hall, Nottingham, Chimneypiece c.1790 (detail)

Since the Square post-dates the chimneypieces by about 40 years, they must have been somewhere else before that – possibly in the original Georgian Capesthorne. One has the *Herculaneum Figures* already mentioned on the *Jambs*, part of the *Aldobrandini Marriage* for the *Tablet*, and quivers and bows in wreaths for the *Blocks*. Both this and its pair have simple fluting for the Friezes. At first sight, the other *Chimneypiece* seems very similar. The figures are the same height, but instead of dancing, one leans on a cross and the other on an anchor. On the *Tablet* is a reclining girl with three babies. We can therefore identify them as *Faith, Hope* and *Charity*. The ecclesiastical symbolism is carried further by the *Blocks,* which show what Croggon elsewhere refers to as "Doves in Glory" – versions of the *Paraclete*. All this suggests that it could have been made for someone in the Church, a Bishop perhaps. But Lady Bromley Davenport's researches have failed to unearth any clerical ancestor.

A near-duplicate of the other Capesthorne chimneypiece, with a variation in the tablet and frieze, was discovered in 1987 at Wollaton Hall, Nottinghamshire. It must date from a late Georgian modernization in this famous Elizabethan house.

Small Ornaments to be assembled at the customer's wishes

There are two sections in the catalogue covering small details. The shorter, consisting of items which seem to have been intended for general architectural use, contains thirty- six items. The other, described as ORNAMENTS to fix on Wood or Stone Chimneypieces, contains as many as 139. The difference between the two groups seems mainly one of size. Ribbon bows, for instance, from 15 down to three inches long, were in the first category, while from five inches down to one inch they came in the second. As can be seen from this example, there were overlaps, and some confusion, and it seems best to discuss all the items together.

Rams' Heads looking front face, or adapted for use on a corner, *Lions' Heads* and *Lions' Paws*, seem mainly for architectural use. Extraordinary capitals of *Rams' Heads* can be seen on the Orangery at Heveningham Hall (James Wyatt). *Lions' Paws* were probably used not only as pedestals etc. in the 18th century, but also came in useful for the Romanized furniture of the 1800s. Bows appear, if the catalogue is correct, to have been available in twenty-one sizes, which seems excessive, even if they appeared in their thousands in late 18th century decoration. At one inch long, they only cost a penny; half a crown was the price of the 15in. size. *Myrtle Wreaths, Cornucopiae, Greek Honeysuckle, Sphinxes, Tripods and Classical Heads* could be supplied from four or five inches down to two. Perhaps the largest selection was of husks, the essential cliché of neo-classical decoration. Mrs. Coade offered festoons of them ready-made (4d. each) and a huge variety of different kinds of husk for the customer to put together as he pleased. One type of husk could be supplied "in 12 sizes from 1 inch to ¼ inch long." This suggests that one size differed from the next by only 1/16th inch, a length which many people cannot measure by eye. To join up the husks, "stalks to be applied to husks" were from 3d. to 6d. a dozen.

All this rich variety has disappeared from view. I hope that some of it survives, hidden under paint, but probably most of it has disappeared entirely. When the Coade factory site was being excavated from the Festival Hall Site, Mr F. J. Collins, then of the Historic Buildings Department of the London County Council, tells me that some of these little motifs came to light, but were lost through the workmen not realising what they were.

Clocks

There is only one clock-case design in the Coade catalogue, but two different designs have appeared in 1987 and 1988. The catalogue number 525 is a "clock-case with two sitting Figures, Spring and Autumn; an Eagle on the Top". It was 1ft 5¼ ins long. This turns out to be an accurate description; the case is covered with a raised diamond pattern with a circular opening for the clock face. The figures sit on each side. The eagle reclines on the top; its relaxed pose suggests to me that it could have softened and sagged slightly in the kiln. It is an elegant piece and is now in a private collection. It is very similar to the clock, designed by Adam, with a movement by Vulliamy and carved by Bacon for George III.

The other is less pleasing. It was sold at Sotheby's, Billinghurst, in May 1987, and is an oval, over 3 feet high, with the hole for the clock face placed off-centre. Low relief figures of Father Time and a reclining girl fill in the background and have a drooping Flaxmanian look. Its present whereabouts is not known. It was included in Coade's Gallery as "An oval medallion over the chimneypiece . . . *Time* moving off with the hours, and Attention watching the moments as they fly", accompanied by a translation of a Greek epigram.

NOTES

1. A noble suite of this kind, by Thomas Chippendale, is at Harewood House.
2. *Etchings of Ancient Ornamental Architecture drwoan from the Originals in Rome and other Parts of Italy during the years 1794, 1795 and 1797.* C. H. Tatham. Published 1799-1800.
3. A. Graves op.cit.
4. Sold 6-9 June 1983 by Christies.
5. CD June 1816 "Honble C. Long, 2 tripod stands 20 gns."
6. CD "Earl Ashburham a candelabra composed of three figures on a pedestal £21. Cartage of do. to Cockspur St. 12/-". Presumably for Ashburnham House Dover St.
7. Mrs. Coade also mentioned that her design of stove had "open work in the dye of it, for letting out the warm air; the smoke may be conducted away underneath, as the stoves at the Bank of England".
8. CO July "Ironwork to be prepared by Mr. Evans".
9. CD February "Stonework for stove 25 guineas".
10. CD "2 descending stoves with brass and ironwork complete" for £118 in May and "stove with dome top and perforated ornament" for 30 guineas in August.
11. Beaumont CD 1817. Gillespie CO. March 10th.
12. See Alison Kelly, "Coade Stone Interiors" the *Antique Collector*, July 1986, pp.50-55.
13. Plaques of the Bacchanalian Procession and the Roman Processions are inset in the walls of a passage at Chicksands Priory and presumably came from chimneypieces. A Roman Procession is also in the chimneypiece at Seaton Delaval which has the same caryatids as Schomberg House and Coade's Gallery, and a Bacchanalian rout in one of those at the Octagon, Washington DC. Both plaques are shown in chimneypiece designs among the Coade etchings.
14. Alistair Rowan *The Buildings of Ireland, NW Ulster,* plate 78. The chimneypiece is not, however, described in the text as being of Coade stone.
15. See below.
16. Company's records.
17. *James Wyatt,* Antony Dale (1956 edition).
18. 2 The Grove, Highgate.
19. Information from Lady Bromley Davenport.

CHAPTER 12

Garden and Park Embellishments

Vases

Though some vases were from time to time used on the cornices and pediments of buildings (Woolverstone Hall, Suffolk;[1] Grovelands, Southgate, Middx;[2] Somerset House, London;[3] Newington Lodge, Winkfield, Berks,[4] etc. etc.) and a few found a place indoors, by far the majority of Coade *Vases* were used in gardens and parks, and it seems convenient to discuss them all here.

There are thirty-four different designs listed in the Coade catalogue of 1784 and, including related oddments such as *Pineapples* and *Vase-chimneys*, the etchings show forty-five, including several evolved after the issue of the catalogue. Several are twins or triplets – the same Vase with more or less embellishment. For instance, "Egg form enriched with trophies of music" could become a *Funerary Monument* (not in the catalogue) with the lyre changed into a circular plaque for an inscription, and a flame, symbolizing resurrection, in place of a small pineapple on the top. Such an ovoid *Urn*, with a snake coiled round it, was used on the tomb of John Sealy in Lambeth Churchyard.[5]

A fluted *Urn*, for a type which was also made by the hundred in lead by John Cheere and others, was often made at Lambeth. It could be made with or without swags of drapery and lions' heads; with both, it was used at Paxton House, Berwickshire (Coade's Gallery 1799); with cherubs' heads in place of lions' heads, it was used on a garden monument erected at Finedon Hall, Northants by John Dolben to his friend Edward Wortley Montagu.[6]

Several models of *Vase* were of a horizontal oval shape. Mrs Coade called them "squat". A pair of them surmount the gateway to Audley End, also in company with a *Lion*.[7] The shape also went well with the horizontal oblong of a tomb-chest, and one can be seen on the tomb in Lambeth of Admiral Bligh[8] and another at St Anne's, Limehouse. This shape continued in popularity during Croggon's régime. In 1818 alone he supplied a pair for Castlewillan, Ireland,[9] two more for Bletchingdon House, Oxfordshire,[10] and, for the architect C. H. Tatham, "2 vases, large pier, squat" for Henerton House, Wargrave, Berkshire,[11] with two crests for the piers with bears and coronets, so that the entrance must have been impressive. It is a pity it has disappeared. One of the bears, much damaged, is now in a private collection.

Charming "squat" *Vases* can be seen on a very unusual church in Dorset. In 1786 George III permitted Thomas Weld to build a Roman Catholic church,[12] provided that it looked like a private house. John Tasker the architect did this with great success, providing an apparent villa in the idyllic setting of the grounds of Lulworth Castle. It has front and back porches decorated with the squat *Vases, Urns* similar to Sir William Chambers' at each corner of the cornice, and very handsome large gadrooned *Urns* in niches. All are catalogue numbers, and can be recognized from the etchings.

East Lulworth Roman Catholic Church at Lulworth Castle, 1786 by John Tasker, Vase 1786

Coade etchings of various Vase designs 1770s-1780s

Coade etchings of several Pedestals and two Urns

Chambers' *Urns* appear in profusion – there are twenty-nine of them on the cornice at Somerset House in the Strand. They have lions' heads, swags, and gadrooned tops. Like other *Urns* and *Vases,* they were quite cheap to manufacture; Croggon was still selling them for 6 guineas each as late as the Regency. A similar design, with flames rising from it, was used for church or commemorative purposes and can be seen at Taplow Court, Bucks, on the piers of a gateway which formerly led to the now demolished church. Duplicates of this pattern, and apparently those to the memory of Henry Thornton, are now at Mottisfont Abbey, Hampshire and are dated 1794.[13]

Croggon's work books are not very informative about *Vase* orders, but the commission for Mr Chamberlayne of Weston Grove, Southampton shows how they were identified. The order book says:-[14] (May 1817) "Vases C and S plate work 108 oval with handles instead of lions' heads at 7 guineas each." C and S is Coade and Sealy, though in fact most of the etchings were issued before Sealy became a partner. A search through the vase designs shows that no.108 is a *Squat Vase* decorated with bunches of grapes hanging from ribbon bows. It must have been improved by having handles instead of the lions' heads, which look pretty perfunctory in the etching; but this is another of the cases where the illustration is much inferior to the actual piece. An example at Ardress House, Co Armagh, Ireland has finely modelled lions' heads, and someone has enjoyed pricking the pores from which the lions' whiskers sprang.[15]

C. H. Tatham brought out two books of classical ornament[16] and at least one of them must have been kept in the Coade office, as a Mr Rhodes, the architect of the Office of Woods and Forests, ordered (it seems for the Office itself) "4 vases with birds per Tatham's book".[17]

One lady revealed herself as the classic maddening customer, as we read Croggon's Day Book for 1814.[18] In April, Lady Cork was charged for "2 vases, fixing and carting". In a few days he noted down "Men's wages taking down and replacing Vases", and then in May, "Men's attending moving and refixing vases"; finally, in July, he wrote "labour and cartage fetching back vases from Burlington Street to Manufactory to be sold on her behalf." She was luckier than she deserved; Croggon was able to dispose of them to Lord Egremont at Petworth, as he had "two vases, Lady Cork" in 1815.[19] He may have disposed of them in his turn as they are not now at Petworth.

There is no space here to detail other *Vase* orders which cannot now be traced, but a word may be said on *Pineapples* and *Pine-cones. Pineapples* were a symbol of hospitality, and often appear on gate-piers. The Coade design is a handsome object, though its leaves are unbotanical. C. H. Tatham had a pair which are lost under the marshalling yards behind St. Marylebone Station,[20] but a fine set can be seen at Ham House, near Richmond, Surrey. These are dated 1800 and 1801. From the evidence of the etchings (I have never seen an actual one) the Coade *Pine-cones* were miserable objects priced at a guinea and not worth more; a far cry from the noble Pigna in the Vatican.

Ham House, Surrey
Pineapples 1799-1800

Coade etchings of Vases and a Pineapple
1770s-1780s

199

I have left to the last the vases which, throughout the history of the Coade firm, proved continuing favourites, and deservedly so. These were copies of the *Medici* and *Borghese Vases*, a near-pair of clasical bell-kraters of large size. Panini includes both vases in a painting of 1757 showing all the works of sculpture most admired by 18th century travellers in Italy.[21]

The Coade copies are 4ft 2ins high. Both have a frieze of figures; the *Borghese* shows Bacchanalian revellers and Apollo, the other a scene with warriors standing about and a girl drooping at the foot of an altar. Mrs Coade described it in the Gallery handbook as the sacrifice of Iphigenia, but I believe that this is now disputed. The revellers on the *Borghese Vase* could be divided into two groups, each of which made a plaque. Examples of these still survive at Latrobe's Hammerwood Park, and existed until 1973 on White Cottages, Ascot, when they were smashed by demolishers.[22]

It will be remembered that Daniel Pincot exhibited a *Borghese Vase* in 1769, and accepted a subscription for another for Stourhead in 1770. His name also appears in 1771 in Matthew Boulton's correspondence concerning the *Medici* and *Borghese Vases* for Kedleston, Derbyshire. Mrs. Coade exhibited a *Medici* in 1777 as her own, but I think it must have been modelled earlier. The Kedleston *Medici* is marked Coade, while the Borghese there has no mark, and was presumably Pincot's.

I have traced more than twenty examples of these *Vases*, and of these the majority are in Croggon's work books. Since these cover only eight years, while both *Medici* and *Borghese Vases* can be found in 18th century orders and also in the period after 1821, I expect that more will eventually come to light. There is no need to list those that have disappeared, but the following surviving examples may be identified: taking the *Borghese* design first, since it was made earlier, the Stourhead, Wilts, specimen must be the earliest, and is possibly the first Lambeth vase. The Kedleston *Borghese* 1771, could well be the second. A *Borghese* from Elvaston Castle, Derbyshire, 1818, is now at Barnby Manor, Nottingham-shire. A fine *Borghese* at Uppark, Sussex may date from about 1800 when Humphry Repton redesigned the grounds. A damaged and restored *Borghese* at Temple Newsam, near Leeds, and one slightly damaged at Chiswick House, West London are not dateable. An interesting pair of vases is at Killerton, Devon, with the figures from the *Borghese Vase* on an amphora shape instead of a krater, and dolphins at the foot. The vases are marked Coade and Sealy (i.e. made between 1799 and 1813). Since John Johnson was the architect of the house, he could have recommended their purchase. Of the Medici design, there is the fine specimen at Kedleston, and two at Kew Gardens. Another is at Chiswick. One of the Kew *Medici Vases* is marked Croggon 1826. The last dated vase I have seen is at Coleorton Hall, Leicestershire, of 1827. The other Kew *Vase* is a splendid object, standing on a superb *Pedestal* with the Royal Cipher, rams' heads at the corners, and a different bas-relief on each side. This is part of a special order for King George IV in 1825, made for Royal Lodge, Windsor. These vases are described in more detail in the chapter on Commissions for the Crown.

Cobham Hall, Kent, Borghese Vase 1801

Fountains

Fountains are characteristic of the Italian type of formal garden, and during Capability Brown's long reign as a landscape gardener were out of fashion. After his death, Humphry Repton cautiously introduced a few formal details. The house no longer rose straight from the grass; it was sometimes allowed to have a terrace, and with the terrace came balustrades and, perhaps, formal fountains or a sundial.

This change of taste is reflected in the Coade publications. No fountains appear in the 1784 catalogue. By the time Coade's Gallery had been established, in 1799, a fountain was once more a subject of interest, and Coade and Sealy took a famous (though, one would have thought, an old-fashioned) model, Bernini's Triton in Rome. Mrs Coade does not give his name, but otherwise describes it accurately as *"The Triton –* a 6ft statue for a fountain, setting [sic] on three dolphins, from the *Piazza Barberini* at *Rome.* His hand holds a conc shell to his mouth, out of which issues a stream of water; and water is spouting also from each of the dolphins". Mrs Coade engagingly adds that "this celebrated statue was modelled from nature", without saying where Bernini might have found a Triton willing to sit for him.

Petworth House, Sussex, Fountain based on a figure by Giambologna. 1809

It is worth stressing that a complicated piece such as this fountain, requiring a large number of moulds, would not have been made as a speculation, so that there must have been a customer for it, prior to 1799. There is no information on who he was, but a number of later orders show that the design was popular. Harry Alcock,[23] of Wilton Castle, County Wexford, ordered a fountain in the style of the Bernini Triton, and another went to Taymouth Castle[24] in 1813, when a "triton for a fountain on coral rock and a bason" cost £157.10.0. More Triton fountains went to the Earl of Northwick[25] at Flambards, Harrow, in 1820, and to C. N. Palmer of Norbiton Place, Surrey in 1819.[26]

None of these fountains has survived, so it is interesting to see one which has, and which, since it is stamped 1809, belongs to the Coade and Sealy period, for which few records are known. It is at Petworth, Sussex,[27] and is superbly modelled; but the most interesting fact about it is that it is *not* the Bernini fountain.

202

It is based on a small scale High Renaissance figure modelled by Giambologna, and later copied full size by Battista Lorenzi, neither being intended for a fountain. So *either* Mrs Coade had moulds for both the Bernini and Giambologna figures, *or* she was mistaken in attributing her fountain to Bernini. I think the latter is more likely. Her design was most probably copied from an engraving, where reversals of a design were frequent, since her figure is the reverse of the original, and holds his conch in his left hand. Strictly, he is not a Triton, who would have had two tails instead of legs, as the Bernini figure has, but a human youth. Dolphins twine themselves about his feet, and originally spouted water which would have dripped into several large shells below. It is one of the finest figures made by the firm, and at this date can, I suppose, be attributed to Panzetta.

Stoneleigh Abbey, Warwickshire, Fountain 1821

In all, Croggon listed thirteen *fountain* orders, mainly with shells and sometimes with dolphins, including an interesting one for Farnley Hall,[28] Yorkshire (there are also two Coade hawks) described as "three basins with lions' heads and legs" 1818. The latter objects are the monopodia fashionable in the Regency for furniture copied from Greece and Rome and which were also used for Coade Sundials (see below). A charming Coade fountain came to light, with no provenance, at a sale at Sotheby's Billingshurst in May 1988 (no.771), stamped Coade & Sealy 1804. A large scallop shell is supported on branches of "coral" and has a base of grotesque masks and further shells. The design appears to correspond to another fountain ordered by Mr. Fector, of Kearsney Abbey, near Dover, in October 1814 and described as "ornamental stone fountain, coral tripod stand, coral top supporting a shell, three shells etc. 35 guineas".[29]

Grotesque Head, probably for a fountain 178? (the last numeral defaced) marked Coades Lithodipyra

One splendid example, in a different style, which is still on view in Dublin, is the Duke of Richmond's Fountain, in Merrion Square.[30] It was designed by H. A. Baker, a pupil of James Gandon. Unlike those which have been described, and which are in essence sculptural, the Merrion Square fountain is conceived as architecture. In the middle there is something like a Roman triumphal arch, with the arch itself filled in to form a background for the fountain. Two round *Medallions* are set in the spandrels of the arch, and there is a *Bas-relief* in the frieze. One of Mrs Coade's *Squat Vases* stands on a plinth on top. Walls each side curve out to piers decorated with further *Medallions*, and topped by tall *Urns*.

Merrion Square, Dublin, the Duke of Richmond's Fountain, H.A. Baker 1791

In 1799, Mrs. Coade mentioned "Statues, Vases, Arms, Fountains etc. at Lord Aldborough's" in Dublin. The house is now a Post Office store, and the *Vases* and *Fountains* seem to have gone, though a *Coat of Arms*, and *Lions* and *Sphinxes* survive on the roof.[31]

Audley End, Essex
Garden Feature with a base usually for a Sundial,
with a tripod copied from Herculaneum on its top 1783

205

Not exactly a fountain, but a sculptural composition presiding over a spring and pool, survives at Sezincote, Gloucestershire, the ravishing house built in the Mogul style by S. P. Cockerell for his brother Sir Charles, who also had Coade *Bulls* and *Elephants*. A stream meanders through the beautiful grounds, and where it begins as a spring, the water has been dammed into a pool, at the back of which rise steps to a high relief *Panel* depicting the Indian Sun God Suraya in a niche. At each side are *Bulls* which I believe to be the surviving Coade ones. Thomas Daniell, the topographical artist who specialized in Indian scenes, helped S. P. Cockerell with the design of the house, and could have provided the design for Suraya. It may be the fountain for which Sir Charles was given an estimate of £27 in November 1813 – if so it was inexpensive for what was provided.[32]

Sezincote, Gloucestershire c.1815. Suraya Fountain Figure, S.P. Cockerell and T. Daniell

206

Gateways

A fine gateway at the beginning of a drive gave the visitor a foretaste of the grandeur to come when he reached the house. Much trouble was therefore taken to make these entrances imposing and many are noble compositions. It will be recalled that the Screen which Robert Adam had designed in 1772 for Syon House had been decorated with his characteristic delicate ornament in a ceramic body, disastrously, by one of the unsuccessful manufacturers mentioned in Chapter 2; and that Mrs Coade had complained that she had been injured by this failure, since the decoration had been assumed to be her own work.

Eventually, the Screen was repaired by the Coade firm; and in 1810 Coade and Sealy were given the opportunity of making a replica of it for Rio de Janeiro.[33]

Similar in design to the Brentford Screen, but made fifty years later, is the entrance to Easton Neston (now the entrance to Towcester Racecourse). It was made by William Croggon in 1822,[34] shortly after he had bought the Coade business from the executors. Both designs have cubical lodges at the ends, linked by a screen of columns to a central arch. At Easton Neston, the centre is crowned by a coat of arms with supporters, and a coronet on top. This, and the capitals, some vases and two hinds which are recumbent on the roofs of the lodges, are all of Coade stone.

Entrance to Easton Neston (now Towcester Race Course) by John Raffield 1822

A fine gateway was, according to Mrs Coade in Coade's Gallery, at Castletown, Co Kildare, Eire. Mr Desmond Guinness, however, tells me that it was never there, but made for Glananea, Co Westmeath, and was designed by Samuel Woolley. In 1799, Mrs Coade described it as "a Colonade and Gateway with the crest (a horse) on it, Capitals, Statues in niches". It was later moved, and partly re-erected at Rosmead. The *Statues* were removed from it, and are now in a private collection in Northern Ireland.

Clumber, Nottinghamshire, has a magnificent composition of lodges and screens of the late 18th century. An undated invoice[35] shows that no less than twenty-five vases, as well as eight "balls and necks" were provided for it, though none survive. The Carburton gate, at the other end of the estate, has Coade *coats of arms* dated 1789, and the *vases* probably date from about this time.[36]

More modest, but pleasantly decorated with Coade stone, are the entrances to Paxton House, Berwickshire (1789) and Preston Hall, Midlothian (c.1794). Both have *Lions*, sitting at Paxton, and combined with vases; and standing with their forepaws on balls at Preston Hall (*Michel-Angelo Lions* to Mrs Coade). (Coade's Gallery List 1799).

Sundials

Coade etchings of Pedestals as at Audley End and Rio de Janeiro

Mrs Coade offered two Pedestals which she thought particularly suitable for sundials, triangular in plan, and with very low relief decoration on the sides. On one, the corners are marked by up-tailed dolphins, and on the other by girls with their arms folded. I have never seen the dolphin version and the only example I know of was sent to Brazil,[37] but the one with the girls proved popular. It seems to have been ordered for Mr Gibbons of the Oaks, Wolverhampton, in 1815,[38] which has been demolished; but four others survive, one at Syon House,[39] one at Wardour Castle, Wiltshire,[40] one at Weston Park, Shropshire,[41] and the fourth at Audley End, Essex.[42] The Audley End example is surmounted by a strange *Tripod* table supported by *Monopodia*. The design of this upper part comes from a table in the House of the Cervi, Herculaneum.[43] As it was supplied as early as 1783, Mrs Coade was up to date with her archaeology.

Garden Buildings

A delightful garden building at Great Saxham Hall, through long known, has only recently been discovered, by Julia Abel Smith, to have been made by the Coade firm. It is Gothic, and since it is marked Coade and Sealy it must have been made between 1799 and 1813. The heavy cornice, like all such Coade pieces, had to be cut out at the back, so that the clay was the same thickness throughout. In the Great Saxham Umbrello this has been done so neatly, in two rows of rectangular depressions, that unless its purpose were known, it would have seemed merely a decoration. As the dome above has long gone, both the inside and the outside can be looked at at once.[44]

Great Saxham Hall, Suffolk. Garden Gazebo, 1799-1813

Such buildings as *Haldon Belvedere, Burton Constable* (see figures) and panels at Croome Court (see External Architecture Ornaments), are more appropriately treated in other parts of this book. However, there is one which deserves to be described here for its sheer fantasy.

Opinion about the guilt or integrity of Warren Hastings' behaviour in India, as first Governor General, was sharply divided when he came back to England; but one man had no doubts whatever. Major Osborne, of Melchett Park, Hampshire must, I believe, have served in India, and had the same enthusiasm for Hindu architecture which Sir Charles Cockerell, a little later, showed at Sezincote for Mogul art. In his garden he set up a temple which has disappeared, but fortunately was described by Britten in the *Beauties of Wiltshire* (the county boundary being then in a different place) and repeated in the *Gentleman's Magazine* 1841, part 2 p.244.

Burton Constable, Yorkshire. Orangery by William Atkinson 1789, Coade Figures and Plaques.

Croome Court Worcestershire. Plaques in Island Temple by Robert Adam 1778

After detailing the pyramid roof and the "decorations peculiar to Hindoo architecture," Britten goes on to quote the inscription on a bust of Hastings inside:

> "Sacred to the Genii of India, who from time to time assume Material Forms to protect its nations and its Laws. Particularly to the immortal HASTINGS, who in these our days, has appeared the Saviour of those Regions of the British Empire, this fane was raised by John Osborne in respect of his pre-eminent virtues in the year MDCCC."

Britten continued:

> "The design of this temple was furnished gratuitously by Thomas Daniell Esq. R.A. after the choicest models of Hindoo architecture, and was executed in artifical stone by Mr. Rossi."

From this it appears that the whole temple was of Coade stone; certainly a pair of Brahmini bulls, like those at Sezincote, are on the front corners of the verandah and Britten also mentions the Indian Gods, Ganesu [sic] and Vishnu. From a plate in the *European Magazine*[45] it can be seen that Hastings' bust, bare shouldered in a Roman style, rises from what Britten calls "the sacred flower of the lotus", in fact a cup of petals, with more downward-curving petals below.

Though Major Osborne dated his temple 1800, this must be the completion date, as it was begun in time to be included in Mrs Coade's 1799 list.

Basket of fruit and flowers made for Wentworth Woodhouse, Yorkshire 1814

NOTES

1. By John Johnson 1776. Coade's Gallery 1799.
2. By John Nash 1797.
3. By Sir William Chambers. 1776-86. Coade's Gallery text refers to "vases on the parapet and various Royal Arms".
4. Mentioned in Coade's Gallery 1799.
5. Though John Sealy most concerns us, the tomb's first inhabitant was Harriett, wife of his brother William, who died in 1799.
6. Now in a private collection.
7. Supplied 1786. Essex Record Office D/DBy A 44/11.
8. CC March 1814 "Admiral Bligh Tomb to the memory of his wife 45 guineas": the inscription on the tomb in Limehouse is not now legible.
9. CD November 1818 "Lord Glerawly, Castlewillan, Ireland . . . 2 squat vases", ordered with two eagles and two Egyptian lions.
10. CO October 1818, Mr Annesley (in fact Lord Annesley) "2 lions couchant, 2 eagles, 2 squat vases".
11. CD May 1818 "2 crests for piers of bears and coronets, coral stand supporting bason, 2 large squat vases £106.5.0. The order had previously been given to Charles Fredk. Johnson Esq . . . for Mr. C. H. Tatham."
12. At this time it was still illegal to build a Roman Catholic church.
13. Information from Martin Drury, National Trust.
14. The bill is recorded in the Day Book for the following November. The house was demolished c. 1920.
15. J. A. K. Dean
16. *Etchings of Ancient Ornamental Architecture drawn from the Originals in Rome and other Parts of Italy*, 1799, which Mrs Coade probably had as she copied a seat from it – see chapter on Mrs Coade's Classicism – and *Etchings representing fragments of Grecian and Roman Architectural Ornaments*, 1806.
17. CD June 1818.
18. CD April 1814 "2 vases, fixing and carting, 16 guineas plus £1.11.6., followed by a bill for 8s. 0d for moving vases, then 16s. 0d. in May, and finally 10s. 6d. in June for taking them back to Lambeth. In August 1815 she paid for a man's attendance in bringing a fountain to her house (15s. 6d.) and in May 1816 for a man's attendance in taking it back to the factory again (10s. 0d.)
19. CO July 1815 "Lord Egremont 2 vases as Lady Cork".
20. C. H. Tatham, Queen St Mayfair. CO August 1817 4 pines for piers $1^1/_2$ guineas each to be delivered to 35 Alpha Road, Lisson Grove. A note of June 1819 says "C.

H. Tatham for 4 pineapples, agreed to be a present". Tatham built this house for himself.

21. At the Staatsgalerie, Stuttgart. A copy in the Metropolitan Museum, New York.

22. On information from Dorothy Stroud I arrived to see them being smashed to pieces.

23. J. E. Ruch "Regency Coade" *Architectural History* 1968, note 40. p.12.

24. 1813 bill from Coade and Sealy, Scottish Record Office, GO112/20/4/9/49. Information from Dr James Macaulay.

25. CD April 1820 "The Earl of Norwich (crossed out) Northwick, Statue of Triton and conc with 2 dolphins for a fountain from the Piazza Barberini in Rome £53.17.0."

26. CD August 1819. "C. N. Palmer, Norbiton Hall near Kingston, Triton figure with dolphins for fountain £131.16.0."

27. See Alison Kelly "Coade Stone at National Trust Houses", *National Trust Studies 1980*. p.104-106.

28. CO June 1818 "Mr. Fawkes, fountain from Mr. Rhodes' drawing 40 guineas". Mr Rhodes was architec t to the Office of Woods and Forests from 1808. Another fountain to his design was supplied to Mr Fector, Dover, in September 1818 for 45 guineas. In CD it is described as "Fountain 3 basons with lions' heads supported by lions' legs (i.e. monopodia) and cost 40 guineas.

29. CO October 1814. Kearsney Abbey has been demolished.

30. Gunnis op.cit. gives the date as 1790. It is mentioned in Coade's Gallery ("Statues for Public Fountains"). *Portrait of Dublin*, Desmond Guinness 1967, has a photo p.81.

31. Informaton from Jeffrey Williams.

32. CD November 1813.

33. "An Expensive Present", Alison Kelly, *Burlington Magazine* September 1984. p.548-553. Information from Dr Colin Shrimpton, Archivist to the Duke of Northumberland.

34. Croggon often stamped his pieces at this period "Croggon late Coade", but only used his own name here.

35. Newcastle MSS at Nottingham University; information from Gervase Jackson-Stops.

36. Information from Martin Drury.

37. CDB October 1820 "Saml. Phillips for the King of Portugal, Royal arms surrounded with wreaths of laurel, the arms supported by 2 colossal statues of Justice and Truth, 2 triangular pedesals, dolphins on corners, 2 vestal statues for lamps £395.10.4."

38. CD May 1815 "Mr. Gibbons the Oaks Wolverhampton, a tripod for a sundial, 3 figures, pedestal for an 18 inch dial 20 guineas".

39. The date of purchase of the Syon example is not known.

40. Information from The Hon. Mrs Jane Roberts.

41. Information from John Duxfield.

42.   Essex Record Office D/Dby A 41/5. The group was supplied for 30 guineas in 1783.

43.   *Furniture of the Greeks, Romans and Etruscans*, G. M. A. Richter.

44.   Julia Abel Smith "Great Saxham Hall, Suffolk" *Country Life* 27 November 1986. p.1698-1702.

45.   1802 p.448.

CHAPTER 13

Commissions for the Crown and Government

Royal Commissions

The Coade firm was lucky in that it produced work which appealed to both King George III and to his son, successively Prince of Wales, Prince Regent and George IV; usually the designers and craftsmen who appealed to the King were disliked by the Prince, and vice versa. It happens that the first Royal work I have been able to trace was for the Prince.

In London, the Prince of Wales lived in Carlton House, the elegant mansion designed for him by Henry Holland. A long colonnade screened the courtyard from the street, and Coade stone *Trophies* broke the line of the cornice. They are described as being *Trophies of War* for the centre of the screen, and four *Naval* and *Military Trophies* for the ends.[1] Bills submitted between 1783 and 1789 include £555 for Mrs Coade.[2] As we learn that the centre *Trophy* cost £150 and the four end ones £300, she must have supplied other work not identified. The house was pulled down, but when Buckingham Palace was built, similar pieces were used there.

In 1786-7, Coade decorations were ordered for the Prince's seaside residence at Brighton. At that time the Royal Pavilion was being erected in its first, chaste form by Henry Holland. There was a large central bow on the garden side, and above it a drum with a shallow saucer dome; a colonnade of six columns curved round it. An aquatint of 1788 shows the delightful composition, with Coade *Figures*, smaller than life-size, standing above every column.

The Royal Pavilion, Brighton, in its first version, 1788 by Henry Holland, showing Coade Figures.

Mr Derek Rodgers, the then Curator of Brighton Museum, to which the print belongs, pointed out an interesting detail to me. The figures are an addition to the plate, and are engraved; and the lines of the aquatint show through them, as if they were ghosts. The design of the building must have seemed complete enough for prints of it to be produced for public sale, when the *Figures* were decided on as an afterthought, and had to be added hastily to the plate.

The Royal Pavilion, Brighton, in its first version, 1788 by Henry Holland (detail showing Coade Figures).

This pleasing decoration did not last long at Brighton. By 1802, long before Nash turned the Pavilion into what a contemporary called a "Hindoo Kremlin", the Coade *Figures* had been taken down. However, Mrs Coade exhibited a duplicate of one of the allegorical *figures, Fortitude,* from the Pavilion in her Gallery.[3] When Buckingham Palace came to be built, there was a bow with a colonnade surmounted by Coade *Figures,* as at Brighton including *Fortitude* again. This seems an odd virtue to have had such appeal to the Prince, and more suited to poor Mrs Fitzherbert than to him.

Not long after this commission for the Prince of Wales Mrs Coade had an entirely different type of order from the King. The architect Henry Emlyn was called in to make alterations at St George's Chapel, Windsor, in the course of which the original screen between nave and chancel was removed, and one in Coade stone substituted. This was a huge undertaking, since the *Screen* extends across the whole width of the nave, and is six feet or more deep. On the front are three four-centred (Tudor) arches with Gothic ornament in the spandrels. Inside the screen, which has a loft above, the roof is fan vaulted in a design exactly copying the vaulting of the aisles, except that at the back the fans spring, not from the wall, but from slim columns standing in front of it. I believe that this feature is Henry Emlyn's own invention, but it is exactly in the spirit of the late perpendicular architecture all round it. Great care was taken to match the Coade stone to the original stonework of the Chapel, and the precision of the vaulting is as true as if it had been carved in stone. Of all the tens of thousands who visit St George's, only those with their Pevsner *Berkshire* in their hands, or the smaller group who have read Miss Ida Darlington's article in the 1955 report of *The Society of the Friends of St George's* can have any idea that they are looking at a vast piece of pottery.[4] "Airy and harmonious" was Horace Walpole's description of the *Screen* (Pevsner, *Buildings of England – Berkshire*) and the words are just.

Windsor, St. George's Chapel Screen, Henry Emlyn 1787-90

St. George's Chapel, Windsor, Berks. Statue from West Front 1799, ancient photograph ex situ.

There are also three Coade *statues* on the West front of the Chapel. The niches in which they stand are part of the original structure of the building, and contained figures of St George, Edward the Confessor and the Virgin Mary. There was an engraving of this front in Pote's 1749 book on *Windsor Castle*, which showed that St George and St Edward were still in place, but that there was an empty niche at the top where the Virgin had been hacked away at the Reformation.[5] Enough may have remained of the two saints to give an idea of the figures to the Coade modellers, and certainly *Edward the Confessor* is designed in a style which is not at all Coade-like. Coade *Statues* are normally tall with very small heads, but *Edward* has the large head and stumpy stature seen in the early 16th century figures in Henry VII's Chapel, Westminster Abbey, which the modeller might perhaps (since it was not far from Lambeth) have been sent to inspect, to get the period feeling.

St George, spiking his dragon, is more ordinary, and seems to me to have been modelled by someone else. The *Virgin* was where the Coade craftsmen came to grief; no-one of course had had much experience of modelling or painting the Virgin and Child in this country since Tudor times, and the original Windsor statue was missing. It was in fact surprising that it should have been replaced at all. Lacking a suitable prototype, the Coade modeller got out the moulds for the *Vestal Virgin*, and combined her with an energetic putto waving his legs and arms, and looking as if he is about to leap into the Horseshoe Cloister. It is fortunate that her niche is at the top of the façade, and not easily seen.

There was originally a Coade *Font* in the Chapel. Mrs Coade was particularly proud of it, exhibited a duplicate of it in Coade's Gallery, and remarked that it had been shown in the Royal Academy, and that the King had asked for it to be sent to the Queen's House (later Buckingham Palace) so that he and his family could look at it at leisure. It was of the same design as that still surviving in Debden Church; and as the Debden example has the date 1786 embossed upon it, while Henry Emlyn did not begin work in the Chapel until 1787, I think that in fact the Debden *Font* was the prototype. It is described in chapter 8, The Gothic Style. The St George's *Font* survived[6] until the time of Queen Victoria and then came to an ignominious end. The Queen wished to put up a monument to the Prince Imperial, son of Napoleon III, in the side chapel where the *Font* stood, and had it smashed up for hard-core to support the monument.

The West front *Statues* were not finished until 1799, and in discussing all the St George's Chapel work together, we have gone past the date of two other Royal orders. For Carlton House the Prince of Wales ordered, in 1795, six *Vases* to be copied in Coade stone from examples in the collection of Sir William Hamilton, for £45.[7] Sir William's collection was of black and red Greek classical pieces; copied in monochrome, their uncompromising shapes are bleak. One came into the collection of Sir John Soane, and is now in the yard behind Sir John Soane's Museum, Lincoln's Inn Fields;[8] it can be seen from the North Drawing-Room window. (The Museum also has a River God *Keystone* shown to me by Mr Peter Thornton, the Curator.)

Also in the 1790s, the Queen's Lodge at Frogmore in Windsor Great Park was rebuilt by James Wyatt. For the house, Wyatt designed a *Torchère* described in the Coade's Gallery handbook as "an elegant tripod or pedestal of three lights". It is referred to in chapter 11, Tripods.

The austerity of Greek Vases was not to the Prince's usual taste; in 1807 the work ordered from Lambeth was of a very different style. Holland with his restrained classicism was dead, and the Prince called on Thomas Hopper to design him a Gothic Conservatory for Carlton House. This seems not to have been a Conservatory as a place to grow exotic flowers, but a kind of Perpendicular promenade. It had a nave and aisles, fan-vaulted with cast-iron tracery. This was an interesting use of a new material, and still more ingenious was Hopper's idea of filling the webs or spaces between the ribs, which would normally have been of stone, with glass, thus giving not only top lighting, but a roof apparently of metal lace. It is illustrated in *Pyne's Royal Residences, 1819*, (Vol II) where we can see not only the Hopper setting, but also some of the fantastic fittings which the Prince ordered from Coade and Sealy to decorate it.

First to arrive was an octagonal *Fountain*, for which the bill was sent in at Christmas 1809. It had eight dragons at the corners "throw'g water into Bason", the same number of Gothic flowers and heads, and, to crown the centre "Bunch of Leeks encircled with Coronet in centre of Bason to throw up ye Stream".[9] Finally, there were Gothic coronets all round. *Ackermann's Repository* vol VI for September 1811, plate 3 opposite page 167, shows the fountain in front of the garden entrance. It was circular in three tiers, with three leaves sprouting asymmetrically from the centre. At the bottom, four of the eight dragons can be seen, with gadrooned bases. £86 does not seem dear for all this. (Windsor Archives 25309).

In July of 1810, some *Statues* were ready, "2 statues of ancient Kings and 2 do. of Bishops and 1 statue of a Pilgrim for niches in the Conservatory".[10] They too seem reasonable at £96.12s.0d. – less than £20 each; but much dearer was a set of ten extraordinary *Candelabra*, the only survivors of all this fantastic ornament, which were sent at the same time.

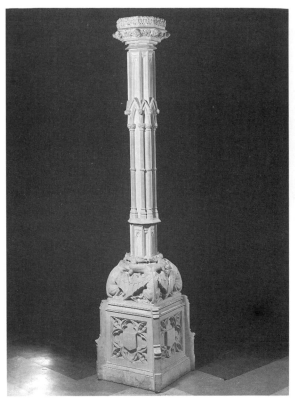

Carlton House, London, Gothic Conservatory by Thomas Hoppen. Gothic Candlestick 1810

They were seven feet high, with slender pointed arches on the tall shafts. On the bases cluster dragons with bats' wings; the huge size of these *Candelabra* made them look specially menacing, as if they had been borrowed from the *Mysteries of Udolpho*[11] or some other "horrid" Gothic novel. They supported brass lamps and stood on black marble plinths; probably it was these features which brought the cost of the *Candelabra* to £500. The tops of the candelabra in Ackermann's print are different from those shown by Pyne. They have metal arms projecting in four directions, each holding what appears to be a fat candle. In the middle is an octagonal Gothic metal feature with an openwork ogee top not unlike the brass top of a 17th century clock. All this had been removed by the time Pyne's plate had been made. (Windsor Archives 25319).

The *Candelabra*[12] went to the Coffee Room at Windsor in 1827, but were later taken out of use. Either this same set, or duplicates with the same date stamp, were sold in 1970. Another is at Athelhampton, Dorset. Another was sold at Christies in 1989, and bought for the National Museum of Wales, Cardiff.

John Nash ordered, in 1825, a fine pair of Coade *Vases* for Royal Lodge, Windsor. The design of the *Vases* was not new, since they were the *Medici* and *Borghese Vases* which had been in production since the 1770s; what made them worthy of a Royal setting was the pair of specially designed *Pedestals*. Each of them had four different panels in high relief on the sides, and a complicated cornice; and modelling each of the eight panels cost 12 guineas each. In addition there was a charge for "modelling Festoons of Laurel, Double G.R., Rams' Heads, Ribbons etc for the Cornices of the Pedestals, and making Moulds for the same". The models, and moulds for them, came to £198; the actual Coade stone Pedestals, cast from these moulds, cost less than half this – £84. The whole bill for the Vases and Pedestals came to £293.6.8. (Windsor Archives 26736.) One is now in Kew Gardens, the other at Wrest Park, Bedfordshire, discovered by Mr John Davis.

Kew Gardens, Surrey, Vase and Pedestal from Royal
Lodge 1825 ordered by John Nash

Wrest Park, Bedfordshire, Borghese Vase from Royal
Lodge, Windsor, by John Nash 1825

From 1825, Nash was busy with the metamorphosis of the Queen's House (Buckingham House) into Buckingham Palace. To help pay for it, Carlton House was demolished and its site became Carlton House Terrace, which is no doubt why the Gothic *Candelabra* were moved to Windsor in 1827. The Palace offered splendid opportunities to William Croggon, since he was paid £5,290 between 1826 and 1828 (over £6,000 in 1828). Details of the bills for Buckingham Palace will be found in the *History of the King's Works* by J. M. Crook, M. H. Port and H. M. Colvin, vol VI pp.271-301. The references are not listed separately here. It will be recalled that the Royal Pavilion, Brighton, in its first form, had a bow with curved colonnade, surmounted by a set of six *Statues of Virtues*. Forty years or so later, Nash was able to repeat the same composition for the King on a larger scale. The *Statues* were the *Virtues* all over again.[13] They were modelled by J. C. F. Rossi and cost £1,386. They were later removed, with the dome above the bow.

Nine *Statues* were designed by John Flaxman, though they were modelled by Edward Hodges Baily. Croggon had £150 each for them in 1827-1828. Originally the Palace was designed (like the original house) round three sides of a square, with the Marble Arch making the entrance at the open front. Each of the three wings had a central pediment with three *Statues, Astronomy, Geography* and *History* on the South, *Painting, Sculpture* and *Architecture* facing them, and *Commerce, Neptune* and *Navigation* in the centre.

To accommodate Queen Victoria's large family, Edward Blore built a fourth wing across the front of the Palace, and started the Coade *Statues* off on a game of musical chairs. He took down the six *Statues* from the side wings, and put *Astronomy, Geography* and *History* on the West (inner) side of his new block. *Sculpture* and *Architecture* he put on the outer side, facing the Mall. He could not think what to do with *Painting*, and she was offered for sale in 1848, but withdrawn. *Sculpture* and *Architecture* were again displaced when Sir Aston Webb built the present façade in 1913; the remaining three *Commerce, Neptune* and *Navigation* survived in their original position until 1948, when they were thought to be dangerous and taken down. What happened to the others is not clear. At Lancaster House, The Mall, two figures from Buckingham Palace are now in the garden each side of a doorway. *Sculpture* holds a mallet and has her arm round a bust of Phidias (?) which stands on a block of natural stone reaching about to her elbow. *Architecture* (now much overgrown by a vine) has half a Corinthian capital at her left side. Both are much over life size – 7-7½ feet. *Architecture* is stamped E. H. Bailey R.A.. sculpt. Croggon Lambeth 1828. Seen August 1988.

Croggon supplied a great deal of other decoration for the Palace. Flaxman designed the *Frieze* of the entablature right round the Palace, and it was not completed on his death. It has a leafy scroll design. Croggon also supplied the *Capitals* on both entrance and garden fronts. There were also Coade stone *Consoles* supporting the balconies of the first floor on the garden front. These are curiously mannerist, with grotesque, open-mouthed faces. Harking back to Carlton House, there were *Naval* and *Military Trophies* (four of each) for the East front towers and *Royal Arms* for the Guard House for which Croggon had £1,260 in 1834.

Buckingham Palace, London. John Nash 1826-29, Frieze by John Flaxmam

For the interior of the Palace he supplied three scagliola *Doorcases* for the Picture Gallery. The Scagliola work at the Palace is discussed in Chapter 19.

On the terrace outside, there are six *Vases* stamped Croggon, Lambeth, and a further six of the same design but said to be of inferior quality, stamped J. Blashfield, Stamford.[14]

These Royal commissions, spanning five decades and three reigns, complete the orders that I have been able to discover for the King and immediate Royal Family.

Government Commissions

The Royal Hospital, Greenwich (now the Royal Naval College) was embellished with Coade ornaments over a long period. Probably the first pieces to arrive were those made for the Chapel from 1779 onwards, after it had been gutted by a fire. James "Athenian" Stuart is credited with the design for the new interior and provided 32 scagliola pilasters which had Coade *Ionic Capitals*, in 1784.[15] William Newton is now, however, considered to be a major designer.

*Royal Naval Hospital
(now College) Greenwich
Altar Figures 1787 in Chapel*

The pamphlet issued by Coade and Sealy in about 1813 to publicise the recently completed *Nelson Pediment* at the Hospital,[16] (see chapter 14) mentions "Statues supporting the Communion Table, four statues of Faith, Hope, Meekness and Charity, six medallions from the life of St. Paul round the pulpit, medallions round the reading desk, panels in the front of the gallery of the chapel," and most of these survive. The altar *Statues* are small figures, now gilded,[17] supporting a semi-circular slab. They are not unlike the much larger figures between the windows at Chelmsford Cathedral, and may have suggested the idea of these 15 or so years later. The four *Statues* of the virtues are in the circular ante-chapel, and stand, above eye-level, in niches. They are about life-size, and are attributable to Benjamin West (he also designed the *Medallions* on the pulpit and the *Nelson Pediment*). Three are figures with their proper attributes, but the fourth is charming and original. It is like the Fishmongers' *Charity* in being a girl with three children, but at Greenwich she sits with the baby on her lap. A two-year-old bounces at her knee, and another stands on the bench behind her, and leans over her shoulder to attract attention.

The *Medallions* on the pulpit are not immediately recognisable as Coade stone. They are inset into the mahogany of an exquisite piece of Georgian cabinet-making, and appear at first glance to be of some yellow wood, perhaps box. This appears to have resulted from the use of some form of varnish. Inscriptions on the *Medallions* tell us in far too obtrusive lettering that they were designed by West and made by Coade. Probably the medallions on the reading desk, which has been removed, were similar. The "panels on the front of the gallery" show the Arms of the Hospital, now painted, on the long sides. The short gallery in front of the organ at the West end has a delightful *panel* of two putti playing a duet on a harp. As the whole is painted in imitation of marble, the Coade stone underneath would not have been recognised if the moulds had not been preserved in the Hospital.

Royal Naval Hospital (now College), Greenwich.
Pulpit 1788 designed Benjamin West P.R.A., with Coade Plaques.

The *Nelson Pediment* is described in detail in chapter 14, but one last Coade piece at Greenwich must be mentioned. Croggon's Order Book[18] for 1814 refers to the "Governors of Greenwich Hospital for Mr. Yenn [the surveyor of the Hospital] Arms of the Hospital with Palms and Laurel, 150 guineas". This large design fills most of the pediment of the Trafalgar Block at the East end of the site, and has the arms supported by a Triton and Hippocampus, with the foliage spraying vigorously on either side.

The Bank of England occupied Sir John Soane for many years. His caryatids have already been mentioned in chapter 7, but he also ordered rather Baconian *Statues* of the *Four Continents* which have been removed to the roof, and *Vases*, which still stand above Corinthian columns in the Lothbury Court. The Coade stone *Stoves* at the Bank,[19] mentioned by Mrs Coade in 1799, have succumbed to more efficient methods of heating. (For more detailed treatment of Soane's Bank work, see Alison Kelly "Sir John Soane and Eleanor Coade", *Apollo*, April 1989.)

Statues of the Four Continents, Bank of England, by Sir John Soane 1801

The Bank and the Naval College retain their Coade stone, but the Custom House lost it entirely. David Laing, Surveyor HM Customs, was given the opportunity of designing a new Custom House in the City early in the Regency, the design of which can be seen in the sumptuous folio he produced in 1818 titled *Buildings Public* and *Private*, but largely consisting of forty engravings of the Custom House. The text includes the excellent description of the making of artifical stone already quoted in chapter 4.

Curiously, though Laing ordered from Croggon a *Britannia*, with *Lion*, a *Neptune* who reclined, as if on a sofa, on the back of a *Seahorse*, and a very large *Royal Arms with Supporters*, for £561.12s.1d., he turned to another maker of artifical stone, George James Bubb, who went into partnership for the purpose with Rossi (who was of course perfectly familiar with working in artificial stone, having worked for many years with Mrs Coade), to make two long strips of frieze with allegorical figures, and a wreath of oak-leaves to go round a clock which was supported by huge figures of Industry and Plenty.[21] There is no reason to suppose that the Coade stone pieces were anything other than their usual cream-colour, or that anything intervened to prevent their being put up – Croggon's bill exists for transporting the workmen and their tools to Custom House Quay to do the job at the end of 1816. Why Bubb was brought in is at present a mystery, and the result was not a success. The *New Monthly Magazine* (1818, p.154) said of the decoration:

> "the process of baking which it undergoes frequently distorts and injures
> the work, it is of a brick-like ferruginous colour and the general effect is
> very unpleasing."

This suggests that what was produced was terracotta. Bubb went bankrupt not long afterwards, and the Custom House had only a few more years of life. In *Georgian London* Sir John Summerson describes the sad end of Laing's building. A pier under the great hall subsided, and the whole centre had to be rebuilt.[22] A new architect, Sir Robert Smirke, replaced Laing's design by his own, and Bubb stone and Coade stone were alike swept away.

Soane kept up his connexion with Lambeth for several more Government buildings. His design for the Royal Entrance to the House of Lords required eight *Scagliola Columns*, and a letter of March 18th, 1826 from Croggon to Soane, now in Sir John Soane's Museum, itemizes the cost of these *Columns* and their *Capitals*, which came to £236.7s.7d. Gunnis mentions that Croggon also did decorative details for Soane's Law Courts (1820-24), and for his Board of Trade building in Whitehall in 1827. The Law Courts and the House of Lords Entrance have disappeared, and the Board of Trade was reconstructed by Sir Charles Barry, so that nothing from Lambeth survives from any of these commissions.[23]

Kensington Palace, London. Heraldic Lion on Gatepier

NOTES

1. *Survey of London.* Vol XX (Trafalgar Square, chapter 8, p59-60).
2. *Buckingham Palace,* H. Clifford Smith, 1931 p.109.
3. "Fortitude, leaning on a broken column, clothed with a lion's skin, executed for his Royal Highness the PRINCE OF WALES, together with five other statues, placed on the outside of his Pavilion at Brighthelmstone in the year 1788". Brighton had not yet been given its present name.
4. *Bulletin of the Friends of St George's,* 1955, Ida Darlington. The front of the screen was replaced in natural stone in the 1920s by the then surveyor of the Fabric owing to a misunderstanding of the Coade material, which he thought unstable. He believed Coade stone was some kind of plaster. Fortunately the front of the balcony was retained.
5. Darlington ibid.
6. Darlington showed a photograph of it.
7. *Survey of London* Vol XX, chapter 8.
8. Information from Miss Dorothy Stroud.
9. The motifs are from the Prince of Wales's heraldry.
10. Plate I of Pyne's book shows the doorway to the garden, with a niche each side with a Coade figure. Plate II shows the entrance to the house, with the statues of the kings in niches each side and the pilgrim above. The text (p.89) says "The West end of the building is finished in tabernacle work, niches and appropriate figures. Behind each cluster of pillars is a candelabrum of Gothic form enriched with devices most tastefully designed and curiously modelled which support elegant lamps of six burners each."
11. By Mrs Ann Radcliffe, 1794.
12. "George IV and the Furnishings of Windsor Castle", by Geoffrey de Bellaigue, *Furniture History* 1972, p.28 and plate 13B.
13. *History of the King's Works* vol VI, by J. M. Crook and M. H. Port, 1973 p.270, 271, 282, 283, 300, 301.
14. Blashfield admired the Coade work, and in his pamphlet "*An Account of the History and Manufacture of Ancient and Modern Terracotta,* 1855, remarked that Coade pieces were normally in "as perfect condition as when first made, while it is common to observe the stonework adjoining or supporting them in a state of mouldering decay, as in the case of the pedestals supporting the terracotta Medici and Borghesi [sic] vases upon the garden terrace at Buckingham Palace. The chief of the architectural enrichments of this palace are of this terracotta, and in making the recent alterations it was found that the only works which had stood

the test of frost, sun and rain were these terracottas".

15.   Mrs Coade detailed what had been done in *Coade's Gallery*.

16.   Scottish National Library Acc.5111 Box 12.

17.   They were gilded to commemorate the Naval Chaplains who were killed in the war. Information from the Rev David Evans, at one time Chaplain to the College.

18.   CD March 1814.

19.   See Chapter on Coade stone in Interior Decoration.

20.   CD December 1816, October 1817.

21.   Alison Kelly, "Imitating Mrs. Coade", *Country Life* November 10 1977.

22.   *History of the King's Works* vol VI p.425 gives evidence that the collapse was due to negligence and deceit.

23.   See Alison Kelly. "Sir John Soane and Mrs Eleanor Coade", *Apollo,* April 1989.

CHAPTER 14

Commemorative Monuments

Visitors to Westminster Abbey and St Paul's threading their way among the monuments, may well feel that Georgian people over-indulged their commemorative feelings; but though their impact is blunted for us today, we should not forget that these monuments expressed important sentiments at the time, and, particularly in the Napoleonic war, were an outlet for patriotic feelings. At the same time, they were very profitable to sculptors and to the Coade firm.

One of a group of Coade Commemorative Monuments I have traced expresses perfectly the sense of position and hierarchy inborn in most people in Georgian times. In 1785 Lord Yarborough put up in his park at Brocklesby, Lincolnshire,[1] an urn on a triangular pedestal supported by three ill-used tortoises. It is inscribed "to the memory of George Holgate of Melton, a tenant and friend, who as a mark of gratitude and regard, bequeathed to him a small estate at Cadhay, and who deserves to be remembered in the class of farmers as a most excellent character, entirely free of affectation of anything above that respectable station in life to which he was so great a credit. He died in 1785". Lady Catherine de Bourgh could not have put it better.[2]

The design of this monument seems to have been popular, since it reappears, with slight variations in the urn, but always with the tortoises, at Mount Edgcombe in Cornwall, at Stanmer Park in Sussex and at Lucan House, Co Kildare, Eire.[3] The Stanmer Park monument commemorates the father of Lady Pelham; the Mount Edgcombe one is in memory of Timothy Brett. The Lucan House monument is to Patrick Sarsfield. All the monuments have a tapering triangular form, with bas-relief *plaques* on the sides, and *urns* of varying shapes on the top. They are particularly elegant examples of Georgian monument form. John Harris, in Pevsner's *Lincolnshire*, attributes them to James Wyatt.

Stanmer Park, Sussex
Monument to the father of Lady Pelham
by James Wyatt c.1775

A particularly delightful commemorative monument, combining Coade stone and landscape gardening, is at Great Amwell in Hertfordshire. In the 17th century, Sir Hugh Myddleton brought water to London by creating the New River; and in 1800 it was decided to commemorate him at the springs from which his river flows. Robert Mylne, architect of the New River Company, devised a charming water garden with streams flowing among several grassy islands. On the main island is an *Urn* to Myddleton, on a smaller one a *pedestal* and *Globe,* with a long poem on the water "which thousands drink who never dream whence flow the streams they bless" etc. With its yew tree and weeping willows, the gently melancholy scene is like a fragment of Gray's *Elegy* in three dimensions.

While working on the Myddleton memorial, Mylne seems to have taken the opportunity of putting a Coade *Urn* on top of his family mausoleum in the churchyard a hundred yards away.[4]

In the same year, John Penn, of Stoke Park, Stoke Poges, Buckinghamshire, put up a monument ot Sir Edward Coke, in a style which was to become a commonplace later, with a figure standing on a tall column. The monument was designed by James Wyatt, who was embellishing the house at the same time for Mr Penn (whose connexion with the great jurist he commemorated I have not so far traced, except that they both lived at Stoke Park). It was modelled by Rossi. Mrs Coade mentioned Stoke in her 1799 list, but puts it in Berkshire, on the wrong side of the Thames.

Another striking monument is Lawrence Castle, Devonshire, a castellated folly put up in memory of General Stringer Lawrence. Inside is a life size statue in Coade stone of the General dressed as a Roman Commander. It is an exact copy of the *statue* of him by Scheemakers previously commissioned by the East India Company.[5] It dates from 1789. The Castle is also known as Haldon Belevedere, and is at Doddiscombsleigh, Lower Ashton, a few miles SW of Exeter, from where it can be seen on the skyline.

George III's recovery from insanity (or porphyria) in 1787 was a matter of general rejoicing, but as far as I know only Sir John Griffin Griffin, by then ennobled as Lord Howard de Walden, put up a monument to it. This was in the park at Audley End, and was called the Temple of Concord. It is a Corinthian temple, originally roofed, but now open to the sky. The *Capitals* are Coade stone and so is the *Frieze*, which on the side facing the house has a *Panel* 8ft long, of 14 figures. In Mrs Coade's words "In the centre is a good likeness of His present Majesty, the figures are emblematical of the Commercial Advantages etc. resulting to the Kingdom from the Graces and Virtues which surround the Throne".[6] As the *Frieze* is only 20 inches deep, the figures are small, and the detail is not easy to see. The *Capitals* are finely detailed.

George III reached the 50th year of his reign in 1809, and this (rather than the 50th anniversary) was taken as the date for celebration. Of the four Coade Commemorative pieces for this occasion, I will take the Weymouth *Statue* first, since though it is dated 1809 on the pedestal, it was in fact made earlier; as Dr Johnson said, "In lapidary inscriptions, a man is not upon oath".[7]

Audley End, Essex, Temple of Concord 1790 by Robert Furze Brettingham, Capitals and Plaque in Coade Stone.

Papers in the Dorset Record Office show that the monument was originally planned as a tribute to George III's continued attendance for the sea-bathing, which he first enjoyed in 1785, to the great profit of the town. It was recognised locally that Weymouth derived the same advantages from the King that Brighton did from the Prince of Wales; and in 1802 a letter from Mr Brown solicited the King's approval for:

> "a statue to be made of Coade and Sealy's composition at Lambeth as large as life and to be placed at the entrance to the town with an inscription under, expressing it to be a token of Loyalty and a Testimony of gratitude for the honour and advantage derived by the place of his Majesty's residence."

Permission was given and in May 1803 John Sealy wrote a hasty note to Mr Brown saying that he had had an interview at the Queen's Palace, to which he and someone else had gone at the unexpected hour of 7am. With them they took a bust, probably partly modelled in terracotta clay.

> "Mr Braune [a Palace page] very politely received us and about half past 8 – the King himself made us a visit – seemed much pleased and I have reason to think approved the work as he stayed about ¾ of an Hour in

231

Conversation with me and we had all ye opportunity of attaining a likeness wch could be expected – when I reminded him that this work for Weymouth was under your Direction – he replied Yes – I know Mr. Brown . . .:

The head of the King, then is modelled from life.

In October 1804 Coade and Sealy sent in their bill. There had been various false starts, Mr Brown having to pay for abandoned designs for the King on top of a Waterworks, and on the front of a Guard House rusticated. Mr Brown must still have been dithering about where to put his statue when a most awkward situation arose; the King paid his last visit to Weymouth in 1805 and the whole purpose of the scheme vanished. The King's fortunate survival gave the people of Weymouth the chance to be grateful to him for reigning over them for fifty years, and must have saved the faces of a number of embarrassed gentlemen. At the base of the plinth there is a small plaque which states that the Mayor called a meeting, and it was agreed that "in the awful times in which we live" fireworks in celebration would be out of the question. A group of gentlemen, including of course Mr Brown, "being possessed of an excellent statute of the King" agreed to donate it to the committee, and subscriptions were invited for its erection at long last.

The *Statue* is an ornament to the Weymouth Esplanade, the King stands on a tall plinth, flanked by the *lion* and *unicorn*, life-size and couchant. He wears Garter robes, and stands in front of an interesting *table* (discussed in detail in chapter 11) bearing his crown and a shield of arms. Since the war, the whole composition has been painted with great success, producing an effect both jovial and marine. The King's hair is brown and his complexion ruddy. He has a blue coat, lighter than the Garter blue of the mantle, and the crown and shield sparkle in heraldic colours, It is just the thing for a Jubilee.

The Esplanade, Weymouth, Dorset. George III Jubilee Statue dated 1809, modelled earlier.

The Bargate, Southampton, Hampshire. George III Jubilee Figure 1809 (as Taplow Court)

Another George III was made in 1809 (as far as is known genuinely) for Southampton. Here the King is seen as a Roman general. The *Statue*[8] stands in a niche rather too small for it, which was previously inhabited by Queen Anne, on the mediaeval Bargate, once an entrance in the walls of the town, but now standing on an island site in the middle of a new shopping centre. The craggy masonry of the Bargate, the classical-style *Statue* and the cars and plate-glass all round make an uneasy combination. A duplicate of this statue is in the forecourt of Taplow Court, Buckinghamshire, unexpectedly dated 1804.[9] This was five years before the Jubilee, and there seems to have been little to celebrate at that date. Dr Ann Saunders has suggested to me that it may refer to the King's recovery from another fit of madness.

Gunnis records that a *Statue* of George III was put up in Portland Square, Bristol. The inhabitants here were dilatory, and the *Statue* was not ready in 1809; they had to put up an obelisk instead, which was replaced by the *Statue* in 1810.[10] It had a short life, since a man called "Orator" Hunt, making a speech in favour of the Princess of Wales, and against the Prince,[11] so inflamed a group of men that they pulled down the figure of the King who by that date was incapacitated, and had nothing to do with the battle between his son and daughter-in-law. It was so badly damaged that it was never put up again.

Another Jubilee *Statue* of the King survives in part in Lincolnshire. In the 18th century, Sir Francis Dashwood put up, at Dunston, a very tall masonry pier with a lantern on its top, a kind of inland lighthouse to guide people over the wolds. In 1810, the Earl of Buckinghamshire decided to replace the lantern by a heroic *Statue* of George III, in crown and robes, which survived with great dignity until 1940. The King was then found to be a danger to aircraft at a nearby airfield, and the *Statue* and many feet from the top of the pier were knocked off. Surprisingly, since this was not a moment for paying much attention to works of art, the pieces of George III were preserved and eventually came to the Museum of Lincolnshire Life. The top third of the figure was relatively undamaged and though the scale of modelling is bold, the detail of the fur of the robes and the Garter chain is precise and impressive. Lincolnshire County Council considered the feasibility of rebuilding the figure to its full height of 15 feet, which involved putting together many dozens of pieces.[12] It was finally decided to use only the bust section of the figure at Lincoln Castle, where it is known as George One-Third. The artist is known for this piece. He was Joseph Panzetta, and since he was the chief sculptor for the firm in the early 19th century, probably the other *George III Statues* are his work.

Dunston Pillar, Lincolnshire. 1809 George III Statue, detail of Garter Chain by Joseph Panzetta.

George III may have been liked by his subjects, but Nelson was adored. The National Maritime Museum at Greenwich displays an immense variety of mementoes, valuable or touchingly cheap, to satisfy the craving for something to keep his memory green. Monuments to him proliferated, and the Coade firm had a number of commissions for them.

Everyone in Great Britain is familiar with the Trafalgar Square Column, with Nelson on its top; far fewer know that this monument was not completed until 1842, while a smaller one in Montreal went up in 1809. A subscription list was started there on the day in December 1805 when the news of Trafalgar reached Canada, and a Coade *Statue* of Nelson eight feet high, and plaques for the plinth of the 50 foot column, reached Montreal in 1808.

Mrs E. A. Collard, who wrote a description[13] of the monument, quotes a pamphlet, now rare, describing a visit by one of Nelson's crew at Trafalgar to Coade's Gallery, where the

Statue was on show before being sent overseas.

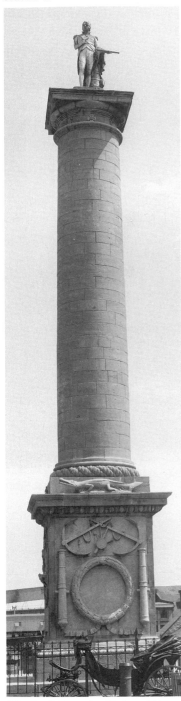

Montreal, Canada, Statue of Nelson, designed by Robert Mitchell 1809

"This is really a grand *figure* of the gallant Admiral" he said to John Sealy, who happened to be there, adding with emotion "I hope it is made of good stuff, and that it will be as lasting as the world". "I have nothing to fear on that score" replied Sealy, "for his Lordship has been in a hot fire for a week without intermission". "Ah, Master!" cried the old tar, "I find you know something of the character of Lord Nelson, for there never was a British Officer who could stand fire better than his Lordship!" No doubt a concocted incident; but it did express a real feeling.

The *Plaques* on the plinth, showing nautical instruments, have been replaced, and there has been some repair to Nelson's head, but the monument remains an impressive conception. The figure was taken down in 1981, being replaced in fibre-glass.

More spectacular, however, and probably the least known of all Nelson monuments, is the Pediment at the Royal Naval College (formerly Hospital) at Greenwich. It was fully described in Hasted's *History of Kent*, and mentioned by Gunnis. It was even photographed in the *Architectural Review* in June 1913, but in recent times it has been wholly forgotten and is not mentioned in any modern architectural book. Though it is in a part of the College which is not open to the public, it can be seen quite well from the windows of the Painted Hall. The Coade firm considered it their most important achievement, and when it was completed, published a pamphlet on it.[14]

The East Section of King William Block has a pediment on its inner side, facing the quadrangle. Wren left this pediment plain, and the corresponding pediment in Queen Mary Block is plain to this day; it was a bold and imaginative idea to fill the empty space with a memorial to Nelson. The pediment is over 40 feet long, and about 10 feet high at the apex. Benjamin West, P.R.A., designed the composition, and it was modelled by Panzetta and West, and took three years to complete. West was paid £1,000, and Coade and Sealy received £2,584.[15]

Coade and Sealy introduced their pamphlet by saying that "allegory was the only proper medium to do justice to the heroic lives" of men who had "signalized themselves in the service of their country", and explaining that West had formed "a design expressive and bold in all respects, which may not improperly be termed an Epic or Heroic Poem in Sculpture."

Royal Naval Hospital (now College), Greenwich. Nelson Pediment, 1810-12, designed by Benjamin West P.R.A.

Royal Naval Hospital (now College), Greenwich. Nelson Pediment, 1810-12, Detail by Benjamin West

236

The composition is centred on Britannia "seated on a rock washed by the Ocean" who is "receiving the dead body of *Nelson*, given up to her arms at the command of Neptune, by a Triton." Beyond Britannia is the British Lion, and then come girls symbolizing the three kingdoms of England, Scotland and Ireland, "in most expressive though disconsolate attitudes . . . reciprocally lamenting their individual and irreparable loss."

It was the firm's finest achievement in modelling, with a breadth, vigour and coherence of design, which combines well with Wren's setting. The units of the composition are enormous, and leave one astonished, as always, at the huge masses of clay which the workmen were able to handle, let alone fire. The figures are in the highest possible relief and in parts detached from the background. I am much indebted to the officers of the Greenwich depôt of the then Ministry of the Environment, who most kindly allowed me to look at the piece at close quarters during cleaning, while scaffolding was in place, and made it easy for me to do so. It was even more difficult in close-up than it was from the ground to appreciate that this great composition is in fact ceramic – the conclusive answer to Pincot's critics who said, "Why stick up earthenware?"

Royal Naval Hospital (now College), Greenwich. Nelson Pediment, 1810-12, by Benjamin West P.R.A.

There were other Coade Nelson monuments. At Great Yarmouth, in Norfolk, there is another column monument, though instead of a portrait *Statue*, it has a ring of Victory *Caryatids*,[16] each holding a bronze wreath, and supporting a cornice on which stands a fine *Britannia*. The design was by William Wilkins, an East Anglian himself, and the figures were modelled by Panzetta (the *Britannia*) and Griffiths (the *Caryatids*). It was near a former Naval Hospital, but is now in a dreary situation among factory sheds and warehouses. *Britannia* faces inland, instead of out to sea; perhaps she looks towards Burnham Thorpe, Nelson's birthplace. She cost £892, and the *Victories* £302.17s.6d., so that the Local Committee were prepared to pay highly for a noble memorial, completed in 1819.[17] The caryatids appear to have been replaced by concrete copies c. 1896, but when the responsibility for the column was taken over by Norfolk County Council in 1974, it was found that apart from the replacement of the arms and part of the helmet, the figure of Britannia was still the Coade stone one, but in very poor condition. It was therefore decided to replace all the figures by fibreglass casts. Britannia had been filled with concrete at some time, and the removal of this reduced the Coade stone surface to rubble; fortunately the head and helmet had not been so filled and so exact moulds could be taken. For stability, the figures have been partly filled with concrete in a galvanized steel armature, and the surface of the fibreglass has been etched to reproduce the original Coade stone colour. The copper wreaths and trident have been replaced. (Norfolk County Architect's Dept.)

Great Yarmouth, Norfolk. Nelson Monument 1819 by William Wilkins Jnr.

At Teigngrace, Devon,[18] there is a remarkable cenotaph to Nelson, with *Fame* rising from the globe, with Nelson's Trafalgar message on a ribbon across it. At Little Marlow, Buckinghamshire, in 1815 Lord Gardner ordered *Statues* of himself and Lord Nelson at 150 guineas each. Croggon's Day Book shows that they were sent off, but Lord Gardner died soon after, and they have been lost. Four very fine Nelson busts survive, one in a private collection and one in the National Maritime Museum, dated 1800. The modeller is not known, but Catherine Andras has been suggested. (See chapter on Statues and Busts.)

Shrewsbury, Shropshire. Lord Hill's Monument by Edward Haycock 1816

During the Napoleonic wars, the British had to nourish themselves very largely on naval victories, since until the Peninsular War the Army had little to do. This imbalance between the Services is reflected in the fact that while Nelson had at least five Coade memorials, I have only been able to find one to an Army commander. (There are two tombs to Army Officers but they are detailed in the chapter on funerary monuments). The *Statue* of Lord Hill, one of Wellington's commanders, near the Abbey Foregate in Shrewsbury, Shropshire, was put in hand not long after the end of the war in 1815.[19]

The *Gentleman's Magazine* (1817.II p.393) gave full details of the design, with an engraving, in a letter from D. Parkes. It was designed by Edward Haycock, with some slight alterations by Harrison. An enormous Greek Doric column 116 feet high, and reputedly the largest in the world, bears a *Statue* of Lord Hill, 17½ feet high. Again, it was modelled by Panzetta, and though it is so high up that it is difficult to see in detail, it fills its position with dignity. "The Town and county of Salop" who, according to the inscription, put up the monument, had to pay £315 for Lord Hill; I cannot account for the discrepancy between this, and the much greater cost for the smaller figure of *Britannia* in Great Yarmouth.

The Napoleonic War in general was commemorated by Mr Henry Collingwood Selby, of Swansfield, Northumberland, who in 1814 ordered a "fine 6ft Statue of Peace and Victory, with wings, a caduceus, olive branch, cornucopia etc." for 40 guineas.[20] He was relying on the fragile Peace of Fontaineblean, and must have had some bad moments during the escape from Elba and the Hundred Days, until the Battle of Waterloo allowed his Peace and Victory *Statue* to come into her own. It has not survived. The column is there, but with a ball on top.

Not far from Mr Selby's monument, and of a similar date, is another column put up for a surprising reason. This chapter began with a monumnen erected by a landlord to a tenant, and it ends with one put up by tenants to their landlord. During the wars, a time of galloping inflation, the Duke of Northumberland had not increased his tenants' rents, and in gratitude the tenants clubbed together to build the Percy Tenantry column, which stands in Alnwick, not far from the station. This, like the Shrewsbury column, is Greek Doric, only much smaller, and was designed by David Stephenson, who had used Coade stone in Newcastle upon Tyne; it was planned in 1816. The Shrewsbury column had four lions at its base, and so has the Percy column, but while Lord Hill's lions are carved in Grinshill stone (the Coade Letter Book shows that Croggon tried hard without success to get the order for them)[21] the Percy *Lions* are Coade stone. Croggon's Order Book for 1817 quotes four lions at £55 each "9 feet clear of tail".[22] He was thinking of the odd Percy heraldic lion, which sticks its tail straight out behind, but in fact the Coade *Lions* sitting at the base of the column have coiled their tails round in the ordinary way. In an unusual pose they turn their heads away from the column. The column is finished at the top with one of the Percy lions, but curiously this one is not in Croggon's work books, and I suppose it must be of natural stone.

Barbara Jones, in *Follies* and *Grottoes* recalls the shocking consequence of the tenants' generosity. Realizing they had money to spare, the Duke raised the rents all round. Gwyn Headley and Wim Meulenkamp, in *Follies* 1986, p.421 give a slightly different version, saying that the Duke had lowered the rents by 25% after the catastrophic fall in agricultural prices after 1814, but put them back to the original figure after the Tenantry Column was completed.

The Tenantry Column at Alnwick
By David Stephenson, 1816
Coade stone Lions.

NOTES:

1. John Harris in *Lincolnshire* (The Buildings of England ed. Nikolaus Pevsner) attributes the design to James Wyatt.
2. Jane Austen, *Pride and Prejudice*, published 1813 but written 1796-7.
3. Probably the earliest of this group, dating from 1775, is the Stanmer Park example.
4. It also is dated 1800.
5. The original still survives in the former India Office, Whitehall.
6. A copy was shown in the Coade's Gallery.
7. Documents in Dorchester County Record Office. D 188B/X3 Archives of Messrs Andrews, Son and Haxtable, Solicitors. Dr Samuel Johnson to Dr Burney, 1775, who repeated it to Boswell.
8. The statue was a gift from the 2nd Marquess of Lansdown. In offering it to the Mayor, he wrote "having been fortunate enough to meet with a figure of the King I think I cannot better dispose of it than by requesting it may be placed in the niche presenting itself in the Bargate". Information by Kay Walham. The figure is a version of a classical statue of the Emperor Hadrian belonging to the British Museum and now in the Orangery at Hampton Court.
9. As this statue was already in existence, and the moulds were therefore available, it would have been quite easy for Lord Lansdowne to "meet with" another copy.
10. Felix Farley's Bristol Journal 28 April 1810 said "the costume, the likeness, the ornaments and the whole detail do the artists Messrs. Coade and Sealy great credit. It is quite as well done, as clean and as minute in its finishings as the chissel of Flaxman or of Nollekens could have made it".
11. At the end of March 1813.
12. Lincolnshire County Council information.
13. E. A. Collard, "Nelson in Old Montreal" *Country Life* 24th July 1969, p.210-211 Robert Mitchell, a London architect who had used Coade stone on other occasions, supplied a design (£58.1s.0d.) and the 8ft Coade stone figure cost £462.12s.0d. The pedestal plaques commemorated Nelson's battles and a crocodile stood on the cornice, representing the battle of the Nile (Aboukir Bay).
14. Scottish National Library Acc 5111 Box 12 "Description of the Grand Model of Neptune giving up the body of Nelson . . ." Printed by T. Romney at the Surrey Printing Office, Westminster Bridge Road Lambeth, price 6d. Dated in pencil 1813, and this date is no doubt correct.
15. Royal Hospital records. Informaton from Rev. David Evans, at that time Chaplain to the Hospital.

16. Notes in the back of CO (no date, probably 1818), "Nelson Trophy Norfolk Column, Mr. Wilkins, Model of statue of Peace, Griffith, model of Britannia Panzetti". Colvin (op.cit. Wilkins Junior entry) says that Wilkins' original design had a trireme instead of Britannia, shown in an etching by Cotman issued to encourage subscriptions. *J. S. Cotman*, S. D. Kitson, fig 30.

17. CD June 1818 Nelson Column Committee six Statues Peace and Victory £302.17.6. CD September 1818 six Grecian Scrolls £99.1s.6d. CD September 1819 Committee of Nelson column Yarmouth, Britania [sic] £892.0s.0d. Copper olive branch for Britannia, wreaths £34.11s.6d.

18. There appears to be no documentation surviving on this piece. As the Templar family of Stover House nearby commissioned the Coade firm for two memorials in the church it seems likely that the Nelson piece also was ordered by them. Stover House (demolished) had a set of Coade Seasons.

19. CD August 1816. "John Beck Esq. Secretary to the committee for erecting a statue of Lord Hill. A colossal statue about 17ft high on a plinth for column at Shrewsbury £315". Fixing (including "carpenter making model of sword £1.5s.0d.") was £66.1.8. *The Courier* 21 August 1816, "Mrs. Coade announces that the 17 foot statue of Lord Hill is now completed and with other works will be on show at the Manufactory".

20. CD December 1814 "a fine 6ft statue of Peace and Victory with wings, a cadeus, olive branch, cornucopia etc £42". In addition there were "4 tablets for inscriptions to fix on column (16 gineas) and cutting letters for 4 inscriptions £21.3s.9d."

21. Letter Book January 1816 p.160.

22. April 1817 "Committee of the Percy column per Mr. Stephenson".

CHAPTER 15

Funerary Monuments

"Man is a noble animal" said Sir Thomas Browne, "splendid in ashes and pompous in the grave."[1] This was a point of view with which Georgian people concurred; a tomb was intended to convey to posterity a man's proper station in life. It was a great age for the monumental mason, and one problem was that there were not enough of them to go round. "Frequent hearses shall besiege their gates" was Pope's curse, and for many this was all too true.[2] Some families kept a special mourning bed, hung with black, to send round to relations in distress, and where it was available it was seldom out of use. With the high rate of continuing demand, and the dignity of the bereaved (and the deceased) insisting that monuments should be as grand as possible, it is not surprising that reputable sculptors could charge a great deal. Sums up to thousands of pounds were paid for the very elaborate compositions.[3]

Those unable to pay such fees had to be content with a plain slab, or a plaque with the minimum of carved decoration. Many must have hankered after a mourning classical figure, or Father Time with scythe and hourglass, or a putto drying his tears on the drapery hanging on an urn. These were the clichés of iconography, repeated by the dozen by such sculptors as Rysbrack, and it is a credit to Mrs Coade's business sense that she was able to supply good examples of them at a price which put them within reach of a wide public.

By the time the etchings and the catalogue were issued, there was a choice of several stock models, besides, of course, any variation the customer cared to order. Most of them can be traced in churches and churchyards up and down the country; and since etchings were only made of pieces already executed, for which the moulds were available, it is possible that the few designs not yet traced may come to light in time. Once in a church or churchyard, a monument had a better chance of survival than the decoration of a house, at risk from changes of fashion. It will therefore be worth mentioning the catalogue designs, and tracing examples of them.

No.509 is an *Elegant Tomb for a Churchyard* at 60 guineas, illustrated in the Guildhall etching book. It is a tomb chest with an urn on top, and infant angels at the corners. The design for it was shown in the Royal Academy in 1784 by Samuel Robinson, and it was presumably first ordered by the relations of Edward Keepe (d.1782) who put up this Coade monument in Woodford Churchyard, Essex. It is now badly damaged, but Katharine Esdaile thought it, in the 1930s,[4] the finest churchyard monument in the country. I am indebted to her son, Edmund Esdaile, for telling me of an almost undamaged duplicate at West Tarring, Sussex. It is to Martha Chivers, who did not die until 1807. The tomb is therefore a quarter of a century or so later than the one at Woodford – evidence of the longevity of some Coade designs.

West Tarring Churchyard, Sussex. Tomb of Martha Chivers 1807.

244

No.510 also described as an *Elegant Tomb for a Churchyard*, can also be traced from the etchings, but I have not found an example yet. It cost 50 guineas, and instead of putti has classical women standing in canted projections at the corners. There is an urn on top, and bas-reliefs of women tending altars at the sides. There is a bow-front, plain in engraving, and no doubt intended for the inscription. Unlike the Keepe-Chivers design, which had figures at the four corners, this design has a flat back, and must have been placed near or against a wall. It was, however, intended to be placed on the ground, whereas a number of designs were intended to be hung on the wall itself, inside the church.

Two, both called *"A Monument consisting of a Sarcophagus, Figures etc. to be placed against a Wall"* were to be had, 9ft high at 30 guineas, and 5ft high at 10 guineas; and an example of the smaller size can be seen in the Cloisters of Westminster Abbey, dedicated to Edward Wortley Montagu. He was the hated son of Lady Mary Wortley Montagu, and a hardly less bizarre character than his mother[5]. Knowing this, it is surprising to find him commemorated by a *Monument*[6] which can only be described as chaste. A plaque with an inscription is surmounted by a sarcophagus bearing an urn. There is a round bas-relief of a mourning woman with a classical lamp beside her, an adaptation of the Mourning Province design. The whole design is a notable example of cool neo-classical taste. *An Historical Description of Westminster Abbey, its Monuments and Curiosities, designed chiefly as guide to strangers.* (No author. Printed for A. E. Newman and Co 1830, p.186,) describing the Cloisters records:- "Near this is a small but very neat monument, made of artificial stone resembling white marble (the only one here of the kind) erected by John English Dolben Esq. The Latin inscription is to the following purport:- To the memory of EDWARD WORTLEY MONTAGUE, who was cast away on his return to England, in 1777, from the West Indies in the 27th year of his age. In memory of their friendship, which commenced at Westminster School, continued for some time at Oxford, not diminished by the greatest distance, scarcely dissolved by death, and, if it please God, to be renewed in Heaven – I E D to whom the deceased bequeathed his books (and likewise appointed joint residuary legatee) erected this monument."

Another Guildhall etching has a much more old-fashioned, rococo character. The sarcophagus is there again, but it has two putti sitting on it, holding drapery which parts like curtains to reveal a medallion, which is plain in the engraving. At the top of the curtains is a frivolous Madame de Pompadour bow of ribbon with fluttering ends. Exactly to pattern, except that the medallion has a coat of arms, this *Monument* can be seen in Desborough Church, Northamptonshire,, in memory of Mrs Pulton, d.1779. (Gunnis.) It is repeated at Montego Bay, Jamaica.

A further wall *Monument*, designed too late for the catalogue, is among the Guildhall etchings, with its size and price written in by hand. it is 9ft long, by 4ft 6ins high, and cost 30 guineas. Two putti perch on the top of a panel intended for an inscription, both of them looking inward and pointing to an oval cartouche with a decorative frame rather like a looking-glass. As a youth, John Bacon worked for a tradesman near Bow church, and either he or Mrs Coade may have been inspired by Wren's doorway at St Mary le

Bow, with its putti and oval cartouche, which Wren himself had taken from François Mansart. In the Coade version the cartouche has been turned round and it is vertical.

Desborough Church, Northamptonshire. Monument to Mrs Pulton d.1779

I have not been able to trace an exact version of this design, but a very interesting variant of it was in Babworth Church, Nottinghamshire. In 1790, Humphry Repton, the most celebrated landscape gardener of his day, was called in to lay out the estate of Mr Simpson of Babworth. In her book on *Humphry Repton* Miss Dorothy Stroud published two of Repton's witty drawings, one showing Mr and Mrs Simpson and their dog being blown along by a gale sweeping over the open wastes of their estate, and the transformation scene in which they enjoy a musical party in the mature wooded landscape he designed for them (plate 33). Poor Mrs Simpson, however, never lived to see this, as she died a year after Repton's visit. He was called in to design her *Monument*, not a usual type of commission for him. Miss Stroud quotes a letter from Anna Seward, the poetess whom her friends, with perhaps too much enthusiasm, called the Swan of Lichfield, saying that she had been asked to compose the epitaph for what she called Repton's beautiful monument (p.50, 51).

The *Monument* has disappeared, but fortunately not before Mr Edmund Esdaile saw and drew[7] it when, as a boy, he went with his mother Katharine Esdaile on her pioneering monument-hunts. He kindly described it to me, and recalled its unique feature, a central oval frame containing a stained glass panel of the Resurrection. This was flanked by putti, similar to those in the etching, and emblems of Mrs Simpson's interest in the arts, an easel and palette, and musical instruments.

Putti in another pose ornament what seems to have been a particularly popular *Monument*.[8] The putto sits on a small fan-vaulted bracket, crouching down in dejection and turning his face from the spectator. Behind him is a draped urn. He appears in three Devonshire churches, Teigngrace (William and James Templer 1803), Holbeton (the Bulteel family from 1801), and Plympton St Mary (William Seymour 1801). He is also to be seen at Buckland Church, in what used to be Berkshire but has now become Oxfordshire (E. Perfect, 1802). A later example is at St Stephen, Norwich (E. Coppin, 1812). All are listed by Gunnis.

Teignmouth Church, Devonshire
Monument to James and William Templar

247

Not in the catalogue, but based on the best-sellng *Vestel* is a Monument which itself was very popular. The figure leans over an urn, with one arm behind it, and the drooping curves of urn and figure combine in a gentle melancholy. The first example I have traced is that dedicated to David Harvey, d.1788, at Langley Marish, Slough, Buckinghamshire; and another copy, of 1791, in Old Battersea Church, London, aroused great interest in the *Gentleman's Magazine* in 1792 (II p.588). The anonymous author clearly thought it was a new design, probably not knowing of the Langley Marish *Monument*. It was dedicated to John Camden, who had died in 1780, and his daughter, wife of Jame Neild, who died in 1791. The figure was immediately recognised as a *Vestal*, which prompted another correspondent to the magazine to complain that a *Vestal* was out of place on the tomb of a married woman. Nevertheless, it appeared again, commemorating another married lady, the next year. Frances Brown was the widow of Lancelot "Capability" Brown, and it stands in Fenstanton Church, Huntingdonshire, of which Brown was Lord of the Manor. Even more unsuitably, according to the *Gentleman's Magazine* the *Vestal* commemorated Sir William Hillman at St James's, Hampstead Road, London. Having lost its church, which was demolished some years ago, the *Monument* is now in the Sculpture Court at the Victoria and Albert Museum. It dates from 1800. Yet more versions of it are at Henstead in Suffolk (G. Mitchell, 1806) and at Wootton, Isle of Wight (Mary Rockfort). She did not die until 1819, and her relations had not yet given the order for it when Croggon's work books finished in 1821, as it is not recorded. The commission must have been given more than thirty years after the Langley Marish order, and again illustrates the longevity of Coade designs.

Monument to Sir William Hillman, 1800
from St. James, Hampstead Road
now in the Victoria and Albert Museum.

An interesting mirror-image version of the design, with the *Vestal* on the left, and the urn on the right, can be seen in the niche on the outside of Paddington Parish Church. The change of pose may have been to allow the figure to look towards the centre of the façade, rather than outwards. It commemorates another man, Joseph Johnson, and was put up in 1802. He was a relation of the architect John Johnson who used a great deal of Coade stone.

Paddington Parish Church, London. Monument to Charles Fryer 1819.

248

Another stock *Monument* which had an extensive sale was a reclining girl, related to Bacon's Naiad, but with a different pose of the head and arm. In the funerary design, the girl has her elbow on an urn, and droops her head to rest it on her hand. The first I have traced is dedicated to Mrs E. Lovett, at Soulbury in Buckinghamshire, of 1786. An exact mirror image of this figure was carved in natural stone by Scheemakers at Powick in Worcestershire and dated 1787.[9] I think it probable that there is a common original for both; for instance one of the *Quattro Fontane* girls in Rome is in a similar pose, though with a more alert position of her head.

The Coade *Mourning Girl* could recline, Mrs Lovett's does, on a cornice, or could be stretched out on a sarcophagus, like the Powick figure. In the latter form are the Coade *figures* at Bassalleg, Glamorgan[10] and at Lawhitton in Cornwall. The Cornish *Mourning Girl* (to Richard Coffin, 1796) is accompanied by putti, and this *Monument* illustrates one of the pitfalls of making up designs from stock units. Mr Cyril Staal, who looked at it for me, points out that the putti are too large in scale for the girl. In Wiston Church, Sussex, the *Mourning Girl* (1796) is by herself,[11] as she is again at Melton Constable. This last *Monument* was ordered in 1814, late enough to be included in Croggon's work books.[12] It commemorated Lady Stanhope. She was only a relation by marriage of Sir Jacob Astley, (who ordered the *Monument*) and so did not rate a place in the family chapel. She reclines in the nave. The figure and plaque cost 80 guineas, and Lambeth workmen had to be sent to Melton for 11 days to put them up.

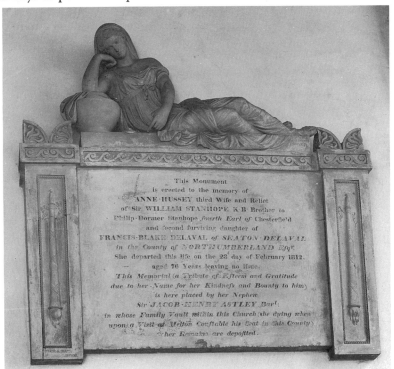

Melton Constable, Norfolk. Monument to Lady Stanhope 1812.

Customers could of course order something entirely original, and the Coade firm would rise to the challenge. Dame Anne Henniker (d.1793) has three Coade *Monuments*. Gunnis mentions one at Great Dunmow, Essex, which I was unable to find,[13] Pevsner[14] mentions another at Worlingworth, which is similar to Edward Wortley Montagu's, without figures, but it is the third, at Rochester, which is the spectacular compositon. A dark pyramid forms the background with Lady Henniker's arms on it. There is a white sarcophagus with *Truth* raising her arm on one side and *Father Time* crouching on the other. The figure of *Time* is particularly fine. This figure is marked Coade, London, 1793, but the *Gentleman's Magazine* of 1794 (I p.410) attributes the design to Thomas Banks. It is, however, among the Coade etchings; either Banks re-used a figure he had designed before, or the design alone of the monument is his, made up of stock pieces. It is the only example I have traced of Banks working with Mrs Coade.

Rochester Cathedral, Henniker Monument 1793, Father Time by Thomas Banks 1793

Twenty years later Mrs Bowes ordered a memorial to her husband General Bowes for Beverley Minster.[16] In front of a pyramid and obelisk with an urn, the *Recording Angel* inscribes Pro Patriae on a roll of honour (Croggon cannot have done well in Latin at school). Flags, cannon balls and cannons carry on the military theme. Below is a large oblong plinth with an inscription, palms and the General's coat of arms. Croggon's Day Book shows that the monument cost Mrs Bowes 150 guineas, with a further 26 for transport and cases; it is a pity that there are no figures for the cost of the Henniker Monument, which compares with it in grandeur. Another military *monument* is to Major Norman Ramsay, a hero who died at Waterloo.[17] His regimental commander ordered a special composition of guns, cannon balls and his roman-style helmet, sword and sabretache for the churchyard of St Michael, Inveresk near Edinburgh. It is in perfect order but has been painted an unfortunate pale blue-grey.

Beverley Minster, Yorkshire. Tomb of General Bowes 1812

Invenesk Churchyard, Scotland. Tomb of Major Norman Ramsay 1816

One of the most touching of the special memorials must have been that to Lady Gardner. Lord Gardner, her widower, had a taste for Coade stone, and had already ordered *Statues* of himself and Nelson. He lived at Little Marlow, a village near the town of Great

251

Marlow in Buckinghamshire. The village, like the town, is on the Thames, and Croggon, in 1815 wrote in his Order Book:

> "To be fixed on a small island at Manor House Little Marlow, a Monument as per model. Her Ladyship with an infant of 3 months old in her arms and another 14 months at her knee".

This sounds very like the Fishmongers' charming *Charity*, minus one child. By October, when the *Monument* was ready, Lord Gardner had moved to Court Garden, Great Marlow, and it was erected there. This house is also on the river, though it may not have had a suitable island. The statue was put up, since Croggon charged for the work, but Lord Gardner was dead by the end of the year, and the Buckinghamshire Record Office, where the County Archivist kindly made a search for me, can find no trace of it.

A simpler form of *Monument* was an *Urn* on a *Pedestal*. The variety of designs for each unit allowed plenty of individual choice. Of the many variations which can be traced, I will take two examples. John Sealy, Mrs Coade's cousin and partner from 1799 to 1813, is commemorated by a pedimented *Pedestal* on which is a medallion in low relief. It is the 'Morning Province' bas-relief from the Palazzo dei Conservatori in Rome. On top is an *Urn* of the type known in the catalogue as Egg-form. A serpent is twisted round it, its coils forming a St Andrew's Cross on the front. It cannot have been perfectly fired, as it is flaking badly. It is in the churchyard of Lambeth Parish Church, indicating that Sealy was Church of England. A number of other Sealys share the monument. The Coades are buried with other Dissenters in Bunhill Fields.

A very fine *Urn Monument* is in Daylesford Churchyard, Gloucestershire. Controversy raged over the conduct of Warren Hastings in India; to Major Osborne (see chapter 12) he was the saviour of the country; to R. B. Sheridan, who made a four day speech at Hastings' trial, he was a monster. After the trial, Hastings retired to Gloucestershire, building Daylesford House and rebuilding Daylesford Church, for both of which he ordered Coade stone. The church has again been rebuilt, but Hastings' *Monument* survives.[18] In the enlightened taste of the Regency, it is austere in the extreme, and so is the inscription. It says only WARREN HASTINGS 1818. In the cloud of assertion and denial, Mrs Hastings confined herself to two non-controversial facts, his name and the date of his death. The *Monument* cost her £55.8s.4d. She could not well have spent less.

Daylesford Churchyard, Gloucestershire.
Monument to Warren Hastings 1818.

Sheridan has no Coade *Monument*, but his widow has.[19] She survived him for only a short time, dying in 1817, and her sufferings are graphically described in the inscription. She was the daughter of Mr Newton Ogle, of Kirkley, Northumberland, who had reposed since 1794 in Ponteland Church under a Coade *Sarcophagus* with trophies on the top. Mrs Sheridan lies in Old Windsor Churchyard, in a plain tomb chest with reversed torches in low relief on the corners. The same design, without torches, was used for a Mr Todd,[20] buried in a romantic situation under a copper-beech tree at the top of Hampstead churchyard in 1821. That survives, but a third copy, ordered by the Dr Fryer[21] who was responsible for the *Barry Busts*, for a relation of his who was buried in Paddington Churchyard in 1819, has not survived the reconstruction there.

A similar design appears at Brighton Parish Church[22] and Speldhurst, Kent (William Nesbit), the latter in very bad condition.

For more modest customers, plain slabs, simply lettered, could be supplied. Charles Carson (1800) and James Bryan (1804) were commemorated by such pieces in Lambeth Church.[23] In Dorset, little Coade lunettes with bas-relief urns, inset in natural stone gravestones, have been found at Winterbourne Stickland (G. Willington 1782) and Dewlish (C. Hill 1792) and are noted in the Royal Commission on Historic Monuments *Dorset* volumes; and there may well be more of these in places not yet studied by the Commission's keen-eyed observers. A similar lunette was in St Mary, Lambeth, with a relief of an urn with putti.[24]

Old Shoreham Churchyard, Sussex. Monument 1828, no dedication.

There are a number of tomb chests with *urns* on the top, but without putti at the corners; one is at St Anne, Limehouse; two more are at the burial ground of Upper Richmond Road, South London and there are other examples.[25]

Probably the most famous, a *Monument* which is mentioned in every reference to Coade stone, is that to Admiral Bligh in Lambeth Churchyard.[26] It is a tomb chest with a flaming urn on top, and was originally erected by him for his wife. He later joined her, and the inscription says that he fought bravely in his country's wars, and brought the breadfruit tree from Otaheite to the West Indies. This project nearly brought the

Admiral's career to a close, since this was one of the many causes of the Mutiny on the Bounty, when he was still Captain Bligh. He provoked another mutiny in New South Wales, but survived that also and died at home.[27]

Lambeth Parish Churchyard, London. Tomb of Admiral Bligh 1814, detail

Lambeth Parish Churchyard, London. Tomb of Admiral Bligh 1814

NOTES

1. Hydrotaphia.
2. Elegy on an unfortunate lady.
3. K.A. Esdaile, *English Church Monuments*, p.87. She quotes £2000 for Rysback's Marlborough Monument, Nollekens' £4000 for the Three Captains in St Paul's, Flaxman's and Bacon's £6000 each for Lord Howe and Chatham respectively.
4. K.A. Esdaile, "Coade Stone", *Architect and Building News* January 19-26 1940, pp.94-96, 112-114.
5. Dictionary of National Biography. The details do not correspond to Dolben's epitaph, and he is likely to have been more accurate.
6. A near duplicate, dedicated to Lady Henniker, is at Worlingworth, Suffolk. See below.
7. He reproduced his drawing in the Letters section of *Country Life*, 5 October 1972, p.824.
8. Not in the catalogue.
9. K.A. Esdaile, *English Church Monuments*, plate 142.
10. Sir Charles Morgan 1806 (Gunnis op.cit.)
11. Sarah Goring 1798. In the Letter Book (p.10) on 22 June 1813 a letter from John Sealy to Charles Goring, Weston, nr Steyning, expresses surprise that he has not yet received back the copy of the inscription as he understood Mr Goring was in a hurry. As there is no other Coade monument in the church the letter seems to refer to the Sarah Goring monument. Festina lente.
12. CD August 1814 "Sir Jacob Ashley [sic] Melton Constable Dereham Norfolks. "A monument to the memory of Lady Stanhope with a figure, inscription table £84.0s.0d., 45 doz letters at 2s.6d. per dozen £5.12s.6d., cases and 11 days attendance at Melton £16.13s.8d."
13. Edmund Esdaile quoted to me Wright's *Essex* which said of the Henniker monuments that "the elevated situation of these monuments prevents the investigation of the arms" so it is likely to be there still.
14. *Buildings of England*, Suffolk.
15. A coat of arms replaces the bas-relief figure.
16. CD April 1814. It was probably being worked on before Sealy's death as it is marked Coade and Sealy.
17. CD 1816 "Major Sinclair Monument to the memory of Major Norman Ramsay, shipped for Edinburgh per Matchless comprising Artillery gun broken wheel, military trophy, helmet, sash, sword etc. 33 guineas . . ."
18. CD April 1819 "Mrs. Hastings, Hastings monument £55.8s.4d."

19. CD July 1819 "Sheridan Esq. c/o H. B. Ogle, Monument to Mrs. Sheridan £63.1s.0d." (This Sheridan must be R. B. Sheridan's son.)
20. CD September 1821. "Clowser for Geo. Todd Esq. Hampstead. To a monument for Hampstead churchyard same as Dr. Fryer's £46.5s.0d."
21. For the Barry busts see chapter on Statues, Busts, etc. CO August 1819 "Dr. Fryer 45 South St. Grosvenor Square, Monument as Sheridan's see letter 31st March." It was for Charles Langley Fryer buried March 6th 1819 (burial book).
22. Tomb of Anna Maria Crouch
23. They have a little very low relief decoration.
24. An old photograph of it, filed in the Sir John Soane's Museum copy of the Coade engravings, is inscribed "Executed for Craven Carden Esq. Templemor, N. Ireland". It was taken from a decayed churchyard tombstone in 1939.
25. Information from F.J. Collins
26. CO March 1814 "Admiral Bligh tomb to the memory of his wife 45 guineas".
27. Dictionary of National Biography.

CHAPTER 16

Fauna

The Coade Zoo is quite extensive. There was a brisk trade in *lions* and *unicorns* for the Royal Arms bought in large numbers for public buildings and for tradesmen, and customers also wanted heraldic animals for their gate-piers and so on. Realistic animals were fewer, but were occasionally made, such as the *Tiger* and its *Companion* for Tehidy Park, Cornwall, or the *elephants* and *Brahmini bulls* modelled for Sezincote. Then there is a large group of animals (lions for the most part) which can be recognised for what they are supposed to be, but whose anatomy might give pain to a zoologist.

Lions

Audley End, Essex. Lion 1786

There are more Coade lions than any other animal. The catalogue offers two couchant designs, a large one six feet long, with a benign expression, and its mouth shut, which could be had for 15 guineas, and a little lion, three feet long with windswept curls for a mane, and its mouth open in what could hardly have been a convincing roar. This could be bought in pairs, with the heads turned to left and right, and such a pair can be seen in the garden at Audley End. They went there in July 1786, together with the big lion to be described later.[1] They were cheap enough at 4 guineas each. Another of them sits on a small watchman's box at the entrance to Stratford Place, off Oxford Street. Originally there were two of these little cabins, but only one now survives, and in fact has been rebuilt recently. Coade's Gallery handbook mentions "Lions, Capitals, Pannels, Vases etc." as having been supplied for Stratford Place, which was built in 1773, by R. Edwin, and other surviving Coade details there are described in the chapter on Architectural Details.

Gosford House, Scotland. Robert Adam c.1790, Lion

More little *Lions* can be seen at Paxton House, Berwickshire. Ninian Home employed the Chippendale firm as his cabinet-makers, and in 1789 wrote to Thomas Chippendale the younger, saying:[2]

> "I propose building a Lodge . . . and may want some figures for ornaments, perhaps two Lions and some Bases. They are sometimes I believe cast in iron and sometimes cut in stone. If you can inform me what they will cost I will be obliged to you. The lions should be couchant and about three feet long".

Chippendale clearly turned at once to Mrs Coade, who supplied exactly what was required, not only *Lions* (no.56) but *Vases* (no.99) *with heads and drapery festoons* (2ft 6ins high, £1.18s.0d.) They stand on top of an open screen of columns and look extremely well.

Sir John Shelley,[3] a relation of the poet, ordered a pair of small *Lions* for Maresfield Park, Sussex from Croggon in 1819 and provided his own transport as they travelled "per Shelley's waggon"; and another pair went to Cullen House, Banffshire. Colonel Grant ordered two *couchant lions* on pedestals 3ft 4ins long. They survive, with an additional rampant lion on the top.[4]

Large couchant *Lions* are more difficult to identify from the Coade and Croggon records, being usually simply called "Lion". Sir Thomas Chapman[5] had one at St Lucy's Athboy, Co Meath, in 1816, which seems to have been lost (the house was demolished) and Lord Annesley[6] had another for Castlewillan, also in Ireland, in 1821, which is now in a private collection in England. A bill for Coade couchant *Lions* for the North portico of Stowe exists among the Stowe papers at the Huntington Library at San Marino, CA. and they can be faintly seen in Seeley's engravings of the house in 1797, but they have now gone. They survived until early this century and can be seen in an article on Stowe (anonymous) on 3 January 1914.[7] The plate on page one of the article shows the North Front. Page two shows a close-up of the *lion*, from the back. The South Front had two *Florentine lions*, pp18-26. A pair of couchant *Lions* survives, however, in situ in Regent's Park. In 1818 Mr C. A. Tulk[8] ordered a pair of Coade *Lions* to be "modelled from a sketch by Mr. Flaxman" for 40 guineas, for his elegant villa designed by John Raffield, St John's Lodge. These most unwarlike beasts now slumber on the cornices of the wings.

The recumbent *Lions* at Alnwick are referred to in the chapter on Commemorative Monuments.

More martial was the specially designed piece ordered from Croggon in 1815 by Geo Palmer[9] of St James' Street. Delivered six months after Waterloo, he had "A large group comprising the French Eagle conquered by the British Lion" for 45 guineas. This splendidly ferocious beast is now outside the Grosvenor Arms inn at Pulford in Cheshire. How it got there is a mystery. Possibly it was on Grosvenor property in London and was later moved to another Grosvenor site on the Eaton Hall Estate.

St. John's Lodge, Regents Park, London. Lion by John Flaxman 1818

The Grovesnor Arms, Pulford, Cheshire. "The British Lion Tramples on the French Eagle" 1815, from St. James's London.

Standing *Lions* were more difficult to make, owing to the problems of supporting the body before the clay had hardened in the kiln, but a number were made. The etchings show a *Lion* standing with one foot on a ball. This is sometimes called the *Florentine Lion*; but a scribbled note, on the stub of a page which has been largely cut away from the Soane Museum book of engravings, says that Coade made the *Michelangelo Lion*, with ball, and the *Northumberland Lion*. *Michelangelo Lions*[10] can be seen on the gate-piers of Preston Hall, Midlothian, a house of about 1794.

Preston Hall near Edinburgh, Scotland. Entrance Gateway by Robert Mitchell c.1791

Northumberland Lions stand with their tails stretched out in a most unnatural way. The *Northumberland Lion* on the gateway at Audley End not only has its bill but also its signature; the bill refers to a "cap of maintenance", and it is at first difficult to see what this is. It turns out to be a formalized object from which rises a plinth with the lion standing on it. It was a Cap of Dignity or Cap of Maintenance, a boat-shaped cap edged with ermine, which was set on a helmet in place of a wreath or coronet. A heraldic animal or other emblem was set inside the Cap of Dignity on top of the helm; without the helm, this is the arrangement at Audley End. The whole composition is decidedly awkward, and one wonders why Mrs Coade should have been so pleased with it that she had the word COADE incised in letters so large that no passer-by could fail to see them.

A handsome standing *Lion* has been bought for Millichope Park, Shropshire,[12] but probably the best known example of all is the huge beast, modelled by the sculptor Woodington in 1837,[13] among the last works of the Coade firm. It was on a brewery near to the factory, but lost its home when the site was cleared for the Festival of Britain in 1951. The late King George VI asked for it to be preserved, and in recent years it has been placed in a fine position on Westminster Bridge,[14] not far from the site of Coade's Gallery. The brewery originally had two more smaller lions. One was destroyed; the other now commemorates the British Lions rugby football team at Twickenham.[15]

Westminster Bridge, London. Lion from the Lion Brewery, Lambeth by William Woodington 1837

All these *Lions* are male, but Mrs Coade did make a female. In the etchings she is called *Egyptian Lioness,* and looks a muscular creature with a disagreeable expression, her lips pursed up in disapproval. The original model can be seen on the Campidoglio in Rome,[16] a pair of Egyptian animals carved from basalt, and brought to Rome in classical times. Their mouths are pursed to hold small tubes through which water feebly dribbles; Mrs Coade copied the expression, but not the reason for it. The Coade beasts on the "Cat Gate" at Culzean Castle turn out to be in fact *Egyptian Lionesses.*[17] They were presumably ordered by Robert Adam; and another distinguished customer for an *Egyptian Lion* (actually Lioness) was Thomas Hope[18] the arbiter of early 19th century decoration. His *Lion* was originally bought from Coade and Sealy (i.e. between 1799 and 1813) but Croggon had to supply him with a new one in 1820, as the first had proved defective in some way. Hope's house,

Deepdene, Dorking, has been demolished, but the *Lion* survives in a private collection in Suffolk. A pair of Coade *Egyptian Lions*[19] was for sale in a Bond Street antique shop a few years ago. Their present whereabouts is not known to me. A pair stamped 1804 was in the hands of an antique dealer in 1988, and four more were for sale in 1989.

Coade etching of an Egyptian Lioness 1770s-80s

Other animals

The *Tiger* and its *Companion* in Tehidy Park were, according to Mrs Coade in her Gallery handbook, modelled from life by John Bacon. It is not clear if the etching of a *Tiger*, sitting up like a cat, is Bacon's model, since the Cornish one has disappeared. The catalogue model cost 8 guineas, and sat about 3ft 6ins high. An example is at Acton Round, Salop.[20] To continue with Indian animals, *Elephants* and *Brahmini Bulls* were supplied for Sezincote, Gloucestershire. In his order from Sir Charles Cockerell, in August 1814, Croggon noted down "4 elephants wants copied from his. The trunks of the four made to be altered and four of the bulls already made to be sent to Sezincote with his Elephant and Basin". In all, eight *Bulls*, of the hump-backed Indian kind, and four *Elephants* were supplied. The *Elephants* have gone completely, and on a bridge the present bulls, which are made of cast iron, must be replacements. Two other *Bulls*, however, which stand by a niche containing the Indian Sun God Suraya are Coade stone originals.

English *Bulls* seem also to have been made, since Antony Dale, in his book on *James Wyatt,* says that the Ridley *Bulls*, the family's supporters, on the gate-piers at Blagdon, Northumberland, are of Coade stone.

263

Sezincote, Gloucestershire by S.P. Cockerell and T. Daniel c.1815. Indian Bulls, copied from Coade originals.

Coade etching of a heraldic White Hart 1770s-80s

Elegant couchant *Antelopes* and *Stags* appear in the Coade etchings. They wear coronets round their necks and must have been designed for some heraldic purpose. I have not seen exact copies, but various members of the deer family appear to have been made. Two White Hart Inns, at Chelmsford[21] and Reigate[22] appear in Croggon's order book for 1815, and on the splendid screen which originally was the gateway to Easton Neston and is now the approach to Towcester Racecourse.

Couchant *Hinds* can be seen on the roofs of the two lodges. The screen is dated 1822.[23]

In an age so reliant upon horses, it is surprising that there is information about only two orders for them in Coade stone, apart from the "Sea-horses" (hippocampi) which were made for the Greenwich pediment (see chapter 14). One was for a plaque in relief, which Croggon's Day Book for March 1821 shows was made for Thomas Rogers, Veterinary Surgeon, Exeter.[24] No address was given, and it has not been possible to trace it.

Mrs Coade did overcome the problem of a horse's delicate legs and achieve a free-standing figure of one, since Mr F. J. Collins found a *Lion* and a *Horse* in Coade stone at Arundel Castle. They came from the bridge at New Shoreham, Sussex.[25] The *Horse* is about the size of a small Shetland pony. Mr Collins found the date 1798 on one of them, and the other is probably contemporary.

Birds

A *Peacock* can be seen on the tomb of Lord Harcourt (see chapter 12) and there was another at Bloxholm Hall, Lincolnshire.[26] This is now a ruin, and the *Peacock* has disappeared, but it survived long enough for Mr John Harris to have seen it, and to refer to it as one of the finest of the Coade works. It was dated 1772.

Swans were bought for public houses. "Mr. Humphrey, Swan Inn, Chichester",[27] ordered one in 1819, together with two Ionic *capitals*, so that perhaps he planned a new porch, with the *Swan* on its top. Another order was for John Lyall,[28] of Chelsea, in 1817, and it is reasonable to suppose that it was for the famous Old Swan Inn there, which disappeared when the Embankment was built. Mr Collins also discovered a *Swan* inn sign at Rickmansworth. The mark on it was damaged, but . . . ADE LAMBETH could still be read upon it. It has now disappeared.

Gosford House, Scotland
Swan c.1790 by Robert Adam

The Vintners' Company is traditionally connected with the ceremony of "Swan Upping" on the Thames, so that it was natural that they should order a pair of *Swans* among their various Coade pieces. They were bought in 1802[29] and survive in excellent condition. Further *Swans* are among the heraldic pieces at Gosford, Lothian Region.

Eagles were supplied on several occasions. Sir George Osborne of Chicksands Priory, Bedfordshire, ordered one in May 1817, "from one in the British Museum", which Croggon referred to as "an antique"; and this was admired, as "Mr. Lautour, Wynne architect" had "two eagles as Sir George Osborne's", 18ins high, in 1819.[30] Mr Lautour lived at Hexton House, Herts. These survive, but the Chicksands one does not, and neither does the "eagle with wings extended", which William Chamberlayne M.P., of Weston Grove, Southampton ordered in 1817.[31]

What sounds like a similar design was the pair of *Eagles* ordered for Castlewillan in 1819. These splendid birds survive on the gatepiers.[33]

An interesting use of *Eagles* was in connexion with the Eagle Insurance Office. Croggon's Order Book of August 1814 noted "Gave Mr. Goldring Eagle Office contract price of an eagle on a ground . . . "rebuilt" under, 5 guineas the first, two guineas each afterwards"; and three, with dates, as well as two undated, were ordered in the next two or three years. Mr Geoffrey Godden has found yet another *Eagle* for the Eagle Office, with the word REBUILT round the bird; this insurance company was in the habit of putting such plaques on premises insured with them, which had been burnt down and rebuilt with the compensation money. It would have been a useful reminder to passers-by that the Eagle Company honoured its obligations.

I only know of two Coade *Hawks*,[34] on the gate-piers of Farnley Hall, Yorkshire. They survive in good condition, and have the distinction of having been drawn by J. M. W. Turner in one of the series of water-colours which he made when visiting the Fawkes family. The water-colour is still in the house.

Mythological Animals

Unicorns, since they appear so frequently in the Royal Arms, are referred to in the chapter on heraldry.

The *Phoenix* was a bird appropriate to fire insurance companies, and specimens of it were ordered for the Phoenix Insurance Company at Charing Cross (before 1799, since it is in the Gallery handbook) and for another firm in Clink Street, Borough in 1819.[35] There was a most elegant Fire Engine House at Chelmsford,[36] in the form of a classical temple with a Coade *Phoenix* on top, dating from 1803, and though the building has gone (with its no doubt useless fire-engines) the *Phoenix* survives as a garden ornament at Brewery House.

Pheonix from the Pheonix Insurance Company   *Pelican in her Pioty from Pelican Insurance Company*

266

Plaque with a Pheonix, issued by the Pheonix Insurance Company early 19th Century

Sphinxes in late Georgian times were of two varieties, the *Egyptian Sphinx* like the Gizeh specimen, a lion's body with a man's head in a Pharaonic headdress, and the *Grecian Sphinx,* a female animal with a pretty head and voluptuous bosom, and the rest vaguely leonine. This is the version in the Coade catalogue and etchings; she has a small tiara, and her long hair curls on her shoulders. At Castle Park Barracks, Dunbar, there is a large winged Coade *Sphinx* which has been there since before 1799 as Mrs Coade mentioned it in her Gallery handbook. Also mentioned there, and still surviving, are the *Sphinxes* in the garden of the house then called Pakenham, in Ireland, but renamed

267

Tullynally.[37] They are females, but wear the pharaonic linen headdress, in this case with a knot on the top. They must date from the 1780s or 1790s, as they are stamped Coade's Lithodipyra. Mr F. J. Collins discovered an interesting hybrid *Sphinx*, a female, but wearing the Pharaonic folded linen headdress, at the Gloucestershire Regiment's headquarters, dismembered, but with all its pieces intact. It dates probably from about 1800.

The largest surviving Coade *Sphinxes* must be those at Croome Court, Worcestershire. They are most impressive creatures, and we probably owe them to James Wyatt . It was A. T. Bolton, as early as 1922 in his book on Robert Adam who first noticed that these *Sphinxes* are Coade stone.[38] Adam designed *Sphinxes* wearing necklaces for Gosford. The drawing is in the SNMR.[39]

Coade etching of a Lion, a Sphinx and two large bas-relief Heads 1770s-80s

Gosford House, Scotland. Sphinx c.1790 Robert Adam

Croome Court, Worcestershire. Sphinxes 1795

There is an agreeable *Mermaid* in relief as one of the supporters of the coat of arms on the lodges at Caledon, Northern Ireland, in 1813,[40] but the really seductive *Mermaids* are those made for Lord Portsmouth at Hurstbourne Priors[41] (and mentioned in the 1799 list) but now removed to Farleigh House, Farleigh Wallop, Hampshire. They support themselves on their graceful coiled tails on top of the gate-piers, and hold bronze combs and mirrors in their hands, in wait for unwary mariners, but rather too far inland.

Farleigh Wallop, Hampshire
Gatepier with Mermaid 1780-5
from Hurstbourne Priors

269

Coade etching of Tritons as used on Watermen's Hall and Borghese Dancers as used at Heveningham Hall Orangery

NOTES

1. Essex Record Office, Audley End Records. A44/11

2. Christopher Gilbert, "Chippendale Senior and Junior at Paxton". *Connoisseur* August 1972, p.256-266.

3. CD January 1819 "2 lions couchant on plinths to Shelley's wagon, H. Wilds builder, Lewes, £15.9s.0d."

4. Co March 1816 "Col. Grant Cullen House Banff or 2 Cleveland Row, 2 couchant lions for pedestals over doorways . . ."

5. CD November 1819 "Sir Thomas Chapman, St Lucy's Athboy Ireland, couchant lion modelled to order, 30 guineas".

6. CD March 1821 "Rt Hon Lord Annesley, Castlewillan, Ireland . . . a large lion couchant 35 guineas".

7. "The Rebuilding of Sto*we House 1770-1777*" by Michael J. McCarthy, *Huntingdon Library Quarterly* May 1973, mentions payment receipted 9 February 1778 of £40 for two lions at the foot of the steps on the North portico; they are visible in photos p. 23, 24 *Country Life* 3 January 1914 and referred to in *Stowe a description of the house and gardens* printed and sold by J. Seeley 1791 p.52.

8. CD August 1818

9. CD January 1816

10. *Coade's Gallery* 1799 "Lions statues etc. Sir John Callender.

11. Essex Record Office, Audley End Records A 44/11.

12. John Cornforth, "Millichope Park", *Country Life* 17 January 1977.

13. F.J. Collins found a note, photographed by him but since lost by others, of the maker etc. inside the lion when it was moved. The date is scratched on its paw.

14. A plaque on the pedestal records the King's interest.

15. Information from F.J. Collins.

16. At the bottom of the Scalinata.

17. Information from David Learmont.

18. CD ". . . for an Egyptian lion supplied to Mr Hope in lieu of one he had from Coade and Sealy damaged, say 16 guineas for 10 guineas"

19. Messrs Arthur Davidson Ltd., 179 New Bond St., London.

20. Its owner says it came from Alton Towers.

21. CO June 1815 "Mr T. Durrant White Hart Hotel Chelmsford, a White Hart 20 guineas from Blue Boar Aldgate . . ."

22. CO August 1815 "for Mr Relf White Hart Reigate Surrey, White Hart 20 guineas.

23. Among the first to be marked Croggon.

24. Though it is in the Order Book, October 1819, Mr Rogers said he had not ordered

it when sent the bill, March 1820. Acrimonious letters are in the Letter Book, ie 27 May 1820.

25. This suspension bridge was built in 1833, so the animals were already 35 years old. The date 1798 suggests they belong to the 11th Earl's rebuilding, On demolition of the bridge, they went back to the Castle.

26. *Lincolnshire*, the Buildings of England ed. Pevsner, p.460.

27. CD September 1819

28. CD June 1817 "John Lyall Chelsea, a large swan including carting and fixing £15.0s.0d."

29. Information from the Company's Archivist.

30. CO November 1819.

31. CC "Wm. Chamberlayne M.P. Weston Grove Southampton . . . 1 eagle with wings extended 25 guineas".

32. CD November 1818 "Lord Glerawly, Castelwillan, Ireland, 2 eagles for piers with wings extended, 2 squat vases, 2 Egyptian lions £97.10s.3d."

33. Information from J.A.K. Dean

34. CD July 1818 "Walter Fawkes Esq. Farnley, Otley, Yorks. 2 Hawks for piers £29.8s.0d."

35. CO June 1819 "James Taylor builder Balham, a phoenix as at Charing Cross, 30 guineas, to be fixed at Messrs Clark and Collins, Clink St Borough on or before 31st July 1819".

36. "A chaste and beautiful model of a grecian temple," according to an early Chelmsford guide. Information from Miss Nancy Briggs.

37. Coade Gallery 1799 "Sphinxes etc. at Lord Longford's." N.W. English informs me they are now at the entrance to the garden.

38. *The Architecture of Robert and James Adam* Vol 1 p189.

39. Information from Miss Catherine Cruft.

40. Shipping note at the end of the Letter Book, "3 August 1813. For Newry 4 cases of 2 sphinx and 2 arms for Earl of Caledon". Letter (p.13) 11th August 1813 sent account for £98.16s.11d. presumably for the above.

41. *Coade's Gallery* refers to Lord Portsmouth's gateway. The house, and presumably the gateway, were by James Wyatt c.1785. Demolished.

CHAPTER 17

Heraldry

The pomp of heraldry,[1] as Gray put it, was still vividly alive at the time when the Coade firm flourished. Sir Walter Elliot,[2] who never willingly read anything by the Baronetage, was far from unique in his own time, and there must have been many like him, who took as much pleasure in the coat of arms displayed in a pediment, or the heraldic supporters rampant upon gate-piers, as in the genealogies in his sacred text.

This meant that there was a wide field for Mrs Coade, and later Croggon, to explore. They had, moreover, a particularly suitable medium for the purpose, since the details of the heraldry could be clearly shown. In books of heraldry, there were conventions for showing the "tinctures", or colours, in engravings; Gules (red) was indicated by vertical lines, Or (gold) by dots, and so on. To cut these lines and dots in natural stone would have been tedious and expensive, and in many types of stone would quickly have weathered away. But it was easy enough to incise them with some sort of a stylus in the Coade clay before it dried out. Once fired, and the clay turned into Coade stone, this detail was permanent and weatherproof. Its presence, combined with a general sharpness of outline, is usually an indication that the viewer is looking at a piece of Coade heraldry, rather than one cut in a natural stone. The heraldic devices were raised from the background, and so stood out boldly; they would have been moulded separately and stuck on with clay slip before firing. In consequence, Coade heraldry was comparatively cheap. Croggon, in 1815, sent the Committee of the New Bethlehem Hospital (now the Imperial War Museum) a bill for £130 for the splendid "King's Arms Couchant, 15 feet long", which we can still enjoy today. This was a good deal of money; but the Committee had enquired into the cost of having the same thing carved in natural stone, and found that it would be £500.[3] (*Kings Arms Couchant* meant that the *Lion* and the *Unicorn* were sitting down, in contrast to the usual Rampant form, when they prance on their hind legs. Couchant animals were essential in pediments, where the vertical space was narrow and tapering.) Another *King's Arms Couchant*, similar in design, but of smaller size, can be seen on the Judge's Lodging at Lincoln, also in a pediment (c.1810).

Coade heraldic designs fall into two main groups – *Royal Arms*, which had a number of official uses, as above, and the *heraldry* of individual customers or corporate bodies. *Royal Arms* were in great demand for businesses which had received the Royal Warrant to supply some commodity or service, including Mrs Coade herself. The Arms were on her factory. Such firms were, and still are, entitled to display the Royal Arms on their premises. These are usually painted today, but in the reigns of George III and George IV, Coade stone, in high relief, offered an attractive and suitably architectural alternative. In 1799,[4] Mrs Coade said that she had supplied *Royal Arms*, presumably to Warrant-holders, in Bond Street, Holborn, Great Queen Street, Charing Cross, Strand, Long Acre, Fleet Street, St James' Street and Piccadilly. In Croggon's work books we can find them by the dozen, and here we also learn the early 19th century cost. Mr Clift of Bedfordshire[5] (Croggon's inadequate address) had "King's Arms ready made, small size, he to pay fixing, 20 guineas" for 25 Holborn, and "do. smaller, 20 guineas including fixing, at 135 Cheapside".[5] (1814) William Harris and Co.[6] of 50 High Holborn, had "King's Arms Rampant, about 4ft 23 guineas" in the same year. In 1818 Mr John Karney,[7] of Dublin, needed something rather grander, and had "King's Arms, 7ft long, 30 guineas". As the length is specified here, I think this could have been a *Couchant Arms*. An amusing order, illustrating a difference in etiquette between Georgian times and the present, was that from a Dr Willis,[8] of Tenterden Street, Hanover Square, who in 1820 ordered a *Royal Arms Rampant* for £46.2s.4d. It would cause distress to the General Medical Council if practitioners with appointments to the Crown were to put up the Royal Arms in Harley Street today.

Taplow Court, Buckinghamshire. George III's based on a statue of Hadrian 1804, Heraldic detail of the Shield.

It would be tedious to enumerate further similar orders from George III's Royal Warrant holders. More will be found in the London section of the Gazetteer. A few can be found of those who were the Prince Regent's Warrant holders, or who wished to display his *Arms*. Marsh and Tatham and Saunders, the cabinet-makers, ordered a large one,[9] not surprisingly since, as Marsh and Tatham, they have supplied most of the furniture for Carlton House. A Mr Harvey,[10] of St Helen's Place, Bishopsgate also had a large *Regent's Arms* 8ft 4ins high in 1814; and the Royal Worcester China Factory,[11] then Chamberlain's, retained its Coade *Regent's Arms,* a fine design with supporters and urns, but oddly enough only two feathers (cost 30 guineas) until 1971, when it was deplorably removed. Another Coade *Regent's Arms*[12] with its Prince of Wales feathers, survives on the Regent Hotel, Leamington Spa, Warwickshire (1820, so it just missed the Regent's accession). R. Payne, of Union Street, Bath had the Arms of Queen Charlotte (Letter, p.328 of April 1, 1818).

These are now on 8 Argyle Street, Bath, and have a wreath of flowers round the oval shield.

William IV's Arms are on the Anchor Brewery, Southwark,[13] and at Somerset House,[14] and Queen Victoria's are in Suffolk Street, behind the Haymarket.[15] The Royal Arms were also, of course, used by the Royal Family themselves. A sprightly pair, with the Lion on one pier and the Unicorn on the other, can be seen at the entrance to Kensington Palace. Their date is not known.

Apart from Royal Warrant orders, a number of Coade *Royal Arms* were needed for our representatives abroad. There are orders for a church in Lisbon[16] (a consulate chapel?) the British Church in St Petersburg,[17] the Hague,[18] (ordered by the Secretary of State) and the island of St Vincent[19] (ordered by its Colonial Agent). Captain Thompson had a ten foot specimen for Gibraltar.[20] It survives on the Court House. All are in Croggon's work books, and it is reasonable to suppose that similar orders were given at other periods in the firm's history.

Official buildings at home also had their *Royal Arms*. Mrs Coade had good connexions with the War Office, since her 1799 list includes Royal Arms for barracks at Aberdeen, Edinburgh, Hamilton, Glasgow, Perth, Northampton and York. Of these the Perth example is in the care of the Dept. of the Environment after the demolition of the barracks, and the York barracks are derelict, but still have the Coade *Arms*. The fine example at Wyvern Barracks, Exeter has recently been restored.[21] Further examples are in the Isle of Man, on guard houses.[22]

The others have gone completely. The best preserved *Royal Arms*, however, may belong, not to the Army, but to the Navy. The entrance to Chatham Dockyard is in a Vanbrughian style, reminiscent of a toy castle, and over the gateway is a huge *Royal Arms* dated 1812. It is now painted heraldically.

Beverley Sessions House, Yorkshire, 1807 Charles Watson. Royal Arms.

Churches in Georgian times were obliged to display the Royal Arms, and surviving Coade examples (all George III) are known to be in Clerkenwell Church London (built 1788-92, so the Coade *Arms* were there from the first), Christchurch, Spitalfields, another East London church, Madingley Church near Cambridge (1802), Petworth Church, Sussex (1812)[23], Tong Church, Shropshire (1814).[24] Others may await identification.[25]

From the rather repetitious theme of royal heraldry, we may now turn to the richly varied field of the arms of individual people or organisations. Heraldry crops up in unexpected places. The *Marquess of Buckingham's Arms*, stamped Coade and Sealy 1805, and the *Swan of Buckingham* appear on Buckingham Bridge.[26] In 1818, General Manners put the *Manners Arms* over the porch of Bloxholm Church in Lincolnshire (1813).[27] At Abbot's Langley Church, Hertfordshire,[28] the church-wardens, in 1814, ordered four shields, with the *Arms of England*, the *St Alban's Abbey Arms*, the *Bishop of London's Arms*, and, to finish the collection the *Arms of Filmer*. Bart; these last because the Filmers were patrons of the living, and had given it to a member of the family in the early 19th century. The collection is not as impressive as might be thought, since constant coats of whitewash have filled in almost all the detail.

The heraldic animals which supported the shields or arms are often, to the layman, more interesting than the arms themselves. The *Arms* supplied in 1813 for the lodges of Caledon,[29] Co. Tyrone, Northern Ireland, are supported by *Lions* and *Mermaids* complete with hand-mirrors. On the Trafalgar Block (1814)[30] at the Royal Naval College, Greenwich (originally the Royal Naval Hospital) the Hospital's *Arms* are supported by a *Triton* and what is called a *Hippocampus* a horse with a mermaid's tail. A splendid swirl of Palm-fronds sweeps out on each side.

Coat of Arms with palm fronds. Beech Hurst, Poole, Dorset 1798

More *Palm-fronds*, which the firm did with great panache, can be seen with a *Shield of Arms* at Beckenham Place,[31] Kent, a mansion of 1774 whose grounds have become a golf course.

They also appear on a house for which I have no documentation other than a reference to the town in Mrs Coade's 1799 list. The house is Beech Hurst, at Poole in Dorset, dating from 1798. It is of brick, and in the pediment is a *Shield* with Tudor roses and a broad arrow in relief, and the representation of the heraldic colours by dots and striations, as mentioned at the beginning of the chapter. *Palm-fronds* fan out at the sides, and every detail is as sharp as when it was put up.

An amusing example of the way Coade heraldry could reflect the social progress of a family can be seen at Saltram, Devon. In 1816, Croggon's Day Book[32] records the sale of a *Coronet* to the Earl of Morley for 6 guineas. It can be seen today above the family's *Shield* with *Supporters* in the pediment of the entrance front. All is now painted white, but the whole of the achievement of *Arms* is considered to be Coade stone. The *Coronet* of 1816 was not an afterthought, but a replacement, since the Earl of Morley had recently been Lord Boringdon – at an earlier date his father had been plain Mr Parker – and the new *Coronet* was an outward and visible sign of his enhanced status.

Further striking family coats of *Arms* are on the gate-piers at Stowe,[33] Buckinghamshire, and at Kidbrook Park[34] (now called Michael Hall) at Forest Row, Sussex. The *Arms* of the Cinque Ports,[35] with demi-lions attached to demi-ships, can be seen at Sandwich.

Stowe, Bucks, Oxford. Gateway by Vicenzo Valdré, late 18th century, Heraldic Details.   *Kidbrook Park, Sussex (now called Michael Hall) by George Dance, Heraldry 1818*

A number of orders for their *Arms* came from the City companies. Among her customers, in 1799 Mrs Coade listed the Skinners, Watermen, Cordwainers, Grocers, Vintners, Armourers and Braziers, Wax Chandlers, Merchant Taylors, and Mercers, for whom she had supplied "Arms, Ballusters, Pannels, Capitals, Statues, etc." Most of these Companies' Halls have been replaced, either through rebuilding or the Blitz, and the Coade work has gone; but the Skinners'[36] and Watermen's Halls[37] still retain the Coade decoration on their fronts with their *Arms*. The Fishmongers still have their charming *Charity* group,[38] (Mrs Coade forgot to mention this Company) and Stationers' Hall (Robert Mylne, 1800, and just too late for the list) is ornamented with Coade *Plaques*. The Vintners' splendid specimen is now indoors; this is now coloured, but the lines and dots symbolising the "tinctures" can clearly be seen under the paint. The Leather-sellers later joined the list of Coade customers; in 1820[39] Croggon sold them their *Arms* for 50 guineas, a price which would have bought a large example, and charged £8 for fixing it. This was a high figure, suggesting to me that scaffolding had to be put up, and so I suppose it would have been on the cornice. The Hall was rebuilt in 1878, at a time when no-one was interested in Coade stone.

Skinner's Hall, City of London. Coat of Arms and Frieze of swags of skins.

Many others could be mentioned and will be found in the Gazeteer, but this chapter has perhaps suggested the range of Coade heraldry. It could be flamboyant, as in the great Hesketh *Arms with Supporters and Coronet* on the Easton Neston gateway,[40] or neat and modest, like the roundels with the Anson *Arms* on the Lichfield lodges at Shugborough. The firm could cater for all tastes.

Sheffield Park, Sussex. Heraldic Plaque 1809
James Wyatt

Debden Church, Essex. Heraldic Plaque 1793
designed by John Carter

NOTES

1. Thomas Gray. Elegy in a Country Churchyard.
2. Jane Austen. *Persuasion.*
3. CD November 1815. Information on the price of the stone carving. F.J.Collins.
4. *In Coade's Gallery.*
5. CO July 1814.
6. CO March 1814.
7. CO July 1818.
8. CD April 1820. As it cost half as much again as Mr Karney's 7 foot example, it must have been huge.
9. CO March 1820. The firm was in Mount St Grosvenor Square.
10. CO April 1814. He also had a "Tablet with crest and words Harvey Place".
11. CD November 1813.
12. CO March 1820 "Charles Smith architect Warwick for the Regent Hotel Leamington. Prince of Wales feathers couchant 8-9 feet and about 4ft 6ins high."
13. Marked Croggon 1832. Information Walter Ison.
14. In store. Information F.J. Collins.
15. No. 6 Marked T. C(r)og(gon) Lam(beth). *Survey of London* vol XXIII p. 61. This is the only known example of Thomas John Croggon's stamp, and must date from 1837 or after.
16. Co August 1815 (ordered by the British Consul).
17. CO November 1819.
18. CO January 13th 1814 "Lord Clancarty . . . a small King's Arms for the Hague". It cost 25 guineas in April 1814 (CD)
19. CD November 1819.
20. CD February 1821 "A Royal Arms about 10ft long at 80 guineas including all expenses".
21. Information J.A. Havill.
22. These had the Royal cipher and Three Legs of Man. Information Peter Kelly.
23. All these belong to periods when there is no Coade documentation.
24. Coade Letter Book. No fewer than 14 dunning letters were written to Mr James Jones, Churchwarden, from October 1814-May 1817. It must be assumed Croggon then gave up.
25. Arms marked Coade and Sealy 1812 at Hinton St George, Somerset appear to be unique, for a church piece, in being bronzed, with some gilt detail.
26. Information George Clarke.
27. *Lincolnshire.* Buildings of England ed. Pevsner. p.460

28. CD September 1814.

29. John E Ruch "Coade stone in Ireland", *Irish Georgian Society Bulletin*. October – December 1970.

30. CD March 1814. It cost £150 guineas.

31. The portico came from Wricklemarsh, Blackheath. John Cator reused it and added his arms. Blackheath is on Mrs Coade's 1799 list.

32. CD January 1816.

33. Oxford Gate.

34. CO April 1818 "Lord Colchester Kidbrooke near East Grinstead Sussex, arms with supporters for a pediment festoons of oak and ribbons".

35. CD November 1818 "Richard Collard Surveyor, Broad Stairs Kent Shield of arms of the towns of the Cinque Ports for a house Sandwich". The shield, painted, appears to be the one now on the Guildhall - rebuilt 1910-12 by E.J. May with old materials. The design of the lions corresponds to Coade examples elsewhere.

36. The Skinners' Hall has festoons of skins instead of cloth.

37. The Watermens' Hall has Tritons, and dolphins on their heads on the Ionic capitals.

38. By John Bacon RA 1790.

39. CD August 1820.

40. Croggon 1822.

41. John Martin Robinson. Remaking the Shugborough Landscape. "*Country Life* 10 March 1977. pp. 578-581. plates 1 and 3.

CHAPTER 18

Coade Stone Abroad

Coade Stone in the United States

Since Coade stone is so little known in its country of origin, where it is still plentiful, it is not surprising that the American examples, most of which have been demolished, have not attracted the attention they deserve from architectural and ceramic historians, and it is not generally appreciated that the three first architects of the Capitol, Dr Thornton, Benjamin Latrobe and Charles Bulfinch, all made use of it. It is the purpose of this chapter to discuss those examples known to me and encourage, I hope, the search for others.

When they opened their exhibition gallery at the end of Westminster Bridge in 1799, Eleanor Coade and her partner John Sealy issued the handbook[1] to the exhibition which has already been discussed in Chapter 5 and in which they listed those places for which they had had commissions during the thirty years of the firm's existence. The sentence which is of most interest to our present enquiry is as follows: "Washington, new Foederal City, Capitals and frizes, keystones, Chimneypieces etc., Philadelphia at William Bingham's Esq., and Mr John Dorsey's etc., Boston, Corinthian Capitals etc."

Let us take Washington first. Two handsome Coade *Chimneypieces* survive in Washington D.C. The Octagon[2], a fine 18th century house administered by the American Institute of Architects Foundation Inc, was built for a Colonel Tayloe by Dr. Thornton, an amateur architect who made the first designs for the Capitol, but was replaced by Latrobe.

The Octagon, Washington D.C., U.S.A. by Dr. Thornton 1799

Thornton was, however, successful in persuading Col. Tayloe to patronize the Coade firm for his house, built between 1798 and 1800.

Inside the house, two chimneypieces survive. The one in the dining room exactly follows no. 518 in the Coade catalogue:

> Pilasters, Anchor, Cable and Seaweed; Ionic Capitals composed of Dolphins etc; the Tablet as no. 262 [a Vase and Seahorses]; Frize as no 263 [a Festoon of Fishing Net]; enriched Cornice, Mantle and Jaumbs.

In 1784, the date of the catalogue, it cost 15 guineas, and would not have been likely to have cost a great deal more at the end of the century. There appears to be no information as to why Colonel Tayloe, presumably a military man, chose all this marine imagery.

The *chimneypiece* in the drawing room, as might be expected, is more elaborate, and has detail in much higher relief than in the dining room. The figures on the jambs are related to the Herculaneum Figures, copied from domestic frescoes discovered there, which had a great vogue in the late 18th century. The Octagon chimneypiece is not a catalogue number, and presumably had not been designed as early as 1784; but there is an engraving, unnumbered (i.e. later than the numbering in the catalogue) which has jamb figures exactly as those at the Octagon, but a plainer frieze. These same figures appear on a chimneypiece dated 1789 at Capesthorne, in Cheshire; (It is illustrated in Chapter 11) Another has recently come to light at Wollaton Hall, Nottingham.

The Octagon, Washington D.C., U.S.A. by Dr. Thornton 1799

The tablet design, shown among the engravings, is no. 268 *Bacchanalian Boys*, but on an oblong tablet. The absence of detail in the upper corners allowed it to be adapted easily to the half-moon shape on the Octagon chimneypiece. I have not seen this adaptation elsewhere. Colonel Tayloe had a drawing sent to him, and presumably this special variation was shown on it. It is perhaps worth emphasizing again how easy it was to build up an individual design from the wide range of Coade details for which moulds were readily available.

By some accident, the mantelshelf of the Octagon chinmeypiece was left out of the packing case, and this provoked an explosion from Colonel Tayloe.[3] He was deeply dissatisfied with Coade's handling of the order and wrote to his London agents, Messrs. Lamb and Younger to tell them so. The mantelshelf of the drawing room chimneypiece "is entirely missing & therefore unless the Piece be immediately sent so as to be put up before the room is finished Coade's bill ought not to be paid, without a deduction for this piece". He enclosed a letter to Mrs. Coade which he addressed in splendid wrath:

> "Mr. Coade – ought to Mr. Shark"

Continuing with heavy irony he wrote:

> "Astonishing as it will appear to you, t'is no less true, that the mantle of the drawing room Chimneypiece (as P the sketch you sent me) has in the packing been omitted, for t'is in neither the three packages sent, and my room without it cannot be finished, you will therefore please send it to me immediately, and inform me through Messrs. Lamb and Younger how it could possibly be omitted. The Portico pieces, as ordered – if not already sent, I wish not now to be sent, for the Building can't wait for them . . ."

The portico pieces may have been in transit at the time, since the handsome *Ionic Capitals* and *Bases* are of Coade stone, but the mantelshelf did not arrive, and has been replaced by wood ornamented with plaster. Examination of the Bretton Hall chimneypiece in 1988 showed that the mantelshelf consisted of a long slab of *natural* stone, carefully selected for colour, with Coade ornament stuck to its front and side edges.

Mr. Glenn Brown's leaflet[4] provides interesting evidence on the durability of Coade stone. Before the American Institute of Architects took over the building in 1899, it had almost degenerated into a slum, and the drawing room was four feet deep in rubbish. The chimneypieces were neither chipped nor scarred.

Mrs Coade could offer nineteen different Ionic capitals, eight of which she illustrated, but the Octagon design does not follow any of these models, nor any I have seen in the United Kingdom; however, it does conform to a characteristic Coade foible. At Watermen's Hall in London, Mrs Coade stressed the watery connexions of this ancient guild by placing dolphins, standing on their heads, between the volutes of the capitals; at All Souls Church, Langham Place, she showed the viewer that this was a Christian place of worship, not a temple, by placing the winged heads of cherubim between the Ionic volutes. It was presumably to the order of Dr Thornton, or his client Colonel Tayloe, that an anthemion was added to each of the Octagon capitals. The bases of the columns, as well as the capitals, are of Coade stone.

The Octagon, Washington D.C., U.S.A. 1799 designed by Dr. Thornton

Dr Thornton remained faithful to the idea of Coade stone, and is said by Glenn Brown[4] to have recommended Coade stone to Thomas Jefferson for the capitals of the buildings in his new University at Charlottesville. It is a pity, and perhaps rather surprising considering Jefferson's receptivity to unconventional ideas, that he rejected Thornton's advice.[5]

Of Mrs Coade's list of items sent to Washington, we have so far identified surviving capitals and chimneypieces. What of the other items she mentions – Frizes and Keystones? By Frizes (modern spelling Friezes) she meant either a narrow band used as a string-course, or something wider and more closely corresponding to the modern meaning of the word frieze. We know that string-course friezes were used at Senator Bingham's house (see below) and I think that if, improbably, any examples survive, they are more likely to be of this type.

One *keystone*, at least, survives. When the Oldest Inhabitants of Washington disposed of their collection of historic items in 1968, they gave a Coade stone keystone to the Office of the Architect of the Capitol, where it remains. It is stamped Coade London 1793, and shows a girl's head, looking to her left, with ivy twined in her hair.[6] While all the keystones in the Coade engravings look straight forward, towards the end of the century a number were made with the heads turned to one side, several of which survive in South London, and the Washington keystone belongs to this group. The nose of the Capitol example is damaged, as the *keystone* is thought to have been used as a door-stop. Following the valuable article *A Search for Coade Stone in America* by Nathaniel P. Neblett FAIA,[7] the Architect of the Capitol, George M. White, wrote to him to draw his attention to the k*eystone*, and say that it had never been used at the Capitol, nor were there any records of any such pieces having been ordered. In England, such pieces were more usually used on domestic rather than public buildings, and the Capitol *keystone* may have decorated some Washington town house. When such keystones are painted, it is impossible (unless the design is recognised) to distinguish them from natural stone or wood, and it is conceivable that some – camouflaged – may survive today.

The date of 1793 on the Capitol keystone makes it clear that this particular example could not have been ordered by the second architect of the Capitol, Benjamin Henry Latrobe, since he was still in England at this time. At about this date, however, he was using Coade stone in Sussex.

Latrobe's work in England, so far identified, consists of two complete houses, and three where he undertook alterations, as well as unspecified work for the London Police Offices.[8] Of these, the two houses, and one of the alterations, are on Mrs Coade's 1799 list. At Sheffield Park, Sussex, there is no information on what alterations he carried out; and as James Wyatt, working as we know, very regularly with Coade stone, was the main contributor to its design, it is unlikely that Latrobe's contribution will be identified. What was done at Hammerwood Park and Ashdown House, as the earliest work of the United States' first professional architect, is of much greater interest, and this is described in Chapter 10, External Architectural Details, with photographs.

With his enthusiasm for Coade stone during his English days, it is surprising that, as far as I know, no references have yet been found to his actual use of it after he arrived in America. Perhaps the intensive work now being done on him will yield new evidence. Talbot Hamlyn's fine biography[9] makes only one reference to its intended use, and that was abortive. Of the Chestnut Street Theater, Philadelphia, finished in 1807, he writes that "over the colonnade the architect had hoped to use an 'emblem' (of English Coade stone) ... but existing engravings show that this was not included." I am indebted to Jeffrey A. Cohen[10] for a letter of Latrobe of 9th July 1806, in which he said:

> The design intended for the front above the cornice consists of a single Blocking . . . in the center of which a raising Block was intended to support the Arms of the State of Pennsylvania, executed in artificial stone by Coade, & formerly the property of Messrs Wignell and Reinagle. This work in artificial stone must still be at the Theater. It is a very handsome and appropriate decoration and if put up will add much beauty to the front.

As this *heraldic piece* was not only made specially, but was actually on the premises, it seems extraordinary that it was not used; presumably some other State body established a prior claim to it.

Most of Latrobe's American career falls into the undocumented period of the Coade firm's work. It would be pleasant to discover that some of Latrobe's elegant American villas were decorated, like his English ones, with Coade stone, but evidence on this would have come from American sources.[11]

If we look back at the 1799 list, we see that Mrs Coade referred to "Philadelphia, at William Bingham's Esq. and Mr. John Dorsey's etc." This, I think, is the moment to refer to one of the minutiae of English 18th and 19th century forms of address, which might escape an American reader. Someone of the upper classes, a gentleman without a title, was referred to as an Esquire. Members of Parliament were considered to be Esquires, and Bingham, being a Senator, the American equivalent, would be thought of by the Coade firm as being an Esquire too. Dorsey, on the other hand, was considered to be lower down the social scale, and so entitled only to be called Mister. And, in fact, it turns out that he was in business. On December 6th 1793,[12] a John Dorsey advertised in the *Pennsylvania Packet* that he could supply:

> "ornamental stone for the enrichment of exterior architecture . . . Fascia in Guiloche; Rustic, Bas-relief and Masked Keys, for the centre of flat or circular arches; medallions of the Seasons; Tablets; wall capping, etc. etc."

There can be little doubt that this John Dorsey[13] is the one mentioned by Eleanor Coade, and no doubt at all that the items described can be found in the Coade catalogue.

"Fascia in Guiloche" is a guilloche string-course, either plain or with a little flower in each loop. Hundreds of yards of it survive in England. Keys are keystones, which could be rustic, i.e. rusticated, bas-relief non-figurative pattern, such as an anthemion, or with a face, like the Capitol example. If designed for square-headed windows or doors (flat arches) they were flat at the bottom – the Capitol keystone was made for a flat arch. If for round-headed openings, the bottoms were curved.

"Medallions of the Seasons" are a set of four circular panels, 20 inches in diameter, showing putti with various seasonal attributes, flowers, corn etc. Several sets survive in England, and are illustrated in the chapter on external architectural details. "Tablets" are the central features of a chimneypiece, as we have seen at the Octagon, oblong, oval or occasionally semicircular. Jefferson used a Wedgwood tablet on a chimneypiece at Monticello. "Wall-capping" seems almost too humble an item to have been worth sending all the way across the Atlantic, when a workman of limited skill would have been able to carve it in situ. Perhaps it went in place of ballast. What Mr Dorsey's "etc., etc." could have been we can only guess, faced with the Coade catalogue's more than 770 items.

In his biography of Latrobe, Talbot Hamlyn quotes a letter from Latrobe to Isaac Hazlehurst, his father-in-law, on 21 July 1806, showing that John Dorsey was acting unprofessionally as an architect, whereas he was only a builder. "There is now building in this city two capital houses by the Fishers, who call themselves my friends. Do they employ me? John Dorsey has now no less than 15 plans now in the progress of execution, because he charges nothing for them. The public affront put upon me as a professional man, in the erection of the Academy of Art from the design of John Dorsey – by a vote of all the men who pretend to patronize the arts of this city – would have driven any artist from it – but one held by the strongest family ties and affections. . ."

John Dorsey's advertisement was put in the newspaper several years after William Bingham's house was completed, and we may perhaps imagine that Dorsey's imports could have been ordered because of the fame of this house, and the wish of other people to emulate it.

Bingham's town house was on Third Street, Philadelphia, and was completed in the later 1780s. He and his wife had toured Europe, and the house is said to be a replica of Manchester House, Manchester Square, London, which they had seen on their travels. Manchester House still survives, in Victorian dress, as the nucleus of Hertford House, home of the Wallace Collection. In its proportions, shape of windows etc, it is related to the design of the Bingham house;[14] however, pre-Victorian illustrations of Manchester House show that it never had any Coade stone decoration on it. I believe that the Binghams got their ideas on such decoration from Home House, a celebrated Adam house only a few hundred yards away. It has the Coade stone *plaques* and *guilloche* string-course used by Bingham. It does not have the doorway chosen by him; for this, he and his wife would have had to take a longer walk of a mile or so to Bedford Square. (See Chapter 10).

Curiously, the interior fittings of the Binghams' house have been described in detail, with their furniture from Seddon and their carpets from Moore mentioned with a slightly uneasy admiration as being too lavish for honest homespun Americans,[15] but the exterior of their mansion does not seem to have been examined with the same attention.

Fortunately, the building interested Charles Bulfinch,[16] the early American architect of eminence, and third architect of the Capitol. He made a very detailed drawing of it in 1789, when it had recently been completed. Though the drawing has been reproduced in recent years, always described as Bingham's house, the fact that the decoration appears to be Coade stone has not, so far as I know, been noticed. This resemblance, coupled with the fact that Mrs Coade listed Bingham as one of her customers, leaves me in no doubt that the Bingham house, for its short career, was decorated with architectural ornaments sent from Lambeth.

Charles Bulfinch's drawing of Senator Bingham's house in Philadelphia showing Coade decoration 1789

Bulfinch showed a front door exactly as the Bedford Square model, with rusticated blocks and voussoirs and a mask keystone with a bearded head of a type used in a majority of the Square doorways. The only differences are that Bulfinch shows some fancy decoration at the side of the door, where in the London houses there are plain strip windows, and above the fanlight, where there is a plain surface in London. Perhaps this was ironwork at the Bingham house. Bulfinch also shows the lines of the impost blocks continuing straight

288

across the top of the door, whereas the Coade fascia, in London, arches over the top of the fanlight. Bulfinch indicates, by little vertical lines, that there is some decoration here, and I suggest that this may represent one or other of the designs used in London, no. 464 "Flute", or no. 433 "Flute and wheatear" with a little ear of corn standing in each flute.

Each side of the front door, running under the windows, there is a string-course. Bulfinch has indicated, by a swift scalloped line of his pen, that there was a swag or festoon pattern here. Though there is no illustration exactly like this, any number of moulds for swags were available and could be strung together on plain strips of Coade stone of the required depth.

Above again, linking the bases of the windows in the middle storey, there is another string-course of a different pattern. Bulfinch's drawing, clear on the left side and getting progressively more scribbly as he approaches the right, shows the Vitruvian Scroll or Running Dog, a wave pattern. Again, this is not among the Coade etchings, but it does exist in Coade stone, at the house of the preacher John Wesley in City Road, London.[17]

In the middle of this storey, and probably lighting a handsome entertaining room, Bulfinch's drawing shows a Venetian window. The details again could have been Coade stone; Eleanor Coade made small capitals, and John Johnson used them in this way for windows at Chelmsford Shire Hall. A variety of friezes could be chosen for the short lengths of entablature above the straight topped sections at the sides of the Venetian window. There is also some form of decoration bordering the round head of the centre of the window. If this had the same radius as the fanlight of the doorway below, Mr Bingham could have bought the Coade flute fascia ready-made with the right curve, as seen on the London doorways.

Under the top storey windows there was yet another fascia design. Bulfinch's little scribbled circles indicate that this was a guilloche pattern, as at 20 Portman Square, London. In the middle of this storey there is a fine lunette window which also appears to have some decoration round it. As its radius is larger than that of any Coade-decorated window of this style that I have seen, I suppose that its decoration, if it came from the Coade factory, would have been a special order.

Between the top and middle storeys of the house, there are four oblong plaques, with ornamented borders. What Bulfinch drew inside them may appear meaningless doodles; but to those familiar with the Coade reclining girl bas-reliefs, his shorthand can be read immediately. The original figures for these plaques were probably designed by the sculptor John Bacon the Elder, and could be modified to suit any circumstances by varying the objects held in the girls' hands. The plaques were about 4 feet by 2 feet, but could be enlarged by ornamental frames, and it is clear from Bulfinch's drawing that these were what was used on the Bingham house. We can be pretty certain that, as was usual in such cases, there were two left-facing and two right-facing ladies; what they symbolized must, at this late date, be left to the imagination.

Senator Bingham had a reputation for sparing no expense, but in spite of the decorative elevation of his house he did not have to pay a great deal for his ornament. The doorway surround, with its keystone, would not have cost more than about £6 - £7. The string-courses, if we allow the frontage of the house to be something like 50 feet, might have cost him £10 each, and the plaques are listed in the 1784 catalogue as 7 guineas each. In all, he might have paid £90 or so, while a sofa or gilt mirror from Seddon could have cost him as much.[18]

Since Bulfinch took the trouble to draw the Bingham house with such care, it has seemed worthwhile to investigate Bulfinch's domestic work, to see if he used any similar decoration of his own houses. There are difficulties; almost all buildings concerned have been pulled down, and though some survived into the age of photography, we have to rely on dim and unfocused images. However, on studying the illustrations published in the *Architecture of Charles Bulfinch*, by Harold Kirker,[19] it seems that Bulfinch used Coade type decorations on the following houses. Whether they were actual Coade stone decorations it is almost impossible to determine today.

Joseph Coolidge (Senior) House, Boston[20]

Based on the Royal Society of Arts building by Robert Adam in London. Built 1791-2, demolished 1843. Had a double swag-and-patera plaque of a type used at Belmont, Faversham, Kent. The plaque at the Coolidge house was above a Venetian window with Corinthian capitals. In her 1799 list, Mrs Coade mentioned that she had sent Corinthian capitals to Boston, though these might have been for the Bank (see below).

Charles Bulfinch House, Boston[21]

Built 1793, demolished 1961. Had single swag-and-patera plaques of the standard Coade type, i.e. as at 20 Portman Square, London. There were also Ionic capitals with necking decoration of a type often made by Mrs Coade. The English architect John Johnson was particularly fond of them and, as we have seen, Latrobe used another version of this type of capital at Ashdown House. One of the plaques has been preserved by the Society for the Preservation of New England Antiquities, and is said to be of wood, so that in this case we can be certain that the plaques were not Coade stone, but lookalikes.

Tontine Crescent, Boston[22]

Built 1793, demolished 1858. In his text (p.90) Professor Kirker refers to panels with swags on them in this Crescent. The photograph in the book does not show any, but clearly other photographs or prints must exist to provide the basis for Professor Kirker's statement, and would allow comparison with the Coade designs.

Joseph Coolidge House, Boston[23]

Built 1795, demolished 1846. The house had the usual swag-and-patera plaques on Coade type. There were also separate paterae and urns on the top balustrades. The Coade catalogue could supply balusters, and any number of different patera and vase designs.

290

Harrison Gray Otis House, Boston[24]

Built 1786, surviving, altered. Professor Kirker's plates of this and the Bingham house show that they were close relations. The main differences were that swag-and-patera plaques were substituted for the figure plaques at Philadelphia, the string-courses appeared to be plain, and the doorway was different. The house was restored in 1916, and has no plaques on it now, but the design calls for them, as the space between the top and middle storey is disproportionately deep.

Ezekiel Hersey Derby House, Salem

Built c.1800, altered 1908. A photograph of the original front shows a long panel with four swags and paterae in the centre of the front, flanked by horizontal oval plaques, each decorated with a vertical oval motif with swags at its sides. Except that it is shown on an oblong plaque, a design among the Coade etchings[25] appears to be very similar to the oval plaques at this house, and we have already seen at the Octagon how easy it was to supply a relief motif on a non-standard ground.

Thomas Perkins House, Boston[26]

Built 1804-5, demolished 1853. This house had a double swag-and-patera plaque, as at the Coolidge Senior House, above a semi-circular window.

Blake Tuckerman Houses, Boston[27]

Built 1814-5, demolished 1902. These had swag-and patera plaques between the top and middle storeys. Professor Kirker's plate 138 shows the houses before their destruction, the plaques being particularly clearly visible. The houses were said to have been built of granite, the first of this medium in Boston, and the photograph shows that the plaques had relief carving of an elaboration which would have been almost impossible to carry out in this intractable material. As the age of concrete and its derivatives had not yet arrived, the plaques must have been carried out in wood (which would have had to be painted), a different stone, or Coade stone.

All these domestic commissions therefore appear to have had plaques etc. of normal Coade design or, in the case of the Salem house, a design slightly modified. It may be that they were all, like the surviving example, made of carved wood, which would have necessitated regular painting, or of natural stone, if Bulfinch had been able to find something suitable.[28] Or they could have been imported from the Coade factory. An interesting, and to me significant fact is that Bulfinch repeated the same design over and over, whereas if he had used something hand carved on the spot he could have made variations as inexpensively as repeats.

Whatever he did for these domestic commissions, we know that Bulfinch did in fact use Coade stone on one public building. In 1793 he had a commission to design the United States Bank in Boston, and Asher Benjamin tells us[29] that the "Balustrades and cornice are of Bath stone; pilasters and arches of marble; capitals and other ornaments, including the Eagle, are of artificial stone". The accompanying engraving by Daniel Raynerd shows that the building had Corinthian pilasters, and a very large eagle holding the United States shield in one claw and an olive branch in the other. Three decorative plaques are just below it; the outer two have paterae with swags each side of them and the larger central plaque has a relief of an anchor and other emblems of commerce. Mrs Coade had a large menagerie of heraldic and naturalistic animals, and at least four eagle commissions are known. Benjamin refers to artificial stone without specifying that it was made by Mrs Coade, but it must have been her product since nobody else was making anything of the sort at this time.

Engraving of the United States Bank, Boston, U.S.A. by Charles Bulfinch 1798

Bulfinch then takes his place, because of this commission, if not for any of the houses discussed, in the long list of architects from Adam to Yenn (if we list them alphabetically) who used Coade stone. His careful drawing of the Bingham house shows his interest in a medium which could not at that time be seen anywhere else in America.

There is another use of Coade stone in the United States to which I have found details. The Owens Thomas House, now a museum, at Savannah, Georgia is described in an article by John Cornforth on Savannah houses[30] as having "what appear to be Coade stone capitals", to the columns of its most unusual serpentine-fronted Ionic portico and his supposition is correct for the columns on both front and back of the house.

The house was designed and built for his relation by marriage, R. Richardson, by William Jay (like Latrobe an Englishman by birth) who emigrated to the United States in 1817. Richardson was President of the Bank of the United States in Savannah, and he may have known of the Coade work at the Boston branch of the bank. Jay designed several more houses in the Savannah area before returning to England in 1824.[31]

Given the scanty nature of the Coade firm's records, and the fact that, as far as I know, there has only been one limited attempt to trace Mrs Coade's work in America,[32] there may well be other examples either surviving or described. I hope I may have stimulated a search for them, and that Dorsey's set of the Seasons, for instance, may come to light in a Pennsylvania house. A *Clio* and a *Urania* (dressed as Flora, with flowers in her hair and hand), were identified at the Essex Institute, Salem, Mass. in 1987, having been there since at least 1820.

In the Metropolitan Museum, New York, there is a *vestal* adapted to represent *Faith* by giving her a chalice to hold, now painted terracotta colour. It is a fairly recent acquisition and its original site is not known.[34]

A pair of *Sphinxes* marked Coade's Lithodipyra 1787 were sold from Ryan Mansion, 858 5th Avenue, New York at the American Art Association's Anderson Galleries, 30 E. 57th Street, New York on November 30th 1933. They had been bought from a Paris gallery in 1914. Their present whereabouts is unknown.[35]

Vase with heraldry on its front. Note the representation of the heraldic "tinctures".

Coade Stone Elsewhere Abroad

By the 1780s the Coade factory was known abroad, and the Leipzig magazine *Journal des Luxus und der Moden*, II, 1787 (p.171-3) included an article 'Ueber Herrn Coade's Lithodipira [sic, it should have Lithodipyra] oder Kunst Backerstein Fabrik zu Lambeth in England' (Messrs Coade's Lithodipira or Artistic Baked Stone factory in Lambeth in England). The Intelligenz Blatt section of the magazine, for August, monthly, through to December 1788, carried the whole of the Coade price list.[36]

I have not been able to find that this public relations effort produced any orders. Cardinal Poniatowski bought Gothic windows and capitals, according to the 1799 list, and I have been informed that there is Coade statuary at the Lazienki Palace in Warsaw, but I think that such commissions came via the close Polish-Russian connections. Also according to the 1799 list, 'statues, busts, Chimneypieces, Vases etc.' were sent to 'Petersburgh Zarsko Zelo'. Catherine the Great, a devoted Anglophile, employed the Scottish architect Charles Cameron to design her a suite of rooms in the Palace of Tsarskoe Selo (now called Pushkin) and the Cameron gallery in the grounds. It has not so far been possible to find out if any Coade works survives. The Palace was burnt in the war, but Coade stone was fired in a kiln at a much higher temperature than anything likely in a house fire, and should not have come to any great harm. The Cameron Gallery contained sculpture, and this might have been the site of Coade statues and busts.

As already mentioned, the Coade firm had excellent contacts with the government and supplied Royal Arms for public buildings at home; it also made them for official buildings abroad. During the short period of eight years of the Croggon records in the PRO, orders are recorded for Royal Arms for Colombo (May 1813), Trinidad (September 1813), The Hague (April 1814), St Petersburgh (August 1815), St Vincent (November 1819), Gibraltar (April 1820), and Lisbon (July 1820).[37] There were doubtless other such commissions for periods for which no records survive.

Funerary Monuments were in demand for places where suitable stone or competent sculptors were not available, and several are recorded for the West Indies. The 1799 list refers to four monuments to Finlater, Lawrence, Minto and Birch. Mrs Lesley Lewis traced the tombs of Elizabeth Minto at St Peter's Church, Vere and Bernard Birch at St James's Church, Montego Bay, both in Jamaica.[38] The Finlater and Lawrence monuments have not been found. At Montserrat, the 1799 list refers to Brownbill and Skerret to which Gunnis adds that of Emma Saunders, 1797. General O'Hara is commemorated by a monument in the Cathedral, Gibraltar; he built the Court House on which the Coade Royal Arms remain.

The purpose of an order for sixteen Ionic capitals for the Cape of Good Hope is not clear (March 1820). The bill was for £104.17s.4d. which meant that they cost £6, or less, each, which would not buy a very large size. No suitable building for them has been found.

'Statue, Bust, Chimnepieces etc.' were sent to Amsterdam, according to the 1799 list. This could perhaps have been for the town house of the wealthy British Hope family. On the outskirts of Haarlam a house was built in 1786-9 by Henry Hope, which has five relief plaques representing the arts and commerce, seen by Mr J. H. Cordingley and thought to be Coade stone. The Hope family had to leave Holland to escape Napoleon, and the son, Thomas Hope, arbiter of Regency taste, used Coade stone at his houses.

The removal of the Elgin marbles from Greece was seen as an outrage by the Philhellene Earl of Guildford who, as well as orders for more conventional Coade figures, commissioned, "to be shipped to Athens, a caryatis [sic] abt. 7ft. high, copied from one in the collection of the Elgin Marbles and packing £67.1s.4d" (January 1818).[39]

Mourning for the death of Nelson caused the Montreal businessmen to start a collection for a memorial on the day they received news of Trafalgar. A column, with a statue of Nelson on top designed by Robert Mitchell, and with symbolic plaques on the base, was put up in 1809, thirty years before that in Trafalgar Square, and survived until the 1970s.[40] (It is now in store and has been replaced by fibreglass.) Also in Montreal, for the Bank of Canada,[41] an order of October 1818 was for "four tablets with emblems comprising commerce, agriculture, navigation and arts and manufactures". These were the Baconian type of reclining girls, by now rather old-fashioned, and were originally set on a late-eighteenth century type of house, between the storeys. They are now indoors in the hall of modern premises of the Bank.

The architecturally minded visitor to the Zoo in Rio de Janeiro may be surprised to enter by what appears to be a duplicate of the Brentford gateway to Syon House, by Robert Adam, and this in fact is what it is. The Regent of Portugal, who had escaped Napoleon by fleeing to the Portuguese colony of Brazil, had asked his old friend the Duke of Northumberland to have a replica of the *gateway* made for him and shipped to Rio for the Quinta da Boa Vista Palace. The Brentford Gate had been decorated with bas-relief ornament of some ceramic kind which failed in the first frosts, and had to be replaced by Coade work. The Duke ordered replica decoration, including the Portuguese Royal Arms, to be made at Lambeth, together with natural stone from the Duke's own quarries and a mason to put it all up in Brazil. In the end he found himself paying all the costs including transport across the Antlantic, instead of merely acting as agent. [42]

Rio de Janeiro Zoo, Brazil, copy of Brentford Gate, Syon House, by Robert Adam 1773, made 1812 for Quinta da Boa Vista.

The Regent, having presumably come into funds, a decade later ordered large figures of "St. George with shield and St. John with eagle", in October 1820, together with statues of Truth and Justice, and the Portuguese Royal Arms again, for the Palace, directly from the Coade firm. He also had statues of *Pomona* and *Flora* for lamps, standing on curious pedestals shown among the Coade etchings, which have dolphins standing on their heads at the corners.[43]

Syon House, Brentford Gate, Middlesex by Robert Adam 1773

In February 1816, Croggon sent a bizarre collection of pieces to Haiti, where the black Emperor Henri Christophe had rid himself of French domination during the Napoloeonic Wars. Croggon sent them as a speculation which he was prepared to sell off at about half price[44] and included a naked *Venus*, a couchant *lion* and a *bust* of Admiral Lord Nelson. What happened to the remainer is unknown, but the *Times* of 6 November 1860 stated that a bust of Nelson (clearly recognisable as the Coade model) was found on "an altar devoted to the fetich worship" as the "Deity of the Mountain Streams".[45]

Perhaps other equally exotic settings for Coade pieces may come to light in time.

Nelson Statue, Montreal, Canada

NOTES

1. Coade's Gallery 1799

2. *William Thornton, Small Star of the Enlightenment*, Beatrice Star Jenkins, published in photocopy in 1982, states that both Dr Thornton and John Coakley Lettsome (sic; the English spelling is Lettsom) came from Tortola in the Virgin Islands. Lettsom was 17 years older than Thornton and became his mentor. Both left the island to study medicine in Great Britain, and Lettsom became one of the most celebrated physicians of his time. Lettsom was a lavish user of Coade stone at his Camberwell house, and he also commissioned two Coade plaques emblematical of medicine, one for his own house and one for the Medical Society of London, which he founded and which still retains its plaque. Though Thornton returned to the United States, it seems likely that it was his friend Lettsom who recommended Coade stone to him for the Octagon.

3. I am much indebted to Mr Nathaniel P. Neblett for providing me with copies of these letters, and for the Virginia Historical Society's Manuscript Department for permission to publish them.

4. Glen Brown. *The Octagon, Dr William Thornton, Architect,* p.14.

5. Information from Professor Dumas Malone, Jefferson's biographer.

6. I am indebted to Mr Neblett for his drawing of the keystone.

7. Published in the *Bulletin of the Association for Preservation Technology* 1972. Again I am indebted to Mr Neblett for a copy of Mr White's letter.

8. H.M. Colvin *A Biographical Dictionary of British Architects* (1978 edition) Latrobe entry.

9. Talbot Hamlyn. *Benjamin Henry Latrobe.* 1955.

10. Architectural Historian to the Editorial Staff of the *Papers of Benjamin Henry Latrobe.*

11. When I asked about Coade stone on any of Latrobe's American houses, Mr Cohen told me that, as far as he knew, nobody had looked for it.

12. Alfred Coxe Prime. *The Arts and Crafts in Philadelphia, Maryland and South Carolina,* Series II.

13. Mr Neblett read the long S, used by Mrs Coade's typesetter, and many of his contemporaries, and easily confused with f or l, as an l, and therefore read Dorsey's name as Dorley; and so did not connect him with the *Pennsylvania Post* advertiser. The text of *Coade's Gallery* is, in fact, quite clear.

14. As drawn by Charles Bulfinch, see below. Both houses are reproduced in *Domestic Architecture of the American Colonies and of the Early Republic,* Fiske Kemball, p.210, 211.

15. Wayne Andrews. *Architecture, Ambition and Americans,* p.54, 56.

16. However, Professor Kirker, the *Architecture of Charles Bulfinch* 1969 mentions that Bulfinch's drawing corresponds precisely to a drawing made ten years later. William Burch's engraving of 1800, admittedly an oblique and distant view, on the other hand does not show the Coade decoration (Kemball, op.cit. p.210). Bulfinch's drawing has been reproduced a number of times – as plate 50 of Professor Kirker's book, for instance, and p.135 of *The Palladian Style in England and America,* Desmond Guiness and Julius Trousdale Sadler.

17. Dorothy Stroud, *George Dance,* 1971, p.136 and plate 19.

18. Comparative prices of good quality furniture can be found in Christopher Gilbert, *The Life and Work of Thomas Chippendale* 1978; i.e. a marquetry commode at £68 and six gilt chairs at £120. George Seddon later became the Prince Regent's cabinet-maker, and would have charged quite as much.

19. Harvard University Press 1969.

20. Kirker, plate 14.

21. Op.cit., plate 32.

22. Op.cit., plate 49.

23. Op.cit., plate 51.

24. Op.cit., plate 74.

25. This Coade plate has no number – i.e. it was issued later than the catalogue of 1784 – and has hand written under it "Each 4ft 4 long by 2ft 6, 5 guineas".

26. Kirker, plate 97.

27. Op.cit., plates 137 and 138.

28. Jefferson planned to use a native American stone for the capitals at the University of Virginia, Charlottesville, but this proved unsatisfactory and he had to import marble from Carrara. Information from Professor Frederick D. Nichols.

29. Asher Benjamin, *The American Builder's Companion,* Boston 1806, p.65. 66. Engraving by Daniel Raynerd. Again I am indebted to Mr Neblett for the reference.

30. *County Life,* January 16th 1975, p.142-3.

31. Colvin, op.cit. William Jay entry.

32. See note 7.

33. (Full details are in "An Expensive Present" by Alison Kelly, *Burlington Magazine,* September 1984.)

34. Information from James D. Draper, Curator. European Sculpture and Decorative Arts.

35. Information from Dona E. Caldwell.

36. Information from Simon Jervis.

37. See Chapter 17, Coade Heraldry.

38. See Chapter 15, Funerary Monuments.

39. See Chapter 9, Statues and Busts.

40. See Chapter 14, Commemorative Monuments.

41. CO October 1818 "John Richardson, Southampton Row, 4 tablets with emblems comprising commerce, agriculture, navigation, arts and manufactures 3ft 101/8 ins deep at 10gns each for the new Bank, Montreal, Lower Canada to be ready by the middle of March". Marc Lafrance in an article on the Bank in APT vol V no. 3 1973 p. 103-8 shows an engraving froma drawing by R.S. Sproule of the original bank, a six bay building like a private house, with the plaques arranged in Wyatt-like manner between the ground and first floor windows. Marc Lafrance mentions that Richardson was a prominent Montreal citizen who was concerned with the commission for the Nelson monument (q. v., chapter on Commerative Monuments).

42. Alison Kelly "An Expensive Present", *Burlington Magazine,* September 1984.

43. CD October and November 1820. Messrs. Samuel and Phillips arranged the order in London, "to be paid on shipment", unlike the Rio gateway.

44. CD February 1816. He listed the items in two columns giving the figure he hoped for and a lower one which I suppose was the lowest he would accept. The *Piping Boy's* asking price was 20 guineas, but he would go down to 6. The *Naked Venus* and the *Nelson* were each 10 guineas with a reserve of 5. Quotation from the *Times* from Jim Saunders.

45. See Chapter 9, Statues, Busts and Medallions. Information from Jim Saunders.

CHAPTER 19

Scagliola

With the bas-relief *Plaques* and *Medallions, Friezes,* and *Paterae Chimneypieces* going out of fashion on the early years of the 19th century, the firm had to rely on *Capitals, Statues* and *Heraldry* for the more austere architecture of the Regency. It was therefore natural that Croggon should look out for a new line to replace those which were no longer saleable. In 1816 he decided upon scagliola, and went into active production in 1818.[1]

Scagliola was not a new invention. Imported scagliola had been used as early as Charles II's time (Ham House), and Robert Adam had used it,[2] the firm he employed being Bartoli and Richter. (Bartoli's name suggests an immigrant Italian, and both the process and its name came from Italy.) Among all Adam's other decoration, scagliola did not play a great part, but when ceilings became plain white again, and walls were either white or a strong colour, the impact of richly coloured marble columns was greatly enhanced. The cost of real marble made it out of the question, but scagliola could imitate it sufficiently accurately, if well made, to deceive even architectural historians.

Scagliola is a form of plaster. A base of wood was covered with a comparatively coarse-grained plaster undercoat mixed with a form of glue, like gesso. On top was a thin skin of lime plaster of some kind. Some authorities say that this had to be selenite – crystallized or foliated sulphate of lime. Others say that marble, spar or granite was included. In 1769, Sir William Chambers wrote[2a] to a friend in Scotland giving a description of scagliola production. First describing a basic layer of coarse plaster, he continues "Then a finer paste of the same composition but with less marble is laid on about one and a half inches thick, and after having beat it for some time then strew in bits of marble of different kinds and beat them into the paste, then when dry put on a paste composed of powder of tiles, lime and soap water for otherwise it never takes a polish, this lay on the thickness of a sheet of paper and smooth and polish it with a polished trowel berfore it drys, then rub it with linseed oyl and a woolen cloth". In 1773, to another correspondent he wrote that scagliola "is an imitation of Marble composed of talk [talc], isinglass and mineral Colours of different sorts. It is when well done nearly as hard as marble and as beautiful in every respect. The price is from five or six to 12 shill. Pr. foot superficial". He remarked that Ritter and Bartoli were the best makers, and concluded that "You find it is not cheap". Expensive marbles were imitated, such as porphyry, (plum-colour or purple), verd antique (greenish) and cipollino (little onion in Italian; green and white like a spring onion).

Croggon was not alone in the field. A firm called Brown had the Royal Appointment for scagliola, and Croggon had supplied them with Coade *Prince of Wales Feathers* for their premises in the very year he began scagliola manufacture.[3] John Ruch[4] relates that Brown accused Croggon of using cheap materials, but that Croggon had the unanswerable reply that he got them from the same source as Brown. Croggon also inveigled one of the chief workman away from Brown and brought him to the Coade factory to instruct the staff in scagliola making. This sharp practise paid off, and scagliola became an important, and lucrative, part of the Lambeth business.

In 1824 (p.381) the *Somerset House Gazette* published an article signed L. describing the Coade factory. He went first to the Coade stone section with "Mr Croggon, who showed us over the different parts of the establishment with perfect politeness". Afterwards, L. was greatly impressed with the scagliola department. "It equals the marble in brilliancy, smoothness and variety of tints . . . The scagliola is chiefly employed in ornamental pillars and pilasters; and as it is not subject to the kiln, can only be used for interior ornaments, as it has not the hardness to withstand the weather . . .

"In forming the pillar, a strong frame is first used, which is covered with the artificial stone, and then coated with a mixture about 1/6 inch thick which gives the imitation of the marble intended. In its rough state it gives no promise of its future beauty, but the first application of the scraper brings out all the rich tints which the artist expects from his process. It is only the rare qualities of marble which are imitated; of this class we saw fine specimens of the Verd Antique, Jaune Antique [usually called giallo antico by Croggon; deep yellow], Lapis Lazuli [blue], Broccata and Brocatella [literally brocaded in Italian, yellow or drab marbles with red veins] . . . It fades a little by exposure to air, but in a very short time a workman restores its brilliancy by merely exposing a fresh surface by scraping it".

L., though intelligent, had never seen the process before, and certainly in one respect was making a mistake. The frame, he said, was covered with the artificial stone, but this cannot be right, since he also told us that the scagliola "is not subject to the kiln." Coade clay, left unfired, would eventually crumble away. I think that, having seen Coade clay elsewhere in the factory, he took the coarse plaster, being slapped on to the wood cores, for the same thing. In other respects his description was accurate, and he understood the thin surface coat, and the way of finishing it, very well.

L. referred to the "strong frame" and Croggon, in his work books, called this the "skeleton". Examination of his Day Book entries shows that "skeleton" cost 1/6 per foot, and that there were six feet of "skeleton" for each foot of column. (At Ickworth, Suffolk, for instance, he charged for four *Columns* 15 ft 6 ins high and 372 feet of "skeleton".)[5] This suggests that six pieces of wood were planed to the correct curve, and set up in a ring to make up the column's core, slimmer that the size finally aimed at, to allow for the two coats of plaster. I am assuming that wood must have been used, though there is one reference to an iron core, in 1819, for a Mr Collingham of Hanover Square.[6] Iron columns were being cast occasionally at the time, but would have been very heavy, and I can find no other reference to them in Croggon's work books.

When the cores had been made, and the two coats of plaster put on, the *Columns* went off to their destination, but they were by no means ready. The Earl of Bristol at Ickworth, for instance, had to pay for the work of two men for a fortnight in putting up the four "yellow

302

antique" columns in his library. This cost him over £13.[7] He had already incurred a bill for £325.10s.4d. for the *Columns* themselves, their *Capitals*, *Bases* and "skeletons". Dubbin had been sent to Ickworth to measure up for eight *Columns*;[8] at this price, it is not surprising that the Earl settled for four.

Ickworth House, Suffolk. Scagliola Columns in the Library 1820, Coade stone Capitals and Bases

As workman seem usually to have been sent for comparable periods to other customers (The Marquess of Downshire,[9] for instance, paid £18., in 1820, for work on four *Columns* and four *Pilasters*), I think that the *Columns* must have travelled in their unpolished state, and that the workman had not only to put them up, but to scrape and polish them.

To complete the *Columns*, Croggon offered *Capitals* and *Bases* in a material which I cannot find mentioned elsewhere, and which he called "statuary scagliola" (or scag°). There was no attempt to make this match the *Columns*; it was the usual Coade cream colour, and on examining it carefully at Ickworth, it seems to me to be just an exceptionally smooth surfaced Coade stone, with slight patina. The *Columns* themselves are a rich brownish yellow, and convincing as marble to the eye, though of course not the touch – not cold enough. Equally fine porphyry scagliola *Columns* are in the hall, bought after 1821, and so not recorded in Croggon's books.

Thomas Dubbin, whose work at Deane church has already been mentioned, seems to have taken over the production of the *Capitals* and *Bases*, and his charges for them are mentioned in the Day Book. For Willey Hall, Shropshire,[10] for instance, Croggon noted "Credit Thomas Dubbin 8 corinthian caps for columns, 4 for pilasters and 6 for flat pilasters £174.10s.0d." They are of very fine quality.

Willey Hall was built by Lewis Wyatt (nephew of the better known James) in 1812-15, but the hall *Columns* were not made until 1818.[11] The hall, with its eight great *Columns*, is most imposing. They are of giallo antico, the idea of verd antique having been abandoned as too expensive. The colours used in making scagliola varied in price, green being the dearest. As it was, and in the cheaper colour, the eight *Columns*, with their *Bases* and a *Frieze*, cost £683.10s.9d. The *Pilasters* and all the *Capitals* added a further £570 to the expense. The Willey scheme, with its attendant problems, is described at length in John Ruch's article, "Regency Coade" in *Architectural History*, 1968 pp.41-2.

Scagliola Columns, Coade stone capitals and bases at Willey Hall, Shropshire, Lewis William Wyatt 1812-15

Giallo antico scagliola was also used for another surviving Croggon commission. In 1819, he made 14 *Pilasters* for the Hall of Downing College[12] for the architect William Wilkins. They were "16ft 10¼ins by 2ft 3ins for projection, same imitation of giallo antique as Covent Garden", i.e. Robert Smirke's version of the Opera House. Being easier to make than *Columns*, they were much cheaper – £340 for the *Pilasters* and £62 for the Bases in "statuary scagliola". There is no mention of the Capitals; they are either marble or else were invoiced after the end of Croggon's work books. (The bill for the *Pilasters* was not sent out until July 1820.)

Downing College, Cambridge, by William Wilkins, Scagiola Columns in the Hall 1819

In 1820, Benjamin Dean Wyatt ordered four angular *Pilasters* of sienna scagliola, which can be seen today in the dining-room at Apsley House;[13] this order, with the three already mentioned, and scagliola columns for the drawing-room at Kilruddery, Co Wicklow, Ireland, are the only ones which I know to survive, though there may well be others both of the Regency and of the 1820s and early 1830s which have not yet been identified. No less than three tenants, for instance, of the newly built Bryanston Square[14] ordered pairs of scagliola *Columns*, probably for their drawing-rooms, in verd antique, brocatella and sienna (yellowish brown). Renumbering in the square had made it impossible to identify the houses.

Right at the end of Croggon's work books there are some orders for narrow *Slabs* of scagliola for Seddon,[15] the eminent cabinet-maker, and for others who were also, I believe, in the furniture trade. I suppose they must have been for narrow console tables for halls etc. They must have been for ornamental pieces, since the scagliola would get badly scratched if used for a functional table; it is frustrating not to know if these orders continued.

In 1818, Croggon[16] had what must have been an interesting commission – for repairing and cleaning the scagliola pilasters in the Chapel at the Royal Naval Hospital at Greenwich. We have seen how Eleanor Coade provided the *Capitals* for these pilasters more than thirty years before; but at that time, of course, she could not make scagliola; and they were provided by Richter. Renewing the firm's long association with the Hospital, and no doubt thinking that he could have made the scagliola better himself in the first place, must have been a gratification to Croggon. There was a good deal to do; it required 303 days' work at 6s.6d. and 58½ days at 4s.0d. (£154.17s.6d) to finish the job. The pilasters still look admirable, but how many times they have been refurbished since Croggon's time I do not know.

As Croggon's records finish in 1821,[17] it is not possible to get any clear picture of what the firm was doing later, and any information has to come from outside sources. We know, for instance, that Soane comissioned scagliola *Columns* for the Royal Entrance to the House of Lords in 1826[18] and for the Freemasons' Hall between 1828 and 1831.[19]

Probably Croggon's most important scagliola commission has only very recently been recognised. The scagliola floor of the Ante-Room as Syon has always been assumed to be Robert Adam's design, carried out probably by Richter and Bartoli. However a bill in the Alnwick Archives, discovered by Dr Colin Shrimpton, shows that it was replaced (among his last works) by William Croggon:

Coade Imperishable Stone, Scagliola and Marble Works
Lambeth January 31st 1832
His Grace the Duke of Northumberland

To William Croggon
    to a rich inlaid Scagliola Floor executed in hard material and various
    Colours, the whole inlaid complete in the Vestibule at Syon House –
    including all expence of Drawings, patterns, carriage, fixing etc. as p
    Estimate – £900.0.0.

                                                                Syon Ms U III.

The bill was quoted in *Country House Floors* (p.26) the catalogue of an exhibition held at Temple Newsam House, Leeds, early in 1987.

Anteroom at Syon House by Robert Adam 1761-5, showing the Scagiola Floor relaid by William Croggon in 1832

307

The reader may recall that William Croggon was supposed, by his Grampound relation, to have done work to a value of "scores of thousands with the royal family, the Duke of York's acct. at one time was £20,000."[20] The King certainly is known to have had three elaborate *Doorcases* in scagliola for the Picture Gallery at Buckingham Palace, which had *Terms*, and *Medallions* of Michelangelo, Raphael and Titian, at a cost of £660.[21] (They have now been removed.) At some date after 1830, since it contained a *Medallion* of William IV who acceded in that year, a similar *Doorcase* was made for the Throne Room, for £253.[22] There were probably other orders for the Crown which I have not traced. It was, however, the Duke of York who was, it seems, Croggon's principal customer for scagliola; I have no reason to doubt Mr Croggon of Grampound's estimate of the sum involved.

Since we have been accustomed, from the time of Queen Victoria, to a Royal Family who pay their debts, it should perhaps be mentioned that George IV, from the time he first had an independent income as Prince of Wales, paid only for a small part of his possessions; he found it more convenient to owe for the rest. He lived in a cloud of debt, and after his death Parliament had sourly to vote huge sums to ensure the solvency of the Crown. The King's employees did, therefore, eventually get their money; but there was no such safety-net for the unfortunate tradesmen working for the King's brother, the Duke of York, whose standard of extravagance was similar.

The records of bankruptcy proceedings of this period have been destroyed, the Public Records Office having kept only certain papers considered to be of public interest; it is not therefore possible to find out the circumstances of William Croggon's failure. However, the following facts may be relevant. The Duke of York decided to build himself a new London house early in the 1820s, and after it had been begun by Smirke, Benjamin Dean Wyatt manoeuvred himself into the position of architect in circumstances of professional scandal.[23] (It was this Wyatt who had ordered scagliola from Croggon for Apsley House.) The house was designed with splendour, which the Duke omitted to pay for. When it was being decorated, in 1827, he died, owing £200,000 and having mortgaged the house to the Government for £80,000. The Commissioners of Woods and Forests sold it to the Marquess of Stafford, losing £8,000 in the sale, and he decided to complete the decorations in a different style, so that anything, such as scagliola, made for the Duke, could not be used. Six years later, the Marquess too died, and it was at this point that disaster overtook William Croggon. The Marquess's son, now Duke of Sutherland did complete the house, and at some time in the later 1830s Sir Charles Barry was employed. Barry had commissioned scagliola from Thomas Croggon for the Royal College of Surgeons in 1836;[24] and magnificent columns of sienna, porphyry and red and orange breccia scagliola decorated the splendid hall and gallery of Stafford House. It would be pleasant to think that some of this might have been William Croggon's scagliola made for the Duke of York, and at last used, but on this point I have no information. Scagliola columns of very large size were among the items in the Coade factory sale of 1843.[25]

After his father's experience, Thomas Croggon may have sought for more bourgeois and reliable customers. A few pieces of Coade stone have been traced from his régime; there is a Coat of Arms of Queen Victoria in Suffolk St., Westminster, a *Font* at Chignal St James, Essex, of 1838, a *Charity Boy* on the Vintners' Hall of 1840, a fine *Warwick Vase* and *Pedestal* of 1840 in a private collection in Hampshire. A life-size *Mercury* figure, copied from a sculpture by Thorwaldsen is now in a private collection in Australia.[26] Within five years or so, however, Thomas John Croggon had left Lambeth, and turned his firm in a different direction.

Scagiola columns, with Coade stone capitals and bases. Kilruddery, Co. Wicklow, Ireland, after 1821

NOTES

1. There was a first example in 1817, for Langham House, Portland Place (pedestals for figures) but 1818 brought 6 orders.

2. I.e. at 20 St James's Square.

2a. Quoted in Treve Rosoman *"Scagliola, the Art of the Masquerade"* *Traditional Interior Decoration* October/November 1988, p.117-125. Mr Rosoman gives a complete description, with illustrations, of scagliola manufacture today. Bits of marble are now not included, and the top thin layer is omitted.

3. Acrimonious correspondence re these arms is in the Coade Letter Book (3.6.1817 (p.270) 25.9.1817 (p.289)), Brown could not pay; Croggon threatened other measures, finally offering to pass on the arms to another customer.

4. John E. Ruch "Regency Coade" *Architectural History* 1968, corresponence re Willey Hall Salop. p.41, 42.

5. CD March 1820.

6. CO August 1819 "Luke Collingham Esq. ordered by Robert . . . (illegible) 2 Doric columns med. yellow antique scag° (for an iron core)".

7. CD April 1821 "Earl of Bristol, time, expenses fixing columns 2 men 14 days each £13.7s.0d."

8. CD March 1820 "Mr. Dubbin's time at Ickworth taking dimensions for 8 columns for the library, 3 days £6.19s.6d."

9. CD April 1820 "Marquis of Downshire, Man's time in fixing scagliola at East Hampstead £18.11s.0d."

10. Work notes at back of Day Book.

11. CD October 1818.

12. CO July 1819. CD July 1820.

13. CD February 1820.

14. CD July 1821 "Col. Graham, Bryanston, Square, 2 scagliola sienna pilasters £31.10s.0d." November 1821 "Col. Graham's columns and capitals £78.15s.0d." CD August 1821 "– Barkes Esq. for 79 BryanstonSquare, 2 pilasters in statuary brocatella £33.10s.6d." CD August 1821 "Genl. Maitland, 30 Bryanston Square, 2 pilasters verd antique, grecian capitals £35.17s.9d."

15. CO April 1821 "Messrs. Seddon 150 Aldersgate St. 1 verd antique slab 3ft 6ins x 8ins x ⅜in thick, front and both ends polished and finished." CO January, April 1821 gives several orders for similar slabs. Miss Johnes, 24 Portman Square also ordered one in June 1818, but may well have been a private customer – related to Johnes of Hafod, who used Coade stone?

16. CD December 1818.

17. Fifteen commissions are recorded for that year.

18. Letter from Croggon to Soane of 18 March 1826, Sir John Soane's Museum, justifies their cost (£236.7s.7d.) Croggon also supplied scagliola for Soane's Privy Council building. Office of Works 5/126 f.123.

19. Bill for the Freemasons' Hall headed "Coade Works Lambeth" for 4 giallo antico scagliola columns (£129.9s.0d) in the Soane papers at Sir John Soane's Museum.

20. See Chapter 1.

21. *Buckingham Palace* by J. Harris, G. de Bellaigue and O. Millar, p.79.

22. *History of the King's Works* vol VI p.283.

23. H.M. Colvin "The Architects of Stafford House", by *Architectural History* 1958 pp.17-30.

24. Gunnis op.cit. Croggon entry.

25. The sale advertisement (Minet Library, Brixton no. 12/24) mentions "fine specimens of scagliola including twelve noble columns 16 feet high". Sale of the 'valuable works in Terracotta of Coade's Celebrated Manufactory, Belvedere Road" ... "FOR SALE BY AUCTION in suitable lots on the premises on Friday July 21st 1843 and three following days, Sundays excepted at 12 o'clock" Messrs. Rushworth and Jarvis, auctioneers, Saville Row, Regent Street and 19 Change Alley, Cornhill. Minet Library, Brixton 12/64.

26. Alison Kelly "Mrs. Coade's Stone", *Antique Collector* August 1981, p.81.-83.
Blanchard advertisement, the *Builder* 29.12.1855.
Victoria and Albert Museum Library.

Library Fireplace, Ettington Park, Warwicks

EPILOGUE

So, for various reasons, therefore, Coade stone was made no longer. The firm had the facilities for making the Victorian type of terracotta, and it could be imagined that, had it been able to survive, it could have been part of the great expansion of the architectural terracotta industry of the mid and later 19th century. As it is, however, the Coade firm's history began in the early years of George III and, continuing into the time of William IV, coincided fairly exactly with the neo-classical period. This gave it a coherence and unity which a later change of style would have destroyed. Eleanor Coade's elegant product reflected the taste of a period in which many people consider that the heights of British applied arts were achieved, and added its own lustre to them.

Mark Blanchard, whose econium of the Coade firm I have quoted earlier (Chapter 3), said as late as 1855 that he was the successor to the factory and user of its formula, and obtained prizes in the Great Exhibition of 1851. It is probable that he bought some of the moulds at the sale of 1843, and I have seen pieces marked Blanchard which, apart from his stamp, could be taken for Coade work. J.M. Blashfield's ceramic work of the 1850s and 1860s also continued something of the Coade tradition, though his designs, apart from the *Medici and Borghese Vases* (for which illustrations were easily available) are not in Coade style, except for the *vases* he made for Buckingham Palace to supplement the Coade pieces already on the terrace there. He did, however, appreciate the quality of the Lambeth product in his *Account of the History and Manufacture of Ancient and Modern Terracotta* (1855) in which he wrote that the Coade stone at Buckingham Palace was the only work there remaining in good condition. (The Palace was hardly thirty years old). Charles Fowler, the architect, in his 1850 address to the R.I.B.A.,[1] was also appreciative of Eleanor Coade, but after this her name and achievements sank into oblivion.

They were so completely forgotten that when Llewellynn Jewitt wrote about the Coade firm in his *Ceramic Art of Great Britain* in 1878 he achieved the high score of eight mistakes in the first paragraph.[2] (The remainder of his entry was more accurate, though he inexplicably mistook the modeller Coffee for an unnamed fire-man). As his book is much respected, these mistakes have often been repeated. Another curious mistake occurs as late as 1910, when the writer of *English Pottery and Porcelain, a Handbook for the Collector*[3] could state that "no authentic specimen of this ware is known".

Knowledge of Coade work became more extensive and more accurate this century. In 1913, J. Tavenor-Parry wrote a good description of the works[4] and gave the only photograph, as far as I know, of the Nelson Pediment at Greenwich. He also showed the Pelican Office group in its original setting.

Mrs Katharine Esdaile wrote two important articles published in 1940,[5] and her enthusiasm brought Eleanor Coade to life. Unfortunately, she believed that Holt's factory and the Coade works were the same, and that Mrs Coade took over the Holt formula, both of which statements turn out to be incorrect, but which have often been repeated.

The demolitions on the South Bank for the Festival of Britain in 1951 disclosed the site of the Coade factory, between the present Festival Hall and the Hayward Gallery, and a short-lived interest was aroused. Mr F.J. Collins, then of the Historic Buildings Department of the London County Council, made a thorough investigation, and with Miss Ida Darlington, Archivist of the Council, began a serious study of Eleanor Coade. The article on the factory in volume XXIII of the *Survey of London,* though unsigned like the rest of these surveys, is by them, and they established the relationship between the Coades and the Enchmarches of Tiverton.

In November 1953,[6] S.B. Hamilton gave for the first time an analysis of the Coade body, until then wrapped in mystery, and believed by many to be so still. He used material taken from the Coade site, where clay, believed to be Coade clay, and many pieces of moulds etc. were found and are now in the Museum of London.

Also in 1953, Rupert Gunnis published his *Dictionary of British Sculptors 1660 – 1851,* which contains by far the most extensive list of Coade pieces so far published.[7] He lists fifty Coade memorials, and while his list of architectural commissions is slighter, it must be remembered that his primary interest was in sculpture.

In the late 1960s, Mr John E. Ruch made a discovery of prime importance in the Public Record Office. Deposited there as evidence in a Chancery case, they consist of Croggon's Order Book and 'Day Book' (accounts) from the time he took over as manager in 1813 to Eleanor Coade's death in 1821, and a Letter Book begun by Sealy in January 1813, and continued by Croggon.[8] For this short period, these papers cast a spotlight on the customers, the orders, their destinations and their costs. Mr Ruch wrote up his conclusions in two articles, "Regency Coade" in *Architectural History 1968* and *Coade Stone in Ireland* in the *Irish Georgian Society's Bulletin* for October – December 1970. Mr Ruch then returned to Canada and ceased to study this rich cache of Coade information.

Through its long years of publication, Sir Nikolaus Pevsner's *Buildings of England* has recorded a large number of Coade pieces. Usually there are one or two references per volume, and only eight contain none. (As all these counties contain Coade work, the omissions will be corrected in later revisions.)

In 1985, Dr Ian Freestone, Miss Mavis Bimson and Mr M.S. Tite of the British Museum Research Laboratory analysed a piece of Coade stone from Eleanor's country house at Lyme Regis,[9] using all the most sophisticated modern techniques. Analysis has advanced a great deal since Hamilton's time, and their conclusions are summarised here in the chapter on the *Making of Coade stone.*

In 1986, Mr John Havill wrote a valuable book on *Eleanor Coade Artificial Stone Manufacturer,*[10] in which he demolished the long-held myth that George Coade and the two Eleanors lived in Lyme Regis before they went to London. Relations were indeed at Lyme, but George went to Exeter at about the time of his marriage and Eleanor II was born there. Kilns at Lyme and work sent to London from there are imaginary. The exceptional amount of Coade work in the Exeter area must result from family contacts.

Ill-informed articles about Coade stone continue to be written, and even today many people believe that the only surviving Coade pieces are the tomb of Captain Bligh, the Westminster Bridge Lion, and the houses in Bedford Square; but it will be seen from what I have written above that an important body of accurate information about Eleanor Coade and her family is already in print in a variety of places. It seemed worth while to bring it all together, and combine it with the results of seventeen years of personal research to produce the first book on Eleanor Coade and her colleagues and successors, and the Coade factory.

Eleanor Coade as well as being an interesting and powerful character, was an important figure in her own day, with commissions, as we have seen, from all the eminent architects of her time, and the Royal Appointment to both George III and George IV, as well as to other members of the Royal Family. The important work which she and her successors carried out in Europe and America is detailed here, and I hope that many examples of her work as yet unknown will come to light as a result. If this book restores her to her rightful place as a pre-eminent in the Georgian decorative scene, the labour and pleasure of writing it will have been worth while.

THE RIVER GOD, a 9 Feet Figure, at COADE'S Lythodipyra, or Artificial Stone Manufactury, Narrow Wall, LAMBETH.

Etching, said to be by William Blake for the River God at Ham House.

NOTES

1. "Some remarks on Terra-cotta and Artificial Stone as connected with Architecture", printed in the *Civil Engineer and Architect's Journal*, vol XIII p.215-216.

2. p.138 – 139, volume I. The whole entry is deleted in later editions.

3. By the Rev. Edward A. Downman, 5th edition, revised and greatly enlarged by Aubrey D. Gunn, p.70.

4. J. Tavenor-Parry "An Episode in the History of English Terra-cotta" *Architectural Review* XXXIII 1913 p.119-122.

5. "Coade Stone" *The Architect and Building News* CLXI, 19 January 1940 pp.94-6 and 26 January pp.112-4.

6. "Coade Stone" *Architectural Review* CXVI, November 1953 p.295-9.

7. Coade entry, p.104-109, Croggon (misspelt Croggan) entry p.116-7.

8. All filed together, with loose papers, as C 111/106.

9. "The Constitution of Coade Stone" by I.C. Freestone, M. Bimson and M.S. Tite, *Ancient Technology to Modern Science* ed. W.D. Kingery, The American Ceramic Society Inc. Columbus, Ohio, USA.

10. 1986. Unpublished. Copy deposited at Exeter University, Metropolitan Museum, New York, etc.

Architects who used Coade Stone and Coade Scagliola

The distinction between an architect and a builder in the 18th century was not as clear as it later became. Some (i.e. Francis Hiorne) combined building with architecture, and there are names in this list who might now be considered solely as builders, quantity surveyors etc. These borderline cases have been included, and only those builders left out who clearly worked under a specific architect (i.e. an entry in Croggon's workbooks "Mr X builder for Mr Y. architect).

In the 1970s, the names and areas of some English counties, and all the Welsh and Scottish counties, were altered. For this architects' list, counties have been given as they were in Georgian times. In the Gazetteer, both old and new county names are given in the Welsh and Scottish sections. As houses and other buildings in these two sections are given alphabetically, and not county by county, that correlation between Mrs Coade's and the present usage should not involve difficulties.

England presents a more intractable problem. The standard architectural works – Pevsner's *Buildings of England* and Colvin's *Biographical Dictionary of British Architects*, were published before the new counties were established, so that anyone searching for a building in the present Avon or Humberside will have difficulty in knowning where to look for it in such volumes. Moreover the Metropolitan Authorities, constructed of bits of various counties put together, are to be disestablished and will presumably return to their component parts. It seems therefore the most practicable answer to use the old county boundaries, giving in addition the changed county name where it occurs. The exception is London. The Greater London Council is to be abolished, but the area over which it presided represents a real entity, and its boundaries have been used for the Greater London section, Middlesex, a real county to Mrs Coade, having disappeared so long ago that it cannot be resurrected.

Fuller details about the buildings listed will be found in the Gazetteer. Many buildings have been traced through Mrs Coade's 1799 list and information from other sources found out about them. Where this is the case, the information will be found in the Gazetteer. Where, however, the 1799 list is the sole source of information, this is indicated here (as CG, the symbol used also in the Gazetteer).

Sir John Soane, Pitzhanger Manor 1800-3. Caryatids

ARCHITECTS WHO USED COADE STONE

* indicates surviving Coade.   x indicates Houses etc open to the public.

CG: *Coade's Gallery* 1799. CO: Croggon's Order Book.

CD: Croggon's Day Book. NP: *The Nelson Pediment pamphlet.* 1813

Gunnis: *Dictionary of British Sculptors,* 1953, Rupert Gunnis.

Pevsner: *The Buildings of England,* Sir Nikolaus Pevsner and others, 1951-74.

RHCM; Royal Commission on Historic Monuments.

The dates of buildings, and their assignment to particular architects, come either from H.M. Colvin's *Biographical Dictionary of English Architects, 1660-1840,* or from the appropriate volumes of the *Buildings of England,* by Sir Nikolaus Pevsner and his associates. These attributions are not individually noted. Other sources of information are given in brackets.

ADAM, Robert, 1728-1792. *Alnwick Castle,* Northumbs., plaques. Brizlee Tower, Lord's Tower, CG. *Croome d'Abitot,* Worcs., plaques Island Temple. *Newby Hall,* Yorks., plaques. *20 Portman Square,* London, plaques, string courses, capitals etc. *Luton Hoo,* Beds., CG. *Culzean,* Strathclyde, Cat Gates. *Bury St Edmunds,* Suffolk, Theatre and Town Hall plaques, vases etc. *The Grange,* Hants., CG. *Audley End,* Essex, Paterae, Ring Temple. *Wedderburn,* Border Region, heraldry. *Caenwood* (Kenwood) London, CG. *Cullen House,* Banff, Grampian Region, heraldry, Vestal in mausoleum. *Dunbar Barracks* (ex Castle), Lothian Region, heraldry. *Glasserton,* Dumfries Region. CG. *Castle Upton,* Co. Antrim, Ireland, plaques, vases etc in mausoleum. *Gosford,* Lothian Region, plaques, heraldry etc. *Admiralty,* London Panels of Tritons. *Woolton Hall,* Liverpool, plaques

ASPRUCCI, Mario, The Younger. Now credited with the design of *Ickworth,* Suffolk.

ATKINSON, Thomas, (of York) ?-1798. *Burton Constable,* Humberside, plaques, figures.

BAKER, Henry Aaron. Dublin, *Merrion Square.* Fountain, urns, vases, plaques etc.

BARRY, Sir Charles, 1795-1860. London, *Lincoln's Inn Fields,* Royal College of Surgeons, scagliola columns.

BEDFORD, Francis, 1784-1858. London, *Denmark Hill, Camberwell,* capitals.

BILLING, Richard, Senior, 1747-1826 and Junior 1785-1853. Builders and architects of Reading. Balusters for site unknown.

BLACKBURN, William, 1750-1790. London, *Watermens' Hall, St Mary at Hill.* Plaques, capitals etc. London, 145 *Denmark Hill,* capitals etc.

BONOMI, Ignatius, 1787-1870. *Lambton Hall,* Durham, Coats of arms.

BONOMI, Joseph, 1739-1808. *Laverstoke,* Hants. CG.

BRAZIER, Edward Bardwell, 1753-?. *Callender House,* Falkirk, Central Region. Figures, vases, chimneytops etc.

BRETTINGHAM, Robert William Furze, c.1750-1820. *Audley End,* Essex, Temple of Concord, capitals, frieze of George III.

BRIDGER, James, ?-1837 (of Aldgate and Chigwell, Essex). Capitals for site unknown, for elliptic columns.

BROWN, Lancelot "Capability", 1716-1783. *Croome d'Abitot,* Worcs. Island Temple with Adam. *Burghley House,* Northants, Lions on Bridge. *Tixall,* Staffs., lions on screen wall. *Redgrave Hall,* Suffolk, Orangery details. *Broadlands,* Hants., Orangery details.

BROWNE, Arthur, of Norwich – Cambridge, *Grove House, Trumpington Street,* capitals and bases.

BULFINCH, Charles. Boston, USA *United States Bank,* capitals, plaques, eagle.

BURN, James. Haddington, Lothian Region, *44 High Street,* Bank of Scotland, plaques and sphinx.

BURTON, James, 1761-1837. London, *Leverian Museum,* Blackfriars Bridge Road, capitals and statue.

BUSBY, Charles Augustus, 1788-1834. Bristol, *Commercial Rooms,* Corn Street, caryatids.

BYFIELD, George, 1756-1813. *Craycombe House, Fladbury,* Worcs., paterae, urns. *Perdiswell House,* Worcester, paterae, urns. *Gaynes Hall,* Hunts., capitals, urns. *Michel Grove,* Sussex Gothic chimneypiece, candelabra. *Salwarpe,* Worcs., CG.

CAMERON, Charles, c.1740-1812 "Zarsko Zelo, statues, busts, chimneypieces, vases etc", CG may have been ordered by Cameron, working at Tsarskoe Selo for Catherine the Great.

CARR, John, (of York) 1723-1827. *Byram Hall,* near Ferrybridge, Yorks. CG.

CARR, James, 1742-1821. *Clerkenwell Church,* London, Royal Arms.

CARTER, John, 1748-1817. *Debden Church,* Essex, Gothic and heraldic ornaments. *Exeter Cathedral,* West Window, Gothic tracery.

CHAMBERS, Sir Wlliam, 1723-1796. *Stanmore Hall*, Middx., CG. *Whitton Place*, Middx., CG. *Rathfarnham Castle*, Co. Dublin, plaques and paterae. *Manresa House*, Roehampton, Surrey, plaques. *Somerset House*, Strand, London, vases. Arbitrated at *Strawberry Hill*, Middx.

CHAWNER, Thomas, 1774-1851. *Chertsey Church*, Surrey, Gothic window tracery and label stops.

CLARKE, W. Tierney. *New Shoreham Suspension Bridge*, Sussex. Incorporated Howard Lion and Fitzalan Horse. Animals now at Arundel Castle.

COCKERELL, Samuel Pepys, 1753-1827. *Sezincote*, Glos., bulls, elephants, statue of Souraya. *Daylesford House*, Glos., paterae. *Gore Court*, Sittingbourne, Kent, CG. *Nutwell Court*, Exeter, CG *Banbury Church*, Oxon., capitals. In restoration of *Sevenoaks Church*, Kent, possibly used Coade stone coping.

COLUMBANI, Placido. *Audley End*, Essex, Library with four Coade figures (previously attributed to Robert Adam) two figures now in hall chimneypiece.

COOLEY, Thomas. Designed the former front hall at *Caledon*, Tyrone, N. Ireland in 1779. The chimneypiece, apart from the "tablet", exactly corresponds to that at *Bretton Hall* q.v.

COUSE, Kenton, 1721-1790. *Normanton Hall*, Rutland, CG.

CRUNDEN, John, 1745-1835. *Portswood House*, Hants., CG *Boodles Club*, St James's, London, paterae, small plaques. *Belfield House*, Weymouth, Dorset? Figure group.

CUBITT, Thomas, 1788-1855. Two sinks, site unknown.

CUNDY, Thomas, Senior, 1765-1825 and Junior, 1790-1867. *Hewell Grange*, Worcs., vases, caryatids. *24 Portman Square*, London, flower troughs, scagliola columns and slabs. *Montreal*, Westerham, Kent, vase, scagliola columns. *Easthampstead*, Berks., Scagliola columns, pilasters. *Ponsonby's house*, St James's Square, London, scagliola.

CUSTANCE, William. *Pemberton's Grove Lodge* and the *Grove*, Cambridge. Possibly for Arthur Browne q.v.

DANCE, George, The Younger, 1741-1825. *Coleorton Hall*, Leics., garden features, vases. *Kidbroke Park*, Sussex, heraldry. *Finsbury Square*, London, plaques, capitals. *47 City Road* (Wesley's house) string course. *St George's Circus*, London S.E., Arms, statues, vases, capitals. CG.

DEFFERD, James, 1750-1813. *Bodorgan*, Anglesey, CG.

DRAPER, George. Plaque of swan and ionic capitals for *Swan Inn,* Chichester. More ionic capitals site unknown 1821.

DUCART, David. *Castle Hyde,* Co. Fermoy. Gatepier sphinxes.

EDWARDS, Francis, 1784-1857. *Lion Brewery,* Lambeth, 3 lions.

EDWIN, Richard, ?-1778. *Stratford Place,* Oxford Street, London. Rusticated houses, porter's lodges with lions. Construction supervised by George Dance, q.v.

ELLIOTT, Archibald, Junior, ?-1843 *Taymouth Castle,* chimneypiece and Triton fountain. *Royal Bank of Scotland,* Glasgow, Royal Arms.

ELSAM, Richard. *Dover Gaol,* Kent, two statues. Designed aisles for *Chertsey Church,* Surrey. Sacked and work completed by T. Chawner, q.v.

EMLYN, Henry, 1729-1815. *St George's Chapel,* Windsor, Berks. Gothic screen, font, three statues. *Beaumont Lodge,* Berks., capitals, figures. Probably *Langley Marish Church,* Slough, Bucks., Gothic screen.

ESSEX, James, 1722-1784. *Strawberry Hill,* Middx., Gothic gateway.

FARRELL, William. *Kilmainham Court House,* Dublin. Royal Arms.

FOULSTON, John, 1772-1842. *Public Library,* Devonport, Devon. Egyptian details. *Egyptian House,* Penzance, Egyptian details. *Egyptian Library,* Devonport, ditto.

FOWLER, Charles, 1792-1867. *Gordon Square,* London, large plaque with Muses, now in *Warburg Institute* on the same site. *Covent Garden Market,* London, statue and plaques. Church in *Lisbon,* Royal Arms.

GANDON, James, 1743-1823. *The Playhouse, Wynnstay,* Denbighshire, two vases. *The Rotunda Hospital,* Dublin. Frieze, panels and pedestals. *Emo,* Co. Laois, Ireland, long plaques, capitals.

GARLING, Henry, 1789-1870. *Grimsthorpe Castle,* Lincs. Royal Arms.

GILLESPIE, GRAHAM James,1776-1855. Gothic candlestick and a vase for own house.

GYFFORD or GIFFORD, Edward, 1773-1856. *Bellevue House, Hale End,* Walthamstow, Essex, figures and vases.

HAKEWILL, Henry, 1771-1830, or his brother James 1778-1843. *Barford House,* Warwickshire, capitals.

HARDWICK, Thomas, 1752-1829. *Wanstead Church,* Essex, capitals. Fountain for Duke of Northumberland, not known for which estate. *St Bartholomew the Great,*

London, repairs to Rahere's tomb. *Bedford Row*, London, fountain. Hardwick organized the Coade copy of Adam's Brentford Gateway at *Syon House* for the Regent of Portugal in Brazil.

HARRISON, Thomas, 1744-1829. *Broomhall*, Fife, three plaques, integral to the house design, though supplied after completion.

HAYCOCK, Edward, 1790-1870. *Nanteos*, Cards. (now Dyfed), urns. *Lord Hill's Column*, Shrewsbury, statue of Lord Hill.

HAYES, Samuel. *Avondale*, Rathdrum, Co. Wicklow, plaques and paterae. *Market Hall, Monaghan*, same plaques as Avondale.

HENDERSON or ANDERSON, William, 1737-1824. *The Old Rectory*, Mountsorrel, Leics., decorated apparently with Coade stone but no documentation.

HOLLAND, Henry, 1745-1806. *Carlton House*, London, trophies of arms, vases. *Brighton Pavilion*, statues. *Debden House*, Essex CG. *Berrington Hall*, Herefs., keystone and paterae. *188-193 Sloane Street*, London. Doorway details. *Stanmore Hall*, Middx. CG. *Broadlands*, Hants., Orangery (may be by Brown).

HOLLAND, Richard, 1752-1827. *Debden Church*, Essex, Font.

HOPPER, Thomas, 1776-1856. *Carlton House Conservatory*, London, Gothic fountain, candelabra, statues. *Alton Towers*, Staffs., three dozen vases.

HORTON, John, ?-1825. *Gun Barrel Proof House*, Birmingham, overdoor composition.

HURST, Aaron Henry, 1762-1799. *Pentonville Chapel*, Pentonville Road, London, paterae, keystones, font. *Wimbledon Lodge*, Southside, Wimbledon, Surrey, decoration on house, gatepiers.

JAY, William c.1793-1837. *Owens Thomas House*, Savannah, Georgia, U.S.A., capitals.

JOHNSON, John, 1732-1814. Chelmsford - *Moulsham Bridge*, balusters, paterae, *Naiad Conduit*, statue; *Shire Hall*, plaques, capitals, etc; *Parish Church* (now Cathedral) Gothic arcade, windows, roof tracery, figures, font. London, *61-63 New Cavendish Street*, 3 rusticated doorways. *Galloway House, St James's*, chimneypiece. *Hatfield Peveril*, Hatfield Place, Essex rusticated doorway. *East Carlton House*, Northants., pediment ornament. *Lewes County Hall*, Sussex, plaques, consoles, vases, etc. *Leicester County Rooms*, plaques, capitals, balusters. *Killerton*, Devon, two vases with Borghese decoration. *Bradwell Lodge*, Essex, plaques, urns, paterae. *Wimbledon Church*, Surrey? pinnacles.

JOHNSTON, Francis. *Charleville*, Co. Offaly, Ireland, pinnacles, crown crockets. Dublin,

Eccles Street, plaques on own house. *Galtrim,* Summerhill, Co. Meath, lions.

JOHNSTON, John. *Rio de Janeiro,* Brazil, erected Coade replica of Adam's Syon gateway at *Quinta da Boa Vista.* Further work at Rio Royal palaces 1813-1820. Possibly related to Francis Johnston.

JUPP, William, ?-1839. *Skinners Company's Hall,* London, capitals, frieze of skins, arms.

KAY, Joseph, 1775-1847. *Bedford Row,* London, vases. Site unknown, Royal arms. *Fisherwick Park,* Staffs., vase.

KNIGHT, Richard, Payne. *Downton Castle,* Herefordshire, four lampholding figures.

LAPIDGE, Edward, 1779-1860. *Norbiton Place,* Surrey, fountain. *Trinidad,* West Indies, coat of arms. Site unknown, two pier tops.

LAING, David, 1774-1856. *Custom House,* London, Royal arms, Neptune, Britannia, lion. *St Dunstan in the East,* London, Royal arms, font.

LATROBE, Benjamin Henry, 1764-1812. *Ashdown House,* Forest Row, Sussex, capitals and bases. *Hammerwood Lodge,* Sussex, capitals, plaques.

LEVERTON, Thomas, 1764-1824. *Plaistow Lodge,* Bromley, Kent, vases, plaques. *Woodhall Park,* Herts., plaques, capitals. *Grocers' Hall,* London, work unspecified. *St James's Place,* London, stove. *Bedford Square,* London, rusticated doorway. *Phoenix Engine House,* Charing Cross, London, CG.

LEWIS, James. *Bletchingdon House,* Oxon. Lions, Gothic statue, vases, eagles.

MARTIN, A. Site unknown, probably London, balusters.

MEADOWS, John. 1732-1791. *Arlington Court,* Devon, CG.

MEDLAND, James? *Beddington House,* Surrey. Coping to "Mr Medland, Architect and surveyor".

MITCHELL, Robert. *Selwood Park,* Berks., lamp-holding figures. *Preston Hall,* Midlothian, lions, lamp-holding figures, pilaster capitals, plaques, coat of arms. *Cottesbrooke Hall,* Northants., plaques on house, plaques, paterae on lodges, bridge. *Nelson Column,* Montreal. Attrib. *Willingham House,* Lincs., capitals.

MYLNE, Robert, 1733-1811. Great Amwell, Herts., *New River Monument* and own *Family Mausoleum* plaques, vases. *Warwick Bridge,* plaques. *Stationers' Hall,* London, plaques. *The Wick,* Richmond, Surrey, paterae. *8 Argyll Street,* London, chimneypiece. *Sundorne Castle,* Shropshire, paterae.

NASH, John, 1752-1835. *Ffynone*, Pembs., capitals. *Llysnewydd*, Cards., CG. *Hafod*, Cards, eagles, garden gateway; fire may have destroyed other items. *Southgate Grove*, Middx., sphinx, urns, capitals. *Casina*, Dulwich, Surrey, CG. *East Cowes Castle*, Isle of Wight, CG. *29 Dover Street*, London, figures. *Sundridge Park*, Bromley, Kent, with S. Wyatt and Repton, work not identified. *Luscombe Castle*, Devon, heraldic plaque. *Witley Court*, Worcs., bill for work unspecified. *Aqualate Hall*, Staffs. Letter re cost of returning packing cases. *Ravensworth Castle*, Co. Durham, chimneypiece. *Charborough Park*, Dorset, heraldic animal. *Lough Cutra Castle*, Co. Galway, chimneypiece. *Royal Lodge*, Windsor, vases and pedestals. *All Souls*, Langham Place, London, capitals. *Villa*, West Cowes, Isle of Wight, Gothic details. *Church*, West Cowes, Isle of Wight, clock surrounds, plaque, coat of arms. *Haymarket Theatre*, London, capitals. *Caledon*, N. Ireland fountain, sphinxes, coat of arms. *Worcester Park*, Surrey, CG. *Market House*, Chichester, town's arms. *Buckingham Palace*, London, friezes, capitals, consoles, vases, plaques, trophies of arms.

NASMYTH, Alexander, 1758-1840. *St Bernard's Well*, Edinburgh, Statue.

NICHOLSON, Peter, 1765-1844. *Corby Castle*, Northumbs, panels and medallions, heraldic lions.

NISBET, James. *Assembly Rooms*, George Street, Edinburgh, four statues.

NOVOSIELSKI, Michael, 1750-1795. *Haymarket Opera House*, also called the King's or Queen's Theatre, London, capitals, arms.

PAINE, James, 1717-1789. Pedestal for sundial by James Paine exhibited by E. Coade, Society of Artists. *Thorndon Hall*, Essex, gatepiers and lodges?

PAPWORTH, John Buonarotti, 1775-1847. *White Knights*, Berks, garden features.

PATIENCE, Joseph Junior, 1767-1825. Completed *Great Saxham Hall*, Suffolk, plaques, coat of arms etc. For Col. Iremonger, site unknown, festoons.

PATTERSON or PATERSON John ?-1832 *Brauncepeth Castle*, Co Durham, CG.

PETO, Henry. *Bryanston Square*, London and *Portland Place*, London, scagliola columns.

PILKINGTON, William, 1758-1848. *Polstead Hall*, Stoke by Nayland, Suffolk, balusters. *Nork House*, Banstead, Surrey, balusters. *New Transport Office*, Cannon Row, London, balusters.

PIRANESI, Giovanni Battista, 1720-1778. Antefixae at *Shugborough*, Staffs, from *Della Introduzione del Progresso delle Belle Arte*, plate I. Capitals at 20 *Portman Square*, London, from *Della Magnificenza ed Architettura de' Romani* plate XX. See Robert Adam.

PLAW, John, c.1745-1820. *Belle Isle*, Windermere, or *Claife Station*, Westmorland, CG. Coade not identified.

PLAYFAIR, James, 1755-1794. *Cullen House*, Banffshire, Mausoleum, figure. *Dalkeith Palace*, Midlothian, figures.

POCOCK, William Fuller, 1779-1849. *Leathersellers' Company's Hall*, London, arms of the company.

PORDEN, William, c.1755-1822. *Upper and Lower Phillimore Place*, Kensington, London, plaques.

POWNING, John, 1763-1832. A keystone sold to "Powning, architect, Exeter".

RAFFIELD, John. *St John's Lodge*, Regent's Park, London, capitals and lions. *Easton Neston*, Northants, gateway, coat of arms, heraldic animals, vases, capitals. Also bought four statues from Coade, for site unknown.

REBECCA, John Biagio ?-1847. *Castle Goring*, Sussex, capitals, plaques, balusters, coat of arms.

REPTON, Humphry, 1752-1818. *Blickling*, Norfolk, ornament on Orangery, *Hill Hall*, Essex, capitals, bases. *Babworth*, Notts, tomb. *Wembley Park*, London, CG. *Sundridge Park*, Bromley, Kent (with S. Wyatt and Nash). *Uppark*, Sussex, with J. Adey Repton, vases.

REPTON, John Adey, 1775-1860. *Uppark*, Sussex, with father; urns. *Bethlehem Hospital*, Lambeth, London, coat of arms.

RHODES, Henry, ?-1846. *Egham Church*, Surrey, vane ornament. *Farnley Hall*, Yorks, fountain. *Whitehall*, London four vases.

RICHARDSON, George, ?-1813. *Stapleford Church*, Leics, Gothic chimneypiece.

ROBERTS, John, (of Waterford) *Curraghmore*, Co Waterford, supporters and crest.

ROBERTSON, William. *Waterford Court House*, Co Waterford, Statue of Justice. *Orchardton*, Kilkenny, Gothic pinnacles.

ROBINSON, Samuel, 1752-1833. *St Thomas's Hospital*, London, arms of hospital, oak and palms. *House in Clapham*, London, relief panels. Site unspecified, vases. *St*

Olave's Grammar School, Tooley Street, London, ? boundary marker. *Woodford Churchyard*, Essex. Tomb.

SANDBY, Paul, 1721-1798. *Bleach Works*, Llewenny, Denbs, reclining figures. *St Leonard's Hill*, Windsor, Berks, keystones.

SANDERS, John, 1768-1826. Capitals, *Brixton Hill*, Surrey.

SANDYS, Francis. *Ickworth*, Suffolk, to design of Asprucci q.v., plaques and frieze from Flaxman drawings. *Chippenham Park*, Cambs, CG.

SAUNDERS, Thomas. *Chapel Royal*, Brighton.

SAXON, Samuel 1757-? *Buckminster Park*, Leics, CG. *Courteenhall*, Northants, CG.

SEARLES, Michael, 1750-1813. *Clare House*, East Malling, Kent, capitals *Paragon*, Blackheath, London, capitals, bases, string course, rusticated quoins. *Paragon*, New Kent Road, (dem.) similar. *Colonnade House*, Blackheath, London, capitals. *Paragon House*, South Row, Blackheath, frieze and plaque. *Surrey Square*, Walworth, London, architectural details.

SIMPSON, Archibald, 1790-1847. *Clydesdale Bank*, Aberdeen, figure and lion.

SMIRKE, Sir Robert, 1780-1867. *Brightling Park*, Sussex (originally called Rose Hill), Gothic garden feature in grounds.

SMITH, Charles S, c.1790-? *Regent Hotel*, Leamington, Warks, Regent's Arms. *Warwick?* Monument for Wratislaw.

SOANE, Sir John, 1753-1837. *Adam's Place*, Southwark, London, frieze. *Pett's Hill*, Sussex, CG. *Earsham*, Norfolk, capitals, medallion. *Langley Park*, Norfolk, chimneypots and paterae. *Cuffnells*, Hants, plaques. *Shotesham Park*, Norfolk, capitals. *Wood Eaton*, Oxon, frieze and capitals. *Tyringham*, Bucks, CG. *Albury Park*, Surrey, capitals. *Bramley Church*, Hants, Gothic window. *Buckingham House*, Pall Mall, London, caryatids. *Brewery*, Bridge Street, Reading, lions etc. *Bank of England*, London, caryatids, vases, statues. *Pitzhanger Manor*, Ealing, London, caryatids, statues, figures. *Moggerhanger House*, Beds, balusters. *Everton House*, Biggleswade, Beds, balusters. 13 *Lincoln's Inn Fields*, London, caryatids. *Royal Hospital*, Chelsea, London, coat of arms. *Board of Trade*, London, decorative details. *House of Lords*, Royal Entrance, London, scagliola columns. *Freemasons' Hall*, London, scagliola columns. *Taverham Hall*, Norfolk. *Board of Trade and Law Courts*, Westminster.

STEPHENSON, David, 1757-1819. *Percy Tenantry Column*, Alnwick, Northumbs, lions. *All Saints Church*, Newcastle, Northumbs, font. *Newcastle Theatre*, trophy of arms. *Scale or Kale Cross*, lions and vases. Originally in Newcastle, given back to *Blagdon House*, now entrance.

STEUART, George, c.1730-1806. Isle of Man – *Castle Mona*, plaques. *Douglas Court House* and *Guard House*, plaques. *Ramsay Court House* and *Guard House*, plaques. *Obelisk Kirk Braddon Churchyard*, plaques.

STONE, Francis, 1775-1835. *Hoveton Hall*, Norfolk, scagliola columns.

STUART, James "Athenian", 1713-1788. *Royal Naval Hospital, Greenwich*, London, Chapel and Antechapel, capitals, figures, coats of arms, plaques, with William Newton. *Belvedere*, Kent, CG.

TASKER, John, c.1738-1816. *East Lulworth Church*, Dorset, urns and vases. *Acton Burnell Hall*, Salop, Ionic capitals, large trusses. *Norfolk House*, St James's, London, 50 Ionic blocks. Site unknown, two rich trophies, 108 balusters. *East Lulworth Castle*, lions.

TATHAM, Charles Heathcote, 1772-1842. *Northwick Park*, Glos, plaque with lion now at Parham, Sussex. *Henerton House*, Berks, two crests, two bases, chimneypots, coral rock. *35 Alpha Road*, Lisson Grove, London, four pineapples, bust of Wesley. The Roman thrones now at *Parham House*, copied from Tatham's engraving.

TAYLOR, James, c.1765-1846. *New Terrace* (now Duncan Terrace), Islington, London, keystones.

TAYLOR, John. *Chessel House*, Hants, CG. *Bannister Lodge*, Hants, CG.

TAYLOR, Sir Robert, 1714-1788. *Gorhambury*, Herts, capitals. *Heveningham Hall*, Suffolk, plaques, figures, lions, capitals, keystones. *Danson Park*, Kent, chimneypots.

TAYLOR, Thomas, c.1778-1826. *Court House*, Leeds, plaques, blocks, vases, capitals, modillions, stove.

THOMPSON, M G. *Harwich Church*, Essex, pinnacles. *Lexden Church*, Essex, pinnacles.

THORNTON, Dr William. *The Octagon*, Washington DC, two chimneypieces, capitals and bases.

TYLER, William ?-1801. *Villa Maria House*, Kensington, London, CG.

UPTON, John. Main block of *Pettshill*, Sussex, added to by Soane, CG.

VALDRÉ (VALDRATI), Vincenzo, c.1742-1814. *Stowe*, Bucks, Lodges at the Oxford Gate.

VULLIAMY, Lewis 1791-1871. *Syston Hall*, Lincs, candelabra on stand. Fountain. Scagliola pedestals, *Pall Mall*, London

WATSON, Charles, c.1770-1836. *The Court House and Gaol* (now called Sessions House), Beverley, Yorks. Royal Arms, Statue of Justice.

– WELLAND and – BOWDEN. *Court House*, Monaghan, Ireland, coat of arms

WILDS, Amon Henry. *Park Crescent*, Worthing, 1829. Triumphal entrance arch, with terms.

WILKINS, William, Senior, 1751-1815. *Donington Hall*, Leics, CG.

WILKINS, William, Junior, 1778-1839. *Downing College*, Cambridge, scagliola pilasters. *Dalmeny House*, Lothians, Gothic battlements, plaques, coats of arms. *Dunmore Castle*, Falkirk, Scotland, scagliola. *Thoresby Hall*, Notts, chimney caps. *Nelson Monument*, Great Yarmouth, Norfolk, Victories and Britannia. *Keswick Hall*, Norfolk. Arms.

WOOLLEY, Samuel. Gateway given as Castletown by Coade but at *Glananea*, Co Westmeath, now rebuilt at Rosmead. *Colonnade*, crest (a horse), capitals, statues, etc.

WRIGHT, Stephen, ?-1780. *Clumber*, Notts, gate screen with 25 vases.

WRIGHT, Thomas, 1711-1786. Wings at *Shugborough*, Staffs, with antefixae from Piranesi qv now removed but surviving.

WYATT, Benjamin Dean, 1775-c.1855. *Apsley House*, London, scagliola columns. For Earl Rivers (site unknown) scagliola columns. *Maresfield Park*, Sussex, crest, two lions. *Bodorgan*, Anglesey, vase. *Bangor*, Caerns, see below.

WYATT, James, 1746-1813. *Heaton Park*, Manchester, capitals, paterae, string course. *The Pantheon*, Oxford Street, London, capitals, paterae, arms. *Sheffield Park*, Sussex, Gothic pinnacles, coat of arms. *Ottershaw Park*, Surrey, lodges, plaques. *Lucan House*, Co Kildare, *Brocklesby Park*, Lincs, monument *Stanmer Park*, Sussex, monument. *Mount Edgcombe*, Cornwall, monument. *Erddig*, Denbighshire, Druid? *Stoke Poges House*, Bucks, plaques and monument to Coke. *Blagdon*, Northumbs, CG. *Bryanston*, Dorset, CG. *Goodwood Estate*, Sussex, coats of arms. *Hurstbourne Priors*, Hants, gateway. *Wilton House*, Wilts, cloister plaques. *Radcliffe Observatory*, Oxford, capitals, plaques, paterae. *Charlton Park*, Wilts, plaques. *Cobham Hall*, Kent, vases, coat of arms. *1 Foley Place*, London, plaques, capitals consoles, balusters.

Pishiobury Park, Herts, chimneypiece. *Milton Abbey Church,* Dorset, font. *Grove House,* Roehampton Surrey, plaques *Henham Hall,* Suffolk, CG. *Heveningham Hall,* Suffolk, Orangery figures and plaques, lodge frieze. *Hothfield Place,* Kent, statues *Town Hall,* Liverpool, Britannia. *Bowden Park,* Wilts, figures. *Chicksands Priory,* Beds, candelabra figures as Frogmore? chimneypiece plaques? *Frogmore House,* Windsor, candelabra figures. *Purley Park,* Reading, Berks, CG *Copped Hall,* Essex, CG. *Croome d'Abitot,* Worcs, Druid, sphinxes, rusticated "Dry Arch Bridge", gateway with vases. *Bangor,* Caerns, CG. *Chiswick House Bridge,* paterae, plaques. *Sunning Hill Park,* Berks, CG. *Elvaston Castle,* Derbys., vase. *Burton on Trent Town Hall,* frieze, coat of arms.

WYATT, Lewis, 1777-1853. *Willey Hall,* Salop, scagliola columns. *Tatton Park,* Cheshire, tripod.

WYATT, Philip ?-1835. *Conishead Priory,* Ulverston, Lancs, (now Cumbria) tablet, statue.

WYATT, Samuel, 1737-1807. *Doddington Hall,* Cheshire, plaques, medallions. *Hooton Hall,* Cheshire, plaques, medallions. *Tatton Park,* Cheshire, tripod, CG. (Completed by Lewis Wyatt), *Temple Park,* Hurley, Berks, CG. *Hurstmonceux Place,* Sussex, plaques, *Kinmel Park,* Denbighs, (now Clwyd) CG. *Penrhyn Castle,* Caerns, (now Gwynedd) CG. *Trinity House,* London, plaques and arms. *Trinity Almshouses,* Mile End road, London, coat of arms. *Birmingham Theatre,* plaques. *Belmont,* Faversham, Kent, plaques, string courses, vases, capitals. *Holkham,* Norfolk, Vinery and East Lodge, plaques, string courses. *Episcopal Palace,* St Asaph, Flints, (now Clwyd) CG. *Shugborough,* Staffs, capitals, plaque? Druid? *Soho House,* Birmingham capitals.

WYATVILLE, Sir Jeffry, 1766-1840. *Belton House,* Lincs, balusters for Orangery. *Longleat,* Wilts, CG.

WYNNE, J. or M. *Hexton House,* Herts ("Wynne architect") urns, basin for fountain, two eagles.

YENN, John, 1750-1821. *Royal Hospital Greenwich,* Arms of Hospital for Trafalgar Block.

AVON (see Somerset)

BEDFORDSHIRE

ALAMEDA, Ampthill. Pair of urns, Somerset House design, placed on gateposts c.1921 by Sir Albert Richardson (Simon Houfe)*

COOPER'S HILL, Ampthill. CG refers to Ampthill. Gunnis mentions urns at Cooper's Hill, but house not traced.

CHICKSANDS PRIORY CG, *Biggleswade.* House altered JAMES WYATT 1813. Gothic quatrefoil frieze appears to be artificial stone, S. and E. sides. Added between 1781 and 1812 – information RCHM.CO December 1815 "Statue of a sleeping nymph on a mattress and plinth £21". Survives, decapitated.* CO March 1816 "Statue of Livia, 40 guineas" only bottom of legs and feet survive in garden. CO May 1817 "An eagle from one in the British Museum £11.2s.8d." Missing. A gothic candelabrum and a group of three girls as West Wycombe in 1890s photo of hall; now both in private collection. Plaques "Roman Procession" and "Bacchanalian Procession" both probably from chimneypieces, built into passage wall.

EVERTON HOUSE, Biggleswade. House altered and extended by *SIR JOHN SOANE.* Demolished. CO, six whole balusters, two half, 42s. 1813.

STOCKWOOD HOUSE, Luton. Demolished 1964. Luton Museum contains coats of arms of the Crawley and Wells families and some scrollwork. Two Keystones ("Greek God and Goddess") now stored by Luton Recreation Services Department. Borough Planning Officer dates the pieces as 1850, comments on late date but believes fairly well established.

LUTON HOO CG, *Luton.* 1763 onwards reconstruction by *ROBERT ADAM.* No Coade work remaining, Undated drawing, Book 39, no.34 R. Adam, Sir John Soane's Museum, shows exterior with statues in niches, roundels above, coat of arms and supporters in pediment.

MELCHBOURNE PARK, (near Kimbolton). CO May 1814 "Lord St John. A bason 3ft 2ins high 1ft 2ins deep. 12 guineas". Piece not identified.

MOGGERHANGER HOUSE, near Bedford, (now Park Hospital.) House by *SIR JOHN SOANE,*

1808. Balustrade (Gunnis).* Soane drawing, Sir John Soane's Museum, Drawer III, 44. Shows balustrade.

SOUTHILL. Very small Coade spaniel,* (Humphrey Whitbread).

WOBURN ABBEY, Woburn. House by *FLITCROFT, HOLLAND* and others. Chimneypots 1789 (Gunnis).

WREST HALL, (now Park) near Ampthill. Jacobean house, rebuilt early 18th century and 1836-7. CG. George IV's vase and pedestal, pair to that in Kew Gardens. No information on how it got there from Royal Lodge, Windsor. (John Davis.)

BERKSHIRE

ALDERMASTON HOUSE, near Newbury. CO June 1815, for William Congreve, "shield 1ft square". Original house mostly burnt.

ASCOT. CG. Two sections of the Borghese Vase bas-relief were on the early 19th century White Cottages, High Street, until demolition in 1973. Information Dorothy Stroud. They may have come from the building referred to in CG which could have been Ascot Place.

ASCOT PLACE. Half hexagon summer house with Gothic decoration. (Roger White and Julia Abel Smith.)

BEAUMONT LODGE: See Old Windsor

BINFIELD PLACE, near Wokingham. CG. CO 1814, "7 balusters as before". CD June 1814 "Mrs Stephenson, Binfield Place, Windsor, balusters etc. £3.4s.8d." Binfield Place is a late Jacobean house, now ruined.

BRADFIELD HALL, near Reading. CG. House of 1763. Coade not traced.

*BUCKLAND CHURCH, ST MARY, near Faringdon (now in Oxfordshire)** Memorial to Elizabeth Perfect, died 1802. Weeping putti by an urn, marked Coade and Sealy (Pevsner).

BUSCOT PARK (*now in Oxfordshire*) X* Pair of life size Egyptian male figures wearing Pharaoh-type headdresses, and with one foot advanced. Marked Coade and Sealy 1800. Copies of the figure of Antinous (now in the Vatican) made for the Emperor Hadrian at the Villa Adriana. Possibly from Thomas Hope's collection since many of his pieces were bought for this house c.1930.

COLESHILL CHURCH, ALL SAINTS near Faringdon * Monument to Mark Stuart Pleydell, 1802. Marked Coade and Sealy wrongly spelt Seeley. "Tall elaborate Gothic canopy" (Pevsner). Information on date from Rev. R.C. Swanborough. Dark grey colour – paint or stain.

EASTHAMPSTEAD, Bracknell. CD December 1819, for the Marquess of Downshire, through his architect Thomas Cundy, "4 scagliola columns and 4 pilasters, with statuary scagliola capitals and bases, £194.6s.0d." House rebuilt, 1860.

FROGMORE QUEEN'S LODGE, Windsor Park. CG "An elegant tripod or pedestal of three lights, with branches of foliage, on lion's feet, and three female figures, or small caryatides, in recesses between the foliage, supporting a vase or lamp, modelled for the Queen's Lodge at Frogmore near Windsor from a design by Mr James Wyatt". Not traced, but see West Wycombe Park, Bucks.

HENERTON HALL. House for C.F. Johnson by *C.H. TATHAM.* Demolished. CO 1817, four fluted chimneypots; 1818, "two crests for piers of bears and coronets, coral stand supporting basin, two large squat vases" for £106.5s.0d. 1819, "a plain vase with vineleaves" 18 guineas. A very battered bear head discovered by R. Breakell.

HIGHCLERE CASTLE (now in Hampshire). CG. Built 18th century, rebuilt by *BARRY* in 19th century. Work not now identifiable – possibly for the park designed by Capability Brown.

HORNTON, near Reading. Letter book shipping notes at end 7.7.1813 "on barge for Reading 2 cases of 4 chimneytop pedestal and 1 case containing a bason for Hornton." Not traced.

MAIDENHEAD. CG. Possibly Oldfield Lodge, Bridge Road, with gate piers with paterae (Pevsner).

NEWBURY. CO for Billing and Son, February 1815 "36 whole ballusters and 6 half, to be directed to Fredk Page Esq, Newbury".

OLD WINDSOR CHURCHYARD*, ST PETER. CD May 1818 for the monument to Esther Jane, widow of R. B. Sheridan. Tomb chest with reliefs of laurel and torches. It cost £63.1s.0d. She was the daughter of Newton Ogle, of Kirkley, Northumberland qv.

OLD WINDSOR, BEAUMONT LODGE* CG. *HENRY EMLYN* had, from Coade, "British Order" capitals of his own invention and ornaments, also statues*. CO, for Lord Weymouth, June 1821, "A fountain with three basins, three dolphins, etc".

PURLEY PARK, Reading. CG. House by *JAMES WYATT.* CO "A.G. Storer Esq. Purley Park, Reading, 2 Venus lamp figures, bronzed £46.4s.0d." Now called Purley House. Letter of 27 August 1813 (p.16) saying that the previous acct presumably the CG reference, was for £101.

BRIDGE STREET (now called Seven Bridges House), Reading. Gunnis "decorative details 1793". House by *SIR JOHN SOANE* 1791. Drawings Sir John Soane's Museum, Drawer II.6. No Coade work remains.

READING. Letter to Messrs Billing and Son, Builders, Reading. Letter Book p.13. Asks for payment of 1812 bill £36.13s.0d. Letter repeated 11.8.1813.

STOKE. CG. Possibly a mistake for Stoke Park, Buckinghamshire, qv.

ST LEONARD'S HILL [sic: actually at Dedworth], Windsor. CG. CD September 1815 "two heads, nun and friar" for – Dawson Esq., for £5.12s.0d." House almost entirely rebuilt.

SELWOOD PARK, Sunninghill. ROBERT MITCHELL for Sir James Sibbald. 1796. Hall exactly as at Preston Hall (same architect) with Coade lamp-holding figures, Engraving in Scottish National Monuments Record (Preston Hall file. X5D 16/3). Demolished.

SULHAMSTEAD, near Reading. CG. Sulhamstead House?

SUNNINGHILL PARK. CG. Altered by JAMES WYATT, demolished. CO April 1814, "Mr. Crawford, Sunninghill, price of piping boy and pedestal, 26gn."

COWORTH HOUSE, Sunninghill. Letter book shipping notes at end. ". . . from Paul's Wharf for Egham, 3 cases containing 12 chimney tops for Mr Wm. Sandleford, Coworth House near Sunning Hill" 21.4.1813. Not traced.

TEMPLE HOUSE, Hurley. (called Bucks by Mrs Coade) CG. House by SAMUEL WYATT, 1790. Demolished.

WHITE KNIGHTS, near Reading. Extensive work done by Coade and Sealy before 1813. Croggon sent bills (undetailed) to the Marquess of Blandford in October 1814 for £387.14s.0d., and in June 1815 for £479.2s.7d. In 1814, Dubbin was sent "to fix shells about the grotto"; in 1815 special chimneypots were supplied for the Hot House, and a Medicean Vase. All the work seems to have been for the famous gardens. Letter book 7.7.1813 Acct rendered £275.17s.0d. and 7.9.1813, Acct rendered £362.6s.0d. Shipping notes 21.4.1813, one case of 25 pipes for Marquis of Blandford Lewis Barge for Reading. Mrs Hofland "*A Descriptive Account of the Mansion and Garden of Whiteknights* 1819, refers to the library (2nd room) with scagliola plasters, sculptures with scagliola bases, 4 lions conchant on scagliola bases, both rooms skirted with scagliola." Croggon?

WINDSOR CASTLE X. *St George's Chapel** CG. Coade screen designed *HENRY EMLYN*, 1790-2. Three statues, on W. front, designed *HENRY EMLYN*, 1799. Font, 1790s, (demolished in 19th century). See chapter on Commissions for the Crown. *Royal Apartments*, Drawing Room. Royal Arms, 1804 (Gunnis). *Royal Lodge*. Medici and Borghese Vases with specially designed plinths* to the order of *JOHN NASH*, 1825 (Windsor Archives 26736). One now at Kew gardens, the other at Wrest Park, Bedfordshire. No information on how they reached these places. *Windsor Barracks*, Royal Arms. NP. Not surviving.

WINDSOR. Shipping notes in Letter Book "Barge for Windsor, 2 cases of 33 Balusters for Mrs Stevenson. 1813." Not traced.

NEWINGTON HOUSE, *Winkfield** CG. Late 18th century house, with two urns and four oval paterae between ground and first floor.

BUCKINGHAMSHIRE

BUCKINGHAM. Bridge. On E. side, plaque with Marquess of Buckingham's arms, marked Coade and Sealy 1805. On the W. side, a plaque with the Swan of Buckingham, marked Coade and Sealy 1809. Information from George Clarke.

DORETON HOUSE (*modern Dorton*) *west of Aylesbury*. CG. Jacobean house altered 1784. Work not now identifiable.

HIGH WYCOMBE, Guildhall*, by *HENRY KEENE*, 1757. Town's coat of arms* added to the pediment at some later date.

ST MARY LANGLEY MARISH CHURCH, *Slough*. CG. Screen of Harvey Chapel*, Gothic, 1792, probably designed by *HENRY EMLYN* (Colvin); Harvey Monument (mourning Vestal)*, 1788. (Pevsner).

LITTLE MARLOW MANOR HOUSE (*also Court Garden, Marlow*). CD. Statues of Lord Nelson and Lord Gardner (150 guineas each) supplied to Lord Gardner and erected at Little Marlow Manor House, April 1815. Statue of Lady Gardner and two children (200 guineas) ordered for the Manor House, April 1810 but erected at Court Garden, October 1815. Not traced. Lord Gardner died the same year. (Buckingham County Archivist, Mr E.J. Davis).

RITCHINGS, near Slough CG. Ritchings estate built over, but reference must be to *Iver Lodge**, Bangors Road South, Iver, on the edge of the former Ritchings estate. Two storey house of S. Wyatt type, bays on front, bows on back. String Course,* of "enriched guiloche" on the bows, extends back to form the window sills. One stamped Coade Lambeth 1792. On the bays, the String Course is slightly set forward and surrounded by a plain band, like a window box. Small oblong panel with griffins* as on Boodles Club St James. In hall a chimneypiece, now heavily painted, with frieze of bucrania,* appears to be Coade.

ALL SAINTS SOULBURY CHURCH, near Leighton Buzzard. Monument to Eleanor Lovett,* 1786. Reclining figure with elbow on an urn. Gothic panel below with inscriptions. (Pevsner.)

STOKE PARK, Stoke Poges. CG. House designed by *JAMES WYATT* c.1801-8. Staircase has plaques "probably of Coadeware stone" (A. Dale, *James Wyatt* p72).* Letter to John Penn, Stoke Park near Windsor 7 January 1813 (p1) offering busts of Chaucer, Lock, Boyle at 12gns each. *Memorial Column* to Sir Edward Coke*, designed by *JAMES WYATT*, 1801. Coade *statue* by Rossi on 60ft Doric column (Lipscomb's Bucks, vol.4, page 552).

STOWE, near Buckingham. Lodges* at Buckingham end of Grand Avenue have Coade plaques and chimneys, the Oxford Lodges* have coats of arms. The "rich Gothic monument with pinnacles etc", CD, December 1814, costing £225, was probably the large Gothic Cross described in handbooks to the house (George Clarke). Only parts of the base remain. There was also a sarcophagus copied from one at Stowe shown in Coade's Gallery, and lions on the portico of the house. Medici lions on the S portico, recumbent lions on the N portico. See *Stowe, a description of the house and grounds* by J. Seeley 1791, p.52. The Oxford Lodges designed by *Vincenzo Valdré* have Coade heraldry.

TAPLOW COURT, Taplow. CG. Urns* on gate piers with flames for Resurrection coming from the tops. Probably originally the entrance to the demolished church.Statue of George III as a Roman Emperor* in front of the house. Marked Coade and Sealy 1804 but same as 1809 figure at the Bargate Southampton (qv). Taplow Court with adjoining Cliveden belonged to Lord Inchiquin. The figure stands on a pedestal like several at Cliveden. (Martin Drury.)

TYRINGHAM, near Newport Pagnell. CG. *SIR JOHN SOANE*, 1792-7 for William Mackworth Praed. Soane drawing, Soane Museum, Drawer III 5, shows balustrade all round roof, panels of Greek key, and very plain Ionic capitals, probably Coade. House much altered c.1900, capitals now different. Figure of Father Time (as Rochester) on sundial.*

WEST WYCOMBE PARK, *near High Wycombe* *X. Four Torchères of three figures each now in dining room, prior to 1781, when described as "4 Composition Therms, Designed and Executed in a Masterly Stile" in inventory.* Probably the James Wyatt design.

CAMBRIDGESHIRE

ANGLESEY ABBEY, *near Lode* X. St George and the Dragon* put on porch in 1926. Six caryatids* marked Coade Lambeth 1793, in garden; originally bronzed and probably from Buckingham House, Pall Mall*. Figure of Father Time as at Rochester, Tyringham.*

CAMBRIDGE *Downing College*ated Designed by WILLIAM WILKINS. CO 1819, "14 flat pilasters, 16' 10ʺ"*, same imitation of giallo antico as Covent Garden", CD columns £340. July 1820. 14 bases in statuary scagliola, £62.* In College Hall.

> *St John's College.* Pedestal for fountain comprising birds, water lilies etc ordered by Professor Calvert, Cambridge. Letter book (p.462) Drawing sent 27.4.1820. Fountain sent 26.5.21 (p.483) CD £28.8s.0d.

GROVE HOUSE, *Trumpington Street.* CO. April 1814 "6 ionic capitals ancient Grecian order at 5gns. each" through Arthur Browne for Christopher Pemberton. *WILLIAM CUSTANCE*, Surveyor and builder of Chesterton, Cambs, probably designed and built 2 Cambridge Villas, *Pemberton's Grove Lodge* and *The Grove.* Colvin II RCHM Cambridge CXXIX pp 347, 354, plate 299.

CHIPPENHAM PARK, *north of Newmarket.* CG. House rebuilt by *F. SANDYS*, 1800. Rebuilt again 1886. Coade work not traced.

ST MARY MADINGLEY CHURCH,* *near Cambridge.* Royal Arms 1802* (Pevsner).

CHESHIRE

CAPESTHORNE*, *near Macclesfield* X. House of 1861 by *SALVIN*. Two Coade chimneypieces from family house in Belgrave Square (Lady Bromley Davenport), but they must have had another setting between their manufacture (1789) and the building of the Square in 1825-40. One has Faith, Hope, Charity and the Paraclete; the other has Herculaneum figures and the Aldobrandini Marriage. (Pevsner).

DODDINGTON HALL*, *south of Crewe*. SAMUEL WYATT, 1777-98. CG. See C. Hussey *Mid Georgian* plates 322, 323. Oblong plaques as at front of 20 Portman Square and round medallions as at back of this house. In centre of bow plaque of the Florentine lion. Another plaque not identified.

HOOTON HALL, *Wirral (now Merseyside)*. SAMUEL WYATT, 1778. CG. House demolished. Pevsner mentions surviving lodges with wreath and garland panels.* Gunnis mentions reliefs by Bacon for Hooton Hall. Henry Clay in *Connoisseur,* p79-87 October 1928, *Coade's Artificial Stone,* shows photographs of the putti on dolphins medallions at Hooton and dates them 1788.

OLLERTON LODGE, *Knutsford, School Lane, Ollerton*. Royal Coat of Arms made for Woollen and Cotton Manufacturers United. Coade and Sealy 1804. 15ft by 5ft 6ins. Now on stables (J. Duxfield and J. Mather).

NANTWICH. CG. Nothing identified

PULFORD, *near Chester*. Grosvenor Arms. Large figures of the British Lion trampling on the French Eagle. Made for Geo Palmer of St James's Street, London qv in 1815 for 45gns. Its route to Pulford unknown.

TATTON PARK X, *Knutsford*. Tripod dated 1815, with sphinxes, bronzed (Brian Austen)*. A replica of this, unbronzed, in a private collection.

CORNWALL

CAERHAYS, *St Michael's Church, near Mevagissey*. Capt Bettesworth, Coade and Sealy, 1812 (bronzed)*. Statue in naval uniform (Cyril Staal). Capt. Bettesworth buried at Howick Northumberland but the figure erected by his Trevanion relations. He was a cousin of Lord Byron who much admired him. Charlotte Trevanion, monument*, 1810; two mourning putti in Gothic gable (Pevsner).

CALLINGTON,*near Calstock*. CG. Nothing traced, probably Whiteford, Callington, q.v.

TRELOWARREN, *Falmouth*. CD November 1813. "V. Vyvyan Esq., two Medicean Vases, 14 gns."* (damaged). Urns not Medicean but similar to Somerset House (R. Breakell).

ILLOGAN. Statue of Farnese Flora, now at Tehidy Park, at Illogan in 1813. (Dugdale's *New British Traveller* 1813 vol 1.)

ST MICHAEL LAWHITTON CHURCH, north of Calstock. Richard Coffin, died 1796. Monument with woman reclining on sarcophagus, and putti at each end*. Putti out of scale (Cyril Staal). Marked Coade and Sealy Lambeth.

MOUNT EDGCOMBE. Cremyll, Torpoint, Cornwall. Monument to Timothy Brett d.1791. Friend of Earl of Mount Edgcombe. Same design as the memorials at Stanmer Park, Brocklesby Park and Lucan House.

THE EGYPTIAN HOUSE, Penzence, Chapel Street. Egyptian figures, columns, winged serpents and mouldings of Coade stone c.1835*. Architect Foulston of Plymouth. (Paul Pearn, architect for restoration.)

ST AUSTELL. CG. but no Coade work found.

TEHIDY PARK, Truro. Statue of Flora,* c.1785. (Gunnis; mentioned Britten's *Cornwall,* page 506.) Surviving but resited from Illogan. *A Tyger modelled from nature for Sir Francis Bassett at Tehidy Park" and "its companion", exhibited in Coade's Gallery 1799, modelled John Bacon (gone). House now a hospital.

TRURO, Assembly Rooms and Theatre. CG. Built 1772. Medallions of Garrick and Shakespeare (Cyril Staal)*. Also a Muse plaque* and an oblong with pair of griffins*. One medallion has been described as Handel, but appears to be Garrick. *Infirmary** Dated 1799. CG. "Over the door is a shield with the Cornish arms supported by "curtains" depending from ribands. Higher is a well-modelled Prince of Wales feathers"* (Cyril Staal).

WHITEFORD, near Callington. CG. House demolished. Garden pavilion, now a farm building, has medallions of Ceres* and America*, battered but still exant (Cyril Staal). Restored by Landmark Trust.

CUMBERLAND

(Now Cumbria)

CARLISLE. CG. Nothing identified. May refer to Corby Castle qv.

CORBY CASTLE, near Carlisle. Pele-tower* remodelled by *PETER NICHOLSON,* 1812-17. CG. Bas-relief of Apollo*, and two medallions* of earth and water, CD August 1815, on lodge, £34.13s, a medallion of Diana*, including case and charges, 12 guineas. CO July 1818. Both orders for the Hon. Henry Howard. Letter book 8 June 1813, shipping notes at end "Two standing lions for Henry Howard Esq. Corby Castle, Carlisle". Also pre-1799 work not identified. Lions* on the two Nicholson fronts of the house.

IRTON PLACE, *near Whitehaven.* Shipping notes at end of Letter book advise despatch of three cases to Irton Esq, Irton Place near Whitehaven, 28.8.1813, and "Mr Irton's two cases" to John Mackinney Esq, Duke St, Whitehaven on 30.9.1813. Not traced.

DERBYSHIRE

BARLBOROUGH HALL Coat of arms*(J.H. Cordingley)

BELPER. CG. 1799. Nothing identified.

ELVASTON CASTLE, *near Derby.* Reconstruction designed by *JAMES WYATT,* carried out 1817. Medicean Vase (35 guineas), two other vases (30 guineas) supplied to Lord Harrington, CD, December 1814. A Borghesian Vase*, £47.3s.2d, CD October 1818. The latter is now at Barnby Manor, Newark, Nottinghamshire, qv.

KEDLESTON X *(Kiddlestone to Coade), near Derby.* ROBERT ADAM, 1765-70. CG. Medicean and Borghesian Vases supplied probably in 1771. At the top of the steps on the south front*.

DEVONSHIRE

ARLINGTON. CG. Probably refers to Arlington Court by JOHN MEADOWS c.1790 for J.P. Chichester (Colvin II). House rebuilt.

BAMPTON, *11 Fore Street.** Coade keystone (J.A. Havill).

BICKLEIGH CASTLE. A vase similiar to that at Killerton (qv) but smaller (J.A. Havill).

BICTON PARK . Three Coade stone busts, of Nelson, Sir Walter Raleigh and Wellington (?) (John Davis). Nelson and Raleigh dated Coade and Sealy 1806 on Orangery.* (J.A. Havill).

CREEDY HALL. CG. Not identified.

DEVONPORT. Egyptian Library by *JOHN FOULSTON* 1823. Details same as those on Egyptian House Penzance qv.

EFFORD. CG. An Efford on the outskirts of Plymouth, nothing identified. Also an Ebford on outskirts of Exeter near Topsham. Home of Matthew Lee, friend of George Coade and agent for Enchmarch family. Nothing identified.

EXETER, (unnamed customer). CO August 1815, "three comic heads for keystones". CO July 1819, "four Ionic capitals in O.S. dia. at top [sic] from Temple of Ilyssus at Athens"; 12 guineas each sent to Exeter per Russett's wagon. CO January 1820 " four Ionic caps at eight gns", £37.3s.8d., including packing.

EXETER CATHEDRAL. "The Great West Window of Exeter Cathedral by Coade about eight or nine years ago, under Mr Soane, was from designs by Mr Carter." (*Gentleman's Magazine,* October 1817, page 365). Actually 1802-3. (Assistant Librarian, Exeter Cathedral Library). No Coade work survives.

MR GOLDWORTHY'S HOUSE, Exeter. CD August 1821, "Goldsworthy Exeter, Statue of Neptune and Seahorse £44". Not traced.

WYVERN BARRACKS, Exeter. Very large Royal Arms c.12' x 10' marked Coade and Sealy 1806.* NP refers to it as Exeter Guard House.

SOUTHERNHAY, Exeter, Small block opposite Devon and Exeter Hospital with lion head keystones.*

SOUTHERNHAY EAST, Exeter. Long terrace with numerous Coade human head keystones to front doors. 1805-1825.*

SOUTHERNHAY WEST, Exeter. As Southernhay East.*

FORE STREET HEAVITREE, near Magdalen Road, Exeter.* Two houses with Coade door surrounds as Bedford Square (Pevsner).

SIDNEY TERRACE, Alphington Street, Exeter.* Door surrounds as at Southernhay (J.A. Havill).

MAGDALEN TERRACE, Exeter. Row of several later 18th century houses with keystones on the wall between windows and doors.*

7 SALUTARY PLACE, Belmont Road, Exeter. Coade details (J.A. Havill)

5 AND 7 PALACE GATE, Exeter. Coade details (J.A. Havill).

6 AND 14 CHURCH STREET, St Thomas, Exeter. Coade details (J.A. Havill).

MR ROGERS, Veterinary Surgeon, Exeter. CO October 1819 "Mr Rogers, Exeter, a horse to be modelled on a panel 5' x 4', 20 gns". The bill was sent to Thomas Rogers, veterinary surgeon, March 1821. Acromonious correspondence in the Letter Book, May 1820, as Rogers said he had not ordered it.

FARWAY, near Honiton THE OLD WATERMILL. Three Coade keystones* added in 1974 on new extension (John Fowles).

HALDON. CG. See Lawrence Castle.

HALDON HOUSE. Rebuilt by Lutyens. Old house had four urns on the parapet (J.A. Havill).

ALL SAINTS HOLBETON CHURCH, south of Plymouth. Bulteel family monument*, 1801. Weeping cherub as Teigngrace (Pevsner).

KILLERTON, near Exeter. House by *JOHN JOHNSON* 1799, later extended. Pair of vases in garden with Borghese figures on large amphora shape. Marked Coade and Sealy and said to be dated 1805, but this mark not seen. Ancient photograph in Sir John Soane's Museum shows one vase with reference to "European Magazine 1802 vol 41 page 2".

LAWRENCE CASTLE, near Dunchideock. Also called Haldon Belvedere. CG. Triangular folly tower built 1788 by *Sir Robert Palk* in memory of General Stringer Lawrence of the East India Company. On ground floor a life size statue of the General exactly copied from the Scheemakers statue of him in Roman armour now in Commonwealth Office. Mark E. CD 1709. (1789)

LUSCOMBE CASTLE, Dawlish. Gothic castle by *JOHN NASH* 1800. Small heraldic panel with two headed eagle on the octagonal tower*.

NUTWELL. CG. Probably Nutwell Court near Exeter by *S.P. COCKERELL.* Not identified.

PLYMOUTH. Letter book 11.8.1813 (p13) to James Gould, Union Place, Plymouth for Edward Lockyer Esq. "Mr Lockyer's frontispiece was ready a fortnight or more since. It will go off in two or three days and is directed to you". Not traced.

ST MARY PLYMPTON CHURCH, near Plymouth. Monument to W. Seymour 1801*. Same putto as Teigngrace (Pevsner).

POWDERHAM CASTLE. Two Coade statues marked 1808*. Urania modified to be a Flora, and a Clio. Found one mile from Castle, 1988 (Anthony Smith, Administrator).

PRINCETOWN. The Royal Farm. Two urns with Prince of Wales feathers, marked Coade London 1797*. House built by Sir Thomas Tyrwhitt, friend of the Prince of Wales, and Duchy of Cornwall employee.

SALTRAM X, near Plymouth. CD. January 1816, "The Earl of Morley, Saltram, a coronet for arms, six gns"*. Completion of arms on south front pediment when Lord Borington became an Earl. Two plaques with heads of Pope and

Gray also in the house*. (Saltram Curator). Gate piers at entrance have horizontal oval paterae, catalogue number 370* (R. Breakell).

THE PARSON'S HOUSE, Sandford, Nr. Crediton. Keystone as Southernhay (J.A. Havill)

SHUTE MANOR HOUSE, near Seaton. CG. House of 1787. two (originally four) urns* with spiral tops (painted) in niches of quadrant walls at front.

STOVER HOUSE, near Newton Abbot. House of 1776 belonged to the Templer family, buried at Teigngrace. CG. Vase and pedestal seven ft three ins high supplied to James Templer, 1794 (Gunnis). Illustrated in *Connoisseur* March 1924, p.162. Ovoid urn with Templer/de la Pole Arms on one side, on under-sized pedestal. Then belonged to Mr R.S. Templer of Barnstaple, now via a descendant in a private collection. Set of Seasons roundels marked 1794 bought from Stover by Roma Cropper 1975.

ST PETER and ST PAUL TEIGNGRACE CHURCH (Stover to Coade) near Newton Abbot. Gothic church of 1786. CG. Monument to William and Charles Templer 1805. Putto weeping by urn, sitting on bit of fan-vaulting*. Monument to James Templer d.1813 with reclining girl*. CD "George Templer Esq, Stover House near Teignmouth, monument 80 guineas". (Unusually deep colour, pinkish brown tint). Cenotaph to Lord Nelson*. Globe with the Trafalgar Order on a ribbon across it rising from palms (?) Angel floats above. All against a dark obelisk. 1805*.

TIVERTON. CG 1799 but nothing identified.

TORQUAY, THE MOUNT and THE TERRACE. Coade doorcases c.1831 and old-fashioned for the date*. Rusticated voussoirs.

TORQUAY. BEACON HILL, nos. 3, 5, 7, 9 have Coade keystones of a cherub (Infant Hercules?) (J.A. Havill).

DORSET

ATHELHAMPTON. Duplicate of candelabrum from Carlton House*, London, qv.

BRIDPORT. CG. Nothing identified.

BRYANSTON, Blandford Forum. House by *JAMES WYATT,* replaced by one of 1890s by Norman Shaw. Victorian photograph (shown by Frances Fergusson at RIBA Seminar, 24 June 1972, shows side with circular medallions or paterae, probably the Coade pieces. Shown in *Neale's Views of Seats* 1818. (Vol. I)

CHARBOROUGH PARK. Entrance gateway with finely modelled deer on top.* (Gunnis file, Conway Library, Courtauld Institute).

ALL SAINTS DEWLISH CHUCHYARD, NE of Dorchester. Headstone to Charles Hill, died 1791, with inset Coade lunette showing putti and an urn, stamped Coade, London, 1792 (RCHM)*.

ST MARY EAST LULWORTH. Roman Catholic church in the ground of Lulworth Castle, by *JOHN TASKER*, has nine Coade vases on the exterior, 1786-7*.

LULWORTH CASTLE. Taylor Pearce Restoration Services cast some copies of Coade lions* from the Castle in 1986.

BELMONT (Bunter's Castle), Lyme Regis.* Mrs Coade took over the lease in 1784, from uncle Samuel Coade. Gate piers now in the back garden show coot, the family crest, in middle of patera. Rusticated blind arcading on ground floor, impost blocks of dolphins (not seen elsewhere) keystone of crowned king over front door (not seen elsewhere), keystones of girls' heads (standard pattern) over ground floor windows, string course, and frieze (standard patterns). Urns on cornice. Inside, string course of flute and patera runs up the stairs, and a doorcase, first floor back, has Coade detail. A fireplace, ground floor front, may have Coade ornament. Survives unaltered.

MILTON ABBAS. Village remodelled by Capability Brown. 17th century almshouses "re-erected 1779" on plaque with coat of arms above which appear to be Coade stone.

MILTON ABBEY, SE of Blandford Forum. CG. Restored by *JAMES WYATT* between 1789 and 1791. Font, a duplicate of those at St George's Windsor and at Debden, supplied probably at his order. Church re-restored by *SIR GILBERT SCOTT*, 1865. Font now removed.

POOLE. CG. mentions the town only. The reference seems to be to BEECH HURST, fine 1798 brick house with shield of arms and palm fronds in the pediment*.

SHERBORNE CASTLE X. Orangery 1779. Panels with oxskulls and paterae (F.J. Collins)*.

ST MARY, SWANAGE PARISH CHURCH. CG. Tomb of Joseph Edmonds d. 1794 in south aisle (reset as church is Victorian). Tomb chest with two putti on top, one mourning (as Teigngrace) other kneeling and pointing to a roundel with ships. Dark pyramid behind.*

WEYMOUTH. CG. Belfield c.1785 by JOHN CRUNDEN. Figure of boy with basket on goat now owned by Mr Legg, 15 High Street East, Dorchester.Statue of George III*, life-size, in Garter robes, with books and the crown on a table behind him. Life-size lion and unicorn lie at the base of the plinth. The monument, though dated 1809, was ordered in 1803, by J.H. Brown. Correspondence in Dorset Record Office. D118B X3.

ST NICHOLAS WINTERBORNE CLENSTON CHURCH*, SW of Blandford Forum. West tower directly above the porch has a panel in the lower stage with trophy of arms in high relief, probably of Coade stone. Church of 1839 (RCHM).

ST MARY WINTERBORNE STICKLAND CHURCHYARD, SW of Blandford Forum. Headstone of George L. Illington, 1782, with inserted Coade lunette as at Dewlish (RCHM)*.

WINTERBORNE WHITCHURCH, WHATCOMBE HOUSE. Armorial design with wreath and shield in lunette at front door. c.1802.*

CO DURHAM

BRAUNCEPETH CASTLE. CG. Bought 1796 by William Russell; rebuilt from 1817. Coade not identified.

LAMBTON HALL, Chester le Street. House by JOSEPH BONOMI the elder 1797, since much altered. CO July 1816 "John George Lambton Esq, Lambton Hall Durham, 19 Piccadilly, 1 shield Lord Jersey's arms, 1 do. Lord Strathmore, 1 do. his own with three crests". They cost £69.14s.8d. Not identified.

RAVENSWORTH CASTLE, Gateshead. JOHN NASH for Sir Thomas Liddell. Demolished. CO July 1814. "A Gothic chimneypiece 140gns". Shipped to Newcastle (CD August 1815 for £14.16s.8d).

SUNDERLAND. CG. Nothing identified.

WHINYARD (now Wynyard) north of Stockton. Bridge with paterae and heraldic medallions in the spandrels*. CG.

ESSEX

AUDLEY END X, near Saffron Walden. February 1772, bill for 16 guineas (Essex Record Office D.DBy A 30/2) for figures not traced; August 1772, bill for Vestal, 15 guineas and a present for Mr Bacon of £2.15s.0d., surviving* with a Sibyl in the hall chimneypiece. Originally in the Library with two others, now lost from *PLACIDO COLUMBANI'S* reconstruction (John Hardy). (ERO D.DBy A 31/9); May 1783 bill for Pedestal and Tripod* 30 guineas in garden north of house (ERO D.DBy A 41/5); bill for 2 small lions",* on steps east of the house; lion and cap of dignity*, 45 guineas, and squat vases*, £5.10s.0d., supplied April to July 1786 (ERO D.DBy A 44/11) – these are on the south gateway. July 1790, bill for packing 12 capitals, £6.10s.9d. (ERO D.DBy A 48/11); the bill for the Corinthian capitals themselves is missing – they are on *ROBERT FURZE BRETTINGHAM'S* Temple of Concord;* bill for modelling two panels* of the King George III and Queen Charlotte surrounded by graces and virtues for the frieze of this temple, 60 guineas (ERO D.DBy A 49/11, May 1791) to celebrate George III's return to sanity. Also by Coade c.1771, paterae on *ROBERT ADAM'S* Ring Temple (Ministry of the Environment)*.

BELLEVUE HOUSE, *Hale End, Walthamstow.* By *EDWARD GYFFORD* or *GIFFORD* for Charles Cooke, shown in *Designs for Elegant Cottages and Small Villas,* 1806. Demolished. CO October 1816 "A Flora and Pomona 5ft. 30 gns each, a fluted Vase, Lion's head and drapery 60s.0d."

BOREHAM HOUSE, *near Chelmsford.* Two chimneypieces, 1771. Gunnis quotes Hoare's Bank archives, but the Bank's Archivist cannot trace the bill.

BRADWELL, BRADWELL LODGE. Extension by *JOHN JOHNSON* 1781-6. Oblong plaques with reclining girls, urns and vertical oval paterae.*

CHELMSFORD, *Moulsham Bridge*.* Designed by *JOHN JOHNSON,* County Surveyor. Unaltered. Bill of 1787 (ERO Q Fab 6 East 521 Packet 25) for four oval paterae with River God's head in the centre, £14, 72 balusters at 7s, £25.4s.0d and 24 half balusters. *Shire Hall*.* CG. By *JOHN JOHNSON* 1790-2, almost unaltered outside. Capitals, large and small, small paterae, three large high relief panels by Bacon. Johnson says "all the ornamental parts in the front, including Plate XIV (detail of the 3 panels) are all finely executed in artificial stone. The last of which were modelled by the late eminent artist, J. Bacon, R.A." *Plans, Sections, Perspectives, Elevations of Essex County Hall at Chelmsford* by John Johnson 1808, plates I, XII, XIII, XIV. *Naiad Conduit*.* CG. Designed by *JOHN JOHNSON,* 1793. The Mildmay Charity "paid Mr. Johnson for Mr. Coad's bill, £108.12s.0d." (ERO) Naiad on a ring of dolphins in the style of Bacon. Originally in front of the Shire Hall. Now restored and in the Shire Hall. (Nancy Briggs.) *Cathedral (formerly Parish Church of St Mary)* Rebuilt by *JOHN JOHNSON* 1801-3. South arcade* rebuilt in Coade stone following the collapse of the church in 1800. Clerestory window tracery*, and draped female figures standing on winged cherubs between the windows also Coade;* the figures and cherubs now gilt. Font* 1801, design as St George's Windsor without the figures, now in Chelmsford Museum. The Rebuilding of Chelmsford Church, *Essex Review*, Vol. XC July 1931, Rev. J.F. Williams, M.A., F.S.A. quotes all bills etc. *Phoenix Fire Engine House.* Classical temple with Coade phoenix on the dome, erected c.1800. The phoenix* survives in the garden of Brewery House. *White Hart.* CO. June 1815. "Mr T. Durrant White Hart Chelmsford, a White Hart 20gns per waggon from Blue Boar Aldgate". Not traced.

CHIGNAL ST JAMES* , *near Chelmsford.* Coade font* 1838. (*Essex Review*, July 1931, Rev. J.F. Williams). Similar to the Chelmsford Font.

COPPED HALL, *Stifford.* CG. Altered by *JAMES WYATT* 1775. Nothing identifiable.

ST MARY THE VIRGIN and ALL SAINTS DEBDEN CHURCH, *near Saffron Walden.* CG. Font*, 1786, as St George's Windsor. Designed by *RICHARD HOLLAND.* Small shields of arms and large quatrefoil panels* with the arms of R.M.T. Chiswell and the date 1793 on the outside of the chancel he added. Designed by *JOHN CARTER.* His Gothic monument* inside. Print in folder entitled *Mint Portfolio Debden* in Essex Record Office.

DEBDEN HOUSE. CG. House by *RICHARD HOLLAND* 1795 helped by Henry, since the house is in his notebook. (Colvin). Demolished. Coade not traced. Print in *Mint Portfolio.*

DEDHAM GROVE *nr Colchester.* Letter to Jacob Elton, Dedham Grove, Colchester of 1.7.1813 (p11) Acct Jan 1813 for £41.11s.0d. Two further accounts rendered. Not traced.

GILWELL PARK, *near Chingford.* Architect *EMIL GODFREY* identified Coade stone chimneypots dated 1797 at this house. They are spiky and painted black, presumably an imitation of Cornish slate. (I.H. Stewart).

ST MARY GREAT DUNMOW CHURCH, *near Thaxted.* CG. Monuments to Lady Henniker, 1793, and Lord Henniker, 1803 (Gunnis)*. "The elevated situation of these monuments prevents the investigation of the arms". *Wright's Essex.* (Edmund Esdaile.)

ST NICHOLAS HARWICH CHURCH*. By *M. G. THOMPSON,* 1821. CD August 1821 "to the Committee for rebuilding Harwich Church, 6 Gothic pinnacles and packing £45.19s.0d" September 1821, "10 Gothic pinnacles 4' high, £63",

"2 pinnacles, 5 cants at 8gns.", October 1821 "gothic octagon pinnacle, 16gns, 3 do. 50gns."

HATFIELD PLACE*, *Hatfield Peverel. JOHN JOHNSON* 1792-4. Essex Record Office D DKE F4 and D DHF T92/76 (Nancy Briggs.) Urns, a frieze of paterae and corinthian capitals. May be copied from Johnson's unused design for Thorpe Hall, Thorpe le Soken.

HATFIELD PRIORY, *Hatfield Peverel.* Hoare's Bank account for John Wright, 22 September 1771 (ledger 84/101) to Miss Coade £8.8s.0d. Do. 20 August 1774 (ledger 90/287) to Mrs Coade £17.8s.0d. (Mrs Cowell.) The 1771 bill probably refers to four urns on pedestals shown in an 18th century print at the corners of the house.

HILL HALL, *near Epping.* CG. CD June 1815 "Sir William Smyth, Bt. Hill Hall, Epping, Mr Dubbin's attendance £3.8s.0d." Elizabethan House altered later. Giant columns on east front have bases stamped Coade Lambeth 1791*, the rest of the columns and capitals being original. In Courtyard, capitals in Coade stone* copy the originals designed by Hans Blum de qvinqve colvmnarvm, Zurich, 1550. *HUMPHRY REPTON* at Hill Hall from end 1791 to c.1795 to remodel courtyard etc. Fiery Salamander* (Smith Crest) will be replaced on gate pier. (Paul Drury.) CD. June 1815.

LANGFORD GROVE, *near Maldon.* Designed by *JOHN JOHNSON,* 1782, demolished 1953. Tripartite doorway with rusticated blocks and keystone as Bedford Square. (Nancy Briggs.)

ST LEONARD LEXDEN *(probably), near Colchester.* CO. July 1821 "Mr. Thompson for Mr. Hayward, builder, Lenden, Colchester, Essex, 2 octagon Gothic pinnacles 2' diam." No price given. Lexden Church was rebuilt 1820-21. Lenden non-existent. The same Mr Thompson designed Harwich Church.

BRIDGE END GARDENS*, *Saffron Waldon.* CG. Gateway with Coade keystone dated 1794 and inside a plaque of Borghese Dancers, Coade & Sealy 1810. House with keystone as Bedford Square.

ST MARY, WALTHAMSTOW. Solly Tomb, sarcophagus with lions' heads.* (F.J. Collins.)

THORNDON HALL, *Brentford.* House *JAMES PAINE* 1770. Gateway presumably contemporary. Cubical lodges* each with roundel with large classical head. Gate piers have 10" frieze with long swags of oakleaves and rams' heads at each corner. On top are the larger size lions with their paws drooping over the edge*.

THORPE HALL, Thorpe le Soken. See Hatfield Peverel

ST MARY WANSTEAD CHURCH*. CG. Classical church built 1790 by *THOMAS HARDWICK.* Ten Corinthian capitals to the arcades inside (bill in ERO D/P 292/28/5 for £66.17s.0d.)

ST MARY the VIRGIN WOODFORD CHURCHYARD. CG. Tomb of Edward Keepe 1782*, stamped "*S.R. ROBINSON* Archt. Coade fecit Lambeth". Much damaged. Same design as West Tarring, Sussex qv with putti at corners, urn on top.

GLOUCESTERSHIRE

BATSFORD near Moreton in Marsh. CG. Nothing traced.

BROCKHAMPTON HOUSE. Two damaged vases of Medici shape but finely-modelled vine decoration. No information on how they got there. (National Trust per J.P. Howarth.)

COMSFORD. CG. Place untraced.

ST PETER DAYLESFORD CHURCH, near Stow in the Wold. Warren Hastings rebuilt the church in 1816. CD July 1817 "Warren Hastings, 2 corbels angels' heads, £5.14s.4d." Church rebuilt again, and corbels gone. Monument to Warren Hastings in the churchyard.* Plain urn inscribed *WARREN HASTINGS* 1818. CD April 1819, "Mrs. Hastings, Hastings monument, £55.8s.4d."

DAYLESFORD HOUSE. S.P. COCKERELL 1790-6. CG (under Oxfordshire). Two Coade paterae on a garden house by the stable block.*

FAIRFORD PARK, Fairford. Orangery with Coade stone plaques,* now demolished, but the National Trust will rebuild it elsewhere. (G. Jackson Stops.)

GLOUCESTERSHIRE REGIMENT'S DEPOT*, Gloucester. Grecian sphinx wearing Egyptian sphinx head-dress.* Dismembered, but all the pieces surviving. (F.J. Collins.)

NORTHWICK PARK, near Moreton in Marsh. CHARLES TATHAM, 1832. On south front of Picture gallery, large plaque of lion, signed Croggon 1832 (Pevsner), now at Parham House, Sussex, qv.

SEZINCOTE, near Moreton in Marsh. By *S.P. COCKERELL* for his brother Sir Charles of the East India Co, as the first Indian style building in England, 1805. Temple Pool with Coade statue of Suraya;* bulls, elephants and a fountain* supplied 1813-14, and four "antique Apollos" at 40 guineas each, one of which seems to have been for East India House, London qv. Elephants gone. Two bulls survive near the Suraya Temple, the rest replaced in cast iron. Fine example of the Borghese Vase* marked Coade Lambeth, no date.

ST EDWARD STOW IN THE WOLD CHURCH. Monument to Leonard Hayward,* 1780 – small urn on bracket (Pevsner).

ST MARY TETBURY CHURCH. 1781 by *FRANCIS HIORNE.* Window tracery Coade stone.* Original contract was for the supply of Tetbury stone throughout, but Hiorne had this altered to "proper and suitable" stone (Gloucester Records Office, ref D 566 R2/5).

TORTWORTH, near Tetbury. CG. House rebuilt 1849 by *TEULON* for Lord Ducie. The Coade presumably demolished.

KINETON HOUSE, Thornbury, near Bristol (now Avon). F.J. Collins saw Grecian sphinxes in pieces in 1952. Sphinxes dated 1840 *COADE LAMBETH* reassembled and sold Sotheby's Billingshurst 1988 to Clifton, Little Venice, London W9.

HAMPSHIRE

BANNISTERS. CG. *JOHN TAYLOR* exhibited at RA a view of Bannister Lodge, Hants., in 1798. Not traced.

BEECH HOUSE. Letter Book 3.8.1813 p12, to Chas Jenkinson asking for payment of £62.0s.0d. for account of December 1810. Addressed to Ringwood, but the house at Bransgore. Not traced.

ST JOHN BOLDRE CHURCH, near Lymington. Tablet to Lieut Philip Bramfield,* died 1796. Urn, cannon, anchor etc. (F.J. Collins, Penelope Chitty.)

ST JAMES BRAMLEY CHURCH. Brocas chapel by *SOANE* 1801. Perpendicular window tracery, subsequently replaced in natural stone. (D. Stroud, *Sir John Soane*). Large drawing in Sir John Soane's Museum endorsed "for one hundred guineas to be complete in three months 27th April 1802 Coade and Sealy".

BROADLANDS X, Romsey. Alterations to Orangery by *CAPABILITY BROWN,* c.1778. Coade urn and enriched frieze.* (Dorothy Stroud *Capability Brown* 1975 p.138). Borghese vase in garden formerly in Orangery.*

CALSHOT CASTLE. Castle built by Henry VIII. CG. Coade work not identified.

CHESSEL HOUSE. CG. Design exhibited by *JOHN TAYLOR* in 1798 (demolished).

CHRISTCHURCH. CG. Nothing identified.

CUFFNELLS. CG. Alterations for George Rose by *SIR JOHN SOANE*, 1795. Demolished. Measured drawing in NMR shows seven plaques; four survive at Stratfield Saye, Hants qv.

ALL SAINTS DEANE CHURCH, near Basingstoke. Built at the expense of Wither Bramston, architect unknown. CO February 1819 lists six Gothic windows* 9ft 6in x 5ft, with labels, £240, four large pinnacles* 10' high, 2ft 3in wide, £72, six small pinnacles*, 5ft 6in high, 48 guineas. March 1819, "Gothic skreen 14'6" high to divide the church from the chancel, £312.19s.4d., Gothic cross for porch and large do. for chancel end of church, £32.17s.6d." All Coade survives except the porch cross.

EMBLEY, Romsey. The twin lodges*, c.1800, have plaques of putti similar to those in Belgrave Square, London (qv) but smaller, and in lower relief. CD May 1815 "Thomas Freeman Esq., Embley, Romsey, Hampshire, small coral fountain with shell, 14 guineas, and a further shell 3' diam, 14 gns." In December 1816 coats of arms were supplied for £9.8s.0d. House demolished in Victorian period.

FARLEIGH HOUSE, Farleigh Wallop. Mermaids with bronze combs and mirrors on gatepiers*, from Hurstbourne Priors, Hants qv.

FREEMANTLE, near Southampton. CG. Demolished. Rusticated blocks for lodge, also a "candelabrum, a most exquisite piece of workmanship, from the marble designed and executed by Mr de Vaere for John Jarrett Esq, at Freemantle near Southampton, 5' 7" high". "Two lodges were built which were surfaced with stone of Coade's manufacture ornamented with figures in bas relief of the same". *Proceedings of the Hampshire Field Club and Archaeological Society* vol 39 1983 (Kay Welham).

GRANGE, near Northington. CG. Soane Museum, *ADAM* drawings, vol. 51, no. 25, shows rusticated bridge with urns in niches, and patera-and-swag plaques as Portman Square. Possibly the Coade was used here. Design for Lord Henley. Present house 1804, reconstructed by *WILKINS*. No Coade stone traced. Inventory of 1795 listed "an artificial stone striped stand richly ornamented (near engine house)" Jane Geddes, "The Grange, Northington," *Furniture History* 1986, p198.

HURSTBOURNE PRIORS, near Andover. JAMES WYATT c.1785 for Lord Portsmouth, demolished. CG "Lord Portsmouth's Gateway". Mermaids from this now at Farleigh House qv. *European Magazine* August 1789 "Reclining girl with sheaf of corn from an original Pannel executed at Coads [sic] Artificial Stone Manufactory for the Earl of Portsmouth in Hampshire".

ITCHEN, near Southampton. CD December 1814. "Rev. I.I. Ogle c/o Nelson Alkin Southampton, for Itchen, near Southampton, monumental Vase with fluted column, ready waiting orders, £31.10s.0d." Probably for a churchyard not traced.

LAVERSTOKE, near Andover (Berkshire to Coade). CG. Built by *JOSEPH BONOMI* for H. Portal, 1799. The Ionic capitals are likely to be Coade.

LYMINGTON. "Summerset" had a Coade bacchanalian procession on a chimneypiece - the plaque bought at auction. (Robin Reilly).

MARWELL HALL, near Winchester. CO August 1817, "Wm. Long, Marwell Hall near Winchester, his arms and crest 3' 6" in height". Supplied for £17.6s.0d.

MELCHETT PARK, near Romsey. CG. Hindu temple in artificial stone with bust of Warren Hastings inside, rising from the sacred lotus flower. Designed by *THOMAS DANIELL* and modelled by Rossi, for John Osborne. Chapter XII. *European Magazine* 1802 p.448 has two plates, the exterior temple, and the Hastings bust inside.

MOTTISFONT ABBEY. Urns marked Coade 1794* believed to be the memorial urns from Battersea Rise in memory of Henry Thornton. With resurrection flames as at Taplow Place. (Martin Drury). Exceptionally gritty stone body as at Stanmer Park Brighton qv.

MOUNT ROYAL. CG. Place not identified.

NEWTON HOUSE CG. Possibly NEWTON HOUSE 1792. *S. Baddisley.* Coade not identified.

NEWTON MANOR HOUSE, near Alton. Probably Newton Valence. CD February 1816 "a damaged Medicean Vase, another damaged vase"

NORTHCOURT HOUSE. Nothing identified. CG 1799.

THE WHITE HOUSE, Northington, near Alresford. Keystone of "Jolly old man wearing a cap"* (i.e. as Bedford Square)? (Patricia Nash)

PORTSMOUTH. J. Owen, Regimental Officer Portsmouth given estimates of Royal Arms rampant and couchant, Letter book 11.6.1813 (p10).

PORTSWOOD HOUSE. CG. *J. CRUNDEN* 1780. Demolished. Nothing traced.

SHEFFIELD HOUSE. CG. Can this be Sheffield Park Sussex? q.v.

SOMERLEY, near Ringwood. Large vase* based on the Warwick Vase marked COADE 1840 near house entrance.

SOUTHAMPTON. CO. March 1815. "four wreaths, 14½" in diam." Customer and site not named. *Bargate* Statue of George III in Roman dress* in trefoiled niche of the mediaeval town gateway. Marked Coade and Sealy 1809 (F.J. Collins). Copy of that of Emperor Hadrian (from British Museum now at Hampton Court). Given by 2nd Marquess of Lansdowne to Mayor of Southampton 18. 8. 1809. Statue of Queen Anne displaced (Kay Welham). *Testwood House.* Shipping notes at back of Letter book "Shipped for Redbridge, three cases 44 balusters for Mr Stringer Bourne Testwood House near Redbridge Southampton 28.5.1813. 5.7.1813 three cases of 36 baluster do. Not traced. *Southampton.* Shipping notes at back of the letter book " five cases for the Rev. Mr Philips containing a pedestal in four cases and a vase in one for Redbridge. 5.7.1813. Not traced.

STONEHAM PARK. CG. Place not traced.

STRATFIELD SAYE, near Bramley. Conservatory embellished in 1951 by the seventh Duke of Wellington with four Coade plaques* – Ceres and Hibernia, both dated 1787, a plaque with an oak garland and one with a harp, dated 1795. All came from Cuffnells, demolished c.1950 (A. Grant). See Cuffnells.

TOWER HILL. CG. Place not traced.

THE VYNE, Basingstoke. Damaged Druid.* (W. Bainbridge).

WESTON GROVE, Southampton. CD November 1817, two vases with handles, 14gns., Eagle with wings extended, 25 gns., two vases from antique, eight gns., two pannels, marriage of Cupid, 28 gns., "for William Chamberlayne, M.P. Weston Grove, Southampton. House demolished.

ISLE OF WIGHT

EAST COWES CASTLE. CG. Built *JOHN NASH* 1799. Coade not identified. CD May 1817 "Shipped for Mr Nash per Newport trader, medicean vase, old stock 11 gns". The vase had been presented to him by Sealy, but had presumably been broken and the replacemant was charged at about half price.

ST MARY WEST COWES CHURCH, Cowes. CD. November 1816. "*JOHN NASH* Esq for George Ward Esq. Four serpents on an outside (?) ground four ft diam. within, 12 gns each.* One pediment with Doves in Glory (the Paraclete?) 16 gns. One shield of arms and crest 18 gns. One round panel with inscription encircled by serpents 25 gns." (Identified by Sir John Summerson.) On church tower.

VILLA, West Cowes. Marine Villa in Gothic style by *NASH* for Sir J. Coxe Hippisley. CD June 1814, "Sir John Hippisley, five octangular pinnacles at 16 gns., £84". Now part of Royal Corinthian Yacht Club; Coade not traced.

ST EDMUND WOOTTON CHURCH, *near Ryde. Memorial to Mary Rockfort died 1819, marked Coade and Sealy*. Vestal figure with urn, cherub's head at foot (Pevsner). See Langley Marish, Bucks, Old Battersea Church, etc.*

HEREFORDSHIRE

(now Hereford and Worcester)

BERRINGTON HALL, near Leominster. HENRY HOLLAND 1778. two Plaques, one keystone* (F.J. Collins).

DOWNTON CASTLE, near Leintwardine.* By *RICHARD PAYNE KNIGHT* for himself, c.1778. Room imitating Pantheon, with niches containing Coade statues, bronzed* (Pevsner).

EYWOOD HOUSE, Presteigne. Letter book 22.1.1813. five cases sent containing 30 balusters. Bill sent 5.8.1813. (p12) £32.7s.0d. Demolished.

LEOMINSTER. CG. Nothing traced.

LUCTON. CG. Nothing traced.

STOKE CASTLE. CG. Possibly Stoke Edith for which *WILLIAM WILKINS* designed lodges 1792. Nothing traced.

HERTFORDSHIRE

ST LAWRENCE ABBOTS LANGLEY CHURCH.* CD. September 1814, "Churchwardens of Abbots Langley Herts., four shields 15" high with Arms of England, Abbey of St Albans, Filmer, Bart., Bishop of London, for waggon from Bull and Mouth Oxford St". The shields, now whitewashed, have been put in the later nineteenth-century porch. The Filmers held the living, one being the vicar in the early nineteenth century.

ST LEONARD FLAMSTEAD CHURCH, near Harpenden. Coat of arms on the vestry (F.J. Collins)*.

GORHAMBURY near St Albans. House by *SIR ROBERT TAYLOR* 1777. Corinthian capitals for portico and pilasters* paid for on April 1782 and March 1873, £342 in all (Hertfordshire Record Office, Account Book of 3rd Viscount Grimston XL 71). On front portico ten capitals for columns, six pilasters. On back four three-quarter columns, four square piers.

GREAT AMWELL, near Ware. Monument to Hugh Myddelton of the New River, by *ROBERT MYLNE* 1800*. In churchyard above, on Mylne's family mausoleum, urn with mask and spiral gadrooning dated 1800*. Plaque with mourning woman on the plinth.*

GREAT NORTH ROAD, 69 Hatfield. Coade door surround (Pevsner). Demolished.

42 FORE STREET, Hertford. Shop building with identical cornice to Egyptian House Penzance. Winged discs over first floor windows*.

HEXTON HOUSE, near Hitchen. (see also 33 Harley Street London). CD January 1820, "Joseph Lautour Esq., Hexton House, Nr. Hitchen, Herts, a fountain triangular rock stand, three basons, three pieces of coral, 40 gns," Gatepiers remain with eagles marked Coade 1820 (F.J. Collins)*. CO "two eagles as Sir George Osborne's, 20 guineas". Architect *JOHN WYNNE.*

NEWSELLS, Barkway, near Royson. CG. House burned 1939-45 (Pevsner). Coade unidentified.

OLD HALL GREEN, ST. EDMUND'S COLLEGE, near Buntingford.* 1795. Three main entrances and two other bays with Coade vermiculated rustication* (Pesvner).

PISHIOBURY PARK, near Sawbridgeworth. Alterations by *JAMES WYATT.* Chimneypiece of artificial stone, probably Coade, with frieze of cornucopiae, scrolls and sphinxes (Anthony Dale *James Wyatt* 1956)*. p52.

SWAN PUBLIC HOUSE, Rickmansworth.* Sign marked . . . ADE, LAMBETH (F.J. Collins). Demolished.

TRENT PARK. Two Sphinxes, with medallions on their bases, of the Seasons, 1785*. (Jacob Simon and F.J. Collins).

WARE. CG. Nothing identified. Possibly refers to Great Amwell, nearby.

ST MARY WELWYN CHURCH. CO July 1819. "James Walker, Churchwarden, Bricklayer,

Welwyn Herts., a font for church at 12 gns." Removed.

WOODHALL PARK, near Hertford*. 1777 by *THOMAS LEVERTON*. CG. Unusual plaques* with crossed arrows, cornucopiae etc. consoles to ground floor windows.* Ionic capitals.*

HUNTINGDONSHIRE

(now Cambridgeshire)

ST PETER and ST PAUL FENSTANTON CHURCH, near St Ives. Monument, mourning Vestal with urn*, 1793, to Frances, wife of Lancelot "Capability" Brown who was Lord of the Manor (Pevsner). As Langley Marish Church qv.

GAYNES HALL, Great Staughton, near St Neots. House by *GEORGE BYFIELD*, 1800. CG. Urn and capitals of Ionic porch, probably Coade*.

HUTINGDON LITERARY INSTITUTE*. Statue of Minerva* (F.J. Collins). Early 19th century building. The large statue in Huntingdon Records Office, Grammar School Walk, Huntingdon, Cambridgeshire, now, 1987, restored to original building.

KENT

ST PETER AYLESFORD CHURCHYARD*.Spong family tomb (Gunnis). CO February 1815, "Mr Spong, Bower House near Maidstone, a monumental vase on pedestal 40 gns including inscription". Shipped per Albion Ferry, November 1815. Not traced at church.

BECKENHAM PLACE - see London.

BELMONT, near Throwley. By *SAMUEL WYATT*, 1792. CG. Plaques with swags,* round medallions of putti with emblems of the seasons,* central plaque of figure with a view of the house and palmtrees,* string course all round,* Ionic capitals,* urns.*

BELVEDERE, near Erith. By *"ATHENIAN" STUART*, 1775. Demolished. CG. CD "Mr Dubbin's attendance at Belvedere in Kent £2.12s.6d.", January 1818. Repeat bill sent November 1819 to Lady Say and Sele.

ASH COURT, Boughton under Blean, Nr Faversham.1801. Bill, undated, from Ornamental Stone Manufactory Coade and Sealy for £30.4s.6d. Coade work not identified. (J.M.L. Booker).

ST PETER IN THANET CHURCH, Broadstairs. Monument dated 1832 (F.J. Collins)* to Captain Richard Burton by John Bacon Junior.

NUCKEL'S ALMSHOUSES, Broadstairs. 1838. Charity figure in pediment*, copy of Charity in the ante-chapel of Greenwich Hospital qv (F.J. Collins).

SUNDRIDGE PARK, Bromley. JOHN NASH, REPTON and *SAMUEL WYATT,* 1799, much altered. CG. Coade not traced.

QUERNMORE SCHOOL, Bromley. Originally Plaistow Lodge, built c.1777 for Peter Thelusson, probably by *THOMAS LEVERTON.* Plaques on entrance front,* vases on back.* (Newman: Pevsner.)*

HOLLYDALE, Keston Mark, Bromley. CO. "Mr. Kirkpatrick, Hollydale near Keston Mark, Bromley, Kent, an oval pannel with Apollo's head and glory, 4'2" x 2'1". Bill sent 22.5.1819 £14.9s.0d. Nathaniel Lloyd's *History of the English House* fig 282 p.266 shows bay with three oblong swag-and-patera plaques, and a sunburst ornament in pediment on front, presumably the "Apollo's head in glory". Appears to have been demolished.

COURT HOUSE, Canterbury. In letter to Mr Robertson of Kilkenny (Letter Book p219) Sealy mentioned two large statues of Justice, one for London, one for the Court House, Canterbury. Sessions House, Longport 1808 by *GEORGE BYFIELD* seems the building, but the figure is now missing.

DOCKYARD ENTRANCE, Chatham. Huge Royal Arms, heraldically painted, marked Coade and Sealy 1812, on main gateway in the style of Vanbrugh, NP (Pevsner).*

CHISLEHURST. Letter Book p13, letter to Dr Jenner, Chislehurst, Kent, 5.8.1813 asking for payment of account of October 1811, £27.6s.0d. Not traced.

COBHAM HALL, near Rochester. Two vases with classical reliefs (Medici and Borghese) dated 1801 in garden on west front (Pevsner).* Probably ordered by Repton. At entrance two Coade coats of arms.*

DANSON PARK, Blexleyheath. House by *TAYLOR,* 1759-62; alterations by *SIR WILLIAM CHAMBERS,* c.1770. Coade chimneypots (Sir John Summerson).*

DARTFORD. CO. June 1814, "Ruth Watson, Dartford Kent, 2 lions' heads, 4 do. feet". Site not identified.

KEARSNEY ABBEY, Dover. CD. April 1819, "Fector, Dover, 8 pilasters green granite (scagliola) £88.17s.6d., 2 pilasters dining room verd antique, £28.7s.0d." CD August 1821. "Exors. of the late Mr. Fector, chimneypiece of statuary marble, verd antique scaliola, black marble slips, £78.15s.0d., ornamental stone fountain, coral tripod stand, coral top supporting shell, 3 shells etc. £36.15s.0d." CD September 1821 "Fountain for the dairy, composed of a stand and large bason, £29.2s.6d." All but one wing of the house demolished (Kent Record Office).

ST MARY'S CHURCH, *Dover.* CG. Coade not traced.

THE GAOL, *Dover.* At end of Order Book, Croggon analysed the workmen's time for making a statue of Faith for Dover Gaol May 1821. He wrote to Mr Fector (of Kearsney Abbey) Letter Book p481, asking if he was concerned with the Gaol as the Surveyor had ordered two statues. Colvin lists the Gaol by *RICHARD ELSAM* as the cause of litigation between Corporation and architect.

CLARE HOUSE* (?), *East Malling.* CG. Villa 1793 for John Larking by *MICHAEL SEARLES.* Colonnaded Tuscan front. Coade capitals and bases, balustrade. Searles also used these elsewhere – see Paragon, Blackheath.

FAVERSHAM. CG. Could be Belmont or Wash Court. Not otherwise traced.

CONGREGATIONAL AND UNIONIST CHURCH, *7 Partridge Lane, Faversham.* Wall monument of sarcophagus with lions' feet, vase with flames above, to John Simmonds, died 31.1.1794 who built the chapel. Coade & Sealy 1805. (John Davies.)

GODMERSHAM PARK, *near Chilham.* CG. Gatepiers of brick with Coade urns on top, dated 1793 (Pevsner).* Fine pair of torchères similar to West Wycombe of three girls but with arms raised. Sold from house by Christies 6 June 1983.

GREAT WIGSELL, *Hawkhurst.* Coade statue (F.J. Collins). Place not traced.

HOTHFIELD PLACE, *near Ashford.* CG. House by *JAMES WYATT,* altered by *JOHN NASH.* Demolished 1954. Statues of Temperance and Justice (Gunnis).

INGRESS ABBEY, *near Dartford.* CG. House demolished 1832. Coade not traced.

MONTREAL, *near Westerham.* CD. April 1815, "dr. Coade and Sealy for a Borghesian Vase sent to Lord Amherst's Montreal to replace one made by them that failed 35gns for £26.5s.0d." House demolished. Vase made 1813 (Letter Book p6). Other things bought for the house as the 1813 account was for £94.1s.0d. (Letter Book p11.)

ST LAWRENCE and ST GEORGE RAMSGATE CHURCH. CG. St George's Church 1824-7, appears to have Coade pinnacles.* The earlier Coade not traced.

RAMSGATE. CD 8.5.1817 "Henry Cull per vessel from Botolph's Wharf, keystone with laughing philosopher's head £1.1s.0d." Keystone survives at 6 Hardres Street.* Also some more, similar but battered, in Boundary Road.

ROCHESTER CATHEDRAL. Monument to Lady Henniker,* marked Coade, London, 1793. *Gentleman's Magazine,* 1794, part I, page 410, attributed the monument to Thomas Banks. (Gunnis.) Father Time and an admonishing lady.

COURT HOUSE, Sandwich. CD. November 1818 "Richard Collard, Surveyor, Broadstairs, Kent, Shield of arms of the towns of the Cinque Ports for a Court House Sandwich, £34.8s.0d." Court House rebuilt 1910-12. Shield replaced on a new building.*

KNOLE–X, Sevenoaks. CG. A Coade vase in the grounds. Kent Record Office. Sackville Mss U269 A243/11. Bill signed Eleanor Coade for Vase, £21, for the Duke of Dorset, 1781. Not traced, but an armorial feature dated 1826 on the Orangery,* and a child and dolphin fountain 1820.*

SEVENOAKS. Letter 13.5.13. (p8) Letter Book to Valentine Hackelton, Seven Oaks, Kent re 26ft of 14in coping and 70ft of 9in coping. Possibly for restoration of Sevenoaks Church by *S.P. COCKERELL* in 1812.

GORE COURT, Sittingbourne. CG. By *S.P. COCKERELL,* 1795. Demolished. Coade not identified.

ST MARY the VIRGIN SPELDHURST CHURCHYARD. Monument to William Nesbit,* marked Coade 1807. "Large flaming lamp on top" (Pevsner). Tomb as Mrs Sheridan, Old Windsor. In very bad condition.

ST PETER and ST PAUL TONBRIDGE CHURCH. Monument to Henry Harpur,* marked *COADE & SEALY* 1800 (Gunnis). Plaque flanked by consoles, cornice above. (Gilbert Hoole.)

LANCASHIRE

BOLTON. CO April 1817 "Mr. Boardman, Bolton Lancs. 2 lions couchant for piers, the plinth 2ft long, 8ins broad at 8gns each". House not identified.

CONISHEAD PRIORY, (Lincolnshire to Coade), near Ulverston. Gothic mansion for R.G. Braddyll by *PHILIP WYATT.* CO February 1819, "a monumental tablet –

gns." March 1819, "A statue of Virgin and Child, small size, 40gns." Coade not identified.

HEATON PARK X, *near Manchester, (Now Greater Manchester). JAMES WYATT,* 1772. CG. Ionic capitals to columns and pilasters,* string course,* paterae.* Now has two bronzed chimneypiece figures made for Mr Locke of Norbury.*

HORNBY HALL. CG. House not identified. There is a Hornby Castle, Lancs, also Hornby Castle, Yorks c.1800.

LANCASTER. Town's Dispensary, (John Champness) 1785 had plaque of the Good Samaritan, now over door of Royal Infirmary.*

LIVERPOOL TOWN HALL – *now in Merseyside.* Reconstruction by *JAMES WYATT,* 1780-92, of John Wood's building. CG. Statue of Britannia on dome, by Rossi,* now gilded, Pevsner. *Monthly Magazine* 1799 p904.

LIVERPOOL – *now in Merseyside.* Letter Book 14.9.1813 (p18) to Mr W. Lewis, 15 Clayton Street, Liverpool, saying that monument had blown up in the kiln, new one being made. Bill, day book, 3.12.1813 for monument £42. 798 letter inscription £8.6s.3d. Not traced. CO 14.3 1815 "Messrs Nuttall, Fisher and Dixon Liverpool. Large Royal Arms ready made 30gns. To be sent per Pickford Grand Junction Canal". Not traced. Woolton Hall,* by *ROBERT ADAM,* 4 round medallions and 7 paterae on front. Drawing in Sir John Soane's Museum (Dorothy Thompson).

MANCHESTER – *now in Greater Manchester.* CG. Nothing traced.

WOOLCOT. CG. Place not traced.

ISLE OF MAN

CG. Guard Houses. *Castle Mona.* By GEORGE STEUART 1801-6 for Duke of Atholl, four round heraldic plaques within laurel wreaths, all different.* (Peter Kelly.) *Douglas* Court House. By GEORGE STEUART, with Guard House. Demolished. Had two plaques as Ramsay, one of three legs of Man, now in Manx Museum.* (Peter Kelly.) *Ramsay* Court House By GEORGE STEUART 1798 with Guard House. Now Police Station, two round heraldic plaques over doors.* (Peter Kelly.) *Kirk Braddon* Churchyard Obelisk to Lord Henry Murray, 5th son of 3rd Duke of Atholl, d1805. Plaque with three legs of Man marked Coade and Sealy,* date obscured by paint. Attributed to GEORGE STEUART. (Peter Kelly.)

BUCKMINSTER PARK, *near Melton Mowbray*. House by *SAMUEL SAXON*, 1790s. Demolished 1950s. CG. CO March 1814, "Lady Manners, fountain 20gns." Coade not traced.

COLEORTON HALL, *near Ashby de la Zouch*. By *GEORGE DANCE* the younger, 1804-8, Gothic. CO April 1817, "Lady of Sir. G. Bowman [sic should be Beaumont] a pair of busts, Milton and Shakespeare, to be finished as terms, 7gns each.* Small elephant to be sent on approval to Coleorton Hall, Leicestershire, 5gns." All three invoiced July 1817, £21.19s.2d. CD August 1817, "A rich Gothic candlestick (de Vaere) £35.16s.1d.* (Now in private collection.) Also in garden, terms of Michelangelo* and Raphael* (see Buckingham Palace) to match the others, and a Medici and a Borghese vase marked CROGGON 1827.* The elephant has disappeared.

DONINGTON PARK, *near Coalville*. By *WILLIAM WILKINS* senior, 1790-1800. CG. Demolished. Coade not identified.

ST MARY'S SCHOOL de Castro, *Leicester*. 1785. Two Charity children c.1788 (Gunnis). Demolished. Figures now in St John's Primary School, 1971 (Pevsner).

COUNTY ROOMS AND ASSEMBLY ROOMS*, *Leicester*. by *JOHN JOHNSON* (see Chelmsford) 1792 (Pevsner), other authorities give different dates. CG. On outside two panels of the Dancing Hours,* Coade capitals to tripartite windows,* balusters (as Lewes County Hall),* small paterae* and small faces in corners.*

LOUGHBOROUGH HOUSE (*Staffordshire to Mrs Coade*). CG. Not identified. Possibly Loughborough Rectory, demolished 1962.

THE OLD RECTORY, *Mountsorrel*. Most elegant late 18th century brick elevation with Coade-style tripod, festoons, paterae etc. All detail very sharp and like Coade stone but the house not on the 1799 list. Attributed to *WILLIAM HENDERSON* I or II. (Edward Saunders.)

NORMANTON HALL, *near Oakham*. By *KENTON COUSE*, 1763-7. CG. Demolished. Coade not identified.

SKEFFINGTON HALL, *near King's Norton*. House 17th century and later. CG. Vase* of the Blagdon and East Lulworth model in garden near front door.

ST MARY MAGDALENE STAPLEFORD CHURCH,* *near Melton Mowbray*. By *GEORGE RICHARDSON*, 1783. (In 1781 he published a *New Book of Fireplaces*.)

Family pew of Lord Harborough has vaguely gothic Coade fireplace*
with plaque of the Sacrifice of Isaac.

LINCOLNSHIRE

BELTON HOUSE X, *near Grantham*. Greenhouse, dairy and Brownlow chapel by *JEFFRY WYATT* (later Wyatville)*. CO May 1819 "Earl Brownlow per Mr Jeffry Wyatt Lower Brook St. 170 whole ballusters 2' 0½" high by 7½" diam at bottom @ 7s.0d. £90.14s.9d." A further 13 ballusters were supplied the next year, all presumably for the Greenhouse, which has a balustrade* all round.

ST MICHAEL BLOXHOLM CHURCH,* *north of Sleaford*. Church altered and added to by General Manners, 1812. His arms, marked Coade and Sealy 1813, over the porch entrance* (Pevsner.)

BLOXHOLM HALL. Very fine Coade peacock, modelled 1772, destroyed 1956 (John Harris). *The Buildings of England, Lincolnshire*

BROCKLESBY PARK, *west of Grimsby*. CG. Holgate Monument, c.1785.* Urn on pedestal supported by three tortoises, vase on top,* erected by the 1st Baron Yarborough. John Harris attributes to *J. WYATT*. See also Stanmer Park, Sussex. Borghese Vase* on pedestal with rams' heads at corners paterae on one side, trophy of armour on the other. (Gunnis Coade file Courtauld Institute.) Now in South Humberside.

COCKERINGTON HALL. CG. Place not traced.

COLSTERWORTH. CG. No site identifiable.

DUNSTON PILLAR, *SE of Lincoln*. Masonry pier with lantern on top erected by Sir Francis Dashwood. George III, over-lifesize statue, modelled by Panzetta, replaced the lantern in 1810. Figure of the King and several feet of the column, removed and broken c.1940. Bust surviving at Lincoln Castle*.

ST MICHAEL EDENHAM CHURCH. Coade Royal Arms rampant* (J.H. Cordingley).

GAINSBOROUGH. CG. Nothing identified.

GRIMSTHORPE CASTLE, *near Corby*. Remodelled for Lord Gwydyr by *HENRY GARLING*, 1811. CD. September 1820, "Lord Gwydyr Grimsthorpe Castle, large Royal arms £49.7s.8d." Not traced.

LINCOLN. *Lincoln Castle*. Bust of George III, the remains of the statue from Dunston Pillar qv. *Judge's Lodging, by Lincoln Castle.* Royal arms,* couchant, in pediment of late 18th century house.

LITTLE PONTON HALL, (Paunton to Coade), near Grantham. Additions to house in late 18th century. CG. No Coade identified.

ST JOHN'S CHURCH, STAMFORD. Plaque of mourning figure with urn*, to John Booth, died 1799. CG. Inscription was changed before firing, and the original text shows through. (RCHM Cambridge.)

SYSTON HALL, near Grantham. CD May 1819 "Sir John Thorold, Syston Park, Grantham, ordered by *MR VULLIAMY*, candelabra or stand to support sundial, £23.11s.0d." Demolished. Stone fountain,* with Greek design, Coade vase above, beside the drive (Rev. Henry Thorold).

UFFINGTON HOUSE, near Stamford. CO December 1817, "Earl of Linsey Uffington House Nr. Stamford, Lincs., 2 coronets 12" diam. at base, £14.1s.10d." House burnt down 1904. Letter Book (p2) says Sealy sent busts of Shakespeare, Addison, Dryden, Prior and Jonson, to Earl of Lindsay 1813. Also offers Emperor and Empress of Russia, life size.

HOLY TRINITY WEST ALLINGTON CHURCH, NW of Grantham. Large heraldic shield in church (Gunnis).*

WILLINGHAM HOUSE N Willingham, near Market Rasen.* House possibly by *ROBERT MITCHELL.* CG. Tetrastyle portico with Ionic Coade capitals, 1790* (Pevsner and Harris, Lincolnshire, p329.)

MIDDLESEX

See Greater London Area

NORFOLK

BARTON HALL, Barton Turf, NE Norfolk. CG. Georgian house, Coade not identified.

BLEACHLEY, (in fact Blicking), Aylsham, near Sheringham. CD September 1817, "Lord Suffield, Bleachley, Aylsham, 84 balusters etc £41.16s.2d." More balusters were later supplied for £22.0s.8d. For Blickling. Orangery probably by *HUMPHRY REPTON*, by 1793, has guilloche frieze of Coade stone by the doors.

DOWNHAM. CG. Downham is the old name for Downham Market. The Castle Hotel, Downham Market, late 18th century, has rocky rusticated blocks, now very coarse looking. Are these local copies of Coade work originally either there or nearby?

EARSHAM,* near Bungay. Additions for William Windham by *SIR JOHN SOANE,* 1784 onwards. Coade mentioned in the Soane account (D. Stroud). Ionic capitals and medallion with flower swags in pediment of Music Room* (originally Greenhouse).

NELSON COLUMN, GREAT YARMOUTH. By *WILLIAM WILKINS* Junior, 1818. On top of column, six caryatid victories, Britannia above, costing in all £1368.2s.6d. See chapter on Commemorative Monuments. CD June 1818, September 1819. Heavily restored.*

GUNTON HALL. CO. 27.6.1817 Lord Suffield, 126 whole Ballusters at 6s.0d. 42 half do. Lord Suffield's Gunton Hall had a balustraded parapet. (Antony Dale *James Wyatt* p58.)

HEYDON HALL, near Aylsham. On extension after 1827, heraldic panel with two shields,* marked Croggon 1830. (Edmund Esdaile)

HOLKHAM HOUSE, near Wells X. VINERY 1780 by *SAMUEL WYATT.* Paterae and guilloche string course.* *EAST LODGE* 1799 by *SAMUEL WYATT.* Plaque with ostrich and wreath of oak leaves modelled by Bernasconi, in pediment (J.M. Robinson, *Country Life,* 21 November 1974).*

HOVETON HALL, near Norwich. Early 19th century house. CO 19.4.1819. "Francis Stone Norwich, 2 scagliola columns porphyry and 2 pilasters, Ionic capitals etc £105.7s.2d." Dubbin credited 18 guineas for capitals. CD May 1820, "Francis Stone Esq. Expenses to and from Hoveton, Nr. Norwich fixing porphyry scagliola columns £5.18s.0d." (Not traced).

KESWICK HALL, near Norwich. Additions to older house by *WILLIAM WILKINS* junior, 1817. CD June 1819, "Hudson Gurney Esq. MP for Norwich, ordered by Mr. Wilkins, 2 shield of arms". The shields may have been for lodges as they do not appear on the main house. Scagliola pillars in the centre room may also be made by Croggon since Wilkins used Croggon scagliola a good deal.

KINGS LYNN. Letter of 10.8.1813 (p13) to Mr W. Newsham, Lynn, Norfolk, saying that two statues of Comedy and Tragedy will come to about 40gns each according to size, and might be less. Adds that those at Covent Garden Theatre were 200gns (presumably referring to carved stone figures).

LANGLEY PARK*, near Loddon. SIR JOHN SOANE, 1785 onwards. CG. Coade supplied paterae and special chimnneypots for the gate lodges in 1791.* D. Stroud. *The Architecture of Sir John Soane* 1961 p32. Alison Kelly, Sir John Soane and Mrs Eleanor Coade. *Apollo* April 1989 p247-253.

ST PETER MELTON CONSTABLE CHURCH,* near Holt. Monument to Lady Stanhope, died 1812; reclining girl, as Lawhitton and Soulbury, qv. Tablet with inscription below. CD August 1814 "Sir Jacob Ashley [should be Astley], Melton Constable, Dereham Norfolks. A Monument to the memory of Lady Stanhope with a figure, inscription table, £84."*

ST STEPHEN, NORWICH. Rampant Horse Street, Monument to Elizabeth Coppin,* 1812, marked Coade and Sealy. Putto by an urn as at Teigngrace, etc (Pevsner). Shipping note at end of Letter Book "Shipped for Yarmouth 3 cases containing a monument for Daniel Coppin Norwich" 4.3.1813.

ST ANDREW THORPE CHURCH, NORWICH. Monument to Elizabeth Meadows Martineau,* 1810. Marked Coade and Sealy. Tablet with a reclining woman (Pevsner).

SHOTESHAM PARK*, south of Norwich. By *SIR JOHN SOANE,* 1785. Brick pilasters with Coade Ionic capitals* D. Stroud. The *Architecture of Sir John Soane* 1961 p32. Alison Kelly, "Sir John Soane and Mrs Eleanor Coade" *Apollo* April 1989 p247-253.

THETFORD, Guildhall. Figure of Justice,* 1799, now at the rebuilt Guildhall (Pevsner). *Borough Offices,* Royal Arms.*

WESTWICK HOUSE, near N Walsham. House, c.1800 (Pevsner). CG. No Coade identified.

NORTHAMPTONSHIRE

BURGHLEY HOUSE X, near Stamford. CG. Ten bronzed sibyls holding lamps in Chapel,* c.1777. Four lions on bridge, to order of *CAPABILITY BROWN* (Dorothy Stroud, *Capability Brown* 1975 p76.) Payment in May 1777 to Eleanor Coade "for four lyons for the New Bridge in the Park £113.12s.0d." (RCHM Cambridge).

CHESTERTON HALL. CG. No record of this house in Northamptonshire. Possibly Chesterton Hall Warwickshire or Huntingdonshire is meant.

COTTESBROOK, north of Northampton. Early 18th century house, with bows added each end, as well as lodges and screen, by *ROBERT MITCHELL,* 1775-9. CG. Coade plaques between 1st and 2nd floors.* Paterae and urns on gate piers* and paterae on bridge.*

COURTEENHALL* (?), *south of Northampton.* SAMUEL SAXON, 1791-3. CG. The Ionic capitals at the back, and the capitals of the window could be the Coade. C. Hussey *Mid Georgian* 1955 plate 468 p228.

ST GILES DESBOROUGH CHURCH. Memorial to Mrs Pulton d1779.* Two putti perch on sarcophagus with an inscription. In the centre, ribbon bow supports a rococo pair of curtains, the folds of which reach out to the putti. In the middle, a coat of arms. Coade catalogue design, no512, 30gns. See also Jamaica, Montego Bay.

EAST CARLTON HALL. JOHN JOHNSON. Demolished. "The artificial stone ornament in the pediment cost 12 guineas". (Nancy Briggs, Leics. Record Office Palmer MSS DG4 (601)). 1781.

EASTON NESTON GATEWAY – *now entrance to Towcester Racecourse.* Central archway* with coat of arms, supporters and Corinthian capitals; screen each side with one oval "squat" urn and two round urns; small lodges at the ends, with a hind couchant on each. Stamped Croggan (note wrong spelling) late Coade 1822 (E. Esdaile). *J. RAFFIELD* given as the architect (*Country Life* 7.11.1908).

FINEDON HALL. Monument to Edward Wortley Montagu erected by John Dolben (see Chapter 14). Like the monument he erected to his friend in Westminster Abbey, this design was also a catalogue number – no. 788 seven guineas. Now in a private collection.

NORTHAMPTON BARRACKS, *Barracks Road.* CG. Thomas Allen, *History and Antiquities of the Parish of Lambeth,* 1826, p306 says that Northampton Barracks have Coade Royal arms. Barracks Road now demolished.

STOKE BRUERNE. Four Vases same design as East Lulworth (Peter Hone).

WEEDON. Phoenix plaque from the insurance company in the gable of the National Westminster Bank.*

NORTHUMBERLAND

PERCY TENANTRY COLUMN, *Alnwick.* Greek Doric column erected 1816, by Duke of Northumberland's tenants. Percy lion on top, four lions at base.* CD 1817 "D of Northumberland's column, *D. STEPHENSON* architect, 4 couchant lions 9 feet in length, packing etc £254.4s.7d." The lion on top appears not to be Coade; there is no mention of it in Croggon's accounts.

ALNWICK CASTLE. CG. ADAM did much work in the Castle in the later 18th century. No Coade identifiable from the Adam drawings in Sir John Soane's Museum. Brizlee Tower and the Lord's Tower, Hulne Priory both have portrait medallions of the Duke and Duchess of Northumberland. Spare copies of the medallions at the Castle are marked COADE on the edge, which would be invisible when the pieces were built in. (J.H. Cordingley.)

SWANSFIELD HOUSE, near Alnwick. CD. December 1814 "Henry Collingwood Selby, Swansfield nr. Alnwick, a fine 6ft statue of Peace and Victory with wings, a caduceus, olive branch, cornucopia etc. £42." Four tablets for the plinth brought the bill to £103.1s.4d. Column still stands, but without figure (Pevsner).

BLAGDON, NW of Morpeth. Alterations to 1735 house by JAMES WYATT, 1778-91. CG. Gardens designed by Sir Edwin Lutyens with rondpoint and a Coade urn*. The Scale, or Kale Cross, given to Newcastle City in 1783 by Sir Matthew Ridley. Returned to him in 1807 and made into entrance, Coade lion and two vases on top* (Lady Ridley). Designed DAVID STEPHENSON. Coade urns from Wallington now in the Quarry Garden.

KIRKLEY HALL, near Blyth. CG. All rebuilt, no Coade identified.

NEWCASTLE THEATRE. CG. Built 1787 by D. STEPHENSON with a large trophy of arms over entrance. Rebuilt 1837. Mackenzie plate V. (R.M. Gard, M.A. County Archivist, Newcastle.)

ALL SAINTS CHURCH, NEWCASTLE CG. Built by D. STEPHENSON, 1786-96. Font as Debden, St George's Chapel, Windsor, etc. Removed. (E.M. Mackenzie, History of Newcastle upon Tyne 1827, p313.)

SCALE or KALE CROSS, NEWCASTLE. See Blagdon.

PONTELAND CHURCH, near Blyth. Monument to Richard Newton Ogle,* died 1794. Sarcophagus marked Coade with trophies on top (Pevsner). His daughter was Mrs R.B. Sheridan, see Old Windsor.

SEATON DELAVAL, south of Blyth. Sir John Delaval bought chimneypieces etc from Christie's 1771 sale of artificial stone. Damaged chimneypiece,* two roman heads* survive.

ALL SAINTS BABWORTH CHURCH, near Retford. CG. Small remains of monument to Mrs Simpson, designed *HUMPHRY REPTON* 1791 and signed Coade and Repton (E. Esdaile). Now mainly demolished, but Mr Esdaile drew it when a young man and published the drawing in *Country Life* 19.4.1973 p1070. It had a stained glass oval panel, putti and emblems of Mrs Simpson's musical and artistic interests.

BARNBY MANOR, near Newark on Trent. Unicorn marked Coade and Sealy* provenance unknown; Borghese vase marked Coade Lambeth 1815* from Elvaston Castle Derbyshire qv.

CLUMBER, near Retford. House by *STEPHEN WRIGHT* 1770. Demolished 1938. CG. CD, January and November 1819, records sale of four ornamented chimneypots to the Duke of Newcastle at about £3 each, and, for the gate screen, 25 vases of six different patterns, with eight balls and necks. The whole bill came to £80.2s.0d. (Newcastle (Clumber) MSS, Nottingham University, undated) (G. Jackson Stops). The screen survives, without vases. Coade arms on the Carburton Gates are dated 1789.* (Martin Drury).

KELHAM. CG. Nothing traced.

NOTTINGHAM. CG. Nothing traced in the town, but the reference may be to Wollaton, a few miles from the town centre.

NUTHALL TEMPLE, east of Nottingham. Copy of La Rotonda by *THOMAS WRIGHT,* 1754, demolished 1929. CG. Coade not identified. Alterations c.1780 by either WRIGHT or JAMES WYATT (Colvin).

THORESBY PARK, near Retford. House by *TALMAN,* rebuilt by *SALVIN,* 19th century. CD June 1819 "Earl Manvers, Thoresby, ordered by Mr Wilkins, a cluster of three chimneycaps £39.10s.10d." They were sent "by water to the mouth of the Trent". (*WILLIAM WILKINS SENIOR.*) Pevsner mentions vase in the garden marked *COADE & SEALY* 1802.

WOLLATON HALL. Elizabethan house, with a Coade chimneypiece almost a duplicate of one of those at Capesthorne, Cheshire, qv. Undated, but likely to be of the 1790s. (D.J.H. Taylor, Museum of Costume and Textiles, Nottingham.)

ST MARY BANBURY CHURCH*. S. P. COCKERELL, 1792-9. CG. Almost certainly the Ionic capitals inside, now painted, are Coade (Nicholas Cooper).* Contractors only paid 25% cash; the rest in 5% bonds. Mrs Coade had two £25 bonds.

BLETCHINGTON HOUSE. Lions, gothic statue, vases, two eagles, ordered by Lord Annesley. CO. September, October 1818.

CAVERSHAM PARK (formerly Berkshire). CG. House reconstructed 1850. Coade not traced.

HENLEY. CG. Site not traced. Possibly refers to Henerton Hall, Wargrave, called Henerton Hall, Henley by Croggon, see Berks.

MIDDLETON PARK, near Bicester. CD August 1814, "Earl of Jersey, a foot for medicean vase in lieu of one of Coade and Sealy, failed. £1.11s.6d." CO May 1815, "Earl Jersey, Rock coping to encompass a bason 10ft diam." House demolished. Coade not identified. Letter to Earl of Jersey 22.5.1813 (p8) saying wagon fully loaded and so could not take two lions, 2 . . . (illegible) and vase from Villa de Medici. Another statue of the Gladiator in hand, and hopes for better luck with it. Would a majestic statue of Hospitality with cornucopia be better?

OXFORD, Exeter College. February 1815, CD "Rev. I.C. Jones Exeter College Oxford, Monument D.B. 35 guineas case etc. £2.3s.0d." Old chapel demolished 1856. Coade not identified. *Radcliffe Observatory. HENRY KEENE and JAMES WYATT,* 1772-94. CG. Plaques of Morning, Noon and Evening on north side;* paterae,* pilaster capitals,* plaques with festoons and the signs of the zodiac,* modelled by Rossi. Antony Dale *James Wyatt* 1956 p83 says moulded ribs and enrichment of dome in the observing room also of Coade.* *St Peter's College, Oxford.* The Master's House, formerly the offices of the Oxford Canal Company, Greek Doric building of 1827-9 in Bulwark Lane. Plaque over the door, a half-moon with drapery flowing down each side. Britannia sits with a shield with the University and Town arms. Behind her are a barge and an excellent relief of the Radcliffe Camera and St Mary's. The plaque predates the building and must have been on a previous Canal Company building shortly after the Canal reached Oxford in 1790. CG.

ST PETER and ST PAUL SHIPLAKE, south of Henley. CD September 1816 "Rev. A.E. Howman, Shiplake, Gothic font 14gns. Sending by Kennet barge £1.3s.0d." Font removed 1869 by the son of the above.

STANTON HARCOURT, west of Oxford. CD May 1814, "Countess Dowager of Harcourt, Rich

Gothic tomb* with figure of the late Lord Harcourt, arms crest, Gothic panels etc. £262.10s.0d. Gothic panels at the foot for full arms and supporters, inscriptions richly wrought with trellis work, pinnacles £84." The whole bill was £374.18s.0d. The tomb is in Viscount Harcourt's private chapel on the south side of St Michael Stanton Harcourt Church.

WOOD EATON MANOR, east of Oxford. Addition of porch with Coade stone details by SIR JOHN SOANE, 1791, based on the Temple of Miletus (Gunnis).* Bill book 4, 1793 in Sir John Soane's Museum shows that John Weyland incurred special charges for having the capitals copied from the Temple of Apollo at Miletus (3gns) as well as making them (10gns). Unusually, the shafts as well as the capitals were of Coade stone. The whole bill came to £49.17s.1d., including 7gns for a vase and pedestal which are now missing. Alison Kelly, Sir John Soane and Mrs Eleanor Coade, Apollo April 1989 p247-253.

SHROPSHIRE

ACTON BURNELL HALL? CD "John Tasker Mortimer St. Two ionic capitals £11.11s.0d., two large trusses finely ornamented with Druids' heads £6.6s.0d." November 1814. JOHN TASKER refronted Acton Burnell Hall in 1814 with an Ionic portico.

ACTON ROUND, near Bridgnorth. Seated tiger,* as catalogue design (Bacon's?). Owner says it came from Alton Towers, probably during JAMES WYATT'S or THOMAS HOPPER'S time there.

LUDLOW. (Herefordshire to Mrs Coade). CG. Nothing identified but possibly refers to Downton Castle, Herefordshire, Ludlow being the nearest town.

MARKET DRAYTON. CG. Nothing identified.

MILLICHOPE PARK. Large Lion in hall.* Recent purchase. Original site unknown (John Cornforth).

PACKINGTON, near Oswestry (in fact PORKINGTON). CO. December 1815 "Mr. Ormesby Gore, Ruabon N. Wales, large shield with 2 crests, ornamental branches etc. 80gns." The CD entry, February 1816, amended the address to Packington, Oswestry. Actually Porkington. Neale's Views of Seats, 1818-23 shows the heraldry. Demolished. Letter Book p211 has reference to a bill of £100.8s.0d. September 10 1816.

SHEFFNAL. CG. Probably Shifnal. May refer to Weston Park qv nearby.

LORD HILL'S COLUMN, SHREWSBURY *Abbey Foregate.* Statue of Lord Hill,* 17ft high on 100ft column, modelled by Panzetta. CD August 1816. "John Beck Esq. Secretary for the committee for erecting a statue of Lord Hill, a colossal statue 17ft high on a plinth for column at Shrewsbury, £315." Erecting the figure and other charges brought the bill to £381. Croggon could not get commission for lions on base (Letter Book January 1816 (p160)). *Courier* 21.8.1816. "Mrs. Coade announces that the 17ft statue of Lord Hill is now completed and will be on show in the Manufactory".

SHREWSBURY. CG. Nothing identified.

SUNDORNE CASTLE. CD. October 1814, "John Corbett Esq., fountain of rock and coral with dolphins, £31.10s.0d." House demolished.

ST BARTHOLOMEW TONG CHURCH*, *near Oakengates.* CD April 1815, "Tong churchwardens, King's Arms Rampant." Dated 1814* (Pevsner). Coade Letter Book, 14 dunning letters to James Jones, Churchwarden, between October 1814 and May 6 1817. Then Croggon gave up.

WESTON PARK, *(Staffordshire to Coade).* Triangular sundial with three figures as at Audley End.*

WILLEY HALL,* *near Much Wenlock.* By *LEWIS WYATT,* 1812-15. Eight columns of giallo antico scagliola, a frieze, and statuary scagliola Corinthian capitals, costing £683.10s.9d, supplied to C.W. Forester, Willey Park,* Broseley Salop (CD October 1818). (Actually Lord Forester). Letter Book 29.6.1818 (p343) "Mr Dubbin has this day sent off the 4 trophys". Good description of the commission, John E. Ruch "Regency Coade" *Architectural History* 1968 p40-42.

SOMERSET

AMMERDOWN,* *near Radstock.* By *JAMES WYATT* for T.S. Jolliffe, 1788. Figures* from the monument to Jolliffe (died 1824) disposed in gardens designed by Lutyens.

BATH, *now in Avon.* The coat of arms with twin shield and supporters on the pediment at the end of *Northumberland Place* (now painted) appears to be Coade. The coat of arms, also painted, on the return end of *Old Bond Street,* facing Milsom Street, may also be Coade. *Union Street,* letter of 1.4.1818 to R. Payne, Union St Bath saying Queen's Arms ready, Letter Book p328.

These arms (of Queen Charlotte, with a wreath of flowers round the arms) now on 8 Argyle St (Geoffrey Beard).

BLAISE CASTLE, now in Avon. Borghese Vases marked Croggon (Nigel Temple)*.

BRISTOL, now in Avon. Portland Square. Jubilee statue of George III erected 28.4.1810 (Felix Farley's Bristol Journal). Statue smashed March 1813 by men inflamed by "Orator" Hunt.

BRISTOL, Commercial Rooms, Corn St 1810. Great Room has caryatids similar to those at the Bank of England, Consols Office (Soane) J.G. Bubb paid £378 for the caryatids, £1388 for all the statuary. Bubb had not yet begun to make artificial stone so these must have been made at Lambeth. The caryatids were an afterthought and the structure could not have supported solid stone figures. (Andor Gomme, Michael Jenner and Bryan Little Bristol an Architectural History) 1979 p233-236.

HINTON ST GEORGE CHURCH. Bronzed coat of arms marked Coade & Sealy 1812 (John Hardy).*

ST JOHN the BAPTIST KEYNSHAM CHURCH, near Bath. Monument to Margaret Simpson,* 1792 (Gunnis). CG.

SOMERTON ENDSLEIGH, Somerton. Early and later 18th century house. CG. No Coade identified.

STAFFORDSHIRE

ALTON TOWERS. Letter (p2) 22.7.1813 Letter Book. Details of three dozen garden vases "Mr Hopper is now proceeding £150.0s.0d." Vases gone, but remains of one triangular pedestal with figures on the slightly concave sides, near greenhouse.

AQUALATE HALL, (Salop to Mrs Coade). JOHN NASH for Sir John Boughey Bt. Gothic. Letter Book 29.1.1813 (p2) J. Boughey told that cases sent back free of charge, would have their cost returned. Demolished. Coade not identified.

BURTON ON TRENT, The Town Hall. CG. The Town Hall was built at the expense of Lord Paget, and carried out by BENJAMIN WYATT, father of James and Samuel. James may have designed it. In July 1771, the Coade firm supplied "4 ornamented patteras and 190ft of Gulochi" and in February 1772 "a Pannel with Arms" for £26.15s.6d. in all. The bill was sent in by Miss Coade – important evidence that she was in charge from a very early date. Staffordshire Record Office D 603/F/3/13/14. (Mrs Randall, Asst Archivist.)

ENVILLE, *near Stourbridge.* House of various dates. CG. No Coade identified.

FISHERWICK PARK. CD. 21.3.1817. Kay, Bedford Street a damaged vase sent to Lord Chichester [sic] £10.10s.0d.

NEWCASTLE UNDER LYME. Theatre Royal, Nelson Place, 1787-8, had a roundel with bust of Shakespeare. The roundel has been placed on a new theatre, 1987. (Gaye Blake-Roberts and Ruth Vincent Kemp.)

SHUGBOROUGH. Ionic capitals to the portico by *SAMUEL WYATT,** 1794. Antefixae* from a design by Piranesi. Artificial stone plaque on the Cat's Monument,* damaged Druid on ruins by river.* Roundels with Anson Coat of Arms on Lichfield lodges.* (Said to be marked CROGAN 34). "E. Coade Artificial Stone £141.5s.0d." in Samuel Wyatt's tradesmen's bills 1792-6. Lichfield MSS Staffs County Record Office D 615/E (H) 2/5.

TIXALL. House by *CAPABILITY BROWN,* 1770s, had Lions on Screen Walls. Demolished 1925. Dorothy Stroud *Capability Brown* 1975 edition p154.

THE OAKS, *near Wolverhampton.* CO. May 1815, "Mr. Gibbons, the Oaks, near Wolverhampton, a tripod for a sundial 3 figure pedestal for an 18" dial." The bill, with carriage, came to £32.15s.0d. House not identified.

SUFFOLK

BOTESDALE, *(Bottesdale to Coade).* CG. House not identified.

BOXFORD, *12 Broad Street.* Egyptian lion* from Deepdene, Surrey qv (Anthony Niner).

BUNGAY. CG. Probably Earsham, Norfolk, within a mile.

BURY ST EDMUNDS. Market Hall and Theatre by *ROBERT ADAM* 1775-8. Plaques of three swags of husks and paterae on all four sides,* niches with urns,* capitals of Coade stone.* (On ground floor, natural stone.)

ST MARY'S CHURCH, CAPEL SW *of Ipswich,* Monument to William Piess, 1809 (Gunnis who calls it Essex). Not visible 1973 (Kelly).

DALHAM, *west of Bury St Edmunds.* Probably Dalham Hall. CO January 1816 "Capt. Murray, Dalham Suffolk, Large size Vestal and Sybil to carry lights 20gns each". Not traced.

GREAT SAXHAM HALL, near Bury St Edmunds. CG. Coade style capitals,* pediment coat of arms and palms,* vases,* plaque as at 21 Portman Square at one end,* round medallions in tympana of triple windows each end.* Plaques* from between ground and first floors now removed and leaning against the house. Great Saxham Hall designed by *ROBERT ADAM,* was burnt and rebuilt by JOSEPH PATIENCE to a different design in 1796 and the Coade work is due to him. The Umbrello garden building is stamped Coade and Sealy, and so later.* See chapter 8 for details. (Julia Abel Smith.)

HENHAM HALL, near Southwold. By *JAMES WYATT* for Sir John Rous, later Lord Stradbroke, 1793-7. Gunnis says "decorative details 1799". Demolished.

ST MARY HENSTEAD CHURCH, near Beccles. Monument to George Mitchell* 1806, marked Coade and Sealy. Sarcophagus with a draped oval medallion of mourning woman by urn (Pevsner). Monument to William Clarke,* 1806. Weeping putto by a draped urn, Teigngrace model (Pevsner).

HEVINGHAM HALL, near Halesworth. Exterior 1779 by *SIR ROBERT TAYLOR* for Sir Gerard Vanneck. CG. On house, urns,* two reclining figures supporting an escutcheon,* plaques with swags, caryatids,* plaques with profiles in relief,* recumbent lions on corner blocks,* corinthian capitals,* keystones,* plaques* with griffins. On the Orangery, designed by *JAMES WYATT,* in 1780s, Dancing Hours plaques,* statues of Flora and Pomona* and "composed" capitals,* and at the entrance, the gatepiers have urns,* and the lodges friezes* and consoles.* (Now stolen.)

HURTS HALL. by *SAMUEL WYATT,* 1803, now neo Elizabethan 1893. CO June 1816 "Hon. Charles Long, 2 vases, same as Evans, 6gns. 2 tripod stands 20 gns each".

ICKWORTH, near Bury St Edmunds X. By *MARIO ASPRUCCI THE YOUNGER* and *FRANCIS SANDYS* 1796-1830 for Earl of Bristol. Part of top frieze of the Rotunda to Flaxman's design and lower plaques in Coade stone*. CD March 1821, "4 Ionic columns in yellow antique* [scagliola] 15' 6" high, skeletons 272' @ 1s.6d., per foot, £325.10s.4d." CD April 1821, "Earl of Bristol, time, expenses fixing columns, 2 men, 14 days each, £13.7s.0d." These columns*, with white "statuary scagliola" capitals* and bases* are in the library. Porphyry scagliola columns* were also supplied for the hall at some later date. Drawing at Chatsworth shows figure frieze.

IPSWICH. CG. Nothing identified. Possibly Woolverstone Hall.

LANGHAM HALL, near Bury St Edmunds. CG. Handsome Georgian house with Ionic doorcase (Pevsner). Coade capitals?

ORFORD LIGHTHOUSE. CG. Not traced.

POLSTEAD HOUSE (now Polstead Hall), Stoke by Nayland. Improvements by *WILLIAM PILKINGTON* for T.W. Cooke, 1816-19. CO May 1814 "188 balusters and 52 half ditto". at 5s. 6d.

REDGRAVE HALL. CG. House by *CAPABILITY BROWN.* Demolished. Orangery, with figures and medallion 1771-3 D. Stroud *Capability Brown* 1975 illustration plate 22b.

SUDBURY. CG. Nothing identified.

TWISTED HALL. CG. House not traced.

WICKHAM MARKET. CD May 1815, "Mr. Ferran, Wickham Market, a column for sundial with heads and drapery for a 15" dial, 7gns." House not traced.

WOOLVERSTONE HALL* (Woolverton to Coade), near Ipswich. By *JOHN JOHNSON* 1776, for the Berners family. CG Capitals,* frieze,* plaque* in pediment, decoration* in blind arches over windows, consoles*, paterae,* balusters* and three urns* (one a chimney pot). The capitals have the beaded volutes of Chelmsford Shire Hall qv (English Heritage).

ST MARY WORLINGWORTH CHURCH, near Framlingham. Monument to Dame Anne Henniker,* 1793. "Very crisp and dainty" (Pevsner). See Rochester Cathedral and Great Dunmow, Essex. Similar to Wortley Montagu, Westminster Abbey.

ST PETER YOXFORD CHURCH. Lunette memorial to Ann Davy, said to have been modelled by Robert Brettingham de Carle 1786, referred to in F. Burgess *English Churchyard Memorials* 1963. (H.H. de Carle.)

SURREY

ABINGER HALL, near Dorking. CD September 1818 "I. Scarlett Esq., Abinger Hall Dorking, 2 Ionic columns and pilasters, scagliola, £63.15s.2d." House now of 1872.

ALBURY PARK. Capitals* on the terrace from the earlier house by *SIR JOHN SOANE* (J.A.H. Kingswell).

BEDDINGTON HOUSE, Surrey. Coping to "Mr Medland, Architect and Surveyor" CO 3. 11. 1814

CAMDEN HOUSE, Beddington. Chimneypiece,* almost a duplicate of one at Capesthorne, Cheshire qv (J.A.H. Kingswell).

ST PETER CHERTSEY CHURCH. Aisles rebuilt 1806-8, by *THOMAS CHAWNER.* Aisle window label stops,* and tracery* are by Coade and Sealy 1806 (Pevsner). Label stops have a variety of motifs, including a crowned skull, cherub's head with wings and a bit of the Laocoon.

COULSDON CHURCH (St John, Bradmore Green, Old Coulsdon). Memorial to Mrs Elizabeth Howard (d1802) with three small cherubs' heads (Ann Saunders).

DEEPDENE, near Dorking. By *THOMAS HOPE,* for himself, with assistance from *THOMAS ATKINSON,* 1819-26. Demolished. CO August 1815 "Thomas Hope Esq. 2 Grecian capitals, 10ins" diam. 8gns each, 2 antics [sic] to do. 4gns., 4 pateras 18" diam. 2gns." CD February 1820, "Coade and Sealy for an Egyptian lion* supplied Mr. Hope in lieu of one he had from Coade and Sealy, damaged, say 16gns. for 10gns." This lion is now at 12 Broad St, Boxford, Suffolk qv.

DENBIES, near Dorking. CD "William Denison Esq. nr Dorking . . . medallion of flora September 1816." (Demolished 1850). Possibly the order for "Arms and crest with wreath of oak on circular ground" of May 1816, £27.16s.6d." sent to Pall Mall may belong to this house.

ST JOHN the BAPTIST EGHAM CHURCH. Church rebuilt, 1817-20 by *HENRY RHODES* (architect of the Department of Woods and Forests). CD July 1818 "Robert Pinney, an ornament for the vane*(?) of Egham Church 8gns." This seems likely to be what Pevsner describes as the tiny tempietto on top of the roof of the belfry.

HAM COMMON, near Richmond. CO January 1815 "Mr. Bernard, 90 Cornhill, one chimneypot bard [sic] 6gns. to be sent to Ham Common, Surrey". House not identified.

HAM HOUSE X, near Richmond. CG. Figure of River God,* 9ft long, on lawn in front of house. Twelve pineapples along forecourt railings,* nine stamped Coade and Sealy 1800, two stamped Coade and Sealy 1799. One stamped Coade.

LEITH HILL PLACE, near Dorking.* Pair of statues* adapted to hold lights, standing on cylindrical bases with neo-classical ornament. 4ft high. Bronzed finish (Martin Drury). Coade 1797.

LYNE CAPLE, near Dorking. CO September 1820. "Jas. Broadwood, Lyne Caple Dorking, a monumental tablet per sketch 40gns." CO May 1821 "a monument for his son 20gns." Place not identified.

MERTON ABBEY, Merton. Croggon, in May 1815, supplied Charles Smith, Merton Abbey, with coping of various widths. House demolished.

MITCHAM. CG. Nothing traced.

NORBITON PLACE, Norbiton. CD June 1818, "C.N. Palmer Esq Norbiton Place, LAPIDGE architect, large masks for keystones, river god and water nymph, £7.1s.0d." CO May 1819 "A triton figure dolphin and shells on coralwork stand 120gns." (Version of Giambologna's fountain). CD September 1819, "A trunk with waterlilies and leaves about 3ft high to cover lead pipes and [sic] fountain £13.7s.0d." Demolished.

NORBURY PARK, near Dorking. In Coade's Gallery (1799) Mrs Coade exhibited two crouching figures Psyche and Hymen, 1ft high "for a chimneypiece of Mr Lock's designed by Bacon". A duplicate pair, bronzed, surfaced in 1984 and is now at Heaton Hall Manchester qv.

NORK HOUSE, Banstead. Altered for Lord Arden by WILLIAM PILKINGTON, 1812-24. Demolished. CD. September 1819 "Lord Arden, 34 whole balusters 10ins", Epsom, loading and delivery £12.15s.0d."

OTTERSHAW PARK, near Weybridge. House and lodges by JAMES WYATT c.1795. House demolished. Lodges remain, with "artificial stone plaques above the windows" (Pevsner).* Now painted in natural colours. CO June 1813 for Edward Boehm "A circular medallion containing coat of arms for dairy ceiling".

PETERSHAM. CG. Probably Park Gate House, with a chimneypiece said to be dated 1794. Not a standard design. (Antique Collector August 1965 p147).

POLESDEN LACEY. Tenant has a medallion of Milton in a wreath,* same style as those at Saltram qv.

REIGATE,THE RETREAT. CO April 1814 "4 squat pier vases, small 5gns each, 2 do. smaller 3½gns. each" for "Wm. Turner, Retreat, Ryegate, Surrey." CO April 1818, "2 5' 6" figures, Summer and Winter, 50gns." House not identified.

THE WHITE HART,Reigate. CO August 1815, "For Mr. Relf White Hart Reigate Surrey, White Hart 20gns.". Demolished.

22 UPPER WEST STREET. Coade decoration on the exterior* (Ivor May).

RICHMOND. CO April 1821, "Saml. Paynter, Richmond, 2 sphynxes for 28gns." CO 1821, "a black and gold pedestal per drawing." Possibly for the house in Richmond, belonging to S. Painter, altered by *VULLIAMY*, 1834. Demolished.

RICHMOND, TERRACE GARDENS X. River God, duplicate of Ham House figure, much damaged.*

RICHMOND PARK. CG. The Wick, by *ROBERT MYLNE* 1775, has apparently Coade paterae (painted) on the front.* It stands at the entrance to Richmond Park, and could be the building referred to.

RIPLEY. CG. Nothing identified.

ROEHAMPTON, GROVE HOUSE (Froebel Institute). Pediment with a large plaque of a female profile set in a wreath.* *JAMES WYATT.* Oblong plaques of festoons over first floor windows.* Similar profile plaques on ends of house.* Much additional work in similar style c.1900. (Anthony Dale.)

ROEHAMPTON, MANRESA HOUSE. By *WILLIAM CHAMBERS*, 1767. Lord Besborough bought four tablets at the Pincot sale at Christie's in 1767.

RUNNYMEDE PARK, Tile Hill, Egham. Back of remarkable house, three storeys in front, two at the back, has seven Coade plaques marked Coade London 1791. Reclining ladies and swags and paterae.

ST ANNE'S HILL. CG. Place not traced.

SUTTON. CD March 1814, "Miss Manners, Sutton, Surrey, fountain, rock, coral, £21." Including erecting the fountain, the bill was for £25.18s.1d. There was a further bill for mending it in 1820. House not traced.

WAVERLEY ABBEY, near Farnham. CG. House c.1770-80. (Pevsner.) Entrance front has typical oblong plaques with swags,* oval paterae.* The pilaster capitals could also be Coade. Garden front has the same plaques* and round paterae,* and coat of arms with putti over door.* A decorated string course* is on both sides.

WORCESTER PARK, Ewell. CG. JOHN NASH built additions to house. Demolished.

SUSSEX

ARUNDEL CASTLE. CG. Lion* and Horse* near the Norman castle mound, one stamped 1798, from New Shoreham Suspension Bridge qv (F.J. Collins).* Relief

378

of King Alfred instituting Trial of Jury, 20ft wide by J.C.F. Rossi 1797. Statues of Liberty and Hospitality 9ft high 1798. (Sold in 1891 and probably the figures presented to the Lambeth Vestry in 1891.) Now lost. Coat of arms, openwork cartwheels in the balustrades by the front door also Coade work. Lost in later 19th century reconstruction. John Martin Robinson, "Magna Carta and Pretty Ladies' Maids" *Country Life,* 7 July 1983, pp46-49.

ASHBURNHAM PLACE, *near Battle.* House of many periods, demolished 1950s. Fountain in dairy c.1800 (Gunnis).

ASHDOWN HOUSE, *near Forest Row.* CG. House by *BENJAMIN LATROBE,* 1795, shortly before he emigrated. Semi-circular Ionic portico with four columns having Erechtheion capitals and bases,* also the pilasters of the rotunda inside.* Upstairs "composed" capitals, now painted, seem likely to be Coade stone.

BATTLE ABBEY, *Battle.* Work for Mr Godfrey Webster, knighted during its progress. CD December 1814, "Sir Godfrey Webster, 22 Gothic corbels, £57.15s.0d."* September 1815, "8 Gothic corbels* £21., large Gothic archway sent this day per waggon* £147." A further eight Gothic corbels were sent in the same month. CD November 1815 "Gothic chimneypiece £42." CD December 1815 "sent this day per waggon for White Hart, Arms and crest on circular tablet, £31.10s.0d."* The archway* is on the front, and the corbels* survive in situ. Further corbels seen lying in the garden now seem to have disappeared (F.J. Collins), the chimneypiece was lost in a fire in 1931. The coat of arms, once over the fireplace in the great hall, now in the garden, broken in two but in surprisingly good condition.*

BIGNOR. CG. Nothing traced.

ST NICHOLAS BRAMBER CHURCH (*Steyning to Coade*). Circular bas-relief of a mourning woman above an inscribed plaque to Ann Green, and Rev. Thomas Green, 1789 (E. Esdaile).* Very small coat of arms below.*

BRIGHTLING PARK. Garden seat with Gothic ornament by Sir *ROBERT SMIRKE* (F.J. Collins and Sir Noel Moynihan). Marked *COADE SEALY* 1803.

BRIGHTON ROYAL PAVILION. CG. Copies of six statues placed on the *HENRY HOLLAND* version of the Royal Pavilion in 1788 were exhibited in Coade's Gallery 1799. They were removed from the Pavilion by 1801 and seem to be lost.

ST NICHOLAS' CHURCH, *Brighton.* Churchyard tomb of Anna Maria Crouch (died 1805) marked Coade and Sealy* (ie. before 1813). Urn* on top, marked Croggon (ie after 1821). Tomb as Mrs Sheridan, Old Windsor qv. Tomb in fair condition though very mossy. Urn in very poor condition. No stamps now visible, but seen by E. Esdaile.

CHAPEL ROYAL, *North Street, Brighton*. By *THOMAS SAUNDERS*, Royal Arms with conchant lion and unicorn dated MDCCXCIII reset on Victorian chapel of 1884-93 (Antony Dale). Site originally the Assembly rooms of the Castle Hotel.

NEW STEINE HOTEL, *Brighton*. Building survives in New Steine Square. Letter to W.R. Mott 18.2.1813 (Letter Book p4) New Steine Hotel Brighton, asking payment of £24.17s.6d. Coade work not identified.

CHURCH ARMY BUILDING, *Brighton*. On the corner of Upper James and Lavender Streets. Two plaques of reclining ladies marked Croggon 1823.* (F.J. Collins 1950s.)

CASTLE GORING, *near Worthing*. CG (as Goring Park). Designed 1790 by *JOHN BIAGIO REBECCA* for Sir Bysshe Shelley, poet's grandfather. Front a mock castle, back a Palladian villa. On the villa side three panels with Bacchus, Satyr and Ceres, coat of arms in pediment, fluted string course, Ionic pilaster capitals, balusters below windows, all in Coade stone. At each end, an extension with Ionic columns with Coade capitals. The figures lean out of their panel frames to an extraordinary extent, unknown elsewhere.*

CHICHESTER. CD May 1821 "James Smart, Chichester, 2 Ionic caps. £13.16s.0d." There had been an order on 16 April for two Ionic capitals for George Draper, a Chichester architect. Was he building the house for Mr Smart, or are the two unconnected?

MARKET HOUSE, *North Street*. By *JOHN NASH*, 1807. Coat of arms of the town marked Coade & Sealy (F.J. Collins).*

SWAN INN, *Chichester*. CO May 1819, "Mr. Humphrey, Swan Inn Chichester, order of Mr. *GEORGE DRAPER*, architect of South St, Chichester, a swan on ground as drawing 14gns." CD September 1819, "Humphries, Swan Inn Chichester, 2 Ionic capitals modelled as drawing at 7gns., £15.14s.8d." for a porch for the inn? Not traced.

PRIORY PARK, *Chichester*, Statue of a Druid, originally from the Conduit, South Street, 1777.* (*Sussex Archaeological Collections*, vol 107, pages 10-11.)

COOLHURST, *near Horsham*. Letter Book (p17) to Earl of Galloway. Drawing sent for "a column for a dial of that simple plan. Dial we suppose 7 or 8gns. in Dolland's charge." No further correspondence or bills.

CRANLEY. CG. No Cranley in Sussex. Cranley old spelling of Cranleigh, Surrey. Nothing traced.

FINDON PLACE, north of Worthing. CD. August 1814, "Arms for pediment £21."* The order specifies that the arms should be 2ft 1⅜ins high, showing the accuracy of size expected from the factory.

FRANT. CG. Nothing traced.

GOODWOOD HOUSE X near Chichester. CG. By JAMES WYATT, 1790-1800. Small coat of arms on Kennels.* Now Golf House. A coat of arms on a drapery background similar to that on estate cottages, unmarked but dated 1771, and so preceding Wyatt's work at the house, now ex situ in a 1960s loggia.*

LILLEY GREEN LODGE, near Goodwood. Coat of arms* (J.H. Cordingley).

HAMMERWOOD PARK, near East Grinstead. CG. By BENJAMIN LATROBE, 1792. Porticos each end with archaic Greek Doric capitals* copies from the "Basilica", Paestum.* Greek inscription on the capitals – see Chapter 10. Bas-relief from the Borghese vase in each portico.*

HERSTMONCEUX PLACE, Near Hailsham. CG. SAMUEL WYATT, 1777. Between the ground and first floor windows a series of 11 plaques,* alternately with urns and swags, also paterae.*

HORSHAM TOWN HALL. Built 1812 by Duke of Norfolk, Arms* of the Howards, George III and the Town. All but this façade rebuilt 1888. George III in Coade stone, Howards and Horsham Arms in a very hard natural stone.

ST MARGARET IFIELD CHURCH, near Crawley. 1801 Tomb of George Hutchinson, 1801.* Coade urn (Edmund Esdaile) and reliefs of the woman of Samaria and angels bearing an urn heavenward (Gunnis).

KIDBROOKE PARK, near East Grinstead. Partly rebuilt by GEORGE DANCE, 1814-15. CO April 1818, "Lord Colchester, Kidbrooke nr. East Grinstead, Sx. arms with supporters for a pediment, festoons of oak and ribbons". It is 12ft long and cost 60 guineas.* House now called Michael Hall.

LEWES COUNTY HALL. By JOHN JOHNSON, 1808-12. Three plaques*, Justice and Boy, Wisdom and Boy, and Mercy and Boy, are identical to those on Johnson's Shire Hall, Chelmsford. R.F. Dell, *Sussex Archaeological Collections*, vol C, page 9, says that Coade and Sealy also supplied 40 balusters,* 10 imposts,* 10 female head blocks* and 60 modillions.* Most of these also used at the Assembly Rooms Leicester qv. Coat of arms.* WSRO QAH/1/7E3 (27) QAH/1/7E1

LEWES, 167 High St. Round arched front door with Coade keystone.*

MARESFIELD PARK, near Uckfield. CO November 1819, "Sir John Shelley, Maresfield Park, Uckfield, Sussex, a crest of a griffin's head on ground 12" x 10" x 2½". "2 lions couchant on plinths to Shelley's wagon", for £15.9s.0d, had been sent in January. House demolished.

MICHEL (or Mitchell) GROVE. Gothic improvements by *G. BYFIELD*. House demolished 1832. CO November 1816, "Richard Watt Walker Esq., a Gothic chimneyps. with centre 180gns." Croggon also supplied "2 rich Gothic candelabras, packing etc." for £81.8s.4d – ie. they were very large; see Carlton House, London.

MIDHURST. CG. Nothing traced.

NORFOLK SUSPENSION BRIDGE, NEW SHOREHAM. 1833. Howard Lion and Fitzalan Horse now at Arundel Castle* on bridge until its demolition in 1933.

ST NICHOLAS OLD SHOREHAM CHURCHYARD. Monument outside north side of chancel signed Croggon 1828.* No name of occupant. Classical altar with bas-reliefs of flowers on sides, stepped base (inscribed FUERUNT).

PARHAM HOUSE X, north of Arundel. In the grounds Bas-relief of a lion from Northwick Park, Gloucestershire* qv. Two seats with winged sphinxes* as in Thomas Hope's *Household Furniture* 1807 (Maurice Tomlin, F.J. Collins and J. Duxfield).

PITSHILL (Pett's Hill to Coade) near Petworth. CG. Late 18th century house by *JOHN UPTON* after Soane 1794. Pevsner mentions panels which could be Coade. Nothing identified.

PETWORTH HOUSE X, Petworth. CG. This early Coade not identified. CO July 1816, "Ld. Egremont offered 3 vases and head, River God for 35gns." Not surviving. Very fine triton fountain, with dolphins from design by Giambologna.* (See Alison Kelly Coade Stone in National Trust Houses, *National Trust Studies 1980*), pp94-111.

ST MARY PETWORTH CHURCH. Royal arms in north aisle,* marked Coade and Sealy 1812 (Pevsner).

RUDGWICK, Hyes. Modern gate piers with standard small Coade urns as at Paxton etc. Clearly ex situ. (R. Breakell.)

SHEFFIELD PARK. House Gothicised for Earl of Sheffield by *JAMES WYATT* 1776-7. Small Coade pinnacles* of early date, small Coade flowers* here and there, a fairly flat Coade coat of arms,* and a very vigorous coat of arms and supporters of 1809.* Work by *B.H. LATROBE* not identified.

STANMER HOUSE, near Brighton. In grounds, near carpark, a Coade monument, as Brocklesby etc, with urns and tortoises.* Said to be designed by *JAMES WYATT* c.1775. Very gritty surface as Mottisfont urns.

ST MARY SULLINGTON CHURCH, near Storrington. CD. August 1814, "Rev. J.V.G. Dixon, monument to the memory of the Rev. Dixon 12gns, inscription and expenses 5gns." Not traced.

UPPARK X, near Petersfield. CO April 1820, "Sir H. Fetherstone Bart., Uppark Petersfield, by Goddard's Petersfield waggon from the Boro, 6 antique vases, 2' 4" high, 4gns each." Not traced. Borghese Vase* on front lawn, probably supplied in connexion with *REPTON'S* landscape gardening in 1805.

WEST DEAN PARK. Two caryatid figures, without capitals on their heads, as at Pitzhanger Manor etc, on fluted square bases. Formerly at Monkton and now used as a memorial to Edward James. Possibly originally at West Dean Park house as this was designed by *JAMES WYATT*, the most frequent user of Coade stone. (M. Heymann.)

WESTMESTON PLACE, near Hurstpierpoint. "In front of the house a handsome Coade stone urn" (Pevsner). Not traced.

WEST STOKE, COPSE COTTAGES, nos 13, 14. Over the doors together a coat of arms on a drapery panel dated 1790.* (F.J. Collins)

WORTHING. PARK CRESCENT by *AMON HENRY WILDS.** Entrance arch with four bearded male terms in the main arch, and female heads in the flanking arches. Market CROGGON. Built 1829. (Peter Hone.)

ST ANDREW WEST TARRING CHURCHYARD, near Worthing. Monument as Woodford, Essex, to Martha Chivers, 1807, but almost undamaged, in churchyard (E. Esdaile).*

ST MARY WISTON CHURCH, near Steyning. Monument to Sarah Goring, died 1798. Reclining figure just fitting into an elaborately detailed Gothic recess.* (Pevsner)

BARFORD HOUSE, * *South of Warwick.* CO February 1817, "Charles Mills Esq., Barford near Warwick, to the care of Mr. John Morris, mason, Warwick, bill to *MR. HAKEWILL,* Lower Brook St., 2 Ionic caps. "12ins diam." The Regency house appears to have four Ionic columns; presumably the other capitals were supplied later.

BIRMINGHAM GUN BARREL PROOF HOUSE. Trophy of arms in a niche over the inscription "Established by Act of Parliament for Public Security Anno dom. 1813." Apparently Coade (F.J. Collins.)*

BIRMINGHAM, SOHO HOUSE. Ionic capitals,* *SAMUEL WYATT* 1787-8 (N. Molyneux)

BIRMINGHAM THEATRE ROYAL. CG. Designed by *SAMUEL WYATT,* 1774. Plaques of Garrick* and Shakespeare* have survived the demolition of the theatre and will be reused by Birmingham Central Libraries. A drawing of the façade shows paterae and oblong plaques which could also have been Coade (Birmingham Reference Library). *New Ladies Magazine* August 1790 plate opposite p405 shows details.

THE RETREAT, Bordesley, near Birmingham. Almshouses c.1790, demolished. Pairs of cottages in a long narrow court, with front doors in twos. Gothic ogee overdoors had Hope seated in left tympanum, and Faith kneeling in the right (N. Cooper).

ETTINGTON PARK, (Eastington to Coade) near Stratford on Avon. CD. October 1817 "Expenses at Windsor, Dubbin taking drawing and dimensions of chimneypiece, £4.10s.0d." CD June 1818, "Evelyn I. Shirley Esq. a rich Gothic chimneypiece copied from one at Windsor Castle 60gns." Fixing it cost £10.16s.0d. In the Library, which retains its Regency Gothic decorations*, though the rest of the house is Victorian Gothic of 1858-62.

HENLEY IN ARDEN. CG. Nothing identified.

HONINGTON HALL ,(Worcestershire to Coade), Shipston on Stour. 17th century house with rococo decoration inside. CG. Nothing identified.

ST JOHN the BAPTIST LEA MARSTON CHURCH (called Hams Hall by Coade and almost underneath Hams Hall Power Station.) CG. Monument to Mrs Adderley* 1784, with roundel of a seated woman and an urn above (Pevsner).

REGENT HOTEL, Leamington Spa. Built 1818-19. CO March 1820, *"CHARLES SMITH* architect, Warwick, for Regent Hotel, Leamington, Prince of Wales Feathers couchant*, from 8 to 9 ft and about 4ft 6in high." The arms survived the bombing of the hotel in 1940 and remain in situ.

MALVERN HALL, *near Solihull.* House altered by *SOANE* for H. G. Lewis, 1790s. CO October 1818, "Henry Greswold Lewis Esq., an Ancient Briton, do. Norman, Vestal, Sybil, for 136gns. per letter." Figures not traced. John Constable's *Correspondence* IV p58 suggests that he transmitted an order from Henry Greswold Lewis in late 1818. (Simon Jervis). Constable had also to paint "my ancestor Humphri de Grousewolde" who came over with the Conqueror, "a correct Norman figure in net armour". (Probably the model for the Coade figure). *Correspondence of John Constable*, ed R.B. Beckett, pp57-58 Vol. IV 1962.

SHIPSTON ON STOUR *(Worcestershire to Mrs Coade).* CG. May refer to Ettington Park. Otherwise nothing traced.

STONELEIGH ABBEY, *near Kenilworth.* House mainly by *FRANCIS SMITH* but altered by *C.S. SMITH* (of Warwick) in early 19th century. CD. September 1820, "James Henry Leigh Esq., circular pedestal green granite scagliola, statuary base and plinth £16.16s.4d." Not traced. CD. July 1821, "Fountain, 2 basins, coral work etc. 30gns. Circular coping 12ft diam. 12gns. Fountain comprising icicles and 3 dolphins and 3 shells supporting large shell, 40 guineas.* Hexagon coping, comprising spar, shells and waterlilies, 24gns." Only second fountain survives (Lord Leigh). Graceless design with awkward centrepiece and little animals — cat etc — worked into the coping.*

WARWICK (?). CD. July 1821, "Wratislaw per *MR C. SMITH* architect Warwick, Monument comprising a pedestal and fluted column with a vase at the top, 70gns." With inscription etc the whole bill was £104. Wratislaw was a Rugby barrister (Warwickshire Record Office).

WARWICK CASTLE — X. CG. Bridge by *ROBERT MYLNE*, with Coade plaques,* illustrated in A. E. Richardson, *Robert Mylne*, 1955, plates 38, 41.

WESTMORLAND

now Cumbria

WINDERMERE LAKE*, *now Cumbria.* CG. Belle Isle, a house by John Plaw 1774 in the middle of the lake would be the appropriate reference, but its Ionic capitals turn out to be of wood, not Coade stone, and no other Coade stone has been found there. Claife Station, built c.1799 on the lake shore near

Far Sawrey as a summer house, might be the place, with its battlemented tower, but no Coade stone remains in the present ruin. (B.N. Dean, Assistant Historic Buildings Representative National Trust.)

WILTSHIRE

BOWDEN PARK, * *near Corsham.* By *JAMES WYATT,* 1796. CG. Oval hall with Coade statues* in niches, dated 1796 on the pedestals. Illustrated *Connoisseur* April 1961, p168.

CHARLTON PARK, * *near Malmesbury.* Alterations attributed to *JAMES WYATT,* 1774. Hall has apse with round Coade plaques,* similar smaller plaques* above the doors Antony Dale *James Wyatt* 1956 p33.

STOKE PARK, Earl Stoke (Colvin) or ERLESTOKE PARK (Pevsner). House by George Steuart 1786-91, the gatepiers with rustication and urns on top appear to be Coade stone (Peter Hone).

FRESDEN, Highworth. Urn from Northwick Park, qv dated 1840 (F.J. Collins).*

LITTLECOTE, near Hungerford. CO July 1814, "Major General Popham, a fountain on coral rock with 2 basins, 30gns. Now removed.

LONGLEAT, near Warminster. CG. Nothing identified.

STOURHEAD X, near Mere. CG. Statue of Urania 1773 (Gunnis): not traced. Borghese Vase, ordered 1770, in Temple of Flora.* Henry Hoare paid £12.14s.6d. for it, 7.5.1772, having already paid Daniel Pincot £5.5s.0d. subscription for it. See Chapter 3 (Kenneth Woodbridge).

WARDOUR CASTLE. Triangular pedestal as Audley End, in garden (Hon. Mrs Jane Roberts).*

WILTON HOUSE, Wilton, nr Salisbury. Plaques of Coade stone on the walls of the cloisters built by *JAMES WYATT* in 1801 Antony Dale *James Wyatt* 1956 p164. Thought to have been removed c.1960. (Earl of Pembroke.)

WORCESTERSHIRE

CROOME COURT, near Worcester. CG. Island Temple 1778, Aldobrandini Marriage (long plaque),* Phrygian Shepherd and Shepherdess* (two roundels) griffins and foliage (long plaque).* Paid for by *"CAPABILITY BROWN"* (John Hardy); but the design of the temple, among *ROBERT ADAM'S* drawings in the Soane Museum, clearly shows the plaques. South front steps two large Grecian sphinxes;* Druid statue, dated 1795;* Naiad by artificial grotto, very badly damaged;* Punch-bowl gateway, with "squat" urns dated 1794;* "Dry Arch Bridge" (carrying a drive over a gully)* with rusticated blocks and voussoirs and fine keystones of bearded heads, 1797. Monument, 1809, to "Capability Brown", very badly damaged* but now restored.Druid cost 25gns, two sphinxes 50gns, bill to the Earl of Coventry 14.8.1795 (Croome Estate Office 21A). Documents concerning all pieces except the Naiad and the Brown monument survive amongst the Croome Estate papers. Round temple with oblong swag and patera plaques and a term as at Chiswick House.*

EVESHAM. CG. Nothing identified. Perhaps refers to Fladbury.

FLADBURY, CRAYCOMBE HOUSE, near Evesham. By *GEORGE BYFIELD*, 1791. CG. Six paterae along the front,* three urns on cornice,* urn in alcove at east end of house.*

HAGLEY HALL, near Stourbridge. CG. Nothing identified.

HEWELL GRANGE, near Tardebigge. Alterations for Lord Plymouth by *THOMAS CUNDY*, 1815. CO March 1814. "2 Medicean and Borghesian Vases with pedestals at 100gns." They were "sent off by Pickford's barge from Paddington by canal". In 1815, the Earl had to have a new Medicean Vase "replacement of one that failed, 35gns." CD August 1821, "2 caryatids 6' 6" high with capitals 45gns. each"*(N Molyneux).

THE LEASOWES. CG. Famous for its gardens. Nothing identified.

SALWARPE (Salwerpe to Mrs Coade). CG. Nothing identified, but *GEORGE BYFIELD* did alterations at Salwarpe Parsonage in 1795. As he used Coade stone at Fladbury, Michel Grove Sussex and Perdiswell Hall Worcester this might have been the place.

WORCESTER, CHAMBERLAIN'S FACTORY (now Worcester Royal Porcelain Co.) CD. November 1813 "Regent's arms, 2 feathers, 30 gns." Survived on former Dyson Perrins Museum (now Reject China Shop) until 1971. Now removed, owing to the Director not knowing it was a scheduled building.

WORCESTER, PERDISWELL HALL, CG. House demolished, gatepiers survive on Droitwich Road, with plaques of Agriculture and Navigation, dated 1788 (Pevsner).* House by *GEORGE BYFIELD*.

WITLEY COURT. Lord Foley incurred charge of £86.14s.0d. on 11 September 1811. Reminder sent (Letter Book p6) on 16.4.1813. Sir John Summerson suggests 1810 for *JOHN NASH'S* remodelling of house – now ruined. *The Life and Work of John Nash Architect* 1980 p49.

YORKSHIRE

ALL SAINTS ASTON CHURCH, * *near Sheffield.* Plaque to William Mason, the poet, died 1797,* with fine portrait in profile in a medallion" (Pevsner). Marked Coade and Sealy 1804.

BEVERLEY, THE MINSTER. Monument to General Bowes.* CD April 1814, "Mrs. Bowes, monument to the memory of General Bowes intended for Beverley Church, comprising a figure representing the recording angel, with military trophies etc. 150gns."

WEDNESDAY MARKET, Beverley. Keystone* and two paterae,* one dated 1790 (Ivan Hall).

SESSIONS HOUSE, New Walk, Beverley. CHARLES WATSON architect 1807. Arms of his Majesty £42,* Statue of Justice £73.10s.6d.* (Ivan Hall has the bill).

off NEW WALK, Beverley. In garden of block of flats, one urn* as Paxton, but lacking finial and base and one large plaque,* swag and patera, as 20 Portman Square, from demolished house in the area (Elizabeth Hall).

31 BUTCHER ROW, Wednesday Market, Beverley. Bacchus keystone dated 1790 (not a catalogue number) and two paterae with Apollo head in centre. Demolished (Ivan Hall).

BOROUGHBRIDGE. CG. Nothing identified.

BRETTON HALL, south of Wakefield. CG. Chimneypiece removed 1946. Sold 1987. See Chapter 11.

BURTON CONSTABLE X (Burton to Coade), NE of Hull. CG. *THOMAS ATKINSON* built an orangery for William Constable 1788-9. Statues, including a Flora, Ceres, Pomona, urns and plaques of Seasons, costing £83.18s.7d., were bought for it (Christopher Gilbert).* Drawing displayed at the house.

BYRAM, near Pontefract. CG. Work by *CARR* of York and *ROBERT ADAM* for Sir John Ramsden Bart. c.1780. Demolished. Coade not traced.

CASTLE HOWARD. Medici Vase* in poor state at entrance to Ray Wood. Bought 1778 for £18. Private accounts of 5th Earl of Carlisle, cat. no. J14/81. (Archivist Eeyan Hartley.)

DONCASTER. CG. Nothing identified.

FARNLEY HALL, Otley. CO June 1818, "Mr. Fawkes, fountain from Mr. Rhodes' drawing 40gns." CD July 1818, "Walter Fawkes Esq. Farnley, Otley, Yorks, 2 hawks* for piers, £29.8s.0d., fountain, 3 basins with lion's heads, supported by lions' legs, £42. 2 shields of arms £29.8s.9d." The hawks on the gatepiers can be seen in a watercolour of the house by J.M.W. Turner, at the house.

FREMLINGTON. CG. Place not identified.

GRANGE (now Beckett Park College), Headingley, Leeds. Attributed to *JAMES PAINE.* CO March 1817 "Sir John Key ordered by Mr. Chippendale for lamps, Vestal and Sybil to be bronzed, 4ft 6ins". CD May 1817 bill to Sir John Lister Kaye for "Vestal and Flora at 20gns each and scagliola porphyry pedestals for them at 6gns each."

GRANTLEY HALL, near Ripon. Two heraldic plaques with blackamoors and crowns* dated 1794 and two Borghese Vases (College booklet).*

HAZLEWOOD CASTLE, near Tadcaster. Sold 15.6.1972 by executors at auction at the house, Lot 760, a recumbent Unicorn marked Coade and Sealy 1801.* Present whereabouts unknown.

HEATON LODGE. CG. Unidentified.

HILLAM HALL. Large dog kennel with bas-relief classical decoration on sides and a cross over the entrance. Marked *COADE & SEALY.* Now in private collection.

HULL. CG. 1799. Plaques,* Spring and Summer, from the Citadel, now in the Grotto in East Park, Holderness Road (Ivan Hall).

KIRKELLA, Hull. Letter Book shipping notes 28.8.1813 "For Hull, 2 cases for R.C. Pease Esq. Kirkella near Hull of companion to Stove and top."

LEEDS, THE COURT HOUSE. By *THOMAS TAYLOR.* Letters to T. Taylor March - May 1813 (pp5, 9, 10, 18). Shipping notes at end of Letter Book. 26.1.1813 six cases to Hull of two Corinthian caps for Court House, 25.2.1813 three cases of a stove and ironwork for do. 18.5.1813 eight cases containing 40 blocks and two angle vases (?) with piece of foliage and two cases with vase and foliage (?). 27.8.1813 two cases for Court House of two pannels foliage. 8.10.1813 two cases of two ionic caps, one case of four modillions. Letter of 1814 (p42) to Mayor of Leeds asking for his intervention as Coades can get no reply from Mr Taylor re the Court House. Corinthian classical building with plaques of City Arms, laurel wreaths and fasces. Demolished, but some Coade decorations from it recently rediscovered. (Adam White.)

MALTON . CG. Nothing identified.

METHLEY HALL, near Leeds. CG. See Temple Newsam entry, below.

NEWBY HALL, near Ripon. CG. *ROBERT ADAM* worked on the house from 1767-80. Coade not identified, probably "Swag and patera" plaques on Adam wings as at 20 Portman Square.*

SHEFFIELD, PHOENIX FOUNDRY. CO July 1820 "Longdon Walker and CO Phoenix Foundry, Sheffield, refer for payment to Mr. W.H. Whiteley, 2 Rosoman St. Clerkenwell, a bust of the Rev. Mr. Westley [Wesley] 5gns."

SLEDMERE X, near Malton. CG. Extensions to the house designed by the owner Sir Christopher Sykes 1781-1788. Plaques* on the SE, SW and NW fronts, also coat of arms on SW front.*

STOCKTON (in the Forest). CG. Nothing identified.

ST MARY SWINE CHURCH. Eighteenth century font; bowl with some Gothic enrichment, standing on clustered columns (M. Edward Ingram).*

TEMPLE NEWSAM X, near Leeds. Borghese Vase* now in hall and restored, from Methley Hall; also from Methley Hall were a group of three boys, a group of two boys, and a set of three vases with bas-relief figures. Purchased 1957; all destroyed by 1961. (C. Gilbert.)

WAKEFIELD. CG. Might refer to Methley Hall (see Temple Newsam). Otherwise nothing identified.

WENTWORTH WOODHOUSE. CG. From Pincot's sale 1767, Lord Rockingham bought a pair of river gods, six keystones and a bust of Antoninus Pius. CD December 1814, "4 figures of Seasons(*), 4' 6", £105., 2 large baskets of fruit and flowers(*), £42, ready waiting orders." The 1814 pieces are now in a private collection as are four larger figures of the Seasons, six vases and two sphinxes ordered in the 1780s-1790s.

WIKEHAM ABBEY, near Scarborough. CG. Eighteenth century house largely rebuilt in 20th century. Coade not identified.

YORK BARRACKS. CG. Demolished between 1971 and 1974. The coat of arms (1796) is in the care of English Heritage, and may be reused (RCHM, York).*

YORK, HESLINGTON HALL, University of York. Statue of Diana as a huntress, with a stag, in the forecourt of the Hall. Destroyed by vandals in recent years. (RCHM, York.)

(b) GREATER LONDON AREA

(including Middlesex)

ACTON GREEN. CG. 1799.

ADAM'S PLACE, Southwark. SOANE'S first dated building 1780-82, had cornice of Coade swags and bucrania, catalogue 186 "Oxhead and festoons of fruit 12/- per foot. Sir John Soane's Museum Drawer 39, Set 1, item 4." (Pierre de la Ruffinière du Prey. *Soane, the Making of an Architect* p225 fig 11.7 1977.)

ADELPHI, Royal Society of Arts. Bust of James Barry, the gift of Drs Clarke and Fryer, June 1819, missing. See St Paul's and Greenwich Park. Copy survives in a private collection.

ADMIRALTY, Whitehall. Screen by *ROBERT ADAM* to Ripley's building. CG, "Pannels with tritons etc." Panels visible in engraving in T.H. Shepherd's *London,* 1829.

ALBION FIRE OFFICE. NP. Royal Arms: place untraced, pre 1813.

150 ALDERSGATE STREET. CO April 1821, "Messrs. Seddon, 150 Aldersgate St. 1 verd antique slab, 3' 6" x 8" x ¾" thick, front and both ends polished and finished." Messrs Seddon were eminent furniture makers.

7 ALDGATE. CO July 1814, "James Bridger, no.7 Aldgate, 2 Corinthian capitals for elliptic columns". A special order.

ALL SOULS, Langham Place*. By *JOHN NASH,* 1822-5. Ionic capitals* for the circular portico (Sir John Summerson). A special order, with tiny winged cherubs' heads between the scrolls.

35 ALPHA ROAD, Lisson Grove. CO August 1817, "C.H. Tatham, Queen St. Mayfair, 4 pines for piers, 1½ gns. each, to be delivered to 35 Alpha Road." A present to Tatham, for his own house. Street gone.

APSLEY HOUSE X. CD February 1820, "Duke of Wellington for Apsley House, ordered by Mr. Wyatt, 25' 4" fluted stringing with plain moulding @ 7s.6d., per foot, 25' 4" in rich guioche @ 10s.6d. per foot, £28.14s.4d." CD, also February 1820 "Duke of Wellington, 4 angular pilasters sienna scagliola, £129.4s.0d."* CD October 1820, "Benjamin Wyatt, 2 bases for columns ornamental stone, 2 for angular pilasters, 8gns."* B.D. WYATT was the Duke's architect. Now in the dining room.

ARCHBISHOP MICHAEL RAMSAY SCHOOL, Farmer's Road, Camberwell. Charity boy,* standard figure, unpainted, from Lambeth Charity School via Archbishop Temple's School.

ARGYLL HOUSE, 8 Argyll Street. By *ROBERT MYLNE.* Chimneypiece, 1783, cost 6½ guineas (R.S. Mylne, *The Master Masons to the Crown of Scotland,* 1893). (F.J. Collins)

ARMOURERS AND BRAZIERS HALL, City of London. CG. No Coade work identified.

ASHBURNHAM HOUSE, Dover Street, Westminster. CD October 1816, "Earl Ashburnham, a candelabra composed of three figures on a pedestal £21. Cartage of do. to Cockspur St. 12s.0d.".

AYBROOK STREET, W1. Coade keystones (F.J. Collins). Demolished 1970s.

BAKER STREET, W1*. Four rusticated doorways,* stretches of guilloche string course.*

BANK OF ENGLAND, City of London. By *SIR JOHN SOANE,* 1795, 12 statues for the dome of the Rotunda, £200 (Gunnis);* 1799, 12 statues for the Transfer Office, £252 (Gunnis);* 1801 Europe, Asia, Africa and America for Lothbury court, £88 each.* CG. 1801 four vases £34.16s.1d., and a repeat order Lothbury Court, "A square pedestal for a stove, with open work in the dye of it, for letting out the warm air . . . as the stoves in the Bank of England . . ." CD November 1818, "18 balusters for the Bank of England, £5.15s.0d." (Curator, Bank of England). The caryatids are all in one hall in Baker's Bank. The four Continents are on the roof.

BASINGHALL STREET. CG. "The White Bear, and other Ornaments". Not traced.

ST MARY'S CHURCH, Battersea (Old Battersea Church). Rebuilt 1775 by *JOSEPH DIXON.* Monument to John Camden,* died 1780, and his daughter Elizabeth Neild; Vestal with urn, as at Langley Marish, Slough, etc.

BATTERSEA RISE. CO May 1815, "Mrs. Thornton, Battersea Rise, a monumental pedestal and vase to the memory of Henry Thornton". Mrs Thornton also had a conservatory decorated with naturalistic Coade flowers (F.J. Collins). The Vase and one to his wife now at Mottisfont Abbey, Hants, qv.

BECKENHAM PLACE, Beckenham, Kent. Cator coat of arms with palms on portico from Wricklemarsh, Blackheath, added to Beckenham Place by John Cator (F.J. Collins).* c.1774.

BEDFORD ROW, Bloomsbury. CO April 1817 "A fountain as per drawing including fixing", for Mrs Doughty, Bedford Row. CD July 1820, "Mrs. Doughty, ordered by Mr. Hardwick, architect, a fountain, 2 circular basins, carriage of same to her house Bedford Row, £24.10s.0d." It is not clear if these entries refer to two fountains, or one which was greatly delayed in making.

BEDFORD SQUARE, *Bloomsbury.* c.1775. *THOMAS LEVERTON* built a few houses, but the original designer unknown. Coade rusticated blocks, impost blocks, voussoirs and keystones to all of the houses.* Keystones are the bearded man and the girl with drapery. In the short west approach street, Bayley Street, the keystones are the bearded man in turban* as at Torquay etc. The Ionic pilaster capitals on the central houses on the north, west and south sides, and the swags in the pediments now painted, are also probably Coade. CG. "Rustic Frontispieces for Doorways, Guilloche Fascia etc." One house damaged in the war, and the Coade replaced by cement.

25 BELGRAVE SQUARE, SW1*. Two long panels of putti engaged in architecture, painting, agriculture, etc.* Originally on 20-21 Wellclose Square, Stepney, the house of the Danish-Norwegian Consul. Now on the Norwegian Embassy. Similar panels at Emo, Republic of Ireland, qv.

BELLMOUNT, *Middlesex.* CG. Not traced.

BELVEDERE ROAD, THE LION BREWERY. 1836, demolished 1950, by *FRANCIS EDWARDS*, near Coade factory. Three lions on top. One now on Westminster Bridge,* qv, one at Twickenham* qv. Third demolished. (F.J. Collins.)

BERKELEY SQUARE, W1. CO May 1821, "Mr. G. Harrison, Berkeley Square, 2 verd antique pilasters, grecian caps, statuary marble plinths."

BETHLEHEM HOSPITAL, *St George's Fields.* See New Bethlehem Hospital.

2-4 OLD FORD ROAD, BETHNAL GREEN. Coade doorcases (Pevsner). Demolished.

BETHNAL GREEN, POLLARD ROW. Keystones marked Coade 1791. Demolished. (F.J. Collins.)

BISHOPSGATE, ST BOTOLPH'S PARISH HALL (*now Fanmaker's Company*). Figures of Charity Boy* and Charity Girl,* from former school. CO January 1821, "Saml. Grimsdale Bricklayer, Builder, 2 Sun St. Bishopsgate, 2 statues of charity boy and charity girl @ 14gns."

7 BLACKFRIARS ROAD. Vase and plaques (Summerson, *Georgian London*). House now demolished. Plaques rebuilt in wall of garage behind, with inscription (F.J. Collins).

BLACKHEATH, THE PARAGON. CG. By *MICHAEL SEARLES*, c.1790. Crescent of semi-detached houses, linked by colonnades. Capitals* and bases* in the colonnades, a fanciful Doric. Flute and patera string course;* rusticated quoins.* Mrs Coade had property here.

COLONNADE HOUSE, South Row, by the Paragon, Blackheath. Surely Searles. Same fancy Doric capitals* and rope moulding bases.*

PARAGON HOUSE, South Row, corner of Pond Road, Blackheath. Probably also Searles, same string course at The Paragon,* "flute and wheatear" frieze* and plaque of sphinxes with vase between.*

TERRITORIAL ARMY HQ, Blackheath. Lion, similar to that on Greenwich pediment, but with differently placed paws.* A trial piece? Tradition, so far unverified, links it with Lady Hamilton's house (F.J. Collins).

BLANDFORD STREET, No 46. Keystone of "laughing philosopher".*

BLOOMSBURY STREET, Nos 36, 38. Porch with a frieze of swags,* and doorway with keystone* as Bedford Square.

BLOOMSBURY, HOGARTH'S HOUSE?. Mrs Diana Shine has keystone,* dated 1792 with "wicked laughing old man" (laughing philosopher?) said to have come from the house earlier occupied by Hogarth. Not identified.

BOND STREET, W1. CG says "various Arms, medallions, pateras, capitals etc". None traced.

BRITISH FIRE OFFICE. NP. Work not specified and place not traced.

BRIXTON HILL. CO "Mr Sanders, Brixton Hill, 12 caps for piers, 1' 6" square, 4" thick." Not traced.

BRYANSTON SQUARE (no number) St Marylebone. CD July 1821 "Col. Graham, Bryanston Square ordered by Mr. Peto, 2 sienna scagliola pilasters, 2 enriched Grecian caps, £31.10s.0d." CD November 1821, "Col. Graham's columns and caps., scagliola £78.15s.0d." The Square by *JOSEPH T. PARKINSON*, 1811.

30 BRYANSTON SQUARE. CD August 1821, "Gen. Maitland, 30 Bryanston Sq. 2 pilasters, verd antique, grecian caps. £35.17s.9d."

38 BRYANSTON SQUARE. CO April 1819, "Mr. Portman, 38 Bryanston Square, a large (old) oval cistern 12 gns." Such cisterns were used as wine-coolers.

79 BRYANSTON SQUARE. CD August 1821, "– Barkes Esq. ordered by Mr. Harrison for No. 79 Bryanston Square, 2 pilasters in statuary brocatella £33.10s.6d."

BUCKINGHAM HOUSE, Pall Mall, SW1. Reconstructed 1790-3 and 1813 by *SIR JOHN SOANE*. Buckingham arms, small and in low relief, in the centre of the balustrade at the roof line (D. Stroud, *Architecture of Sir John Soane*, plate 54). Eight caryatids supporting the lantern of the stair well (Stroud, op cit, plate 55). Demolished. Six caryatids probably from here at Anglesey Abbey Cambs, qv.* Sir John Soane's Museum, Soane bill book No.5, 1793 gives full details of the cost of coat of arms (45 guineas) and figures (15 guineas each) and of putting them up – £202.11s.0d. Alison Kelly, "Sir John Soane and Mrs Eleanor Coade" *Apollo* April 1989 pp247-253.

BUCKINGHAM PALACE. By *JOHN NASH* 1826-37. Nine statues for pediments facing the courtyard (150 guineas each), four military* and four naval trophies* for the east front towers, Royal arms for the Guardhouse,* frieze of the entablature round the Palace by Flaxman,* consoles on west front,* set of Virtues (statues) for west front bow by Rossi (1836), Corinthian capitals, four scagliola doorcases with portrait medallions, six vases in the garden*. The courtyard statues have been removed; the statues from the west front have been dismantled but survive; the doorcases have been removed. Croggon was paid £6003 between 1827 and 1828, and £1323 in 1833 (H.M. Colvin ed *History of King's Works* vol VI J.M. Crook and M.H. Port), pp271-301. Two statues at Lancaster House qv – see Commissions for the Crown, Chapter 13.

BUNHILL FIELDS CEMETERY, City Road, E1. Monument to Henry Hunter,* stamped Coade and Sealy 1804 (F.J. Collins). The Coade family tomb is also here, but is not of Coade stone. George Coade died too soon for any Coade tombs to be ready. Daniel Pincot is also buried here (Bunhill Fields Register, Guildhall Library).

BURLINGTON ST, W1. CD April 1814, "Lady Cork, fountain with rock, coral, shells etc. 18gns., 2 vases, fixing and carting, 16gns." Croggon sent in bills for taking down and refixing the vases, for refixing them again, and finally for bringing them back to the factory. The fountain was also sent back. Croggon finally sold the vases to Lord Egremont at Petworth, Sussex, qv.

9 CADOGAN PLACE. See Lough Cutra Castle, Ireland.

86 CAMBERWELL ROAD, SE. One oval and two oblong plaques, with reclining allegorical figures in Baconian style.* Ex situ, on a building of uncertain date. From Dr Lettsom's house (Sir John Summerson).

CAMBERWELL GROVE, Grove Hill. Dr Lettsom's house, demolished. Lettsom Grove presumably marks the site. Coade's Gallery exhibited a statue of Contemplation by Bacon for him. The house was ornamented with plaques of the four Seasons, plaques of Music, Painting, Architecture, Commerce, Peace, Plenty, Law, Truth and Prudence, all Baconian reclining ladies, and an emblematic plaque of Isis and Egyptian symbolism, as Medical Society of London, qv. *New Lady's Magazine* April 1790 p194, an Account of Grove Hill near Camberwell, and Rev. Thomas Maurice *Grove Hill* 1799, p38, note C, p40 note F, p43 notes P and Q. William Harnett Blanch *The Parish of Camberwell* 1877 print opp p280. J. Edwards *A Companion from London to Brighthelmston in Sussex* 1801, p12 describes Grove Hill.

CARLTON HOUSE, *Westminster*. By *HENRY HOLLAND*, 1783-5. Demolished. Trophies of war for the centre of the screen, four naval and military trophies for the ends, copies of six of Sir William Hamilton's vases, costing £495. One vase* survives in Sir John Soane's Museum (*Survey of London*, vol20, chapter 8). For *THOMAS HOPPER'S* Gothic conservatory, octagonal fountain with eight dragons etc costing £97.1s. 0d., two statues of ancient kings, two bishops and one pilgrim, £96.12.s0d., ten Gothic candelabra 7ft high, £500.* (Windsor Archives 25309 and 25319.) The candelabra or their exact duplicates, were sold at Christie's in 1970. Present whereabouts unknown. A matching candelabrum at Athelhampton, Dorset. The NP also mentions commissions for the garden, unspecified. W. H. Pyre *History of Royal Residences* 1819 vol. II plates 1, 2. *Ackermann's Repository* vol. VI September 1811, plate 3.

CARPENTER'S HALL, *City of London*. CG. Coade not identified. Rebuilt.

CASSLAND ROAD, *Hackney*. Terrace of houses dated 1792. (F.J. Collins). See Hackney.

6 CAVENDISH SQUARE, W1. CD lists, for "Mr. Hanlet, Prince's St. and 6 Cavendish Square", two yellow antique Ionic columns for dining room £76.18s.0d., two Corinthian columns for staircase, yellow antique, £69.2s.3d., two Ionic brocatella columns for staircase, £74.10s.3d, and two Ionic columns for drawingroom, verd antique, £81.16s.0d. Whole bill, including fixing, £331.6s.6d. Demolished.

CHANDOS HOUSE, *Chandos Street*. *ROBERT ADAM* 1770-1. Round medallion* in hall by Bacon, in an artificial stone (Coade?) of Aeneas and Anchises, from Sir William Chambers' house in Berners St (Dr Rosser).

11 CHANDOS ST, *Lettsom House, the Medical Society of London*. Founded by Dr Lettsom of Camberwell, qv. He gave a huge plaque* originally at the Society's Bolt Court premises, now in the Meeting room, marked Coade 1787. Special design with the Great Pyramid, Isis and other medico-Egyptology. (The Secretary, the Medical Society of London.)

CHARING CROSS. Recognisably a street before the construction of Trafalgar Square. CG "various Royal Arms, the figure of the Phoenix at the Engine House, statue of Minerva at the Fire Office, and all their marks." Demolished.

CHARLES STREET, W1. CD January 1818 "Sir John Lubbock, Charles St. Westminster, 2 Ionic caps, 11gns." Not traced.

CHARLES STREET, St James's Square. Galloway House, Charles St by *JOHN JOHNSON* for the Earl of Galloway. Coade chimneypiece, probably that exhibited by E. Coade at the Society of Artists in 1774 "a chimneypiece in artificial stone for a nobleman's hall from a design of Mr Johnson's" (A. Graves).

22 CHARTERHOUSE SQUARE, City of London. Satyr Keystone.* George Coade and his friend Mr Lee of Exeter lived in the square in the 1760s. (John Havill.)

135 CHEAPSIDE, City of London. CD July 1814 "Mr. Clift Bedfordshire, King's arms ready made, smaller 20gns including fixing at 135 Cheapside." Demolished. See 25 Holborn.

CHELSEA, ROYAL HOSPITAL. Royal arms on Infirmary by *SIR JOHN SOANE.* Bombed 1941 Dorothy Stroud. *The Architecture of Sir John Soane* 1961 p110.

OLD SWAN INN?, Chelsea. CD. "John Lyall Chelsea a large swan including carting and fixing £15." The inn demolished 1873.

CHISWICK HIGH ROAD, nos 247, 249. Pair of houses c.1800, with two female head keystones.*

CHISWICK HOUSE, Chiswick. CD June 1814 "Duke of Devonshire, taking away a damaged vase, substituting a better one, £1.5s.0d." CD October 1817, "Duke of Devonshire, Chiswick, repairing Medicean Vase, £8.7s.0d." Its companion Borghese Vase* has a damaged rim. Both restored.* The Bridge by James Wyatt has medallions, oval paterae and small lion-head motifs.* Parts of four terms with girls' heads in store.* (Peter Hone).

47 CITY ROAD, E1. John Wesley's house, next to his Meeting House. String course, Vitruvian scroll pattern.* March 1779, Wesley petitioned the City lands Committee to be allowed to use Coade's artificial stone or Liardet's cement, instead of Portland stone, for the houses he was planning to erect. The Committee agreed, and the houses were put up "according to *Mr. Dance's* new elevations." (D. Stroud, *George Dance, Architect,* 1971 page 136).

CLAPHAM, GILMORE HOUSE, 113 North Side, Clapham Common . CD July 1818. "Nash re Noah Chivers Esq Clapham Common, 2 high top vases with Satyrs' heads

£27.1s.0d." CO July 1818 "2 Gothic stones for pedestals, 2 square stone for do." One vase survives in the garden;* busts of Shakespeare and Milton* (painted) appear to be Coade stone (E. E. C. Smith).

CLAPHAM, NOTRE DAME ESTATE, South Side, Clapham Common. Orangery dated 1792 with capitals and ornamental Coade stone.* Survives but badly damaged E.E.C. Smith. *Clapham* p68, 1976.

CLAPHAM, 52 RECTORY GROVE, Clapham Common. Coade doorcase survives.*

CLAPHAM, Nightingale Lane. Clapham College, formerly Hollywood, 1800. Coade doorway.* (Pevsner, London South p382).

ST JAMES CLERKENWELL PARISH CHURCH*. By JAMES CARR, 1788-92. Coade Royal Arms.* CG.

CLINK ST, WHARF BUILDING, Southwark. CO June 1819 "James Taylor, builder, Balham, a Phoenix as at Charing Cross 30gns, to be fixed at Messrs Clark and Collins, Wharf Building, Clink St Borough on or before July 31st 1819." Not traced.

COADE FACTORY – See Lambeth

COADE'S GALLERY – See Lambeth

COAL EXCHANGE, City of London. CG. "Capitals, ballusters etc." Demolished 1840s.

COLEMAN STREET, 4 King's Arms Yard, City of London. CO May 1819 "a small King's arms, 25gns. Mr. Nash, 4 King's Arms yard, Coleman St." Demolished.

15 COMMERCIAL ROAD, E1. Coade doorway (Pevsner). Demolished.

CONDUIT STREET, W1. CO August 1814 "McGraw and Brett, Plate Glass Manufacturers, Conduit St. Royal arms, 5' 6", 20gns." Not traced.

39 CONDUIT STREET, W.1. 1770. Bedford Square type of doorway (Pevsner).

CORDWAINERS' HALL, City of London. Shield of arms and cornucopiae in pediment. CG. Shown in T.H. Shepherd's *London*, 1820. Demolished.

27 CORK ST., W1. CO April 1815 "Messrs. Wood, 27 Cork St. a British Lion with shield etc., complete 35gns." Not traced.

47 CORNHILL, City of London. CO July 1818 "Charles Hill, 47 Cornhill, a fluted vase with lion's head and drapery." Not traced.

CORNHILL, UNION ASSURANCE OFFICE. 1819 "ornamental decoration" (Gunnis). Demolished.

COVENT GARDEN MARKET, WC2. By *CHARLES FOWLER,* 1828-30. Three figures of Agriculture etc on east end* (Dorothy Stroud). Plaques of Agriculture etc.

CROSBY HALL, *formerly in Bishopsgate, now in Chelsea.* Fifteenth century hall. Statue of Sir John Crosby (original owner) 1835 (Gunnis). The statue apparently did not accompany the Hall to Chelsea and seems to be lost.

CUMBERLAND PLACE. Probably in the City as the present Cumberland Place not yet built. CD – Osborne Esq New Broad St Court June 1817. "Repairing, cleansing and bronzing three figures and a pedestal – 5gns plus cartage." Men's time cartage to Cumberland Place and fixing 12/6.

CUSTOM HOUSE, *City of London.* By *DAVID LAING,* 1817. CD October 1817 "Henry Peto for the New Custom House, Royal Arms Rampant, Neptune on Seahorse, Britannia Lion and Shield, £561.12s.1d." These supplied but J.G. Bubb and J.C.F. Rossi also made a frieze in their own artificial stone (Alison Kelly "Imitating Mrs. Coade", *County Life* 10.11.1977). The building collapsed 1825. Rebuilt by *SMIRKE* with no artificial stone.

DENMARK HILL, *Camberwell.* CO June 1817 "Mrs. James Horne opposite the Fox, Denmark Hill, a pair of Lions' head Vases with Drapery to be sent and fixed £8."

62 DENMARK HILL. Survey of London St Mary Lambeth Part 2, vol XXVI p149, Coade doorway of Bedford Square design.

DENMARK HILL. CO October 1818 "2 Ionic capitals of 12½" diam at 5½gns to be sent to John Curtis Esq Denmark Hill, Camberwell, *FRANCIS BEDFORD* architect." Not traced.

154 DENMARK HILL. WILLIAM BLACKBURN architect 1785-6 Portico with four columns frieze of swag and patera.* *Survey of London* vol. 26, plate 53, p146.

78 DEODAR ROAD, Putney, Thornhill Galleries. Had a duplicate of the Capesthorne chimneypiece, marked Coade 1790.

HABERDASHERS ASKE'S SCHOOL, Pepys Road, Deptford. Statue of Robert Aske* stamped Croggon 1826. Life-size statue in early 18th century dress. Inscription on pedestal says that the school was rebuilt in 1826. Now in front of a Victorian school on a different site.

TRINITY ALMSHOUSES, Deptford. Splendid shield of arms with appropriate globes, quadrants and flags. Sailing ships in all quarters. Above, helmet with demi-lion holding sword. Inscription Trinitas in Unitate. Photographed by F.J. Collins in January 1953, but the piece was destroyed before the LCC Historic Buildings Dept took over the building. CG.

13 DEVONSHIRE PLACE, St Marylebone. Three paterae between 2nd and 3rd floor windows, early 19th century.*

1 DEVONSHIRE TERRACE, St Marylebone. Jupiter keystone.* Dickens lived in the Terrace (demolished) and the keystone is now at the Dickens Museum, Doughty Street, WC2.

DOBSON (?) ROAD, Vauxhall. CO April 1814 "Mr. L. Phillips, Exhibition of fruit trees Dobson(?) Road Vauxhall, small fountain, coral and shell at 3' high, 14gns." William Blackwell granted lease "to maintain the garden ground in a husbandlike and gardenlike manner and to keep about 200 standard fruit trees . . . in good heart" *Survey of London* vol 23, p69

DORSET PLACE, Clapham Road. CO October 1819 "Mr Notley, Dorset Place, Clapham Road. a circular fan to go over a door 3'4" by 1'8", and a keystone." This is the only fanlight in the Croggon records and probably bought in.

DORSET ST W1. East Side. 2, 18, 19 fascia by door, 20-27 Coade keystones of various designs. West side, keystones of old man design on all houses except 40, 41.

29 DOVER STREET, W1. By *JOHN NASH* for himself, 1798. CD April 1814 "John Nash Esq. Dover St. 2 figures of Sculpture and Architecture, 4 do Geometry, Music, Painting and Poetry 150gns." The attic storey had four figures and three oval windows (Terence Davis, *John Nash,* plate 38, 1966) which could have been the above set. Bombed 1941.

11 DOWNING STREET, SW1 etc. CG says "Pedestals for stoves at the Secretary of State's and the Chancellor of the Exchequer, free from the noxious effects of cast iron, and at other places." Removed.

DRURY LANE, WC2. CO March 1814, "Biddell, Drury Lane, King's arms 20gns." Not traced.

DRURY LANE THEATRE. CD September 1819 "Elliston, Drury Lane Theatre, Arms of Prince of Wales, cartage from manufactory to theatre 9s.6d." Removed.

1A DUKE ST, Manchester Square.* Bearded head keystone.*

DULWICH. CO October 1814, "Mr. John Wills, Dulwich, an old figure of Britannia 10gns." Site not traced.

DULWICH, THE CASINA. By *JOHN NASH* for Richard Shaw, 1798. CG. Balustrade and Ionic capitals? (see Terence Davis, *John Nash,* page 35). Demolished 1906.

EAGLE OFFICE, City of London. CO August 1814, "Gave Mr. Goldring, Eagle Office, contract price of an eagle on a ground, 14" square, under 5gns. the first, 2gns.

each afterwards." CD June 1817 "Medallion with eagle, 7gns. CO June 1818 "Eagle Office, a circular tablet and date 1818." CO August 1819 "A medallion with eagle and inscription *Rebuilt by Charles Johnson* 1819." CD September 1819 "2 circular medallions, each with Eagle and inscription 7gns." Geoffrey Godden had yet another Eagle plaque inscribed "Rebuilt by Eagle Insurance company 1823";* it seems therefore that the Eagle Insurance Co provided plaques to be put on buildings burnt down and rebuilt with their insurance cover.

EAST INDIA HOUSE, Leadenhall Street. By *RICHARD JUPP* and *HENRY HOLLAND,* c1800. CD September 1815, "Sir Charles Cockerell Bart for carting and fixing figure of Apollo at India House this day £3.6s.8d." Cockerell was an official of the company; in 1814 Croggon had supplied him with "4 antique Apollos, on a ground richly ornamented with tablets of horses and small figure in a niche at 40gns each" and other things for Sezincote, Gloucestershire, qv. CD November 1817 "East India Company, Font, highly wrought, with cherubs 35gns." The font was sent to India, the bill to East India House. The Apollo probably the same design as at Corby Castle, Cumberland (Cumbria) qv.

EAST INDIA HOUSE?. CO October 1814, "Black Parry and Co., Arms of the East India Company in manner and about the same size as Harris Holborn 25gns."

EAST INDIA DOCKS. CD June 1819, "R. Walker Esq. to attendance at E. India Docks taking instructions for model of ship in artificial stone 2gns." Probably something similar to the ship model for West India Dock qv.

ELTHAM. CG. Nothing identified.

EMBROIDERER'S HALL, Gutter Lane. "Embroiderer's Hall . . . is a modern building the entrance of which is of artificial stone rusticated, over which are the arms of the company". (Henry R. Thomas *The Ancient Remains . . . and recent Improvements of the City of London.* 1830.) (Cyril Staal).

ENFIELD, Clay Hill. CO October 1816 "Mr. Edward Harman, Clay Hill Enfield, Gothic chimney pcs at 40gns." The bill, by July 1817, had gone up to 50gns; in August Croggon invoiced "Wilson's attendance 3 days, taking down and refixing in another room a Gothic chimneypiece." CO October 1820 "Mr. Edwd. Harman, Clay Hill, a Gothic chimneypiece similar to Sir H.A. Liddell." It was invoiced a "rich Gothic chimneypiece with pinnacles, £109.15s.0d." House demolished.

FANMAKERS' COMPANY – See Bishopsgate

FENCHURCH STREET, *Mr Palmer's premises.* Plate 27c Dorothy Stroud *George Dance, Architect 1741-1825,* 1971 shows shop front with plaques as 20 Portman Square qv.

FINSBURY SQUARE, *Terrace of west side.* By GEORGE DANCE, 1779-90. Demolished. Dorothy Stroud, *George Dance, Architect,* 1971, plate 41a (1910 photograph) shows swags, oval bas-relief plaques and capitals to pilasters, all, apparently, of Coade stone.

FINSBURY, 6 MOUNT PLEASANT. Phoenix Brass Foundry. See under Phoenix.

FISHMONGERS' HALL, *London Bridge Approach.* Statue of Charity,* four chimneypieces and plaques with nereids and dolphins, 1790, costing £205 – Company Notebook no.5 – (Gunnis) destroyed in rebuilding of 1831.

33 FITZROY STREET. Keystone at 33.* (F.J. Collins)

FLEET STREET. CG "Royal Arms, Lions, Capitals, Fascias etc." All demolished.

1 FOLEY PLACE, *formerly Queen Anne Street East, W1* By JAMES WYATT for himself before 1783. Demolished. CG mentions "Pannels, Capitals, Consoles, Trusses, Ballusters etc. at the house of Mr. James Wyatt". some of this decoration* now on Syon Lodge, Isleworth (Pevsner).

FOUNDLING HOSPITAL, *Bloomsbury.* CG mentions "Vases and Pedestals for chimney tops, keystones, imposts etc." Possibly embellishments for buildings of the 1790s on the Hospital's land. Hospital rebuilt. No Coade traced. Surviving portable font of 1804, classical tripod shape with lambs' head monopodia, dated 1804 (F.J. Collins).*

FREEMASONS' HALL, *Great Queen Street, WC2.* By SIR JOHN SOANE, 1828-31. Demolished. Undated bill in Sir John Soane's Museum, for Freemasons Hall, from Coade works, Lambeth, for four Ionic columns 12ft 5in, giallo antico scagliola, £120, capitals 6 guineas, bases 3 guineas.

FULHAM, THE GRANGE, *North End Road (Burne Jones' house).* CG. Allowed to fall down 1950s. Coade medallions on the back (Pevsner); three panels in care of the Borough Council 1957 (F.J. Collins).*

GEORGE STREET, *St Marylebone.* Durrants Hotel. Guilloche string course, radiating paterae as Home House, composed pilaster caps*

24 GEORGE STREET *next door*.* Keystone of old man in a cap at front door.

36 GERRARD STREET, *W1. Survey of London,* St Anne's Soho volume, mentions the representation of the Admiralty's Great Seal, with a trophy of sea horses, flags, gun barrels and other nautical symbols, all probably in Coade

stone, believed to have been put up by the firm of Giles Walkeling, suppliers to the Admiralty 1821-70. Decoration damaged by fire and removed 1950.

GLOUCESTER PLACE, W1. Nos 48, 84 have doorways as Bedford Square.

GOLDEN SQUARE, W1. CO March 1814 "Thomas Stephenson, Lower John Street, Brewer St. Golden Square, 12 trap stones." Site not identified.

GORDON SQUARE, Bloomsbury. House of Charles Fowler, now replaced by the Warburg Institute qv. Long plaque of Apollo and the Muses from his house now in the Warburg Institute Hall (Sir John Summerson).

GOWER STREET, WC1. CO August 1816 "John Shaw Esq. Gower St., 4 Corinthian capitals at 10½" diam. as Lord Grosvenor's 48gns." Not traced.

GOWER STREET, between Store Street and Chenies Street*. CG mentions "rustic frontispieces for doorways, guilloche fascia, etc."* All the doorways have been altered. The fascia remains in the block on the west side between Chenies St and Store St.

5 GREAT ELBOW LANE, College Hill, City of London. CO January 1820, "Joseph Minett and Co, 5 Great Elbow Lane . . . a lion couchant for a porch or gateway 23' high 10' wide." Not traced.

GREENWICH PARK. CD May 1819, "Drs. Clark and Fry, Greenwich Park, modelling bust of the late James Barry, 12gn; bracket with inscription, the above placed in St Paul's Cathedral 2 busts of do. delivered to Dr. Fry, 10gns, 1 do. to be placed in the Great Room of the Society of Arts and Sciences Adelphi, 5gns." See St Paul's Cathedral and Royal Society of Arts Adelphi. They were Dr Fryer and Dr Clarke.

GREENWICH, ROYAL HOSPITAL, now Royal Naval College Chapel. Interior reconstructed by *"ATHENIAN' STUART,* 1780s, and William Newton Thirty-two capitals for pilasters,* 1784; six medallions of the life of St Paul on the pulpit, 1789*; four medallions of prophets 1789; medallion of Elymas the sorcerer, 1789; six angels, now gilt, supporting the altar*; four statues, Hope, Meekness, Charity, Faith, designed Benjamin West, PRA in ante-chapel*. In December 1818, CD "Repairing cleaning scagliola in chapel, 303 days at 6s.6d., 58½ days at 4s.0d., £154.17s.6d." Large panel of putti playing harp on organ loft,* panels with arms of the Hospital on side galleries.* Plaques from demolished reading desk in store.*

Pediment, quadrangle, King William Block*. Composition, 40ft by 10ft, with statues 8ft to 9ft, of

Neptune handing over the body of Nelson to Britannia, accompanied by hippocampi, tritons, England, Scotland and Ireland, a British sailor and a lion. Designed by Benjamin West, modelled by West and Joseph Panzetta, 1812. *Nelson pediment pamphlet* published to describe it. Scottish National Library Acc 5111 Box 12. Not dated, probably 1813. *Gentleman's Magazine* 1812 vol. 2 p490.

Trafalgar Block. CD March 1814, "Governors of Greenwich Hospital for Mr Yenn, Arms of the Hospital with palms and laurel 150gns."* CD July 1817 "Mr. Dubbin sent to Greenwich Hospital to repair antique galley 1½gns." What could this be?

GROCER'S HALL, *Prince's Street, City of London.* 1800 Decorative works £182 (Gunnis, from Company records). Not traced. G. Richards *New Vitruvias Britannicus* II plates 5, 6, 1808.

GUNNERSBURY PARK. Reclining nymph, survived until 1950s (F.J. Collins). Now destroyed.

HACKNEY TERRACE, Cassland Road. Pediment with palms (F.J. Collins). Handsome terrace with fine armorial ornament in central pediment, with the arms of Fellowes, Shillitoe and Pickering, all in oval shields, and palm branch ornament (Andrew Byrne and Isobel Watson, *Country Life* Nov 12 1987 pp192-4).

HADLOW STREET, Burton Crescent. CO July 1829 "Mr Langdon, Surveyor, Hadlow St Burton Crescent, offered to execute for Mr Langdon . . . 14 corinthian capitals in Oct, 22" for 20-25gns. if possible." Not traced.

HALE END, Walthamstow. CO October 1816, "Cooke, Bellevue House, Hale End Walthamstow, a Flora and Pomona, 5ft 30gns each, a fluted vase, lion's head and drapery 60s." By *EDWARD GIFFORD* or *GYFFARD*. Demolished.

HAMMERSMITH, Lower Mall.* Kent House, Lower Mall, has oblong plaques of swags over upper floor windows, horizontal oval paterae by front door. Plates 37 and 38, *Survey of London*, VI, Hammersmith volume.

ST JOHN HAMPSTEAD PARISH CHURCH. CD July 1817, "Mrs. Milligan for Wilson and Thomas's attendance at Hampstead repairing monument, painting, do. railings, 15gns." CD April 1820, "Miss Milligan Hampstead for cutting inscription on tomb Hampstead churchyard £3.5s.6d." Both entries presumably relate to the same tomb, which has not yet been traced. CD September 1821, "Clowser for Geo. Todd Esq. Hampstead, to a monument for Hampstead church yard same as Dr Fryer's." Dr Fryer's was in Paddington churchyard and is lost; it was the same as Mrs Sheridan's, Old Windsor, qv. Todd's* is in the newer part of Hampstead churchyard, opened in 1812. "G. Todd of Belsize in this parish aged 67". 1820.

HAMPSTEAD, *Admiral's House.* Three reclining figure plaques, *Architecture, Geometry, Sculpture.* (Sir Colin Anderson 1973). It is not known if the plaques are still in situ.

HAMPSTEAD, *4 Gainsborough Gardens.* Charity figure and boy, as the Marine Society, qv marked Coade Lambeth, 1793 (F.J. Collins).*

HAMPSTEAD, *North End Road, The Old Bull and Bush (carpark).* Statue of Venus with two dolphins.* Unusual pose with both arms raised, holding a scarf. Complete until 1960s. (F.J. Collins) the figure lost an arm in the 1970s. Shattered 1980s. Remains, minus the head, in a private collection.

HANOVER SQUARE, *Tenterden Street, W1.* CD, "Dr Willis, Tenterden St. Hanover Square, a Royal arms rampant £46.2s.4d."

HANOVER SQUARE, *W1.* CD March 1814 "Lord Harewood Hanover Square, 4' 6" statue of Flora 20gns. cartage 10s." (For Harewood House, Hanover Square).

HANOVER SQUARE, *W1.* CO August 1819, "Luke Collingham Esq., Hanover Square, ordered by Robert . . . (illegible) 2 Doric columns yellow antique scago (for an iron core) with statuary scago caps and bases, total 9' 0¾", 1' 2" at top, 1' 5" at bottom, two pilasters to same, return 4"." Demolished.

33 HARLEY STREET. CO November 1819, "Mr Lautour 33 Harley Street (*Wynne* architect) 2 small urns on plinths, 2 eagles as Sir George Osborne's, 18" high, 20gns." These were invoiced to Mr Lautour at Hexton House, Hitchin, Hertfordshire (qv), where the eagles, copies from the British Museum, survive on the gate piers. CD November 1820, "Joseph Lautour Esq. 2 Doric columns and 2 angular pilasters in scagliola brosetta 10' 2½", £95.8.3." For Hexton House or for Harley Street?

71 HARLEY STREET, W1.* Lord Andover, or Lord Vise of Andover (Croggon tried both), at 71 Harley Street, had "a basin for a font, 2gns." in June 1818. This house survives, with Coade ornament.

HARLEY STREET, various houses between nos 66 and 145.* Forty houses in this part of Harley Street have Coade stone on the doorways, and sometimes other decoration. This street illustrates very well the variety possible from a few standard units. There are 16 different combinations of keystones, voussoirs and impost blocks.

FLAMBARDS, *Harrow.* Alterations by *JOHN SHAW* for the Earl of Northwick, 1820. CD April 1820, "The Earl of Northwick, statue of Triton and conc with 3 dolphins for a fountain from the Piazza Barberini in Rome £53.17s.0d." This Bernini fountain design was shown in Coade's Gallery from 1799. Flambards survives, separated from its park, now Northwick Park. Fountain not traced. Possibly the same design as at Petworth which is *not* Bernini.

85 HATTON GARDEN, Holborn. CO June 1818, "Mr Edwards Taylor, 85 Hatton Garden, an old statue 5gns."

HAYMARKET OPERA HOUSE, *called the King's or Queen's Theatre.* CG, "Royal Arms and Capitals for the colonnade at the Theatre." Built 1790-1 by *MICHAEL NOVOSIELSKI.* Reconstructed *NASH* and *REPTON* 1816. Rebuilt after fire, 1867.

HIGHGATE, 2 The Grove*. Chimneypiece with Vitruvian scroll frieze, central plaque, caryatids (Article *The Queen,* 24 August 1955, F.J. Collins).

50 HIGH HOLBORN. CO March 1814, "Wm. Harris and CO 50 High Holborn, King's arms rampant abt. 4', 23gns." Not traced.

HOLBORN, 6 MOUNT PLEASANT. Bower and Co., Brass Foundry. Plaque marked Coade and Sealy 1808 (F.J. Collins)*. Removed to SE London. See Phoenix Brass Foundry.

25 HOLBORN. CO July 1814, "Mr. Clift, Bedfordshire, King's arms ready made, small size 20gns., he to pay fixing, 25 Holborn." See also 135 Cheapside.

HOLBORN. CG mentions "Royal arms, Lyons, Capitals, Fascias etc." Not traced.

HOPE FIRE OFFICE, *new premises, Oxford Street.* Croggon notes, November 1818, "Hope Office, statue of Hope". The order was given as "A statue of Hope, with anchor, 55gns." Demolished.

HORNIMAN MUSEUM GARDEN,* *London Road, Forest Hill.* Figure group* from the Pelican Life Insurance Office, Union Assurance, Cornhill. Designed by 1799, as an illustration of it is the frontispiece of the *Coade's Gallery Handbook.* Six figures. Said by Mrs Esdaile (*Architect and Building News,* January 1940 pp94-6, 112-114), to have been executed by de Vaere from designs by Lady Diana Beauclerk. Hughson's *London,* p523, 1807. The Pelican was the life insurance counterpart of the Phoenix fire insurance.

HOUSE OF LORDS, Palace of Westminster. Royal Entrance, by *SIR JOHN SOANE* 1823, burnt down 1834. Letter in Sir John Soane's Museum from Croggon to Soane of 18 March 1826, giving details of the estimate – eight scagliola columns, £163.16s.0d., eight plain Ionic capitals, £37.16s.0d., eight moulded bases, £16.16s.0d. With the materials for the 'skeletons" and men's time, the bill came to £236.7s.7d., with an extra 12 guineas for the capitals.

ISLEWORTH, Syon House –See Syon House

ISLEWORTH. CG. Nothing traced unless this refers to early work at Syon House.

ISLEWORTH, Syon Lodge*. Has details from Foley Place, James Wyatt's house, qv.

ISLEWORTH. CO May 1814, "Dr. Bates, Isleworth, 12 half ballusters, 1' 9", 3s.6d. each, 40ft. of coping, 2 coinc (quoins) 1s.3d. per ft." Not traced.

ISLINGTON, CUMMING STREET off Pentonville Road. One house with Coade decoration (Pevsner). Demolished.

ISLINGTON, nos 50-58 DUNCAN TERRACE*. Coade keystones,* mostly Minerva, and impost blocks.*

ST MARK KENNINGTON CHURCHYARD*. CD October 1819, "Peter Bayley, 14 Kennington Green, Monument to Mrs. Bayley in Kennington Church Yard, vase and pedestal, 40gns."* The order refers to a "Monument as Hastings" – ie., Warren Hastings at Daylesford, Gloucestershire, qv.

KENNINGTON ROAD*. A variety of Coade keystones. 362-366, 350-352, 354 (*Survey of London* vol. XXVI).

KENNINGTON ROAD, MONTFORD PLACE. Triangular indentation off Kennington Road. Fine semi-detached houses, keystones,* arches supported on rams' head consoles,* one keystone* built into a garage. Adjacent to 366.

KENSINGTON, HOLLAND HOUSE. Fountain marked Coade Lambeth 1797, demolished late 1940s (F.J. Collins).

KENSINGTON PALACE*. Gatepiers with lion and unicorn supporting Royal Arms.*

KENSINGTON, VILLA MARIA. By *WILLIAM TYLER* for the Duchess of Gloucester, design in Royal Academy 1800. CG mentions "Villa Maria-House, the Duchess of Gloucester's." Two uneven blocks linked by a colonnade; possibly the caps of this are the Coade items. Water-colour drawing in Kensington Public Library. Demolished.

KENWOOD, Highgate. CG as Caenwood. *ROBERT ADAM* 1767-9. The capitals of the portico, on the north side, the frieze of festoons of husks and paterae, and the medallion in the pediment (subject not yet traced), may be of Coade stone, now painted.

KEW GARDENS. Medici Vase near the Pond and Palmhouse, stamped Croggon Lambeth 1826.* Another Medici Vase, on elaborate plinth corresponding to that ordered by George IV for Royal Lodge Windsor, qv in 1825.* Its pair at Wrest Park, Bedfordshire qv. Bill in Windsor Royal Archives 26736.

LAMBETH CHURCH AND CHURCHYARD ST MARY*. James Moore, 1781 (Gunnis). Robt Wilmot, 1799, "A handsome monument erected by Coade" in the church. (Robt. Allen, History and Antiquities of the Parish of Lambeth, 1826.). Charles Carsane 1800, in the church, inscribed slab with low relief cherubs. James Bryan 1804, inscribed slab with very slight decoration as Carsane. William Sealy, John Sealy and other Sealys from 1800, tomb in churchyard, with urn with snake twisted round it.* Admiral and Mrs Bligh, 1814, in churchyard, sarcophagus with flaming urn on top.* CD July 1814 "Admiral Bligh, Monumental tomb to the memory of his Lady £47.5s.0d." Semi-circular medallion with urn, portrait medallion and three putti, taken from a memorial slab in the churchyard and now in the west end of the north aisle. See Templemor, Northern Ireland.

LAMBETH, LION BREWERY. Large lion 1837 now on Westminster Bridge. Small lion now at Twickenham Rugby Ground. Other small lion broken on the demolition of the factory late 1940s (F.J. Collins).

LAMBETH, COADE'S GALLERY, Westminster Bridge Road. The Gallery was one of a row of houses, Coade's Row, erected in 1798. Over the front door was a bas-relief 9ft x 8ft, enlarged from the firm's trade card by John Bacon and four terms. Over the other door was a similar panel describing the firm. Demolished 1908. Survey of London vol XXIII plate 1, p69.

LAMBETH, COADE FACTORY, Narrow Wall – later Belvedere Road. The exterior was decorated, first with a plaque of Phoebus and his chariot, later with statues, lions, the Royal arms and a trophy of flags and weapons, and finally with two statues, a balustrade and a lion. The basic structure was a dwelling house, with a yard and kilns behind. Survey of London Vol. XXIII, plates 38a, 39a, 48. Chapter 15, p58-61.

LAMBETH ROAD, ARCHBISHOP TENISON'S SCHOOL, 55 Kennington Oval. Charity Boy from the Lambeth Ragged School (Survey of London, vol XXIII, page 59). Via Archbishop Temple's School, the figure has now reached Archbishop

Michael Ramsay School, Camberwell, qv. On the way a companion Charity Girl has been lost.

LANCASTER HOUSE. Statues of *Sculpture* holding a bust of Phidias, and *Architecture* with half Corinthian capital at her side, from the pediment of Buckingham Palace, now in the garden. Both are 7 to 7½ feet. *Architecture* is stamped E. H. Bailey Sculp. Croggon Lambeth 1828.

LANGHAM HOUSE, formerly at south end of Portland Place. By *JOHN NASH*, 1813, demolished 1864. CO January 1817 "Sir James Langham, Bart., Langham Place, Portland Place, 4 figures to carry lights, 4' 6" Vestals and Sybils, 20gns. 4 pedestals abt. 3' with his arms on the front of each, 2 figures of Flora and Pomona to carry lights at 5' 6", 30gns." All bronzed. CD April 1817 charged £60.9s.0d., for the scagliola pedestals.

LEADENHALL STREET. See East India House

LEATHERSELLERS' COMPANY HALL, Bishopsgate Street. CD August 1820, "Leathersellers Company's Arms £52.10s.0d. Fixing at their hall in Bishopsgate St. £7.14s.0d." Demolished.

LEE, ST MARGARET'S CHURCH, Near Lewisham. Original church in ruins; churchyard full of 18th and early 19th century monuments. Sir John Call,* 1801 (Gunnis). ([Sic.] Actually Sir John Gale, pyramid with coat of arms (F.J. Collins)). William Chivers, 1807* (Gunnis).

LEVERIAN MUSEUM, Blackfriars Road, later called the Surrey Institution. By *JAMES BURTON,* 1786. CG says that a statue of Contemplation, and the capitals of the portico were by Coade. Demolished.

LINCOLN'S INN FIELDS. Royal College of Surgeons, *SIR CHARLES BARRY,* Scagliola columns.

LINCOLN'S INN FIELDS, SIR JOHN SOANE'S MUSEUM, See Sir John Soane's Museum

LIVERY COMPANIES' HALLS. CG list Coade at the Skinners' qv, Watermens' qv, Cordwainers', Grocers, Vintners' qv, Armourers', Waxchandlers', Stationers' qv, Merchant Taylors', Mercers' qv and Carpenters' Halls. Leathersellers' added 1820 qv. All except the Skinners', Stationers', Watermens' and Vintners rebuilt. The Fishmongers' Hall qv also has Coade work.

LOMBARD STREET, PELICAN OFFICE. See Horniman Museum.

LOMBARD STREET, POST OFFICE. CG mentions capitals at the Post Office. Demolished.

LONDON ASSURANCE OFFICE. CG mentions statue of Britannia at the London Assurance Office. Not traced.

LONG ACRE, WC2. CG mentions "Royal Arms, lions, capitals, fascias etc." in Long Acre and neighbouring streets. Apparently none surviving.

LOTHBURY, 8 TOKEN HOUSE YARD. CO July 1818, "I. Smith Esq., 8 Token House Yard, Lothbury, sketches for Charity Boy and Girl about 4' 4", 4gns. each". Not traced.

MANCHESTER SQUARE, 1 DUKE STREET. On the corner of the Square. Keystone of bearded man with turban. Strip of fascia with upright feathers across top of door from impost to impost.*

MANCHESTER STREET, W1. Small-size Coade keystones,* Minerva, girl (head sideways), satyr, laughing philosopher (several), girl and drapery, all on quite modest houses. On Durrant's Hotel side door, laughing philosopher keystone.*

8 MANSION HOUSE STREET. CD September 1814, "Beck and Cowan, Beehive and flowers etc. 5gns, gilding and painting 1½gns." The street has disappeared.

THE MARINE SOCIETY, 5 Clark's Place EC2. CG "Charity, a group of two figures, modelled by Bacon, for the Marine Society of London, under the direction of Jonas Hanway, 4' 3" high".* Still in the Society's possession (F.J. Collins). Mrs Esdaile (op cit) said that it was at Lloyds, confusing it with Lloyd's own Charity group, in metal and modelled by Flaxman.

MERCERS' HALL, Cheapside. CG. St George and Dragon, marked Coade Lambeth 1792 (F.J. Collins).* Now moved to the storage department of the Museum of London.

MERCHANTS TAYLORS HALL, Threadneedle Street. CG. Rebuilt.

MILE END ROAD, TRINITY ALMS HOUSES. Coat of arms Trinity House (F.J. Collins). Survived the war. Destroyed before the LCC Historic Buildings Department took over maintenance of the building. Possibly belonged to *SAMUEL WYATT'S* construction of a new quadrangle in 1806.

MORTLAKE. CO March 1815, "Mr. Pembroke, Mortlake, oval tablet with inscription with arms and supporters. Not traced.

64 MOUNT STREET, W1. CO, May 1821, "Gen. Phipps, 64 Mount Street, Park Lane, small porphyry pedestal with black marble plinth". A scagliola piece with natural marble base. Not traced.

MOUNT STREET. CO March 1820, "Marsh and Tatham and Saunders, Mount St. Grosvenor Square, Royal arms 8ft long, 11in. thick". The Prince Regent's favourite furniture makers. New arms for his accession.

MUSEUM OF LONDON. Collection,* almost entirely of plasters, from the Coade factory site, formerly in the basement of County Hall. Mostly in store.

NARROW WALL, LAMBETH. CD July 1817 "F. Fowler, Narrow Wall, a kitchen sink £1.14s.0d". For one of Croggon's Lambeth neighbours? Street now Belvedere Road.

NATIONAL MARITIME MUSEUM, Greenwich. Bust of Nelson,* former site unknown.

NEW BETHLEHEM HOSPITAL, now Imperial War Museum, Lambeth. CD November 1815 "Committee of New Bethlehem Hospital, ordered per *MR REPTON* King's Arms couchant(*), 15' long including . . . (illegible) and fixing 130gns." The Committee had turned down an estimate for £500 for carving the arms in Portland stone. The arms are in the pediment.

NEW BOND STREET, 12 W1. CO April 1814, "Mr. Hillhouse, 12 New Bond St. Princess Charlotte of Wales' arms 4' high, 5" thick, not to exceed 20gns."* On art market 1988.

NEW CAVENDISH STREET, 61-63 W1.* Two houses treated together to form a feature on the axis of Mansfield Street. Three arches (door, window, door) with rusticated voussoirs and blocks, and bearded-head keystones. By *JOHN JOHNSON, 1778* (D. Stroud).

NEWHAM, STRATFORD LIBRARY, Romford Road. Statue of Shakespeare from Opera House Haymarket (F.J. Collins).*

NEW ROAD, now Marylebone Road. Croggon's showrooms, address sometimes given as 6 Palace Row, New Road, in the Trade Directories, 1826-1833. The overdoor plaque from Coade's Gallery, qv still in situ in 1891 (*The Builder* August 22nd 1891) at end of Tottenham Court Rd.

NEW ROAD, now Marylebone Road. CO May 1821, "Richard Wade, New Road, Portland Place, 2 rustic doorways, imposts, a Jupiter mask." Not traced.

NEW ROAD, now Marylebone Road. Acrimonious correspondence in the Letter Book (pp270, 289) with Brown, Scagliola maker. "Unless the arms are paid for will take other measures". "Will deliver the arms on payment of 35 guineas". Finally, "Mr. Groves, fishmonger, of New Bond St has applied for arms, will let him have the Brown arms if he will give them up and pay expenses". June to October 1817.

NEW TRANSPORT OFFICE, afterwards the India Board of Control, Cannon Row. By *WILLIAM PILKINGTON.* CD April 1815, "Mr. Smith for New Transport Office, 38 whole, 8 half balusters." Not traced.

NORFOLK HOUSE, St James's Square. See St James's Square.

NORTHUMBERLAND HOUSE, on site of Northumberland Avenue. CD August 1821, "Duke of Northumberland, for men's time and materials, cleaning and repairing and repolishing a rich inlaid scagliola chimneypiece, £31.10s.0d." Probably the chimneypiece designed by *ADAM,* * taken to Syon House on the demolition of Northumberland House.

NUN HEAD GREEN, Peckham. CD March 1819, "Mr. Golding Nun Head Green 4' 6" Flora on pedestal £28.7s.0d." Not traced.

OXFORD STREET, 176. CO January 1821, "Ferguson and Co. 176 Oxford Street for Jn. Martin Esq. a verd antique slab 3' 4" by 1' 4", rounded a little the front corners". Further similar orders were given by this firm in 1821. Of London and Lancaster "late Gillows". Cabinet maker and upholsterer. (*Dictionary of English Furniture Makers 1640-1840*, 1986, p297)

OXFORD STREET, 9 Hanway Yard. CD November 1819, Wade and Wilson, 9 Hanway Yard, Oxford Street, sheaf of wheat 4ft high, 16 guineas. Probably the shop's sign. Not traced.

ST MARY PADDINGTON PARISH CHURCH. By *JOHN PLAW,* 1788-91. Monument to Joseph Johnson, marked Coade and Sealy 1802; he was the son of architect *JOHN JOHNSON* (Nancy Briggs); Vestal with urn in niche on south side.* CO March 1819 "Dr Fryer, 45 South Street Grosvenor Square, monument as Sheridan's, see letter." It was to Charles Fryer, and cost £56.2s.0d. See Hampstead Church and Old Windsor Church. Monument now lost in reconstruction of churchyard.

5 PALACE ROW, New Road (now Marylebone Road). CD January 1821, "John Mullane, 5 Palace Row, New Road, a verd antique slab 5' 6" by 1' 2" by 1½"." Similar orders in April 1821, probably for furniture. Site not traced.

PALACE YARD, Henderson Hotel. CO May 1817, "Offer to erect 4 chimneyshafts for Mr Crofton, Henderson Hotel, Palace Yard, 3ft. high 12gns. each." Not traced.

PALACE YARD. CD May 1819, "Mr. Hunt, 2 Ionic caps, £10." Not traced.

PALACE OF WESTMINSTER. House of Lords Entrance. *SIR JOHN SOANE* scagliola columns. Letter from Croggon to Soane 18.3.1826 Sir John Soane's Museum 2 XI

H5. Croggon charged £236.7s.7d. (*History of the King's Works* VI p505). Demolished. *Law Courts. SIR JOHN SOANE*. Royal Arms in Coade stone for King's Bench. (History of King's Works VI p505.)

83 PALL MALL, Christie's Auction Rooms. Sale 24 February 1809. "An eminent publisher retiring from business put up for auction Coade busts of Venus and Caracalla". (Gunnis)

PALL MALL Messrs Ransome, Morland and Hammersley. Sir John Soane's Museum, Soane Bill Book 1791-2 p56 (very faint) 1791 November 7. "To 30 balasters 2ft. 2in at 5s.0d. £7.10s.0d., 6 halves at 3s.0d. 18s.0d., Cartage to Pall Mall 2s.0d." Not traced.

PALL MALL, 74 CO April 1819, "Estimate to *MR. VULLIAMY* 74 Pall Mall a candelabra in artificial stone from 18-29gns." CD June 1819, mentions four scagliola pedestals for Justice [sic; should be Justin] Vulliamy, and a further eight in September for £10.5s.0d.

PALL MALL, 80-82 Schomberg House. Porch, supported by male terms, duplicates of those at Coade's Gallery*, with a plaque symbolising painting*. The Polygraphic Society, copiers of pictures, put up the porch in 1791. One term dated 1791.

PALL MALL, 90 CD October 1816. William Dennison "sent to Pall Mall small Laocoon bronzed". 10 guineas. CD July 1816 "Arms and crest on a circular ground with wreath of oak 3ft 8in diam £27.19s.6d."

PALL MALL, BUCKINGHAM HOUSE – See Buckingham House

PALL MALL, The Picture Gallery. CG refers to Pannels, Ballusters and caryatids at the Picture Gallery, Pall Mall. This could be either Dalton's House, on the site of the United Services Club, first exhibition gallery of the Academy, or Christie's premises, also used for exhibitions, see above. Both demolished.

PANTHEON, THE Oxford Street. By *JAMES WYATT*, 1770-2. Burnt and rebuilt 1795. CG mentions capitals, pateras and arms. for the 1st or 2nd Pantheon? Demolished.

PARAGON, THE New Kent Road. By *MICHAEL SEARLES*, 1790s. Probably similar to surviving Paragon (Blackheath, qv) also by Searles. CG. Demolished. Gate piers now at Royal Arsenal Woolwich (English Heritage 1988.)

PARSON'S GREEN, Henniker House. Keystone on doorway of late 18th century house, now part of Lady Margaret School*.

PECKHAM, GROVE BAPTIST CHAPEL, Camberwell Grove. CO May 1819, "offered to . . . (illegible) for Peckham Baptist Chapel, an oval tablet of about 2' 7" by 1' 8" with the words "erected 1819", 8gns impost strings plain, 4s.6d., per foot, do. ornamented, 5s.0d. coping 1s.3d., Ball and Foot 2½gns each. The oval shield with date* cost the committee £9.11s.0d. Pesvsner remarks on the pretty late Georgian Chapel, built 1819 by *ROPER.* CD.

PENLINGTON PLACE. CO October 1814, "Mr. Penlington, a tablet with Penlington Place 1813". Not identified.

PENTON RISE, WC1. Pevsner refers to Coade bits; area now demolished.

PENTONVILLE CHAPEL, Pentonville Road, N1. 1787. Two horizontal oval paterae over central door; girl's-head keystone in arch above; flat Ionic pilasters with capitals probably Coade; porches each side with girl's-head keystones. All very battered (1972). Gunnis refers to a Coade font, c.1793. By *AARON HENRY HURST* (Colvin). Demolished by 1988.

PENTONVILLE, 2 Queen's Row. CD "Hancock, 2 Queen's Row, Pentonville, a group of charity girl and boy 20gns." The street has disappeared.

PHILLIMORE PLACE, Upper and Lower. In Kensington High Street, 1788 onwards, by *WILLIAM PORDEN.* Uniform houses with swags and paterae. George III called the terraces "Dishclout Row". (*Survey of London, North Kensington* p58ff). Demolished.

PHOENIX BRASS FOUNDRY, Herne Hill. Trophy of Arms* now on Bowen & Co's works, with gun barrels, cannon balls etc 1808 from foundry at 6 Mount Pleasant Finsbury. (F.J. Collins)

PHOENIX ENGINE HOUSE, Charing Cross. Probably similar to that at Chelmsford qv. Designed by *THOMAS LEVERTON.*

PICCADILLY, Pulteney Hotel. CD May 1815 "Colossal bust of the Emperor of Russia with arms and hands in military uniform 40gns." The Emperor Alexander had stayed at the hotel in 1814 (Isobel Rae). Fixing the bust, on what was later Hertford House, cost Mr Escudier 2 guineas.

PICCADILLY. CG mentions "various Royal Arms." Not traced.

PICCADILLY, 144-145 By *S.P. COCKERELL* for his brother Sir Charles. CD August 1818, "For labour of boring through a candelabra to admit of gas. Jones and horse and cart, bringing it from Piccadilly and taking it back again, 4gns." House demolished 1972.

PICCADILLY, K4 Albany. CO June 1814 "Manuel Sarrateau K4 Albany House, to Mr Evans Crutched Friars, a stove oval shape to pattern, no hobs, a figure at top. Ironwork to be prepared by Mr. Evans. 50gns. 15% off." Two Eagles marked Coade and Sealy, Lambeth, 1803 (F.J. Collins).

PITZHANGER MANOR,* Ealing. SIR JOHN SOANE'S house, altered by him. Caryatids in breakfast room*, caryatids as Sir John Soane's Museum. 1802.* Two figures in Eating Room.* Sir John Soane's Museum Box 7 Parcel G, bill for the outside caryatids, six vases and 73 balusters £62.0s.0d. and "4 cariatide figures* as per agreement, 8 blocks with raffle leaf in the dyes circular and oval . . . £21."* The Breakfast Room figures were taken from a chimneypiece design, no.516. The round blocks were above and below the figures, the oval ones on their sides. The two figures in the Eating Room were originally called Urania and Clio. They are now accompanied by plaster duplicates. (Emmeline Leary.)

PORTLAND PLACE, Langham House. See under Langham House

PORTLAND PLACE see also NEW ROAD. Now Marylebone Road, Portland Place.

PORTLAND PLACE, W1. CD August 1818 "Mr. Peto Little Britain for house Portland Place, 2 Ionic columns with 2 do. pilasters in porphyry scag° with caps and bases of statuary scag°. Invoiced at £42.12s.6d." Not traced.

PORTLAND PLACE. European Magazine May 1787 refers to "two lions of this [Coade] manufacture" at the corner of Portland Place. Probably means Stratford Place qv.

PORTLAND PLACE, Camberwell. CO May 1814, "Law and Font, Portland Place Camberwell, 8ft circular coping at 1s.8d." Presumably for a fountain basin. Untraced.

PORTMAN SQUARE,20 AND 21 W1. No 20 by *ROBERT ADAM*, 1775-7; 21, part of the same composition externally, reputedly by *JAMES ADAM*. CG "Pannels of oak, capitals, medallions, ballusters etc."* The panels, now painted white and blue, are oblong with swags on the front, and round with figures on the back. Also surviving are guilloche string-courses,* round paterae on the front,* the capitals of the back porch* and probably the front one, and possibly the bucrania on the front porch.*

PORTMAN SQUARE, 24 CO June 1818 "Miss Johnes, 24 Portman Square, a small verd antique slab." Probably for furniture. Not traced.

PUTNEY BURIAL GROUND, Upper Richmond Road, rear of nos 205-213. Monument to Harriet

Thomson, marked Coade London (F.J. Collins)*. Tomb chest with attached shafts at corners. Oval medallions on sides.

QUEEN STREET. CG. Mentioned with Long Acre qv.

QUEEN'S GUARD HOUSE, St James's Park. NP mentions royal arms. Demolished.

REGENT STREET, Argyll Rooms. By *JOHN NASH,* 1818, burnt 1830. CD "John Nash Dover St a cup in artificial stone for a figure and man's time fixing in Argyll Rooms 12s.0d."

REGENT'S PARK, St John's Lodge. CD July and August 1818 "C.A. Tulk Esq. Marylebone Park, 2 corinthian pilaster caps. 16gns." "2 couchant lions 4' long, modelled from a sketch by Mr. Flaxman £42." House by *J. RAFFIELD* 1818-19, altered by *BARRY* 1846-7. Pilaster capitals removed by *BARRY,* and the lions put on top of the wings.

RICHMOND AVENUE, N1 (?).* Regency terrace with Egyptian sphinxes on front steps. All now painted, but apparently of artificial stone. Coade? (A. Kirk Wilson).

ROYAL COLLEGE OF SURGEONS see LINCOLN's INN FIELDS. Scagliola pillars in 1836 for Sir Charles BARRY (Gunnis). Later removed.

ROYAL HOSPITAL CHELSEA – See Chelsea.

ST ANNE, LIMEHOUSE. Tomb with urn in churchyard, marked Coade and Sealy London (F.J. Collins)*. Urn is the Wyatt design with swags and bunches of grapes. Name illegible.

ST BARTHOLOMEW THE GREAT, Smithfield.* Rahere's tomb,* c.1500. CD October 1815 "Churchwardens of St Bartholomew The Great, August, September, October, to Men's time and materials in cleaning and restoring a rich Gothic monument including sundry new pinnacles, corbels, etc., in the church of St Bartholomew the Great, 50gns."

ST BOTOLPH, Bishopsgate – See Bishopsgate

ST DUNSTAN'S IN THE EAST City of London. Rebuilt by *DAVID LAING* and *W. TITE,* 1817-21. CO July 1820, "St. Dunstan's church East ordered by Mr. Laing, a font abt. 25gns, a Royal arms abt. 20gns." Bombed.

ST GEORGE'S HANOVER SQUARE, CHURCHYARD OF off Bayswater Road. CD July 1818, "Mrs. Hughan for repairs of monument in St George's Burying Ground, Hanover Square, £31.10s.0d." Not traced.

ST GEORGE'S FIELDS. St George's Circus layout and radiating streets, by *GEORGE DANCE*

THE YOUNGER, from 1769. CG. "Arms, Statues, Vases, Capitals etc., at the Circus." All rebuilt.

ST HELEN'S PLACE Bishopsgate. CO 1.4.1814 John Harvey and . . . [illegible] Prince Regent's Arms. Feathers 8' 4" high 20gns. Mr Harvey, St Helen's Place, Bishopsgate St. Tablet with crest and words, Harvey Place 14gns.

ST JAMES, HAMPSTEAD ROAD. Monument to Sir William Hillman,* dated 1800, now in Victoria and Albert Museum. Vestal as at Battersea, Langley Marsh, Fenstanton. Church demolished.

ST JAMES'S PARK, New State Paper Office. SIR JOHN SOANE 1829-33. Royal Arms (D. Stroud *The Architecture of Sir John Soane* 1961, Plate 223.)

ST JAMES'S PARK. See *QUEEN'S GUARD HOUSE*.

ST JAMES'S PLACE, off St James's Street. CD February 1814 "Sir John Lubbock, St. James's Place, stonework for stove, £26.5s.0d." House not traced.

ST JAMES'S PLACE. CD September 1815, "The Hon. Frederick North, 6 4ft 6in statues, of Minerva, Fortitude, Flora, Contemplation and 2 Vestals at 20gns. £126. Cartage to St. James's Place £5.5s.8d." CO October 1816, "In six months a statue abt. 7ft copy of Caryatis from one of the Elgin Marbles in the British Museum at 50gns. to be copied as it now appears." Sent to Athens but apparently never used as a replacement for Elgin's caryatid.

ST JAMES'S SQUARE, SW1. CD September 1816, "Duke of Norfolk, sent to Norfolk House by order of *TASKER*, 50 Ionic blocks £12.10s.0d., fixing etc. 17s.0d." CO December 1816 "Duke of Norfolk for Norfolk House, Cap of Maintenance £26.5s.0d." House by *MATTHEW BRETTINGHAM*, demolished 1938.

ST JAMES'S SQUARE. CO June 1818 "Edward Boehm Esq. St. James's Square, Amersham Park per Messrs. Chapman, a circular medallion containing coat of arms for dairy ceiling". Not traced.

ST JAMES'S SQUARE. CD July 1821, "Ponsonby St. James's Square per *MR. CUNDY*, 2 columns, 2 pilasters in green granite scagliola and enriched Grecian caps. £82.8s.6d." Not traced.

ST. JAMES'S SQUARE, 5 Four statues, one marked Coade Lambeth 1792 (F.J. Collins)*.

ST JAMES'S SQUARE. CG mentions "various arms, medallions, pateras, capitals, etc. in the Square". Not identified.

ST JAMES'S SQUARE, Charles Street (now King Charles Street). Galloway House (demolished) for the Earl of Galloway by *JOHN JOHNSON*. Coade chimneypiece in hall (F.J. Collins), probably that exhibited by E. Coade in 1774, "a chimneypiece in artificial stone for a nobleman's hall from a design of Mr. Johnson's".

ST JAMES'S STREET. CD January 1816 "Geo. Palmer St. James's Street, a large group comprising the French Eagle conquered by the British Lion, 45gns." Almost certainly that at Pulford, Cheshire,* qv.

ST JAMES'S STREET, Boodles Club. By *JOHN CRUNDEN*, 1775. has paterae, now painted, on front, with characteristic Coade faces in the middle.* Also small griffin plaques.* CG mentions "various arms, medallions, pateras, capitals" in the street.

ST JAMES'S STABLE YARD. CD August 1816, "Hunt, Stable Yard St James's Unicorn on plinth 6gns. Men's time carrying and fixing do. Strand 8s.0d."

ST LAWRENCE, Brentford. Monument to Rev. Wm. Cooke 1810 (Gunnis).*

ST MARK'S, Clapham Road. Churchyard Monument to Mrs P. Brayley, 1819. Mentioned in Pevsner *London South*, p336, but vanished by May 1986.

ST MARY'S, Battersea – See Battersea

ST MICHAEL'S, Cornhill, City of London. Monument to Mrs Asperne, 1806 (E. Esdaile).* Tablet curved round a half column in north aisle.

ST OLAVE'S, Hart Street, City of London. Monument to the Davison and Newman families with reclining figure of Commerce (*History of St Olave, Hart St* by Porah, E. Esdaile). Figure as at Melton Constable, but figure rests arm on large volumes (ledgers?). Below, a sarcophagus "Sacred to the memory of Monkhouse Davison Esq. and Adrian Newman Esq." Weeping putti on sarcophagus. Bombed.

ST OLAVE TOOLEY ST SCHOOL. Oblong plaque found at New Malden and believed to be a boundary marker. Marked Coade's LITHODIPYR St OL, therefore probably 1780s-1790s. Shows Schoolmaster and boys in attempted Elizabethan scene representing school's date.* (F.J. Collins) Present whereabouts unknown.

ST PANCRAS OLD CHURCH, Midland Road. Tomb of Isabella Jackson Hernon, marked Coade and Sealy 1813. Tomb seen by F.J. Collins in 1950s. Not found 1984.

ST PAUL'S CATHEDRAL. Monument to James Barry, with portrait bust, in crypt near the tomb of Wren, 1819.* See Royal Society of Arts, Adelphi and Greenwich Park.

ST PAUL'S CHURCHYARD. CG mentions "pateras, vases, etc., at the School and at Newbery's." Whole area blitzed. School removed 19th century.

ST PETER, Cornhill. CD October 1820, "Gascoigne, Leadenhall Street, monumental tablet to be fixed in St. Peter's church Cornhill to the memory of Miss Amelia Murphy £15.2s.6d." Not traced.

ST THOMAS'S HOSPITAL. CD July 1814 "St. Thomas's Hospital Governors, Arms of the hospital with festoons of oak leaves, acorns, lions' heads etc. 30gns. Fixing, carting £2.4s.6d." For St Thomas's at Southwark, demolished 19th century.

SIR JOHN SOANES MUSEUM, Lincoln's Inn Fields. In *SIR JOHN SOANE'S* house, reconstructed by him. Caryatids based on those at the Erechtheion, 1812, £40 (Gunnis).* Vase from Carlton House (qv).* Museum has proof copy of the Coade etchings, many pages cut out. River God keystone.

SKINNERS' HALL, Dowgate Hill. By *WILLIAM JUPP,* c.1808. CG. Pediment design with frieze of swags* which are animal skins. Also capitals* and the Company's coats of arms.*

SLOANE STREET, Chelsea. Keystones* at nos. 88, 89, 90. "Bedford Square" doorway, no.91.* Similar doorway with relief of vase in tympanum,* no.93.

SMITH STREET, Chelsea. Nos 2, 5, 22, 48, 49, 50, have small crowned head keystones. Very small modest houses.

SOHO SQUARE, W1. CG mentions "capitals, ballusters, pateras, arms, etc." Nothing identified.

SOMERSET HOUSE, Strand. By *SIR WILLIAM CHAMBERS,* 1776-86. He designed the vases for the parapets; 29 supplied by 1787 for £193 (Gunnis)*. In basement, coat of arms dated 1831 (F.J. Collins)*.

SOUTH AUDLEY STREET, Plate 80b *Survey of London* vol. XL 1980 p305 shows three Coade plaques on the back wall of yard, one round, two oblong, reclining ladies.*

SOUTHGATE, Grovelands. By *JOHN NASH,* 1797. CG. Extant Ionic capitals to columns and pilasters, Coade*. Terence Davis, *John Nash,* plate 6, shows print of house with two large urns on the portico and a sphinx on the cornice, now removed, almost certainly Coade.

SOUTH STREET, 8 Finsbury – See Rio de Janeiro, Brazil

SOUTH LAMBETH ROAD, 57, 59, 268-274. Early 19th century Coade keystones.*

SOUTHWARK, Anchor Brewery, Park Street. Coat of arms of King William IV, 1832, marked Croggon (W. Ison).

SOUTHWARK, Holy Trinity. Survey of London vol. XXV p111. Statue* by NE side of church partly ancient and partly restored in artificial, probably Coade stone. May be King Alfred one of an ancient pair in the garden of Carlton House, or one of eight medieval statues which disappeared which Soane cleaned the N front of Westminster Hall in 1820-5. In situ by 1830.

SPITALFIELDS, Christchurch. Royal Arms* 1822 "from Coade's ornamental stone and scagliola works £66.14s.0d." (*Survey of London* vol. XXVII p166).

SPITAL SQUARE, 20 Doorway as Bedford Square, frieze and cornice. Demolished. (*Survey of London* vol XXVII p65).

STAMFORD STREET. CD February 1801, "Benevolent Society of St. Patrick, Stamford Street, Royal arms £40.19s.0d." Thomas Allen *History and Antiquities of the Parish of Lambeth,* 1826 shows house with the arms on the porch. Now gone.

STANMORE HALL, Stanmore. By *SIR WILLIAM CHAMBERS,* 1770 for John Drummond of Drummond's Bank. CG. Demolished. Nothing traced.

STANTIONERS' HALL, Ludgate Hill, EC4. By *ROBERT MYLNE,* 1800. CG. Set of four putti as four Seasons, nos 314-317,* a large patera* and an oblong plaque of griffins and ornament.* Three plaques marked Coade, three unmarked (F.J. Collins).*

216 STRAND, 216 CG says that Coade supplied "Chinese Figures and Lion at the Tea Warehouse, Strand". A classical doorway has the name TWININGS in the frieze remaining from the original building. Chinese figures sit on the pediment with the lion above. The colouring and gilding of the figures are modern (Sir John Summerson).

STRATFORD PLACE, W1. By *R. EDWIN,* supervised by *GEORGE DANCE,* 1773. CG. Rusticated blocks and voussoirs on house no 16 on west side* (as catalogue no476). At south-east end, a porter's lodge with lion couchant on top* and a small plaque of "griffins and ornament"* on the south side. There was a matching construction at the south-west end, demolished.

STRAWBERRY HILL, Twickenham. Horace Walpole's house. CG. Gothic gateway designed by *JAMES ESSEX* from tomb of Bishop de Luda, Ely, 1771. The subject of an argument between Eleanor Coade and Horace Walpole, 1772, on cost – £150. (Gunnis) (Illustration *Architectural Review* November 1950 plate 15). A medallion of Thomas Gray in a wreath,* same as at Saltram qv, on the exterior.

ST LEONARD STREATHAM CHURCH YARD. Monument to Joseph Hay, 1808 (Gunnis).* CD September 1817, Boyce, 2 North Audley Street, cutting inscription on tomb in Streatham Church Yard, and repairs 1gn." CD October 1820, "Boyce, new top stone to the monument in Streatham Church Yard, repairing the monument £11.14s.3d." To John, not Joseph Hay; (F.J. Collins). Similar to Bligh, Lambeth. Boyce's may be the badly crumbled tomb of similar design nearby.

SUFFOLK STREET, 6 Westminster. Coat of arms of Queen Victoria* inscribed T. C(r)og(gon) Lam(beth). *Survey of London* vol. XXIII p61).

SURREY SQUARE, Walworth, off Old Kent Road. Coade decoration in pediment.* (Surry to Coade.) By *MICHAEL SEARLES,* 1794.

SURRY SQUARE, Southwark. CG refers to rustication at 28 Surry Square.

SYON HOUSE X, Isleworth. Brentford Gateway, by *ADAM,* 1773.* Decorations in another composition restored by Coade. CD March 1814 "Sundry work on Syon Gateway, £450." CD November 1818, "D, of Northumberland, Syon, small fountain, rock forming triangular support, 2 basins coral, £39.9s.0d." Triangular base for sundial* as Audley End. Also surviving two urns* near house, an urn* said to commemorate a monkey and two portrait plaques* (Duke of Northumberland.) The scagliola floor in the Ante-room, believed to be the original designed by Adam and executed by Bartoli, has been found to be a replacement by Croggon of 1831-2. Syon MS U 3 8m "His Grace the Duke of Northumberland to William Croggon. To a rich inlaid Scagliola Floor executed in hard Material and various Colours, the whole laid complete in the Vestibule at Syon House – including all expense of Drawings, Patterns, Carriage, fixing etc. as pr. Estimate £900." (Dr Shrimpton Alnwick Archivist, and C. Gilbert, J. Lomax and A. Wells Cole *Country House Floors* 1987 p26).

TANNERS HILL, Deptford. Brunswick House. Coade medallion, figure sacrificing, design not otherwise known on decayed house. Built 1789 for Thomas Slade (Cherry & Pevsner, *London South* 1983 p409).

TEMPLE, THE Fleet Street. CO July 1814, "Sir A. Shee c/o T. Collins Esq. Brick Court Temple, Monument with naval trophies and inscription at 25gns." CD shows that it was "to the memory of Lieut. Jones". It is not in the Temple, and has not been traced.

THAYER STREET, 12 W1. Girl's head keystone,* small and very simple front door.

TOOLEY STREET. CD February 1821 "Newman Bridge St. House, square pedestal verd antique scagliola including deal base painted stone colour £13.1s.6d."

TOTTERIDGE, near Barnet. CD July 1819, "Mrs. Pugh, Totteridge, clothed Venus figure £7." Not traced.

TOWER HAMLETS, Court of Request. CG "Statues of Justice and Model of the White Tower." Not traced.

TOWER OF LONDON. NP "Coat of arms in the Office of Ordnance." Not traced. Cutting, Minet Library 12/64, probably from *European Magazine* January 1802, refers to the resistence of Coade stone to fire "demonstrated at buildings which have been burnt down or damaged by fire – such as the Ordnance Arms in the Pediment of the Tower of London".

TRINITY HOUSE, City of London. CG mentions "Arms, statues etc. at Trinity Houses at Water Lane, Tower St. and Tower Hill". Water Lane site not traced. Tower St and Tower Hill must refer to the present Trinity House, in that area, by *SAMUEL WYATT*, 1792-4, bombed, but rebuilt. Allen, *History of the Parish of Lambeth*, 1826, says the Royal arms* were Coade. Portrait medallions and plaques of putti and lighthouses may also be Coade.

TURNHAM GREEN, Waterloo Cottage. CD July 1818, "James Baxter, Waterloo Cottage, Turnham Green, A statue of Time with scythe and hour glass complete with rustic plinth, £18." In 1819, removed to Chelsea, not traced.

TWICKENHAM, Rugby Union Headquarters, Whitton Road. Lion* from the Lion Brewery, Belvedere Road given to the Rugby Union Headquarters for its centenary. (F.J. Collins.)

UPPER GROSVENOR STREET, W1. CD March 1820, "For Earl of Grosvenor, Upper Grosvenor St., 2 large giallo antico scag° pedestals £28.11s.0d." Not traced.

UPPER GROSVENOR STREET, 43 CD May 1821, "Bethell, 43 Upper Grosvenor Street, 2 scagliola pedestals 3' 3" high, marble bases, £35.2s.0d." Not traced.

UPPER MALL, Hammersmith, near Weltje Road. Coping on river wall stamped Coade in 1950s (F.J. Collins). Wall now raised and the Coade coping removed.

UPPER RICHMOND ROAD CEMETERY, Wandsworth – See Putney Burial Ground

UPPER SEYMOUR STREET, 58 W1. CD August 1820, "Edward Synge Cooper Esq. M.P. Monument comprising pedestal and vase with drapery etc. and cipher £64.19s.6d." Site of monument unknown. CD September 1820, "Edward S. Cooper Esq. M.P. a shield of arms and a crest £23.18s.1d." Site also unknown.

UPPER WIMPOLE STREET, nos 8, 10, 13, 20*. Doorcases.

UXBRIDGE, Belmont House. CG. Statue of Ceres* holding cornucopia and bunch of grapes marked Coade Lambeth. In grounds of a house on the site of Belmont House. (*Industrial Archaeology* 1968, part 2, pp206-8).

VERE STREET, Oxford Street. CO August 1815, "Underwood, Woollen Draper, Vere St, Oxford St. Arms of the Duke and Duchess of Cumberland, 6' long, one shield". Area rebuilt.

VICTORIA AND ALBERT MUSEUM, SW7. Monument with mourning Vestal* from St James, Hampstead Road.

VINTNERS' HALL, Upper Thames Street. CG. Balustrades renewed by Coade and Sealy, 1799, £260.10s.0d. (removed in later reconstructions). Pair of swans, 1800-1,* £13.10s0d., now in entrance. Coat of arms with supporters, November 1802, £32.19s.0d., in original position in the Hall.* (Elizabeth Glover, Company Archivist). Charity Boy dated 1840 on exterior.* Charity Girl missing.

WALTHAMSTOW, ST MARY'S CHURCHYARD. Solly Tomb, 1819, supported by lions' masks and feet (F.J. Collins).*

WANDSWORTH COMMON. Letter Book p19, 5.10.1813 to Richard Clarke Burntwood Lawn(?) Wandsworth Common asking payment for coping £24.17s.6d.

WANDSWORTH, 52 Rectory Grove. Doorcase (Pevsner).* See Clapham Common Rectory Grove.

WANDSWORTH ROAD, 30 Brunswick House. Elliptic porch with Coade swags in frieze* (Dan Cruickshank and Peter Wild).

WAPPING, SCANDRETT STREET SCHOOL. Charity Boy and Girl (F.J. Collins).* Derelict, figures surviving in store, and will be put on new building.

WARBURG INSTITUTE, Woburn Square, Bloomsbury. Oblong panel of the nine Muses in the Hall (Sir John Summerson).* From the architect *CHARLES FOWLER'S* house on the same site. (Bertram Hume.)

WATERLOO PLACE. CD March 1819. "Rivington Waterloo Place, a Bible and Crown £13.7s.0d."

WATERMENS' HALL, St Mary at Hill, City of London. By *WILLIAM BLACKBURN*, 1778-80. Plaques of tritons,* central plaque of badge and oars,* pilaster capitals,* frieze of swags and drops below pediment* (Gunnis from Company records).

WAX CHANDLERS' HALL, City of London. CG. Rebuilt.

WELBECK STREET, W1. Coade details at nos 12, 28, 44, 45.

WELLCLOSE SQUARE, Stepney. See Belgrave Square. A keystone, old man's head at 36 Wellclose Square seen in the 1950s (F.J. Collins). Lost in the demolition of the Square. The plaques now at 25 Belgrave Square are from Wellclose Square.

WEMBLEY. CG. Wembley Park altered and Gothicized by *HUMPHRY REPTON*, 1790-5. Demolished. Coade not traced.

WEST INDIA DOCK. West Indiaman over the entrance, 1804 "The extraordinary dimentions and elegant execution afforded a very superb and handsome spectacle" (*Monthly Magazine*, 1804, page 75). The ship model given by the Port of London Authority in 1932 to Poplar Borough Council, and put in Poplar Recreation Ground. A full-sized wooden replica in the PLA Cutler Street Museum, in early 1950s. Museum now given up (Trinity House).

WESTMINSTER ABBEY, W side of Cloisters, near to Abbey door. Monument to Edward Wortley Montagu,* 1777. Sarcophagus with central bas-relief medallion, catalogue design, marked Coade. The gift of J.E. Dolben Similar design to monument at Worlingworth, Suffolk, qv. *An Historical Description of Westminster Abbey, its Monuments and Curiosities designed chiefly as a guide to strangers.* No author. 1830 p186 (pub. A.E. Newman), gives details and a translation of the Latin inscription.

WESTMINSTER BRIDGE, East end. Lion designed by W. F. Woodington,* from the Lion Brewery beside the Coade factory, demolished 1950. Dated 1837 on one paw, and said to weigh seven tons (F.J. Collins). Now placed near the site of Coade's Gallery. Preserved through the intervention of King George VI.

WESTMINSTER BRIDGE, Toll House. CG. "Vases, pannels, chimneytops, keystones etc. at the Westminster Bridge Toll House". Demolished.

WESTMINSTER BRIDGE ROAD AND ORDNANCE TAVERN. CG "Arms, pannels etc. in the

Road and at the Ordnance Tavern". Demolished. Probably refers to Coade's Row.

WESTMINSTER BRIDGE ROAD. Survey of London, Lambeth (vol. XXIII p69) mentions a plaque on a terrace inscribed "Coade's Row", surviving until 1908.

WESTMINSTER BRIDGE ROAD. Coade's Gallery see *LAMBETH* Coade's Gallery.

WESTMINSTER LAW COURTS. By *SIR JOHN SOANE,* 1820-4, demolished 1883. "Decorative details" (Gunnis). See Palace of Westminster.

WHITTON, Middlesex. CG. Whitton Place was Sir William Chambers' own house. Demolished 1935. Nothing traced.

WHITEHALL, Department of Woods and Forests. CD June 1818, "*RHODES,* architect's office, Woods and Forests, Whitehall, 4 vases with birds per Tatham's book £38.2s.0d." Untraced.

WHITEHALL, Board of Trade. By *SIR JOHN SOANE,* 1827, reconstructed by Barry. "Decorative details" (Gunnis). Untraced.

WHITEHALL GARDENS, 6 Vestal Virgin marked COADE EXCUDIT (unique stamp) seen by F.J. Collins 1950s. Now destroyed.

WIMBLEDON ST MARY'S CHURCH. Rebuilt by *JOHN JOHNSON,* 1788. CG. CD September 1818, "Sold for cash, a Gothic pinnacle for Wimbledon church". Tomb of Gérard de Visme. Stone pyramid with Coade stone heraldic plaque inset, churchyard.

WIMBLEDON, Wimbledon Lodge Southside. House built for Gérard de Visme (whose Coade portrait bust is now in a private collection) designed by *AARON HENRY HURST* in 1792 (Colvin). The elevations are in the RIBA drawings collection. It had sphinxes on the roof, a long plaque with classical figures and a pair of Florentine lions, which are now at 42 High St, Wimbledon. The remainder destroyed (Lady Hartopp, Wimbledon Museum Committee).

WIMBLEDON. Bridge over Wandle demolished 1959. Keystone with bearded head marked COADE LAMBETH 1792. (Lady Hartopp, Wimbledon Museum Committee.)

WIMPOLE STREET, W1. Sixteen houses survive with Coade decoration between nos 19 and 56.* (19, 33, 34, 36, 39, 42, 44, 45, 46, 47, 48, 51, 53, 54, 55, 56.)

WIMPOLE STREET (Upper). Nos 8, 10, 13, 20 have Coade decoration.*

WOOLWICH Royal Arsenal. Gatepiers from the Paragon New Kent Road qv (Frank Kelsall English Heritage).

(c) WALES

(listed in alphabetical order of places with the present as well as the historical counties)

BANGOR, Caerns (now Gwynedd) CG. Site not identified. *SAMUEL WYATT* designed Library, Registry and Organ Loft for Bangor Cathedral 1776-86, B/DG/V/3. Chapter Acts and Accounts 1749-81 (J.M. Robinson *The Wyatts* 1980 p256.)

BASSALEG CHURCH, Monmouthshire (now Gwent). Monument to Sir Charles Morgan,* 1806. Reclining girl on draped sarcophagus with Sir Charles's arms on it. Inscribed plaque below flanked by reversed torches (Douglas Hague).

BODORGAN, *Anglesey (now Gwynedd).* Probably by *BENJAMIN WYATT*, 1779-81. CG. One damaged Coade vase, very large, and of "squat" shape, with swags, stamped Coade London 1791.* Originally one of a pair, it is thought (Douglas Hague).

BARON HILL, BEAUMARIS, Anglesey (now Gwynedd). By *SAMUEL WYATT*, 1776-9. CD "Lord Bulkeley, shield of his arms, to be sent to Park St. August 1814". Not traced.

CAERNARVON, Caernarvonshire (now Gwynedd). CG. Nothing traced.

DOWLAIS HOUSE, Glamorgan (now South Glamorgan). CD October 1818, "Josiah John Guest, Dowlais House, Cardiff, Monument, vase and pedestal, inscription in memory of his wife, £47.8s.4d." Not traced. Letters pp333, 346, 355, 368 on the progress of the monument. Completed September 1818.

ERDDIG See Wrexham

FFYONE, Pembrokeshire (Cardiganshire to Coade) (now Dyfed). By *JOHN NASH*, 1792-4. CG. Two Corinthian capitals, 16 guineas, 1796 (Gunnis)*. Plan in Terence Davis, *John Nash*, 1966 pp25, 26 shows columns at end of dining room, now library. Surviving?

HAFOD, Cardiganshire (now Dyfed). By *THOMAS BALDWIN*, 1783 and *JOHN NASH*, 1794, etc. CG. House burnt 1807. Font 1792 (Gunnis). Gateway in garden of Adam and Eve (as Bedford Square) (Sir John Summerson). Auctioneers John Francis, Thomas Jones and Sons sold a pair of eagles originally from Hafod some years ago (P.G. Francis).

KINMEL PARK, *Denbighshire (now Clwyd). By SAMUEL WYATT and THOMAS HOPPER.* Demolished 1866. CG. Coade Egyptian lions from original house now on gatepiers (Peter Hone)

LAUGHARNE CHURCH, *Camarthenshire (now West Glamorgan).* CD January 1818, "Miss Elliott, Laugharne . . . monumental tablet with vase £25.10s.1d." Not traced. 1799, George Elliott, monument (Gunnis).

LLANARTH, *Cardiganshire (now Dyfed).* CG. Nothing traced.

LLESNEWYDD *(actually Llysnewydd), Henllan Bridge, Cardiganshire (now Dyfed).* CG. "capitals etc." By *JOHN NASH,* c.1798. Plan in Terence Davis, *John Nash,* shows columns dividing hall and clustered columns on porch, which probably had the Coade capitals. House now altered.

LLEWENNY HALL, *Denbighshire (now Clwyd).* CG. "Large statues of Sabrina a Water Nymph, and the Thames, a River God" (Catalogue numbers, given special names). For the Bleach Works, designed by *PAUL SANDBY* at Llewenny. Plate 7 of *European Magazine* 1789 shows River God. Peter Howell, "Country Houses in the Vale of Clwyd." *Country Life* 29.12.1977, pp1966-1969.

NANTEOS, *Cardiganshire (now Dyfed). EDWARD HAYCOCK* worked on mid 18th century house in 1830-40. Coade urns on parapet.* (Douglas Hague).

PENGWELL, *Flintshire (now Clwyd).* CG. Nothing traced.

PENRHYN CASTLE, *Caernarvonshire (now Gwynedd).* CG "Arms, supporters, Gothic ornaments etc".* The 18th century house was replaced in 1827-47 by *HOPPER,* but the arms survive* (Douglas Hague).

ROCH CHURCH, *Pembrokeshire (now Dyfed).* Monument, 1790,* to the Rev. John Grant (Gunnis).

RUPERRA, *Glamorgan (now West Glamorgan).* CG. Nothing traced.

ST. ASAPH, *Denbighshire (now Clwyd).* CG. Nothing traced.

TREMADOC, *Caernarvonshire (now Gwynedd). Town Hall.* Keystones and two roundels (F.J. Collins).*. *Church.* Perpendicular Gothic gateway to churchyard, with battlemented towers, gargoyles and elaborate tracery (Douglas Hague).* Richard Fenton *Tours in Wales 1804-1813.* says "The Gateway is of Coad composition, most superb and elegant . . . not at all in accord with the other parts of the Building". (E. Beazley).

WREXHAM, ERDDIG, Denbighshire (now Clwyd). CG. "Medallions, chimneypieces etc." These not traced, but Coade vases* on the garden front, and a decapitated Druid in the garden (Douglas Hague).* Possibly connected with *JAMES WYATT'S* work 1773-4.

WYNNSTAY, Denbighshire (now Clwyd). CG. "Paid Mrs. Coade for two vauses of artificial stone for the niches of the Playhouse at Wynnstay". Wynnstay Collection, 115/4 Acct book 1771, 16 June (F. J. Collins). Demolished. Print of the theatre showing the vases *Country Life* 6.4.1972, p852 fig 7.

(d) SCOTLAND

(listed in alphabetical order of places, SNMR is the National Monuments Record for Scotland)

ABERDEEN, Clydesdale Bank By *ARCHIBOLD SIMPSON.* Statue of Ceres with Lion and Cornucopia* designed by James Giles (J.H. Cordingley and J. Macaulay).

ABERDEEN, Barracks. CG, "Royal Arms and Trophies". Demolished (SNMR).

ARNISFIELD, Haddington (now Lothian Region). CG, "Arms and supporters, Pannels, medallions etc. at the Earl of Wemyss." House demolished 1929 (SNMR). The present Earl believes that some of the plaques now at Gosford may be from Arnisfield.

BLAIR ATHOLL, Perthshire (now Tayside). White Horse over entrance to stables of Atholl Hotel* (SNMR). Horse now moved to the Crafts Museum (R. Breakell).

BROOMDALE (should be Broomhall), Fife (now Fife Region).* Designed by *THOMAS HARRISON* 1796-9. Bow window with three reclining-figure plaques.* (J. Mordaunt Crook, "Broomhall," *Country Life,* 29.1.1970, figure 2 p242). Letter Book has regular dunning letters from 1813-17 for payment for "3 pannels at £43.12s.0d."

CALLENDER HOUSE, Falkirk (now Central Region). Entrance lodges by *EDWARD BARDWELL BRAZIER* 1787-88. Sphinxes, vases for chimneytops, eight vases, statues of Flora and Ceres. (Forbes family correspondence GD 171 Box 14, 16, 58. John Hardy). All now late Victorian.

CROMARTY HOUSE (now Highland Region). CG, "Statues, etc." Hall has niches with Coade figures,* including the Vestal and Sibyl (Michael Nightingale).

CULLEN HOUSE, Banff, (now Grampian Region) Entrance Gateway* designed by *ROBERT ADAM* (Adam drawings, *Soane Museum,* vol. 36, pp68-70) not carried out until 1816. Arch with Ionic columns, frieze of swags and bows, two couchant lions, rampant lion on top. Couchant lions ordered March 1816 CO. Lord Seafield's arms and supporters supplied June 1817 for 40gns CD. Mausoleum with Vestal* c.1790 inside (Gunnis, Coade file, Conway Library, Courtauld Institute).

CULZEAN*, *Ayrshire X (now Strathclyde Region)*. By *ROBERT ADAM*, 1777-90. The Cat Gates have piers surmounted by Egyptian Lionesses one marked COADE LAMBETH 1802 badly decayed. (David Learmont).* Coats of arms over two garden archways.*

DALKEITH PALACE *(now Lothian Region)*. CG, "Statues and Pedestals at the Duke of Buccleugh's". *JAMES PLAYFAIR* worked for the Duke at Dalkeith, 1786. Statues now removed, possibly to other Buccleugh houses (SNMR).

DALMALLEY, *(now Strathclyde Region)*. CO July 1814, "2 shields of arms at 1' 6" high, 18 or 20gns. Earl of Morton, Dalmalley near Edinburgh". Not traced.

DALMENY HOUSE* X, *Linlithgow (now Lothian Region)*. By *WILLIAM WILKINS* Junior, 1814-17. Coade stone chimneys,* battlements,* plaques,* coat of arms,* pinnacles* etc. The most extensive Gothic Coade work surviving on a private house, costing £3,800, plus nearly £1,000 for packing. Details in Croggon's Day Book, over a period of about three years.

DUFF HOUSE, *(now Grampian Region)*. CG, "Monuments, Arms and Supporters, Statues and Gothic Pinnacles, the Earl of Fife's." The Mausoleum has the Gothic pinnacles,* and other Gothic detail. The other items not traced (SNMR).

DUNBAR *(now Lothian Region)*. CG, "Large winged sphinx, crest of the Earl of Lauderdale".* On Castle Park Barracks, in fact the crest of the Earl of Dunbar (SNMR). Building originally Dunbar Castle, *ROBERT ADAM* 1790-2, for the Eighth Earl of Lauderdale.

DUNMORE CASTLE, *Falkirk (now Central Region)*. By *WILLIAM WILKINS Junior*, 1820. CD "Lord Dunmore, ordered by Mr Wilkins, Dunmore Castle Falkirk Ireland, [sic] 4 columns, 4 pilasters giallo antico . . . £249.5s.0d." From the plan in the SNMR these scagliola columns were in the library. Demolished.

DRYBURGH ABBEY, *Kelso (now Border Region)*. CG, "Statue of a Piping Faun at the Earl of Buchan's." CD August 1819, "Apollo Belvedere, a circular pedestal with the 9 muses modelled in the die, enriched with laurel wreaths £119.4s.0d." The Apollo was for the Temple of the Muses. It has been removed. (SNMR)

EDINBURGH, Barracks. CG. "Royal Arms and Trophies". Not traced.

EDINBURGH. CO May 1814, "Charles Ritchie Edinburgh, price of sphinx 3' long, 24 gns." Not traced.

EDINBURGH, The Theatre. CG, "Statues of Shakespeare* and the Tragic and Comic Muses." Shakespeare taken to Bonaly Tower, near Edinburgh, on the demolition of the theatre (SNMR) where it survives in the garden.

EDINBURGH, Assembly Rooms, George Street. CG "Four statues for holding lights survive in storage (Edinburgh City Council).*

EDINBURGH, George Street. CG. Medallions of Flora and Pomona. Possibly at 113 George Street, decorated by JAMES NISBET (SRCHM).

EDINBURGH, St Bernard's Well. 1789. CG, "Statue of Hygeia 9' high." Though the Roman temple in which it stood survives, the statue has disappeared, though visible in an early 19th century painting (SNMR).

EDINBURGH, Register Office. By *ROBERT ADAM* and *ROBERT REID,* 1774-92. CD May 1814, "Lord Frederick Campbell, 2 descending stoves with brass and ironwork complete including packing and expenses on board, £110." CD August 1814, "Stove with dome top, perforated ornament £31.10s.0d" The stoves have disappeared (Edinburgh City Council).

EDINBURGH, 34 Albany Street. CD April 1817, "*GILLESPIE*, architect, Gothic candlesticks". CD May 1817, "Damaged vase £19.7s.0d." Almost certainly for *GILLESPIE-GRAHAM* who had not yet hyphenated his name. (G. de Bellaigue.)

EDINBURGH, London Street. CO June 1816, "J.C. Gordon Esq., W.S. [Writer to the Signet] London Street, Edinburgh, write him of the departure of Major Ramsay's monument, the mont to be left in the care of the ship's company until Mr. G. gives orders." CD August 1816, "Major Sinclair, Monument to the memory of Major Norman Ramsay . . . artillery gun, military trophy, broken wheel, helmet, sash, sword, etc . . . £52.19s.1d."* See St Michael's Church, Inveresk, Musselburgh, Lothian Region.

GLASGOW, Barracks. CG, "Royal Arms and Trophies." Not traced.

GLASGOW, Royal Bank of Scotland. CO May 1819, "a large Royal Arms, 35gns. directed to John Thomson Esq. Royal Bank Glasgow, to be sent by a Grangemouth vessel from Glasgow Wharf Wapping." Not there now (SNMR).

GLASGOW. CG, "Lions at Mr. Mair's." Presumably for Plantation House, Glasgow. Demolished (SNMR).

GLASGOW. Mr Love's. CG, "Statue of Hope at Mr Love's."

GLASSERTON, Wigtown (now Dumfries and Galloway Region). House 1787 by *ROBERT ADAM.* CG, "A statue for a lamp etc." Demolished c.1950. Alistair Rowan *Designs for Castles and Country Houses by Robert and James Adam* 1985 plate 17 shows figures in niches each side of front door, swagged frieze below Diocletian window in middle, paterae each side of this. All this could be Coade stone.

GOSFORD, Lothian Region. House 1791-1800 by *ROBERT ADAM.* CG, "Arms and supporters, Pannels, Medallions etc. at the Earl of Wemyss". Plaques and roundels on stables (special designs).* Sphinxes in garden.* Coat of arms with supporters on house.* 12 plaques* and 11 roundels* with large heads discovered by Miss C. Cruft in the grounds. Possibly from demolished wings, or from Arnisfield.

HADDINGTON (now Lothian Region). Couchant lions on houses in Haddington* thought to be artificial stone – one which fell off Distillery Park House is known to have been Coade stone (C. Cruft).

HADDINGTON, Bank of Scotland, 44 High Street. Villa of 1802 possibly by *JAMES BURN.* Sphinx on cornice,* reclining girl plaques on wings.*

HAMILTON BARRACKS (now Strathclyde Region). CG, "Royal Arms and Trophies." Demolished (SNMR).

HENDERSYDE PARK (now Border Region). 1803. House had medallions of Flora and Ceres* in pediments on south front and a medallion and scroll of the Waldie arms and crest on the pediment of the north front.* Three vases on the corners of each pediment.* (Ian Gow via Miss C. Cruft SRCHM.) Demolished.

ST MICHAEL'S CHURCH INVERESK, near Musselburgh. Tomb of Major Norman Ramsay,* in churchyard near the south entrance to the church. Sarcophagus with inscription, and on it a gun, as Bowes memorial Beverley, cannon balls and other gun impedimenta, sword, sabretache and splendid Roman type helmet with plume. Unfortunately painted grey-blue, though apparently in good condition. Tomb apparently paid for by fellow officers. See Edinburgh, London Street.

INVERNESS (now Highland Region). CG, "Nova [?] Arms and Supporters at Sir Hector Munro's". Not traced.

MONTROSE (now Tayside Region). CG, "Vases for piers at John Brand's Esq." Not traced.

PAXTON HOUSE (now Border Region). CG, "Arms and Supporters." These were not for Ninian Home of Paxton, but his cousin Patrick Home of Wedderburn, qv. The Coade decoratons, lions* and vases* at the front entrance of Paxton House were probably ordered through Thomas Chippendale the Younger in 1789. (Christopher Gilbert.)

PERTH, Barracks (now Tayside Region). CG. "Royal Arms and Trophies." The arms* were in the pediment over the front entrance. Barracks demolished, but the arms in the care of the Department of the Environment (SNMR).

PRESTON HALL, (now Lothian Region). By *ROBERT MITCHELL,* c1794. CG, "Lions, statues etc. Sir John Callender's." Florentine Lions on the gate piers.* Four lampholding figures in the hall.* (See also Selwood Park, Berkshire). Four pilaster capitals with necking of acanthus, coat of arms, and two ornaments of swags of material held up by masks on the garden front.*

TAYMOUTH CASTLE, (now Tayside Region). Bill 1813 from Coade and Sealy for Gothic chimneypiece for Baron's Hall £200, and Triton for a fountain on coral rock and a bason £157.10s.0d. Arms and crest for chimneypiece £8.8." (Scottish Record Office GO 112/20/4/9/49, via J. Macaulay.) Work of *ARCHIBALD JAMES ELLIOTT* 1806-10. Wilson and Harris were sent from the factory to put up the pieces (64 days at 9 shillings per day plus their expenses and fares £20.8s.6d.) CD November 1815. Letter 7.9.1813 (p7) saying they were on their way. For Earl of Breadalbane. Demolished.

TILMOUTH PARK, (now Border Region). CD August 1821 "Sir Francis Blake M.P., Tilemouth Park, Berwick, 4 pilasters and 2 wall pieces between pilasters for arch in dining room in brocatella scagliola, grecian caps £148.5s.0d." Two richly ornamented centres for chandeliers, a scagliola niche, and the men's time in fixing the scagliola, cost nearly £72 more. House demolished in 19th century.

UPSETTLINGTON near Coldstream, (Border Region). Lady Kirk House, Archway with lion with extended tail – ie., Northumberland lion.*

WEDDERBURN, (now Border Region). By *ROBERT ADAM.* CG. The arms and supporters* mentioned under Paxton belong here, in the tympanum of an arch over a triple window. Eagle supporters and an inscribed ribbon below. A lion on the North Lodge Gateway* (Mrs Home Robertson).

(listed in alphabetical order of places, Northern Ireland and the Republic of Ireland together. Mrs Coade's list is, of course, set out in this way, and architectural historians such as the Irish Georgian Society usually deal with both parts of the island together; this arrangement therefore seemed the most practical).

ARDBRACCAN CHURCH, Navan, Co. Meath. Inscribed tablet ordered by Bishop of Meath, early 1813. (J. Williams.)*

ARDRESS HOUSE, Co. Armagh. Squat oval urn* (F.J. Collins). The design, with ribbon swags and pendants of grapes, is offered in the Coade catalogue as a wine cooler. Very fine detail (J.A.K. Dean RIBA).

ATHENRY FRIARY, Galway. Ruin, containing "smoking" ie with the finial of flames symbolizing resurrrection, urn of baroque style marked Coade London 1790.* Design not known elsewhere (F.J. Collins). Also Bermingham family mausoleum with Coade plaques and other decoration, 1790, standing in chancel (N.W. English.)*

AVONDALE, RATHDRUM, Co. Wicklow. By *SAMUEL HAYES* for himself, c1800. Round paterae and swag-and-patera oblong plaques below first-floor windows.* Plaques of griffins over windows in end walls* (J. Williams).

BALLINATRAY, near Waterford. Statue of St Molanfide,* [sic] representing Mr Bryce Smyth in Augustinian habit, in the ruins of Mola Abbey, supplied July 1821 for £42. Mrs Smyth also had a scagliola slab for eight guineas. St Mola n'Faidh was a sixth century bishop, founder of the Abbey.

BARRONSTON, Co. Westmeath. House of Lord Sunderlin, mentioned CG. House burnt and rebuilt, no Coade surviving (J. Williams).

BATTINGLASS CHURCH, Co. Wicklow. Stratford Tomb, ordered by the Earl of Aldborough. Vestal with urn, 1796 (J. Williams).*

BELVIEW PARK, Co. Galway. Pediment had Lawrence coat of arms and trophies marked Coade London 1791. House demolished (J. Williams). Entrance gates with coat of arms dated 1792 and sphinxes survive. (N.W. English.)*

BELLEVUE, Delgany, Co. Wicklow. House of Peter la Touche, mentioned CG. House c1791, now demolished; photos show urns on parapet. Surviving lions couchant on gate-piers (J. Williams).*

BLESSINGTON COURT HOUSE, Co Dublin. Small coat of arms in pediment (J. Williams).*

BOLTON CASTLE, Co. Kildare. Crest of Earl of Aldborough marked Coade London 1795.* Moved c1835 from Belan House (N.W. English).

CALEDON, Co. Tyrone. Additions by *JOHN NASH,* 1812. Two Grecian sphinxes supplied for gate-piers,* and two coats of arms for the lodges,* in 1813. (£98.16s.11d. Letter Book page 13.) (Illustrated John Ruch *"Irish Coade", Irish Georgian Society Bulletin,* autumn 1970.) CD October 1815, "small fountain, stand, with water leaves and small bason, 10gns." Not surviving. Letter Book bills repeated September 1816 (p214) and again in January 1818. Chimneypiece illustrated Alistair Rowan, *The Buildings of Ireland and NW Ulster,* plate 78 shows design as Bretton Hall Yorks qv except for a plaque of "Griffins and ornament". Coade stone (J.A.K. Dean RIBA). Three intertwined dolphins remain from a fountain* (Dr D.J. Griffin).

CASTLEBLAYNEY, Co. Monaghan. Coade order supplied in 1808. Still not paid for in 1816, when a dunning letter sent at Mr Blayney's request to Col Freeth of Aylesbury. Coade not specified (Ruch, op. cit.) House rebuilt. No Coade surviving (J. Williams).

CASTLE CONNELL, the Hermitage, Co. Limerick. CG "Hermitage, Arms, Capitals etc." There were urns on the gateway, also statues. All removed before demolition of the house c.1965 (J. Williams).

CASTLE DALY or DUNSANDLE, Co. Galway. Both houses belonged to Peter Daly. Mentioned in CG. Castle Daly demolished. Dunsandle partly demolished. No Coade remaining (J. Williams).

CASTLE HYDE, Fermoy, Co. Cork. Sphinxes on gate piers.* By *DAVID DUCART* (?) c.1790, ill. M. Craig and D. Fitzgerald, *Ireland Observed,* 1970 (J. Williams).

CASTLETOWN, Co. Kildare. Mrs Coade wrongly sited the Glananea gateway (qv) at Castletown.

CASTLE UPTON, Co. Antrim. Mausoleum by *ROBERT ADAM* for Lord Templetown, 1785.* Two medallions of mourners,* ill. *Georgian Society of Dublin,* vol 2, 1910, and M. Craig and D. Fitzgerald, *Ireland Observed,* 1970. *Country Life* 13.7.1978 p126, fig 2, also shows vases in niches* and urn on top.* Gives date 1789.

CASTLEWELLAN, Co. Down. CD November 1818 "Lord Glerawly, Castle Willan Ireland, 2 eagles for piers with wings extended, 2 squat vases, 2 Egyptian lions, £97.10s.0d." March 1821, "A Gothic statue about 5' high, £42. Large lion couchant 35 guineas. Six vases and feet as per drawing, £37.16s.0d." The eagles* are on piers leading to yard; lions couchant* are in private collection, Newcastle; the vases and statue have disappeared (J. Williams) (J.A.K. Dean).

CHARLEVILLE, Co. Offaly. Pinnacles and crown crockets sent to the Earl of Charleville, August 1813, shipped to Johnson, Eccles St Dublin (Ruch, "Coade stone in Ireland", *Irish Georgian Society*, Oct-Dec 1970, p6). On the gate piers which have tracery as Tremadoc, Wales, but pinnacles on top. Architect, *FRANCIS JOHNSTON* (J. Williams).

CRESCENT, THE *Clontarf, Co. Dublin.* Sphinxes (in bad condition)* c.1790 (J. Williams).

CORK. CO March 1821, "Wrote Mr. Connor building a Catholic Chapel at Cork, to make 3 statues of Faith Hope and Charity for 160gns. about scagliola etc." Not traced.

CORK. *Grand Parade City Garage* had Coade keystones* panels and swags. All except keystones now removed. (Dr D.J. Griffin who has seen other Coade keystones in Cork.)

CURRAGHMORE, Co. Waterford. CG "At the Marquis of Waterford's Arms, Supporters and crest."* House by *JOHN ROBERTS* of Waterford, interior, *JAMES WYATT.*

DAWSON GROVE, Monaghan. Hon Mrs Dawson had an urn on a column in 1811 for £29.4s.0d. Reminder letter, (p6) on 15.4.1813. J.A.K. Dean FRIBA discovered a "Chambers" urn, with remains of flames (ie funerary) on a ruined lodge, probably the 1811 piece,* and also a keystone stamped Coade and Sealy, of a bald-headed man.*

DRUMCREE. CO April 1814, for William Smyth Esq. Estimate sent for seven figures Britannia, Hibernia, Victory etc 8 ft high, appropriate drapes and devices at 180 guineas each, one do. Fame 9ft 200 guineas, four basso relievos 12ft long, 4ft high, of battles, 100 guineas, eight small do. 8½ft long 4ft high 80 guineas – 2500 guineas. Not unexpectedly, there appears to have been no follow-up.

DRUMSILL, *near Armagh.* CG, "Tomb in churchyard with statues in the angles." Place not traced; only Drumsillan Church, which has no tomb of this kind (J. Williams).

DUBLIN. CD. July 1821 "J.E Devereux, Bury St, St James's, a Gothic monument 60 guineas. Inscription to the memory of the Rev. Henry Swann. Shipped per "Susanna" of Peters for Dublin." Tomb not traced.

DUBLIN, *The Court House, Kilmainham.* By *WILLIAM FARRELL*, Coat of Arms (drawings in the collection of Maurice Craig) (J. Williams).

DUBLIN, Lord Aldborough's House. CG, "Statues, Vases, Arms, Fountains etc. at Lord Alborough's". Lions* and sphinxes* remaining on roof of surviving wing. Also coat of arms* and swag plaques* (J. Williams). Illustrated Desmond Guiness, *Portrait of Dublin* p58.

DUBLIN, Eccles Street.* House by *FRANCIS JOHNSTON* for himself. Plaques* on facade (J. Williams).

DUBLIN, 13 Henrietta Street. CG, "Arms of the Bishop of Meath." House now a tenement. Arms gone before 1910 (J. Williams).

DUBLIN, Henry Street. CO July 1818, "John Karney, Henry Street, Dublin, a King's arms 7ft long, 30gns." Not traced, probably a shop.

DUBLIN, Lea Mount. Letter Book 7.10.1813 to Robert Alexander of Lea Mount Dublin about a complaint of a defect in his Egyptian lions.

DUBLIN, Merrion Square, Duke of Richmond's Fountain. CG, "Statues for Public Fountains." Fountain by *H.A. BAKER,* 1791. Triumphal arch shape. Squat urn* in centre, smaller vases* at ends, oblong plaque,* round plaques* with profile heads, round plaques* with figures,* The house on the corner of Merrion Square and Clare St had an urn which is now on the fountain (Dr D.J. Griffin).

DUBLIN, Mountjoy Street. Letter to John Peacock 29.7.1813 repeating account of December 1812, £32.7s.0d. Letter Book (p12).

DUBLIN, The Rotunda (Lying-In Hospital). By *JAMES GANDON,* 1786. CG ("Oxskulls, Pannels and Drapery etc. at the Rotunda").* Drum-shaped building with frieze of bucrania and drapery* and oblong panels with swags below.* Illustrated Desmond Guinness, *Portrait of Dublin* p9. Urns also survive (J. Williams).* Also pedestals in the hall of the Hospital.*

DUBLIN(?). CO August 1814 "Mr. Blaquire of Dublin, 7 Weymouth Street, Portland Place, Pair of monuments, 150gns." Mr Blaquire also had a house at Leighlin, Co. Carlow. Tombs not there, and not traced in Dublin (J. Williams). Letter Book p70 15.10.1814 says Coade firm has made model and sent drawing but had heard nothing. Not carried out?

DUBLIN, Clonmell House, Harcourt Street. CG, "Oxskulls, Pannels and Drapery etc. at the late Earl of Clonmell's." House survives without any Coade (J. Williams). Plaques in Mews* (Dr D.J. Griffin).

DUNGANNON, Co. Tyrone. CG, "King's Arms at the Sessions House." Illustrated in *Court Houses and Market Houses of Ulster* C.E.B. Brett 1973.

ECHLINVILLE (now called Rubane), Co. Down. Keystones with grotesque heads on the arched windows of the library (*Down Survey*, J. Williams).*

EDENDERRY RECTORY, Co. Armagh. Urn with a frieze of quatrefoil flowers (F.J. Collins).*

EMO, Co Laois. CG "Groups of Boys on Pannels at Lord Portarlington's". See Belgrave Square, London, for near duplicates. House by *JAMES GANDON*, 1790, illustrated Desmond Guinness, *Irish Houses and Castles* p9. Panels* and also capitals* and coat of arms* in pediment survive (J. Williams).*

FURNESS, NAAS, Co. Kildare. Entrance piers with very small paterae (J. Williams).*

GALLEN, Co. Offaly. CG, "Mr. Armstrong, Arms and Trophies in the Pediment".*

GALTRIM, near Trim, Co Meath. By *FRANCIS JOHNSTON*, c.1810. Coade stone Lions, dated 1802 (Maurice Craig. *Classic Irish Houses of the Middle Size* 1976 p157, 158 J. Williams).

GALWAY, Court House. John Behan ordered Royal Arms for the Galway Court House in 1816 (Ruch, "Coade Stone in Ireland," *Irish Georgian Society* Oct-Dec 1970, p6). (Probably removed in 1922). Now in University College Galway.* (N.W. English).

GLANANEA, Co. Westmeath CG (incorrectly referring to it as Castletown). "A Colonade and gateway with the crest (a horse) on it, Capitals, statues in niches."* Gateway designed by *SAMUEL WOOLLEY,* now dismantled and rebuilt at Rosmead. The statues have been removed and are now in private collection. Swags,* Keystones,* Urns* etc remain (Desmond Guinness).

HARRISTOWN – See Marlay

KILLYAN, Co. Galway. Coat of arms* of family of Cheevers in ruins of mediaeval church (N.W. English).

KILLYBALLYOWEN, Co. Limerick c.1800, demolished 1965. Similar decoration to that at Avondale, qv. Eight oblong swag-and-patera plaques, and griffin plaques in tympana. See *Thomond Archaeological Society Records* (J. Williams).

KILKENNY COURT HOUSE, Co. Kilkenny. CD "*Wm. ROBERTSON* architect Kilkenny per Supply to Waterford, Statue of Justice 7' high with copper scales and steelyards complete for the Court House Kilkenny £63."

KILRUDDERY, Co. Wicklow. Country Life* 27.7.1977 "Scagliola columns in the drawing room cost £320 from William Croggon, the well-known London scagliola maker"* (E. Esdaile).

KNIGHTSTOWN, Co. Laois. Gates with urns and swags on piers* (J. Williams).

LIMERICK. Mr Thomas Monsoll Tervoe (or Iervoe) sent 2nd account for £45.14s.0d. Letter Book p6 13.4.1813. Letter 21.6.1813 saying payment of £35 made, £10.14s.0d. still due.

LOUGH CUTRA CASTLE, Galway. CD December 1818 "Lord Gorst [sic, should be Gort] a rich Gothic chimneypiece from one at Windsor Castle 50gns. Shield of arms 30gns. By *JOHN NASH.* Later Victorianized, but chimneypiece survives (J. Williams).*

LOUTH HALL, Louth. House of Lady Louth, mentioned CG. Extant, but no Coade traced (J. Williams).

LUCAN HOUSE, Co. Dublin. Plaques and medallions in Coade stone on bridge and gate piers, by JAMES WYATT c1795. The memorial to Patrick Sarsfield, though the same design as those in Coade stone at Stanmer Park, Sussex, Mount Edgcombe, Cornwall and Brocklesby Park, Humberside has been discovered by Dr D.J. Griffin to be of Portland stone.

MARKREE CASTLE, Co. Sligo. Monument of vase and pedestal for E.S. Cooper. "Cooper's monument" and "Arms for Pediment", mentioned in Croggon's work notes (Ruch, op cit p8). House surviving, Coade gone (J. Williams).

MARLAY, Co Dublin. House of the La Touche family of bankers. Photo plate 13 p147 Maurice Craig, *Classic Irish Houses of the Middle Size,* shows "squat" urn on roofline, paterae with mullets,* frieze of festoons and bows,* all Coade designs. Urn now removed (Dr D.J. Griffin).

MONAGHAN COURT HOUSE, Co. Monaghan. By *WELLAND* and *BOWDEN,* 1820, for Lord Rossmore. Coat of arms in the pediment, see C.E.B. Brett, *Court Houses and Market Houses of the Province of Ulster,*1973 (J. Williams).*

MONAGHAN MARKET HALL, Co. Monaghan. By *SAMUEL HAYES* for Lord Rossmore, c.1800. Plaques and paterae as at Avondale, qv and Rossmore coat of arms.* C.E.B. Brett, *Court Houses and Market Houses of the Province of Ulster* 1973 p94 shows the plaques and paterae in place but says, unexpectedly, that they have been replaced by Portland stone.

MOTE PARK, Ballymurray, Co. Roscommon. Triumphal arch, with central block to the cornice having a long swag and patera and a Florentine lion on top.*

ORCHARDTON, Co. Kilkenny. By *WILLIAM ROBERTSON,* c.1820. Rosettes on the underside of Gothic cornices.* There were also pinnacles, now removed (J. Williams).

PAKENHAM, Castlepollard, Co. Westmeath (called Tullynally since 1961). CG. "Sphinxes etc. at Lord Longford's." Sphinxes* survive in the garden. Marked Coade's Lithodipyra, they must belong to the 1780s or 1790s (J. Williams). Also two urns of Sir William Chambers pattern.*

PORTLEMAN. CO 21.3.1821 Devereux at 21 Bury St, St James's a Gothic monument (old style) £65, with inscription additional. CD July 1821 J.E. Devereux, Bury St, St James's, a Gothic monument 60gns. Inscription to the memory of the Rev Henry Swann, shipped per Susannah of Peters for Dublin. Tomb not traced. (Dr D.J. Griffin)

RATHFARNHAM CASTLE*. Interiors by *SIR WILLIAM CHAMBERS,* 1770-1. CG, "Pannels of the Sciences, patteras etc." House surviving (M. Craig, D. Fitzgerald *Ireland Observed*). A Coade stone head keystone on the gate (Dr D.J. Griffin).*

ROSMEAD (Glananea). Remains of arch with keystone and Corinthian capitals, Sir William Chambers' urns, figures.* (J.A.K. Dean.)

RUBANE, Ards, Co. Dublin. Gatepiers with paterae and small plaques (J. Williams).* Keystones marked Coade's Lithodipyra London one with date 1787.* (C. Norman)

ST. LUCY'S (now Killera), Co. Westmeath. CD November 1819, "Sir Thomas Chapman, St. Lucy's Athboy, Ireland, Couchant lion modelled to order 30gns." House gutted. (J. Williams.)

SANDY MOUNT, near Dublin. House of R. Alexander. An Egyptian lion sent there late in 1813. (Ruch op cit p11 note 20). Not traced (J. Williams).

SANTRY COURT, Co. Dublin. House of Lord Domville. Plinths of statues with paterae*(?). The sphinxes here may be of Coade stone (J. Williams).

SKIBBEREEN, New Court. Lord Riverston, mentioned in CG, lived here. House demolished (J. Williams).

TEMPLEMORE ABBEY, Co. Tipperary. CD December 1817, "Denis Ryan, Templemore, Ireland, a vase with arms as per drawing £17. including 10% discount". Ruch (op cit p6) refers to correspondence about the price of this vase. House demolished and rebuilt (J. Williams).

TEMPLEMOR, Northern Ireland. Old photograph in Coade book of engravings at Sir John Soane's Museum shows semi-circular Coade medallion with urn with portrait medallion with three putti, one holding coronet, inscribed "St.

Mary's Churchyard, Lambeth, executed for Craven Carden Esq. Templemor, N. Ireland." See Lambeth Church, London.

THOMASTOWN PARK, *Athlone, Co Westmeath*. Ruined gate lodge, with random masonry. Six paterae* strung out unevenly, apparently re-used from somewhere else (N. W. English).

THOMASTOWN PARK*, *Ballydongan, Co Galway*. Gatepiers with paterae* and small plaques* (J. Williams, also N.M. English).

TOLLYMORE, *Co Down*. Lord Clanbrassil, mentioned CG, lived here. Enrichments to a fountain called the Lion's Mouth – a lion's mask and circular panels*; Coade? (J. Williams).*

TULLYNALLY – *See Pakenham*

TYNAN, *Armagh*. Mr Purden, Newry, sent letter 14.5.1813 (p7 Letter Book) saying that three cases containing three heads modelled in relief (?) for Sir James Strong sent per Prince Regent. Bill for £41.13s.0d. to Strong 1.5.1813.

WATERFORD. CD "*WILLIAM ROBERTSON* architect Kilkenny for Waterford. Statue of Justice £77.2s.1d." Not traced.

WILTON CASTLE, *Co. Wexford*. Ruch (op cit) p8 says that Henry Alcock ordered a copy of the Barberini Fountain. Building now ruined. It was not in fact the Barberini Fountain but from Giambologna: see Alison Kelly "Coade Stone at National Trust Houses", *National Trust Studies* 1980 pp94-111.

(f) FOREIGN PARTS

(listed in alphabetical order of countries)

AUSTRALIA

Statue of Mercury, copy of Thorvaldsen, 1830s, sold 1981. Private collector. New South Wales. Illustrated Alison Kelly "Mrs Coade's Stone" *Antique Collector* August 1981.

BELGIUM

BRUSSELS. CD March 1821 "The Earl of Clancarty, Bruxelles, Royal Arms, £46.10s.9d." Not traced.

BRAZIL

RIO DE JANEIRO. Copy of Syon Gateway* presented to the Regent of Portugal then in exile in Brazil by the Duke of Northumberland in 1812. Now the entrance to Rio Zoo. (Alison Kelly "An Expensive Present", *Burlington Magazine* pp548-553. September 1984.)

RIO DE JANEIRO, probably for the Palace at Rio de Janeiro. CD October 1820. "Saml. Phillips for the King of Portugal. Royal Arms surrounded by wreaths of laurel, the arms supported by 2 colossal statues of Justice and Truth, 2 triangular pedestals, dolphins on corners, 2 Vestal statues [actually Flora and Pomona] for lamps £395.10s.4d." CD November 1820, "Saml. Phillips, statue of St. George with shield, St. John with eagle, shipped by their lighter, £155.18s.4d." Gunnis also records, 1812, capitals and friezes for the Royal Palace, Rio. No information received from Brazil on the survival of these pieces.

CANADA

MONTREAL, Statue of Nelson on a column, Place Jacques Cartier.* By *ROBERT MITCHELL.* Sent 1808, erected 1809. Figure of Nelson stood until the late 1970s on a Doric column. Now a fibreglass replacement. On the plinth, three bas-relief plaques of the battles of Copenhagen, the Nile and Trafalgar. Copies now on the monument. A fourth plaque, said to have been restored or replaced, c.1900, records the erection of the pillar. A model crocodile, symbolizing the Battle of the Nile, sits on the plinth. See C. J. Pullen, *Canadian Geographical Journal*, vol. LXXIV no 2, Feb. 1967 p.58-64. Figure now in the care of the City Engineer.

MONTREAL, the Bank of Montreal, Head Office. CO October 1818, "John Richardson, 51 Southampton Row, 4 tablets with emblems comprising Commerce, Agriculture, Navigation, Arts and Manufactures, 3' 10½" by 2' 6" at 10gns. each for the New Bank, Montreal, Lower Canada to be ready by the middle of March." All adaptations of Bacon's reclining ladies, see Stratfield Saye, Hampshire etc. Originally on a Wyatt-style house with the plaques between ground and first-floor windows. On the demolition of the Bank, the plaques* were on a post office on the same site. Now in the Bank's modern head office.* (Article by Ida Darlington in STAFF, *Bank of Montreal*, 1965). Three plaques marked Dubbin and Panzetta (F. J. Collins). Marc Lafrance says however (APT vol. V, no.3, 1973, pp103-8) that all four are marked Coade and dated 1819; he points out that John Richardson was also connected with the Nelson monument.

CEYLON now SRI LANKA

COLOMBO. Shipping note at end of Letter Book 14 May 1813 "Shipped in the Albina, Rob. Wetherall Master, . . . 19 cases directed to the Hon. John Rodney, Colombo, Ceylon, containing 2 King's Arms."

GIBRALTAR

Court House, Supreme Court. Built 1819 by General Don. CO April 1820 "G.B. Thompson Esq Captain Royal Engineers, Inspector . . . [illegible] work, Gibraltar. A Royal Arms about 10 ft long at 80gns, including all expenses."*

King's Chapel. Monument to Major General Charles O'Hara 1802, plaque with his arms.* (F.J. Collins and Richard Garcia.)

GREECE

ATHENS– intended for the Erechtheion (?). CD January 1818, "The Earl of Guildford, to be shipped to Athens, a caryatis abt. 7ft. high, copied from one in the collection of the Elgin Marbles and packing, £67.1s.4d." Not traced. Lord Elgin's caryatid was replaced by a pile of stones until the mid 19th century. A replacement terracotta figure was then put up, but it has not been possible to connect this with Lord Guildford's figure.

HOLLAND

AMSTERDAM. CG "Statues, Busts, Chimneypieces etc." Not traced.

THE HAGUE – British Consulate (?). CO January 1814 "Lord Clancarty for Mr. Bandenetts (?) at the Secretary of State's Office, a small King's Arms for the Hague". Bill for 25gns. CD April 1814. Not traced.

WEGLEGEN, on outskirts of Haarlem. House built by Henry Hope. Five reliefs of arts and commerce behind the portico.* (J.H. Cordingley.)

POLAND

WARSAW, Lazienki Palace. Coade statuary (F.J. Collins). Not traced. Palace of King Stanislaus August Poniatowski, relative of Cardinal Poniatowski. (Mary Curry)

WARSAW(?). CG, "Poland, Gothic Window, Capitals etc. for Cardinal Poniatowski." Not traced.

PORTUGAL

LISBON – Consular Chapel(?). CO July 1820, "Mr. Charles Fowler, for a church in Lisbon, a 3' 6" Royal Arms on a ground." Not traced.

RUSSIA

ZARSKO ZELO (Tsarskoe Selo, now called Pushkin). CG, "Statues, busts, chimneypieces, vases etc." These may have been in Charles Cameron's apartments, or the Cameron Gallery, built for Catherine the Great. Palace gutted 1940s.

ST PETERSBURG (now Leningrad) British Church. *CD August 1815, "Sir Danl. Bayley, British Consul in St. Petersburg for British Church there, Royal Arms rampant, £42." Not traced.*

SOUTH AFRICA

CAPE OF GOOD HOPE. CD March 1820 "16 Ionic caps. shipped for Cape of Good Hope, £104.17s.4d." Not traced.

UNITED STATES OF AMERICA

BOSTON. CG, "Boston, Corinthian capitals etc." Almost certainly the capitals on the United States Bank, by *CHARLES BULFINCH*, 1798; this also had an American eagle with flag (N.P. Neblett).

NEW YORK, Metropolitan Museum. Figure of Faith,* a Vestal amended to turn her into Faith by the addition of a chalice, an alternative emblem to the more usual cross. The piece has been stained a terracotta colour at some time. The Museum has no prevenance earlier than 1964, when it was in the hands of a New York antique dealer. (James David Draper, Curator, European Sculpture and Decorative Arts.)

EX NEW YORK. From Ryan Mansion 858 5th Avenue. Pair sphinxes marked Coade's Lithodipyra 1787 sold at American Art Association Anderson Galleries 30 E 57th St New York, sale no4066 30 November 1933. Present whereabouts unknown. Bought from a Paris gallery in 1914. Originally on limetone plinths with putto medallions which look the size of the Seasons (Dona E. Caldwell).

PHILADELPHIA Pennsylvania. CG, "Philadelphia at William Bingham's Esq. and Mr. John Dorsey's etc." Bingham House (demolished) had extensive Coade decoration; drawn by Charles Bulfinch in 1789. Desmond Guinness and Julius Trousdale Sadler Jr. *The Palladian Style in England, Ireland and America,* 1976 p135. John Dorsey was a dealer who had Coade plaques etc on sale. He was also a builder.

SALEM MA Essex Institute. 132 Essex Street. Figures of Clio* and Urania* dressed as Flora with sheaf of flowers and flowers in her hair. Damaged, but being restored. An engraving of 1820 shows the figures in a Salem garden. (Alison Cornish).

SAVANNAH, Georgia. Owens Thomas House. Ionic Coade capitals* (John Cornforth) Country Life 16.1.1975. Architect *WILLIAM JAY.*

WASHINGTON DC, The Octagon. Capitals and bases for the columns of the porch,* and two chimneypieces supplied, 1801.* (N.P. Neblett and Historical Society of Richmond, Va.) One chimneypiece closely related to those at Capesthorne, Cheshire.

WASHINGTON DC. CG, "Washington, New Foederal City, capitals, frizes, key stones, chimneypieces, etc." The capitals and chimneypieces might be those of the Octagon, ordered some time before delivery. No friezes have so far been traced. One keystone* is now in the care of the Architect to the Capitol, though it does not appear to have belonged to that building. it is dated 1793, and has the girl's head, turned ¾ face, known in London, but with ivy leaves in the hair, not so far traced in England (N. P. Neblett). Long used as a doorstop, and damaged on the nose.

WEST INDIES

HAITI. CD February 1816 "Invoice of 11 cases shipped on board the ship Sir Joseph Banks . . . at my own account and risk". Croggon sent a mixed collection of figures and animals, including a bust of Nelson, as a trading venture and valued them at £40.1s.3d. *The Times* 6 November 1860, recorded that in an old house, among the Acul Mountains, there was found on an altar devoted to the fetich [sic] worship, a bust of Lord Nelson which had been worshipped for half a century as the Deity of the Mountain Streams. The bust was minutely described, and though it was described as marble, the impressed mark COALE AND LEALY, misread from Coade and Sealy, identified it without doubt as the one sent by Croggon. (Jim Saunders.)

JAMAICA, Montego Bay. CG, "Four monuments to Finlater, Lawrence, Minto and Birch." E. Minto tomb at St James's Church marked Coade London 1790. Tomb chest with putti sitting on it holding out drapery tied in a bow at the top* (Gunnis, Coade File). Bernard Birch died 1782; at St Peter's, Vere, plaque of the "Mourning Province" and urn with a putto on it* (Gunnis, Coade File).

MONSERRAT. CG, "Monument to Brownbill and Skerrett." Lesley Lewis in *Commemorative Sculpture in Jamaica* (bound with *Commemorative Art, Sculpture in Jamaica* in Victoria and Albert Museum Library) says that the memorials to Brownbill and Skerrit were not mentioned in Lawrence Archer's *Monumental Inscriptions in the British West Indies* c1875, and she wonders if they were ever erected. Gunnis also refers to a monument, 1797, to Emma Saunders at St Andrew's.*

ST VINCENT. CD November 1819, "James Colquhoun, Colonial Agent for the island of St Vincent large Royal Arms, £55.4.4."

TRINIDAD. Letter Book (p7) to Mr Lapidge, architect, Green St Grosvenor Square 14.9.1813 saying the Arms for Trinidad were ready. Shipping note 4.11.1813 "For Trinidad 1 case King's Arms."

BIBLIOGRAPHY

(Works are published in England except where stated)

ABEL SMITH, JULIA Great Saxham Hall, Suffolk. *Country Life* (27th November 1986 p. 1698-1702)

ACCADEMIA ERCOLANENSE Antichita di Ercolano (Naples 1755-92)

AGIUS, PAULINE *Ackermann's Regency Furniture and Interiors* (1984)

ALLEN, THOMAS *History and Antiquities of the Parish of Lambeth* (1826) Another ref. calls him Robert.

ANON. *Picture of London* (1804)

ANON. *History of Lambeth* (n.d. c1821) Minet Library, Brixton 12/64

ANON. *A Historical Description of Westminster Abbey, its Monuments and Curiosities.* Designed chiefly as a Guide to Strangers. (1830. p. 186)

ARCHER, LAWRENCE Monumental Inscriptions in the British West Indies (c.1875)

ASHER, BENJAMIN *The American Builder's Companion* (Boston 1806)

BARTOLI PIETRO SANTI Admiranda Romanorum Antiquitatum (Rome 1693)

BAYLEY, REV. Sussex Archaelogical Society Proceedings (1969)

BEARD, GEOFFREY *Craftsmen and Interior Decorators in England 1660-1820* (1981. p. 252)
The Work of Robert Adam (1978)

BEAZLEY, ELIZABETH *Madocks and the Wonders of Wales* (Faber 1967)

BELL, C.F. *Annals of Thomas Banks, sculptor* (Cambridge 1938)

BETJEMAN, JOHN AND PIPER JOHN *Murray's Buckinghamshire Architectural Guide* (1948)

BLANCHARD, MARK *Catalogue,* undated but after 1850.

BLASHFIELD, J.M. Catalogue of Five Hundred Articles (1857)
An Account of the History and Manufacture of Ancient and Modern Terracotta and its use in Architecture as a durable and elegant Material for Decoration. (1855)

BOLTON, A.T. The Architecture of Robert and James Adam (1922)

BOTTARI, G.G. *Musei Capitolini* (vols 1-3 Rome 1775)

BRIGGS, NANCY "Woolverstone Hall" Suffolk Institute of Archaeology and History

BROCKETT, ALLAN *Nonconformity in Exeter* (1650-1875) Manchester U.P. 1962. p. 134

The Builder (22 8 1891 p. 140-1)

BURGESS, F. *English Churchyard Memorials* (1963)

BURT, M.G.E. "Anglesey Abbey" *Connoisseur* (June 1949, p. 88-93)

BYRNE, ANDREW and ISOBEL WATSON "Hackney Terrace," *Country Life* (12th November 1987 p. 192-4)

CAMPBELL R.H. Carron *Company* (1961)

CAVACEPPI, BARTOLOMEO Raccolte d'antiche statue, busti teste cognite ed altre sculture antiche (3 vols Rome 1768-72)

CAYLUS, COMTE DE *Recueil d' Antiquités egyptiennes, etrusques, grecques et romaines* (7 vols. Paris 1752-67)

The Man at Hyde Park Corner. Sculpture by John Cheere (1709-1787) Catalogue by Terry Friedman and Timothy Clifford of exhibition at Temple Newsam, Leeds and Marble Hill House, London. (1974)

CLAY, HENRY "Coade's artificial stoneware." *Connoisseur* (LXXXIII 1928. p. 79-87 and March 1924 p. 162 Stover Vase

CLIFFORD SMITH, H. *Buckingham Palace* (1931 p. 109)

CLIFFORD, TIMOTHY, "John Bacon and the Manufacturers" *(Apollo* October 1985)

CLIFTON TAYLOR, ALEC *The Pattern of English Building* (1962-1965)

CLIFTON TAYLOR, ALEC and IRESON A.S. *English Stone Building* (1983)

COADE FACTORY *Etchings of Coade's Artificial Stone Manufacture.* British Library. (Dated in pencil 1777-1779, probably c1785.)
    A Descriptive Catalogue of Coade's Artificial Stone Manufactory at Kings Arms Stairs, Narrow Wall, Lambeth (1784) British Library.
    Description of the Grand Model of Neptune giving up the body of Nelson with the Dominion of the Sea into the Arms of Britannia from a Design by Benjamin West Esq. for Greenwich Hospital at Coade and Scaly's ornamental works, prob. 1813 Scottish National Library Acc 5111 Box 12. Coade's Gallery (1799) British Library

COLLARD, E.H. "Nelson in Old Montreal." *Country Life* (24th July 1969)

COLLINS, F.J. "Coade stone" *Museums Journal.* Vol 57 No. 2 (May 1957 P. 37)

COLVIN, HOWARD "The Architects of Stafford House." *Architectural History* (1958 p. 17ff)
    A Biographical Dictionary of British Architects 1600-1840 (1978)

CONSTABLE, JOHN *Correspondence* Vol IV (ed R.B. Beckett 1962 p. 57-58)

CORNFORTH, JOHN "The Owens Thomas House, Savannah" *Country Life* (16th January 1975 p. 142-3)
    Millichope Park *Country Life* (17th January 1977)
    English Interiors 1790-1848 The Quest for Comfort (1978)

COX JOHNSON, ANN *John Bacon RA* (1961)

CRAIG, MAURICE and FITZGERALD, DESMOND *Ireland Observed* (1970)

CROKER, J.W. "Lord Elgin's Collection of Sculptural Marbles" *Quarterly Review* (1815-16 XIV pp. 513-47)

CROOK, J. MORDAUNT "The Custom House Scandal" *Architectural History* VI (1963)
    "Broomhall, Fife" *Country Life* (29th January 1970)
    The Greek Revival (London 1972)

CROOK, J. MORDAUNT and PORT, A.S. *History of the King's Works* Vol VI

CRICKSHANK, DAN and WILD, PETER, *London, The Art of Georgian Building* (1975)

CRUNDEN, JOHN *The Chimneypiece Maker's Daily Assistant* (1766)

CURL, JAMES STEPHENS *The Egyptian Revival* (1982)

DALE, ANTONY James Wyatt (1956)

DARLINGTON, IDA Bulletin of the Friends of St Georges (1955)
    "Bank of Montreal 'plaques.'" *Staff - Bank of Montreal Journal* (1965)

DARLEY, MATTHEW and EDWARDS, R *A New Book of Chinese Designs* (1754)

DAVIS, TERENCE *John Nash (1966)*

DEAN, WILLIAM *A Historical and Descriptive Account of Croome d' Abitot* (1824)

DE BELLAIGUE, GEOFFERY. HARRIS, JOHN. MILLAR, OLIVER. Buckingham Palace (1968)

DE BELLAIGUE, GEOFFREY. "George IV and the Furnishings of Windsor Castle" *Furniture History* (1972 p. 28 and plate 13B

DELL, R.F. "The County Hall, Lewes" *Sussex Archaeological Collections* Vol C (p. 9)

DESGODETZ, ANTOINE *Les Edifices antiques de Rome dessinés et mesurés très exactement* (Paris 1682)

Devon and Cornwall Notes and Queries (1971-3 Vol XXXII p. 221-2) (1974-7 Vol XXXIII p. 26-8 226-7)

Dictionary of National Biography (1888 Vol 2 p. 361 (Bacon))

DOWNMAN, REV. E.A. *English Pottery and Porcelain* 5th ed. revised by Gunn, A.D. (1910)

DUCAREL, DR *History and Antiquities of Lambeth* (1785 or 86, Vol 6 of *Bibliotheca Topographica Britannica*

DU PREY, PAUL DE LA RUFFINIERE *Soane, The Making of an Architect* (1977)

Ecclesiologist, The Vol I no. VIII (May 1842 p 27) Circular from Austin and Seeley "Austin and Seeley beg to add that their work is executed without the application of heat"

EDWARDS, JAMES *A Companion fron London to Brighthelmstone in Sussex* 1801 (Pamphlet in V and A Library)

EMLYN, HENRY *A proposition for a new Order of Architecture with Rules for Drawing the several Parts* (1781)

ESDAILE, KATHERINE A. *Englist Church Momuments* (1946) "Coade Stone" *The Architect and Building News* CLIX (19th January p. 94-96, and 26th January p. 112-114, 1940)

European Magazine (1786) Print of interior of Coade Kiln
(August 1789) Print of a panel of Agriculture for the Earl of Portsmouth from the original pannel executed at Coad's [sic] Artificial Stone manufacture
(1802 p.71 or 7) *Account of Coade. Sealy's Gallery* (p. 448 has 2 plates of Melchett Park temple to Hastings.)

EVELEIGH, D.J. *Firegrates and Ranges* (1983)

FENTON, RICHARD *Tours in Wales* (1804-1813) Tremadoc

FLEMING, JOHN *Robert Adam and his Circle* (1962)

FOGGINI, P.F. *Musei Capitolini, tomus quartus* (4th Vol, 3 earlier by Bottari (1782))

FORDYCE, WILLIAM *Memoirs concerning Herculaneum the Subterranean City* (London 1750)

FOWLER, CHARLES "Some remarks on Terracotta and Artificial Stone as connected with Architecture" *Civil Engineer and Architects Journal* (Vol XIII p. 215-16 1850)

FOWLER, JOHN and CORNFORTH, JOHN *English Decoration in the 18th Century* (1974)

FREEMANTLE, nr Southampton Lodges described by writer unknown in *Proceedings of the Hampshire Field Club* and *Archaeological Society* (Vol 39 1983)

FREESTONE, I.C, BIMSON, M and TITE, M.S "Some Recent Research on Coade Stone" *English Ceramic Circle Transactions* (1986 p. 203-205 plate 122)
"The Constitution of Coade Stone" *Ancient Technology to Modern Science* (edited by W.D. Kingery, The American Ceramic Society Inc. Columbus, Ohio 1985)

GALT, JOHN *The Life, Studies and Works of Benjamin West Esq.* (London Edinburgh 1820 (first published 1816))

Gentlemen's Magazine (1794 Part I p. 140) Lady Henniker's monument, Rochester

Georgian Society of Dublin (Vol 2 1910-1913)

GIAMBOLOGNA, Sculptor to the Medici 1529-1608 (Catalogue edited by Charles Avery and Anthony Radcliffe of the exhibition held at the Royal Scottish Museum, Edinburgh and the Victoria and Albert Museum 1978)

GILBERT, CHRISTOPHER "Chippendale Senior and Junior at Paxton" *Connoisseur* (August 1972 p 256-266)
    The Life and Work of Thomas Chippendale (1979)

GILBERT, CHRISTOPHER and WELLS-COLE, ANTHONY *The Fashionable Fireplace* (1985)

GILBERT, CHRISTOPHER. LOMAX, JAMES. and WELLS-COLE, ANTHONY *Country House Floors* (Temple Newsam 1987)

GLOSSOP, W *The Stove - Grate Maker's Assistant* (London 1771)

GORI, F *Museum Florentinum* III (Florence 1737)

GORI, FRANCESCO *Admiranda Antiquitatum Herculanensium descripta et illustrata ad annum MDCCL* (2 vols. Padua 1752)

GRANT, MAURICE, H. *A Dictionary of British Sculptors* (1953 p. 64)

GRAVES, A. *Dictionary of Artists* (1893 p. 57, 80)
    The Society of Artists of Great Britain (1760-91), *The Free Society of Artists* (1761-83), *A Complete Dictionary* (1907)

GUINNESS, DESMOND *Irish Houses and Castles* (1971)
    Portrait of Dublin (1967)

GUINNESS, DESMOND and SADLER, JULIUS, TROUSDALE, SADLER *The Palladian Style in England, Ireland and America* (1976)

GUNNIS, RUPERT *Dictionary of British Sculptors* 1660-1851 (1953)

HALLETT, DANIEL,T. *Index of Artists* New York (1948 p. 82)

HAMILTON, S.B "Coade Stone" *Architectural Review* CXVI (November 1953 p. 295-9)

HAMLYN, TALBOT *Benjamin Henry Latrobe* (*OUP* 1955)

HANSFORD, F.H. "Eleanor Coade of Lyme Regis" *The Dorset Year Book* (1960-61 p. 27)

HARRIS, JOHN *Sir William Chambers* (1970)

HARRIS, EILEEN *The Furniture of Robert Adam* (1963)

HARRIS, JOHN. MILLAR, OLIVER and DE BELLAIGUE, G. Buckingham Palace. (1968)

HASKELL, FRANCIS and PENNY NICHOLAS *Taste and the Antique* (1981)

HAVILL, JOHN Eleanor Coade, *Artificial Stone Manufacturer* (1986) Typescript at University of Exeter

HEPPLEWHITE, GEORGE *The Cabinet-Maker and Upholsterer's Guide* (1788)

HITCHCOCK, HENRY-RUSSELL *Early Victorian Architecture in Britain* (1958)

HOLT, RICHARD *A short treatise of artificial stone as t' is now made and converted into all manner of curious embellishments and proper ornaments of architecture* (1730)

HOPE, THOMAS *Household Furniture and Interior Decoration* (1807)

HOWELL, PETER "Country Houses in the Vale of Clwyd II" *Country Life* (29th December 1977 p 1966-69)

HOWLAND, RICHARD. M and SPENCER, E.P. *The Architecture of Baltimore* (1953)

HUGHSON, DAVID *London* (1811 p. 538-545)

HUSSEY, CHRISTOPHER *English Country Houses* Mid Georgian (1760-1800) (1955)
   English Country Houses Late Georgian (1800-1840) (1958)

HUTCHISON, SIDNEY. C *The History of the Royal Academy* 1768-1968 (1968)

IRWIN, DAVID *John Flaxman* 1755-1826 (1979)

JENKINS, BEATRICE STAR *William Thornton, Small Star of the Enlightenment* (Published in photocopy 1982)

JEWITT, LLEWELLYNN *The Ceramic Art of Great Britain from Prehistoric Times down to the Present Day* (1878 ed. p. 141)

JOHNSON, JOHN *Plans Sections Elevations of Essex County Hall at Chelmsford* (1808)

Journal des Luxus und der Moden II (1787) "Ueber Herrn Coade's Lithodipira oder Kunst Backerstein Fabrik zu Lambeth in England." Leipzig. (Also Aug-Dec 1788 Coade's total price list in English)

KELLY, ALISON *Decorative Wedgwood* in Architecture and Furniture (1965)
   "Decorative stoneware in Disguise" *Country Life* (29th November 1973 p. 1797-1800)
   "Furnishings from the Coade Factory in Lambeth" *Furniture History* (1974 p. 68-70)
   "A Bust of James Barry" *Journal of the Royal Society of Arts* (November 1975)
   "Mrs Coade's Gothic" *Country Life* (2nd June 1977 p. 1514-16)
   "Imitating Mrs Coade" *Country Life* (10th November 1977)
   "Mrs Coade's Stone" *Connoisseur* CXCVII (January 1978 pp. 14-25)
   "A Camouflage Queen by the River" *Country Life* (25th January 1979 p. 244)
   "Coade Stone in National Trust Houses" *National Trust Studies* (1980 ed. Jackson Stops, G.
   "Mrs Coade's Stone - stoneware, statues and ornaments" *Antique Collector* (August 1981)
   "Mrs Coade's Stone" *Transactions English Ceramic Circle* (1982)
   "An Expensive Present: Coade Stone in Rio de Janeiro" *Burlington Magazine* (September 1984)
   "Coade Stone in Georgian Architecture: *Architectural History* (1985 p. 71-101)
   "Coade Stone Interiors" *Antique Collector* (July 1986 p. 50-55)
   Dictionary of English Furniture Makers (ed. Gilbert, C and Beard, G) 1660-1840 (1986) "Eleanor Coade" (p. 180-181)
   "Coade Stone in Sussex" *Sussex Archaeological Society Collections* (1988)
   "Coade Stone in Georgian Gardens" *Journal of the Garden History Society* (1988)
   "Sir John Soane and Eleanor Coade" *Apollo* (April 1989)
   "Eleanor Coade" , "William Croggon" *Craftsmen and Interior Decoration in England* 1660-1820 (by Geoffery Beard 1981)

KESSELS, S.H "Coade Stone : A Lost Secret" *Country Life Annual* 1955)

KIRKER, HAROLD *The Architecture of Charles Bulfinch* (Harvard UP 1969)

KITSON, S.D. *The Life of John Sell Cotman* (figure 30 1937)

KNIGHT OF GLIN and JOHN CORNFORTH Kilruddery *Country Life* (21st July 1977 p. 146-149)

LAFRANCE, MARC *APT*, vol V, no 3 (1973 Montreal).

LAING, DAVID *Plans etc. of Buildings, Public and Private, executed in various parts of England, including the Custom House* (1818)

LATROBE, BENJAMIN HENRY, *The Papers of* (in process of publication, Baltimore)

LEWIS, LESLEY *Commemorative Sculpture in Jamaica* (1965-67)

LINSTRUM, DEREK *Sir Jeffry Wyatville* (1972)

LLOYD, NATHANIEL *History of the English House* (1931)

LONDON, J.C *An Encyclopaedia of Cottage, Farm and Villa Architecture and Furniture* (London 1833)

LOUKOMSKI, GEORGES *Charles Cameron* (London 1943)

MACAULAY, JAMES *The Gothic Revival* (1975)

McCARTNY, MICHAEL J "The Rebuilding of Stowe House" 1770-1777 *Huntingdon Library Quarterly* (May 1973 p. 267-98) U.S.A.

MACKENZIE, E.M *History of Newcastle upon Tyne* (1827 p. 313)

MAJOR, THOMAS *The Ruins of Paestum* (1766)

MALLETT, J.G.V "Nicholas Crisp, Founding Member of the Society of Arts" *Journal of the Royal Society of Arts* (December 1972 p. 28-32 January, 1973 p. 92-6 February, 1973 p. 170-4

MARCHANT, NATHANIEL *A catalogue of One Hundred Impressions from Gems* (London 1792)

MEMES, J.S *Memoirs of Antonio Canova* (Edinburgh 1825)

MONTFAUCON, BERNARD DE *L' Antiquité expliquée et presentée en figures* (5 Vols Paris 1719) *Supplément* (5 Vols Paris 1724)

Monthly Magazine (1799 p. 904)

MYLNE, R.S The Master Masons to the Crown of Scotland (1893)

NEALE, JOHN PRESTON *Neale's Views of Seats* 1818-1823 Second series 1824-29

NEBLETT, NATHANIEL P. FAIA "A Search for Coade Stone in America" *Bulletin of the Association for Preservation Technology* (1972)

NICHOLAS, JOHN *Bibliotheca Topographica Britannica* MDCCXC inc. *Ducarel's History of Lambeth* (1780-90 8 Vols)

PAIN, JAMES *The Builder's Golden Rule* (1782)

PENNANT, THOMAS *Some Account of London* (1791 p. 32 4th ed. 1805)

PENNY, N.B *Church Monuments in Romantic England* (New Haven, London 1977)

PEVSNER, NIKOLAUS Studies in Art, Architecture and Design (2 Vols 1968)
    The Buildings of England (1951-1974)

PHILLIPS, RICHARD *The Picture of London* (1804)

PINCOT, DANIEL *An Essay on the Origin, Nature, Uses and Properties of Artificial Stone.* (1770)

PIRANESI, GIOVANNI BATTISTA *Vedute di Roma* (Rome 1748)
    Diverse Maniere d' Adornare i Cammini (Rome 1769)
    Della magnificenza ed architettura de' Romani (Rome 1761)

PRAZ, MARIO *An Illustrated History of Interior Decoration* (London 1964)

PRIME, ALFRED COXE *The Arts and Crafts in Philadelphia, Maryland and South Carolina* (Series II 1929–33) U.S.A.

Proceedings of the Hampshire Field Club and Archaeological Society (vol 39 1983) Note on Lodges at Freemantle, near Southampton.

PULLEN, C.J *Canadian Geographical Journal* (1967) Nelson Column, Canada.

PYKE, E.J *A Biographical Dictionary of Wax Modellers* (Oxford 1973)

PYNE, W.H *Royal Residences* (Vol II 1819)

PORAH *History of St Olave, Hart St*

QUINEY, ANTHONY *House and Home,* a history of the small English house (BBC 1986)

RAE, ISOBEL *Charles Cameron, Architect to the Court of Russia* (London 1971)

RASPE, R.E *Descriptive Catalogue of a General Collection of Ancient and Modern Engraved Gems, cast in coloured pastes, white enamel and sulphur* by James Tassie, modeller. (2 Vols London 1791)

REDGRAVE,SAMUEL *A Dictionary of Artists of the British School* (G. Benn & Sons 1878 p. 182)

REILLY, ROBIN and SAVAGE, GEORGE *Dictionary of Wedgwood* (1980)

RICHARDSON, A.E and GILL, C LOVETT *Regional Architecture of the West of England* (1924 p. 107)

RICHARDSON, GEORGE *Book of Ceilings,* composed in the style of the antique grotesque (1776)
    A New Collection of Chimneypieces (1781)
    Capitals of Columns, measured from the Antique (1793)

RICHTER, GISELA MARIA AUGUSTA *Furniture of the Greeks, Romans and Etruscans* (1966)

ROBERTS, GEORGE *History of Lyme Regis and Charmouth* (1823 p. 181)

ROBINSON, JOHN MARTIN "Estate Buildings at Holkham" *Country Life* (21st November 1974 p. 1554-1571)
    "Remaking the Shugborough Landscape" *Country Life* (10th March 1977 p. 578-81)
    "Magna Carta and Pretty Ladies' Maids" *Country Life* (7th July 1983)
    The Wyatts An Architectural Dynasty (1979)

ROWAN, ALISTAIR *The Buildings of Ireland* : NW Ulster (1979)
    Designs for Castles and Country Houses by Robert and James Adam (1985)

ROWSE, A.L *The Byrons and the Trevanions* (1978)

RUCH, JOHN P "Regency Coade" *Architectural History* (1968)
    "Coade Stone in Ireland" *Irish Georgian Society* (1970)

SAUNDERS, ANN *The Art and Architecture of London* (1984)

SEELEY, J *Stowe, a description of the house and gardens* (1971 p. 52)

SEELY, BENTON. *Guidebook to Stone* (1744 and later)

SHERATON, THOMAS The Cabinet Maker and Upholsterer's Drawing Book (London 1791-94)
    The Cabinet Maker, Upholsterer and General Artist's Encyclopaedia (London 1804)

SINGER, C and HOLMYARD, E.J *A History of Technology* (1958 p. 446-7, 470)

SMITH, J.T *Nollekens and his Times* (2 Vols London 1828)

SMITH, GEORGE *Household Furniture* (London 1808)

SOANE, SIR JOHN *Royal Academy Lectures on Architecture* (ed. A.T. Bolton)

Somerset House Gazette (1824 Article by L. p. 381)

STEIGHLITZ, CHRISTIAN LUDWIG *Plans et dessings [sic] tirés de la belle Architecture ou Representations d' Edifices exécutés ou projettés en CXV planches Avec les explications nécessaires* (Paris 1801)

STROUD, DOROTHY *Capability Brown* (1950, 1975)

"61-63 New Cavendish St" *Institute of Psychoanalysis Report* (1953)

The Architecture of Sir John Soane (1961)

Humphry Repton (1962)

Henry Holland (1966)

George Dance, Architect 1741-1825 (1971)

STUART, DONALD R "James Essex" *Architectural Review* (November 1950 plate 15)

STUART, JAMES and REVETT, NICHOLAS *The Antiquities of Athens* (Vols I, II. 1762, 1789)

Suffolk Ladies Memorandum Book (1814) quoted *Country Life "The Year at a Glance"* by Pauline Flick (3. 12 1981 p. 2026)

SUMMERSON, SIR JOHN *Georgian London* (1945 and 1969 etc.)

Architecture in Britain 1530-1830 (1953)

The Life and Work of John Nash, Architect (1980)

The Classical Language of Architecture (1980)

Survey of London Vol VI Hammersmith (Plates 37, 38)

Vol XX Trafalgar Square, Coat of arms in street behind Haymarket

Vol XX chapter 8 St Martin in the Fields (vol 3)

Vol XXII Kennington Area St Saviour, Southwark

Vol XXIII St Mary Lambeth, South Bank

Vol XXVII Christchurch Spitalfields (p. 166)

Vol XXIX St James Piccadilly (I) (p. 375-6)

Vol XXXVII North Kensington (1972)

TATHAM, C.H *Etchings of Ancient Ornamental Architecture* drawn from Originals in Rome and other parts of Italy during the years 1794,1795 and 1797. (published 1799-1800)

Etchings representing Fragments of Grecian and Roman Architectural Ornaments (1806)

TAVERNER PARRY, J "An Episode in the History of English Terracotta" *Architectural Review* XXXIII (1913 p. 119-122)

TAYLOR, JEREMY "Charles Fowler 1792-1867 : a centenary memoir" *Architectural History* (1968 p. 57-74)

THOMAS, HENRY R *The Ancient Remains and recent Improvements in the City of London* (1830)

THORNTON, PETER *Authentic Décor : the domestic Interior 1620-1920* (1984)

TIMBS, J *Curiosities of London* (1885)

Universal Magazine, The (1804 p. 70)

VALPY, N and KELLY, A "Advertisements for Artificial Stone" *English Ceramic Circle Transactions* (1986 p. 206-226)

VASI, MARIANO *Description du Musée Pio Clementin et de la Galerie des tableaux du Palais Vatican* (Rome 1792)

WANKLYN, C Lyme Regis (1927 p. 123, 151-3, 244-5)

WATKIN, DAVID The Life and Work of C.R Cockerell (London 1974)

Thomas Hope and the Neo-Classical Idea (1968)

Athenian Stuart (1982)

WELLDON, W and J *The Smith's Right Hand . . . near Forty genteel, new and beautiful Designs for Stoves* (London 1765)

WHINNEY, MARGARET *Sculpture in Britain* (1964)
    Home House No. 20, Portman Square (1969)

WHINNEY, MARGARET and GUNNIS, RUPERT *The Collection of Models* by *John Flaxman RA at University College, London;* A Catalogue and Introduction (1967)

WILLIAMS, J.D *Audley End : The Restoration of 1762-97* (1966)

WILLIAMS, REV. J.F. Chignal St James Font *Essex Review* (July 1931)
    "The Rebuilding of Chelmsford Church" *Essex Review* Vol XL (July 1931 p. 100-166)

WILLS, GEOFFREY *English Looking Glasses* (1965)

WRIGHT, T *History and Topography of Essex* (1836)

YOUINGS, JOYCE *Tuckers Hall, Exeter* University of Exeter (1968 p. 28 ff)

YOUNGSON, A.J *The Making of Classical Edinburgh* (1968)

INDEX

(Illustrations in **bold** type. Book titles in *italics*.
Names of Coade pieces in *italics*.)

LONDON